D1526363

THE
LONG
GESTATION

Irish Nationalist Life
1891–1918

THE LONG GESTATION

Irish Nationalist Life
1891–1918

Patrick Maume

St. Martin's Press
New York

DA
960
.M38
1999

The Long Gestation
Copyright © 1999 by Patrick Maume

All rights reserved. No part of this book may be used or reproduced in any
manner whatsoever without written permission except in the case of brief
quotations embodied in critical articles or reviews. For information, address:

St. Martin's Press, Scholarly and Reference Division,
175 Fifth Avenue, New York, N.Y. 10010

First published in the United State of America in 1999

Printed in Ireland

ISBN: 0-312-22549-0

Library of Congress Cataloging-in-Publication Data

Maume, Patrick.
    The long gestation : Irish nationalist life, 1891-1918 / Patrick
Maume.
            p. cm.
    Includes bibliographical references and index.
    ISBN 0-312-22549-0 (cloth)
    1. Ireland—Politics and government—1910-1921. 2. Ireland-
-Politics and government—1901-1910. 3. Ireland—Politics and
government—1837-1901. 4. Nationalism—Ireland—History—20th
century. 5. Nationalism—Ireland—History—19th century.
I. Title.
DA960.M38   1999
941.5082'1—dc21
                                                        99-22052
                                                        CIP

41017422

CONTENTS

INTRODUCTION

S cholarly coverage of nationalist politics between the death of Charles Stewart Parnell in 1891 and the downfall of the Irish Party in 1918 is patchy; perceptions are dominated by the Parnell split and the final struggles from the 1910 elections, through the home rule debates and the Easter Rising, to the triumph of Sinn Féin and the establishment of the Irish Free State. Some leading figures have been the subject of biographies, but these focus on the end of the period, devoting little attention to the eighteen-nineties and the first decade of the twentieth century.

Two dominant approaches see the period in the light of what came afterwards. The first, developing the views of contemporary separatists, predominated in the decades after independence. Its exponents—principally skilled amateur historians and memoirists—see Irish history as the story of nationalism, equated with separatism. Parnell and the Land League become honorary separatists, but the post-Parnell Irish Party is dismissed as irrelevant. It is equated with John Redmond, who is seen as a corrupt and deluded fool or, in versions drawing on Redmondite apologetics, honourable but naïve; Irish nationality was kept alive by the Irish Republican Brotherhood and the Gaelic League until Easter 1916.[1]

The rival interpretation, popular among academic historians, draws on the apologias of surviving Redmondites and Sinn Féin moderates, reflecting on the refusal of republican hard-liners to compromise after 1922 and the difficulties of self-government. This stresses the achievement of post-independence governments in maintaining a stable democracy and emphasises the political education provided by nineteenth-century constitutional nationalist movements and the creation and maintenance of a professional civil service in the last decades of the Union and the opening years of the new state.[2] This view plays down physical-force separatism, emphasising how the new state built on the achievements of the Irish Party and on local continuity between old and new elites. Some versions regard the fall of the Irish Party as a historical accident and suggest that home rule would have evolved peacefully through dominion status to full independence. The view that home rule would have been preferable to full independence is rarely argued.[3]

This study is closer to the second approach than to the first, though the first has unappreciated merits. Physical-force separatism was stronger than is often supposed, and the extent to which it had a common discourse with constitutionalism is under-estimated. Nonetheless, both view the period in the light of what came afterwards rather than in its own right—though neglect of this period affects understanding of subsequent years, since many participants in later events saw the world from the point of view of their political and intellectual formation. The residual power of the *ancien régime* and the influence of unionists outside Ulster in the last decades of the Union are often neglected, and with them an understanding of the extent to which pre-1914 nationalists could credibly see earlier nationalists such as Thomas Davis and John Mitchel as possessing contemporary relevance, because attacking opponents whose successors were recognisable. Arthur Griffith and Eoin MacNeill are seen as 'moderate', whereas in the early years of the twentieth century they were extremists; the Gaelic League is identified with separatism, though some separatists at first distrusted it.

This book tries to provide a narrative with a strong analytical framework. It argues that the Irish Party and Sinn Féin had a similar social role, using broadly based nationalist agitations to prevent the British government managing the Catholic community through selected lay and clerical notables. The political activists of both movements were drawn from a growing class of urban Catholic white-collar workers whose social opportunities were restricted by structures of privilege; but since the Irish Party also drew on local notables, such as shopkeepers, large farmers, parish priests, and newspaper proprietors, who were displacing landlords as wielders of local patronage, it was vulnerable to accusations of becoming part of the 'whig' management structures it originally attacked.

The difference between the two movements reflected a dispute over nationalist strategy going back to Young Ireland and Daniel O'Connell. The dominant elements in the post-Parnell Irish Party favoured the strategy adopted after Gladstone's conversion to home rule and sought to revive a 'Union of Hearts' with British progressive forces. Sinn Féin invoked not only the Fenian and IRB tradition but also the earlier Parnellite strategy of 'independent opposition' embodied in the polemics of United Ireland against Earl Spencer and revived by Parnell in his last campaign.

The final defeat of the Irish Party reflected resentment built up by the residual strength of the old regime in fighting off the onset of home rule and the reluctance of the British political class to reshape the United Kingdom so as to accommodate Irish Catholics within it, and the persistence of a sense of Irish separateness strong enough to limit willingness to make sacrifices for compromise with Britain. The failure of nationalism to win the allegiance of most Protestants, and the post-independence ascendancy of a narrow version of national identity, which denied significant elements in Irish culture, reflect a failure of Irishness; refusal to adapt the structures of the Union state to accommodate its most conspicuous discontented minority, and the preservation of those structures at the cost of the secession of most of Ireland, can be seen as a failure of Britishness.

B ritain is traditionally a union state rather than a unitary state, with local elites managing the regions and mediating their requirements to the centre. Ireland under the Union saw a series of attempts to establish an elite acceptable to the British state, the Protestant minority, and the Catholic majority. The traditional Anglican landed governing class delayed Catholic emancipation until increased politicisation of the masses made accommodation considerably more difficult, and it was too dependent and divided for the British state to underwrite the all-out repression of resistance to ascendancy rule demanded by hard-line opponents of emancipation.

Thereafter, despite protests from defenders of Protestant ascendancy, British governments tried to secure Catholic loyalty by developing and co-opting Catholic lay and clerical elites, whose status rose with the increasing power and prestige of the church leadership and the growth of a class of provincial traders and large farmers supporting Catholic professionals drawn from their own families and gaining local patronage as they challenged the landlords' dominance of institutions such as the boards of guardians.[4] The high points of this policy can be seen as the alliance in the eighteen-thirties between O'Connell and the Melbourne government,[5] and the first Gladstone government, which seemed for a few years after 1868 to have made Liberalism the political vehicle of Irish Catholic and Presbyterian identities and grievances against the old regime, as it harnessed national feeling in Wales and Scotland through deploying central power for reformism against particularist Tory aristocracies. Liberalism dominated the Irish parliamentary scene, even establishing a base in Tory-dominated Ulster. Catholic representation in the higher levels of the administrative and judicial machine reached levels not regained until the first decade of the twentieth century; competitive examinations allowed surplus children of the Catholic middle class, trained by the growing Catholic public schools, to compete for civil service jobs in Ireland and the empire.

Ireland's economic requirements, however, could not be assimilated to those of Britain. The Famine was exacerbated by a British belief that Irish problems would be solved by assimilation to the British social and economic system and that inter-vention would only delay the euthanasia of predatory spendthrift landlords and ignorant subsistence-level tenants.[6] Only in 1870 was legal recognition extended to differences between the Irish and English land systems, and this was too limited to satisfy tenants' discontent.[7] For much of the century the existing elite remained indispensable to British governments for administration at local level, though such events as the Tithe War of the eighteen-thirties and the Fenian Rising (which produced highly visible crisis flights from remote Big Houses into towns) showed their vulnerability before the Land War.

Elite persistence reflected not only government bias towards the landed classes but distrust of potential nationalist allies. The restrictions on the borough corporations, opened to nationalist control by local government reforms in the eighteen-thirties, were a lasting grievance, cited up to the end of the Union to counter unionist charges about the shortcomings of nationalist local authorities. There were also limits to the appeasement of the Catholic hierarchy, which was prepared to co-operate with the government to safeguard its power in such areas as education but remained apprehensive of government intentions and lay (possibly anti-clerical) Catholic political leadership. The Catholic lay elite were not immune to the social glamour of the older Protestant elite and its institutions, or to commercial advantages that might derive from it; the Trinity Catholic became recognisable, and some Catholic professionals and tradesmen, especially in Dublin, became Freemasons. Advanced nationalists replied to clerical talk of godless Continental revolutionaries by retorting that collaboration with the government only benefited a corrupt lay elite whose unprincipled place-seeking tarnished their clerical sponsors. No government would allow the sort of episcopal control over a Catholic university— and hence recruitment of a Catholic professional elite—the bishops desired; and though ameliorated by the establishment of the Royal University of Ireland as an examining body, the university question limited the system's ability to co-opt the hierarchy and recruit upwardly mobile Catholics.

Above all, Irish Liberalism was a politics of elites: moderate groups within the older Anglican landed elite and the rising Nonconformist denominations and a relatively small Catholic elite, whose advancement conferred few obvious benefits on most of their co-religionists and could be seen as buying off individual adventurers rather than advancing a previously excluded group as a whole. John Sadleir and William Keogh—who obtained popular support by appealing to Catholic and nationalist feeling, then broke their pledge against taking office, retained episcopal support by offering Catholic influence in government, and ended as suicides after criminal fraud (Sadleir) and anti-clerical outbursts (Keogh)—were symbols of clerical shortsightedness and the moral bankruptcy of 'whiggery'. The Catholic upper classes and some church leaders might see themselves as Catholic aristocrats and fantasise that Ireland's problems could be solved by a Catholic ruling class 'naturally' sympathetic to their poorer co-religionists;[8] but though this vision, disseminated by schools such as Clongowes Wood,[9] influenced Catholic middle-class attitudes well into the twentieth century, it had few attractions for those consigned to the base of the pyramid.

Another political alternative similarly had few attractions but influenced the nationalist ideological synthesis. A variant of Anglican Toryism presented itself as defender of Irish peculiarities against remorseless centralisation, just as Scott and his Tory disciples claimed that Liberalism destroyed everything distinctively Scottish. They idealised the gentry as natural leaders of the country, presenting Liberalism as an unholy alliance with ambitious priests and Catholic upstarts to disrupt Irish society,[10] replacing local allegiances and affections with bureaucracy and soulless utilitarianism, and crushing ancient Irish institutions in the name of an official neutrality that undermined all religion. These defences of Protestant ascendancy incorporated critiques of ascendancy and government in existing (as distinct from ideal) forms that could be exploited by nationalists. Laments that landlords were seduced by metropolitan glamour into neglecting hedonistic local paternalism, nostalgia for Grattan's parliament and regret that the Union rendered the aristocracy dependent on Britain and allowed their natural leadership to be usurped by calculating lawyer-demagogues let nationalists say that even Tories recognised the Union as disastrous. Unionist critiques of the greed and social climbing of the Catholic elite and claims that home rule would produce new and worse exploiters could be taken up by advanced nationalists; separatists and unionist populists could join to attack the political pretensions of the Catholic clergy and their expensive new churches, full of imported ornamentation.

Some Protestant nationalists dreamt of leading an inclusive nationalism. Davis marked out his difference with O'Connellism by deprecating calls for a British Whig government to intervene against anti-Catholic discrimination in a historic Irish institution, arguing that it should be reformed voluntarily by appeals to patriotism;[11] the contradiction between Butt's early Toryism and subsequent invention of home rule is less than supposed. Douglas Hyde and Standish O'Grady had similar backgrounds as sons of backwoods Tory clergymen building careers in a metropolitan environment, nostalgic for their rural youth yet alienated from many childhood beliefs. O'Grady—a representative though eccentric example of the socially insecure unionist activist-journalist—and Griffith maintained strong mutual respect.

Beneath the higher reaches of the Liberal elite and the lukewarm nationalism of Dublin Catholic merchants and the *Freeman's Journal,* a populist politics identified nationalism with resentment at the repression, privilege and favouritism that were the other side of the paternalist ethos. Mass literacy in English let these views be spread by the Sullivan brothers' *Nation,* with its Catholic lower-middle-class orientation, the neo-Fenian papers of Richard Pigott, and cheap and didactic popular literature on the Young Ireland model disseminated by such publishers as Duffy of Dublin and Cameron and Ferguson of Glasgow. The Land Leaguer and MP William O'Brien described these publishers as a rival system of national education, countering the denationalising effect of the official system.[12]

The Young Irelanders were less remote from *fin de siècle* Ireland than they seem in retrospect. Charles Gavan Duffy, who did not die until 1903, found his quarrel with Mitchel revived in the literary politics of the eighteen-nineties. Separatists like Griffith saw Mitchel as their contemporary and when attacking parliamentarianism claimed that the Young Ireland critique of O'Connell's Whig alliance was as valid for the nineteen-hundreds as for the eighteen-forties.[13]

The core of the United Irishmen in the seventeen-nineties, of the Young Irelanders' Confederation in the eighteen-forties and of the IRB in the eighteen-sixties was the class of urban artisans, formed by a producerist ethos centred around pride in skills, which marked them out from the unskilled, made them relatively independent of the patronage and dependence relationships of the establishment, and allowed them to despise the professional and merchant classes as consumerist parasites. With traditions of organisation for craft, social and benefit purposes, and threatened with de-skilling by economic changes that reinforced the view of the Union as the cause of economic deterioration, they had a high literacy and an ethos of educational self-provision outside the state system and, to some extent, the control of the church. These revolutionary movements were offshoots of an enduring network of social and literary clubs, reading-rooms, and semi-political benefit societies. (In 1906 the Tralee Young Ireland Society claimed continuous existence from the eighteen-forties.)[14]

Similar institutions under church control could also be political springboards. The autodidact Dublin tradesman William Field MP, son of a Young Irelander (he kept contact with the IRB up to 1900), attended evening classes for workmen in the Catholic University and began public life in a church-run dramatic and debating society,[15] as did the Limerick pilot Michael Joyce (MP for Limerick City 1900–18).[16] Such institutions could easily become mere social or drinking clubs for young men,[17] and indeed physical-force separatism was often presented by conservative nationalists as an adolescent phenomenon of patriotic rhetoric working on inexperienced minds;[18] and it would be as unwise to idealise them as to underestimate, looking backwards from an age of state-provided welfare, the ability of the 'deserving poor' of an earlier era to create institutions of their own and their role in disseminating and supplementing the mass literature of nationalism.

In smaller towns and the countryside this milieu blended into Ribbonism and agrarian secret societies. Ribbonism combined the function of a benefit society with its more notorious activities, a tradition carried on into the twentieth century by the constitutionalist Board of Erin and the separatist Irish-American Alliance. The Old Guard Benevolent Union, a benefit society of old Fenians in the larger towns, reported its proceedings in newspapers in the eighteen-nineties and nineteen-hundreds and paraded openly on national anniversaries.[19]

Arthur Griffith, perhaps the last great spokesman for this milieu, was born in a tenement house in 1871, left school at twelve through economic necessity—

though the Christian Brothers had hoped he might remain at school long enough to sit the civil service examination[20]—was apprenticed to the printing trade, whose strong craft identity was reinforced by the relative slowness of its technical change, and continued his education by immersing himself in the nationalist literature of preceding generations at the National Library[21] and in the clubs. (His teacher in an evening class on Irish history was Kate MacBride, John Devoy's sister.)[22] Griffith first came to public notice in 1885, when he won a book prize in a competition run by one such club.[23] In 1887 he founded the Leinster Literary Society among readers of a young people's column written by the separatist poet Rose Kavanagh.[24]

O'Brien recalled Parnell saying that Fintan Lalor might have founded the Land League in the eighteen-forties if railways had been available to bring his message directly to the people.[25] The Irish Party of the eighteen-eighties and its ancillary organisations can be seen as creatures of the railways and the newspapers produced by mass literacy in English and the growth of a Catholic middle-class clientele. The upheavals of the eighties were accompanied by increased numbers of nationalist provincial papers. Many owners—such as Jasper Tully of the *Roscommon Herald,* J. P. Farrell of the *Longford Leader,* and the Doris brothers of the *Mayo News*—became significant political figures in their own right, and political influence added to profitability through advertisements and printing contracts transferred from older, unionist papers.[26] The party's local leaders were large farmers and tradesmen, while its professional leadership and organising staff were recruited from the lower reaches of the professions and the British and Irish journalistic world, with some members of the Catholic higher professional class and a few dissident landlords and Protestant professionals. By alliance with the Fenian tradition and by channelling the grievances of small and large tenants, Parnell's party mobilised the bulk of the population and, unlike earlier attempts at an independent Irish Party, monopolised the political representation of Catholic Ireland. Vertical bonds of patronage and deference to landlords and the state apparatus were defined as corrupt and degrading and ritually broken, to be replaced by membership in a national organisation entitled to treat non-members as traitors. The Royal Irish Constabulary, widely seen as an attractive source of careers and husbands, was boycotted, and Land League courts were set up to judge local disputes without reference to state machinery.[27]

This response was not universally effective. League machinery was often misused in personal disputes, and it could not maintain effectiveness for very long. Long after Parnell's death, small-town citizens angered advanced nationalists by presenting addresses to landlords and testimonials to retiring or transferred policemen.[28] Nonetheless, the scale of disruption, the concessions it produced and a continuing decline in agricultural prices fatally undermined the old regime. Sinn Féin saw this period of nationalist defiance of Liberal coercion as the essence of Parnellism.

The blow to landlord political and social power in 1879–82 was followed by a campaign aimed at politically displacing or co-opting the professional and commercial elites that dominated Catholic society. Later commentators found it anomalous that the Kilmainham Treaty was not immediately followed by a Liberal-Nationalist alliance and attributed this to the Phoenix Park murders; but the continuing Liberal-Nationalist tensions under Spencer reflected not only government attempts to criminalise nationalist politics[29] but also the Irish Party's drive to dominate nationalist Ireland by co-opting or marginalising conservative notables—accompanied by a move to the right as more aggressive elements left the country or were sidelined.[30] Land agitation tactics had been toned down as the Land League spread to the more prosperous tenant-farmers of the east and south; after 1882 its original County Mayo base sank into quiescence and localised IRB-linked agitation until 1898.[31] The *Freeman's Journal,* organ of moderate upper-class nationalism, was brought into line by the threat of transforming the aggressive Parnellite weekly *United Ireland* into a rival daily paper.[32] The leadership of the Catholic Church—with a few stubborn exceptions—recognised the Parnellite party as guardians of church interests, despite uneasiness with a powerful lay leadership.[33]

At the same time, publicists such as Tim Healy and William O'Brien pursued an outspoken populist campaign against the Spencer administration, focusing on miscarriages of justice under emergency legislation and the sexual misdemeanours of Castle officials,[34] whose violations of decorum were compared to the political pornography of the French revolutionary press.[35] This mixture of unbridled abuse against opponents with high-flown praise of readers for their religion, idealism and bravery would be ridiculed by a new generation of nationalists, such as D. P. Moran and Arthur Griffith, as proof of intellectual vacuity; in fact Moran and Griffith imitated this rhetorical strategy of separation from opponents and consolidation of sympathisers, congratulating readers on their 'hardheadedness' or 'idealism', contrasted with the 'selfishness' of unionists and the 'corruption' and 'folly' of the Irish Party. They played down any suggestion that Liberals were preferable to Conservatives by presenting both as governed by landlords and the Dublin Castle bureaucracy.

In the 1885 general election the Irish Party co-operated with Ulster Conservatives to eliminate Liberal MPs.[36] *United Ireland* took over the role of the weekly press as critic of lukewarm mainstream nationalism, displacing the separatist *Irishman* and marginalising the *Nation*, which promoted Parnell's rise but saw itself as ally rather than follower.[37] By the use of a theatre of defiance, presenting the flouting of authority as equivalent to victory in battle,[38] Parnellism claimed continuity with older traditions of revolt—disgusting separatists like the Invincible P. J. P. Tynan, who jeered that Caesar, Hannibal, Alexander and Bonaparte combined won fewer battles than these gentlemen claimed to have won by talking.[39]

By driving home the idea of the powerlessness of the authorities and by eliminating alternative collaborators outside the hard core of landlord-led Tories, scarred by defeats since 1829, who emerged as leaders of the unionist minority in this Parnell-driven realignment, the Irish Party aimed to show that only by dealing with them could nationalist Ireland be governed without the use of naked force on a politically unacceptable scale. Separatist support for the New Departure assumed that Britain would use such force rather than compromise, and the Parnellite movement was paving the way for a separatist uprising against such a British response.[40] O'Brien claimed that until Parnell told him of Gladstone's conversion he expected to end in insurrection and the gallows.[41]

The price of Irish Party co-operation was substantial autonomy: entrusting Ireland to the party leadership instead of the older elites and bureaucracy—though it was suggested that the administrative experience and economic power of the minority made it indispensable to a new Irish government.[42] The Gladstone-Parnell alliance was presented as the basis of a new union of consent rather than force. Publicists such as Barry O'Brien, whose youthful Fenian sympathies were moderated after Liberal reforms convinced him that some Englishmen meant well to Ireland,[43] constructed a genealogy for Gladstone's home rule proposals as a logical culmination of previous Liberal reforms, seen as fatally limited by British ignorance of Ireland and unwillingness to trust the Irish majority.[44] Irish MPs—some of whom had been Fenians—toured Britain declaring that the British people, once fully informed, would support home rule; the Irish Press Agency, headed by the North Dublin MP J. J. Clancy, joined Liberal organisations in putting the nationalist case to a British audience, while Liberal delegations visited Ireland. At the same time the Plan of Campaign was launched to counter agricultural distress caused by the continued fall in prices and to show unionist bankruptcy by making Ireland ungovernable.[45]

Many Irish Party MPs and activists belonged to the Irish community in Britain—whether born there or, more often, as immigrants—and felt a natural affinity for Liberalism or for groups further left that co-operated with the Irish Party and the Land League in the early eighteen-eighties and assimilated the Irish struggle to the Liberal and radical image of the 'British democracy' facing a landed Tory elite ruling both countries. Davitt's involvement in labour politics is the most prominent example. In some instances, such as that of the Manchester city councillor Dan Boyle and the Glasgow newspaper proprietor Charles Diamond, nationalist involvement was combined with a local political base in Irish ghettos.[46]

As members of Parliament were unpaid until 1911, many Irish MPs lived in London, supporting themselves by professions such as journalism. In the long run this produced its own tensions, with left-wing Irish elements in Britain resenting the Liberal alliance and the dominance of Irish politics in Britain by traders and professionals,[47] while in Ireland those members who lived in England were denounced as Anglicised adventurers. The connection with London journalism contributed to this image: T. P. O'Connor, pioneer of the 'new journalism', whose Catholicism was known to be nebulous, whose marriage had broken down, and whose printing of society gossip on the pretext of insights into human nature outraged Catholic sensibilities,[48] became a useful stick with which to beat his political allies. As early as 1892, unionists publicised a priest who excluded O'Connor's paper, the *Sun*, from the parochial reading-room.[49]

This strategy staked everything on Liberal victory in the election that was due by 1893 on a sufficient scale to overawe the House of Lords. The sense of impending victory brought the Irish Party to the height of its stature; Pearse's child-hood image of O'Brien and Dillon as twin godlike heroes fighting for Ireland dates from this period.[50]

The residual strength of Irish unionism, which included most Protestant Liberal support among Ulster tenant-farmers and the professional and business classes as well as Orange Tory traditionalism, was greater than admitted by nation-alist commentators, who brushed it aside with facile references to sweating in the linen industry and landlord manipulation of religious bigotry, which did not by themselves account for the existence of the unionist coalition. The belief that nationalists were simply incompetent to govern Ireland and maintain the rule of law had clear racial and religious (as well as class) overtones; and in a semi-democratic society strongly influenced by elitism, the image of nationalists as incompetent dema-gogues was a major inspiration of unionist resistance. The mobilisation of Ulster unionism posed problems for nationalism recognised by Joseph Chamberlain, who called for a provincial government for Ulster as part of an extremely limited scheme of autonomy. He intended to undercut Gladstone's proposals and undermine the claims of an Irish legislature; the plan was disavowed by Conservatives and seems unlikely to have been seriously proposed.

In 1893 Unionist conventions in Dublin and Belfast, called to oppose the second Home Rule Bill, denounced partition;[51] in 1907 the biographer of a Church of Ireland archbishop felt his readers needed reminding that such a curious idea was ever proposed.[52] The tactical nature of these partition proposals, and the theatrical nature of threats of military resistance by Ulster to home rule in 1893, when the bill was clearly doomed,[53] helped to blind nationalist leaders to their potential con-sequences when it was renewed between 1910 and 1914. Edward Carson and Bonar Law consciously said nothing in 1912–13 that unionist leaders had not said in 1892–3.[54]

Despite literary fantasies about Ulster volunteers reconquering Ireland from the forces of barbarism,[55] unionism outside Ulster clearly depended on British support. Here again the 'Union of Hearts' assumed that the British unionist majority of 1886 could be overturned by a Gladstonian crusade. The Conservatives had only once won an overall majority since 1841; Liberal unionists had failed to dislodge Gladstonian domination of Liberalism, and many were returning rather than face dependence on Conservatives. On this assumption, tenants on Plan of Campaign estates were invited to risk eviction in the hope of rapid reinstatement. When faced by a determined Dublin Castle administration under Arthur Balfour, however, the nationalist theatre of defiance could be presented as squalid and ridiculous bluff, reinforcing the unionist presentation of the Irish question as law versus anarchy. Just as home rulers pointed to Tory intrigues with the Irish Party in 1885 as showing awareness that home rule was inevitable, unionists pointed to former Gladstonian denunciations of Parnellites as criminals and to separatist statements by Parnellites suggesting that the Gladstonian conversion derived from Gladstone's personal influence and hunger for power at any price. The *Times* noted that Spencer was proclaiming men who called him the 'Duke of Sodom and Gomorrah' worthy to govern Ireland; O'Brien's fulsome declarations that Spencer had been blamed unjustly for subordinates' misdeeds and that he (O'Brien) wished to black Spencer's boots as a form of apology did little to remedy this and was quoted against him thereafter.[56]

The notorious lukewarmness of most Gladstonian leaders on the issue, seen as a diversion to be got out of the way rather than a moral crusade, was emphasised by unionists and glossed over by Parnellites, who presented visiting Liberal delegations (naturally the greatest enthusiasts) to Irish followers as proof that Britain was under-going a permanent moral transformation—though their gamble on a short-term strategy reflected awareness of the implications of Gladstone's death or retirement. Many Liberal enthusiasts had unrealistic expectations of total transformation in Irish attitudes. Unionist propagandists, such as Violet Martin's brother Robert, who in *Punch* and the music-halls incorporated Leveresque portrayals of tenant and landlord united in sport and intoxication into propaganda for the Irish Unionist Alliance, while living in English suburbia, mocked the culture gap between Liberal temperance reformers and the Irish peasantry. Martin, like the Ulster Unionist leader Edward Saunderson, presented himself in terms of British fantasies of the blissfully amoral stage-Irishman to support claims that the Irish were not suited for self-government.[57]

The future separatist Alice Milligan, active in the Plan of Campaign, was annoyed by the condescension of visiting Liberals, their expectation of boundless admiration and gratitude, and their reluctance to join overt defiance of the law. After the debacle, the Liberal by-election victories and Liberal Unionist reversions, once presented as proof of British repentance, acquired new significance; advanced nationalists claimed that victims of coercion had been sacrificed for a Liberal election cry.[58]

I t will never be known whether the Gladstonian-Liberal alliance might have triumphed without the Parnell split. There was a widespread perception that by
1890 the Unionist government was under severe pressure from parliamentary
warfare, the drift of Liberal support back to Gladstonianism, and the reaction of
opinion in favour of Parnell after the exposure of the Pigott forgeries.[59] Frank
Callanan notes that British by-elections after the split continued the earlier trend of
a definite but not overwhelming Liberal swing,[60] and Margaret O'Callaghan points
out that post-Pigott lionisation of Parnell may reflect consolidated Gladstonian
support rather than a conversion of opponents, and that unionists could present the
overall report of the Parnell Commission as confirming nationalist criminality.[61]
Perhaps the unionist problems of 1890 were simply mid-term difficulties; but the
government was helped by the collapse of Irish obstruction as members of the Irish
Party fought among themselves in Ireland, by the deflation of Liberal rhetoric, and
by Parnellite tactical support for Conservative land legislation, which the party previously delayed—giving rise to accusations that Parnell as a landlord was helping
legislation favourable to his class.

The Parnell split strengthened the image of nationalist incompetence and subservience to clerical power and revived separatist perceptions of Liberal treachery
and constitutionalist weakness. Parnell appealed to the pre-1885 rhetoric of
independent opposition, his irreplaceable personal ability and charisma, the urban
Fenian tradition, and the possibility of drawing elements of Protestant opinion into
the nationalist orbit by conciliatory gestures towards landlords and Ulster
Protestants.

It is debatable how far this represents Parnell's personal project as distinct from
the tactic, regularly used in internal nationalist and unionist disputes, of attributing
the persistence of unionism or nationalism (as the case may be) to the incompetence
of the existing leadership and implying that if matters were placed in different
hands all Irishmen would soon see the self-evident truth. The majority of Protestant
home rule MPs opposed Parnell, though some were Liberals recruited to the party
and loyal to Gladstone rather than nationalists in the full sense.

Anti-Parnellites appealed to the Liberal alliance and the plight of evicted
tenants who risked everything on its basis, the principle that the party should be
greater than any individual, visceral hatred and fear of the mob among middle-class
and clericalist conservative nationalists, and outspoken Catholic (or, in individual
cases, Nonconformist) moralism. Further research is needed to confirm or disprove
Callanan's suggestion that the split played a vital part in the crystallisation of this

world view, but some features of the split suggest that it had deeper roots. Just as some anti-Parnellite leaders argued that Parnell was deposed on public rather than private grounds, Parnellites combined the assertion that Parnell's private life was irrelevant to his leadership abilities with denunciations of the sexual habits of individual anti-Parnellites and the British people generally. Griffith was to make extensive use of this tactic.

Divisions among anti-Parnellites—encouraged by Parnell's tactical use of negotiations—further complicated matters. The volte-face of certain anti-Parnellites after at first supporting Parnell encouraged rumours and wishful thinking about possible changes of allegiance, and their disappointment bred resentments lasting for decades; many believed that O'Brien had played Parnell false, while Redmond was periodically accused of having planned to desert Parnell before the Chief's death.

It is questionable whether Parnell could have regained the nationalist leadership lost in the split; he might have shared the discredit attached to his former lieutenants in factional squabbles after the shattered hopes of the second Home Rule Bill and remained vulnerable to accusations of sacrificing home rule for self-gratification. His death removed him from the consequences of the split and preserved intact the memory of his victories, free from comparisons drawn by the generation of Pearse and Joyce between childhood images of heroes and the squalid quarrels dominating their growth to full political awareness. Many of these revolved around the question whether the definitive Parnellite achievement lay in the oppositional politics of the early eighties and the split or the post-1886 Liberal alliance.

Irish politics after Parnell were also shaped by the continuing presence of the older regime and its success in provoking collaboration or resentment. The correspondent of the conservative *Birmingham Daily Gazette,* visiting Ireland in 1893–4, rejoiced in the military and political power of Belfast and the commercial success of the southern unionist middle class, contrasted with the dirt and ignorance of the west, the fiasco of New Tipperary, the quarrels of 'Breeches O'Brien and Horsewhipped Healy,' and the suppression of independent thought by the boycott mentality. He mentioned the old Fenian John O'Leary as a symbol of an older, more honourable nationalism and sneered at the claim to separate nationality by a people who had not kept their own language alive, without realising that he foreshadowed the following decades' cultural politics.[62]

1

'AFTER AUGHRIM'S DREAD DISASTER' 1891–1900

The death of Parnell in Brighton in October 1891 did not end the Parnell split. The Parnellites' sense of identity had been hardened by the bitter hostility they had experienced, including boycotts, intimidation, and clerical denunciations amounting in some cases to excommunication; and Parnell was seen as a martyr killed by treacherous friends. His colleagues organised a ceremonial funeral, one of the greatest political demonstrations of nineteenth-century Ireland, in the Parnellite stronghold of Dublin, then issued a manifesto reaffirming Parnell's claim that the issue at stake was not his personal position but the existence of a nationalist party independent of British political dictation.

They justified their refusal to accept the majority decision of the Irish Party by claiming that the anti-Parnellites were no longer an Irish party but an extension of the Liberals, the successors of the job-hunting 'nominal home-rulers' whom Parnell had driven from Parliament in the early eighteen-eighties. Claims that their actions were endangering the Liberals' ability to deliver home rule at the forthcoming general election were met by the reply that without Parnell to pressure the Liberals, any form of home rule they would concede would be insufficient to satisfy Irish demands.

John Redmond, the new Parnellite leader, resigned his seat in North Wexford and stood unsuccessfully in the Cork city by-election resulting from Parnell's death. This was the fourth consecutive by-election defeat for the Parnellites since the split; but the death soon afterwards of the MP for Waterford city led to a bitter contest, in which Redmond defeated Michael Davitt, who had been drafted in after it became clear that no local candidate could defeat Redmond.

Redmond's victory confirmed that the Parnellites would maintain their existence after the impending general election and remain a thorn in the side of the alliance between anti-Parnellites and Liberals. Meanwhile the anti-Parnellites themselves were being divided by rivalries between Tim Healy and the more moderate John Dillon and William O'Brien. The Parnellites looked on with satisfaction, proclaiming that both factions were equally guilty of Parnell's murder.

The general election of 1892 left the Parnellites with a third of the vote but only nine seats; they were strongest in Dublin, Waterford, some other towns, and parts of Leinster and the west.[1] Violence and clerical intimidation were widespread, especially in the diocese of Meath, where spiritual intimidation of Parnellites led to elections in North and South Meath being invalidated. The same diocese saw a clerically organised boycott against the Parnellite *Westmeath Examiner,* whose proprietors, the Haydens, only survived commercially through a pact between Unionists and Parnellites on Mullingar Board of Guardians, dividing advertising between Parnellite and unionist papers and excluding the clericalist *Westmeath Independent.*[2]

Such alliances recurred elsewhere; William O'Brien argued that under home rule 'Orange and Ivy minorities' would protect one another.[3] Unionists took advantage of nationalist divisions to win two middle-class seats in Dublin as well as the Ulster marginals of Derry city and West Belfast, defeating the anti-Parnellite leaders Thomas Sexton and Justin MacCarthy. A small-scale increase in the Liberal vote in Ulster as some Liberal Unionists returned to Gladstonianism from discontent at Tory-landlord dominance of the Unionist coalition[4] delivered little more than propaganda about not all Protestants being unionists.[5]

In the United Kingdom as a whole the Liberals failed to secure an overall majority but took office with nationalist support. Their campaign in Britain emphasised the 'Newcastle programme' of social reform. Any hope of a home rule mandate strong enough to overawe the House of Lords disappeared. The first session of the new Parliament was taken up with the passage of the second Home Rule Bill through the House of Commons, filibustered by Unionists, while Parnellites lost no opportunity to criticise details though avoiding outright opposition. Nationalist critics of the third Home Rule Bill were to quote Redmond's complaints about the limitations of the second.[6]

The formation of a government in favour of home rule, and detailed discussion on how home rule might be implemented, were vital in working out technical details needed for its revival and preventing the Liberals dropping the issue completely; but defeat in the House of Lords and the decision to proceed with further British reform measures to the House of Lords rather than risk immediate dissolution strengthened Parnellite charges of Liberal betrayal.

Added grounds for discontent were the failure to help the evicted tenants of the Plan of Campaign, the refusal of the Home Secretary, Asquith, to release Irish prisoners jailed for dynamite activities in Britain—exploited by Parnellites and separatists in the Amnesty Association[7]—and the numerous middle-class nationalist or Catholic activists appointed to justiceships of the peace and minor administrative positions.

William O'Brien defended anti-Parnellites against Redmondite charges of place-hunting, claiming that this was necessary to counteract a former Tory bias.[8] The origins, social pretensions and alleged favouritism of 'Morley magistrates' produced considerable sarcasm from unionists[9] and advanced nationalists, exposing a fault-line going back to O'Connell. Given the extent to which power and privilege had historically been in the hands of the Protestant landed class, any movement seeking to mobilise Catholics must address the issue but could be seen as benefiting only a few and placing recipients and sponsors under obligation to the government. Some separatists even called Catholic emancipation disastrous, because it drew Catholics into the British political system,[10] though this assumed that the Irish people could achieve complete separation, and thereby complete equality, at any time if sufficiently determined.

The hypocrisy surrounding this issue was exemplified by Redmond's decision that while he could not name Parnellites for appointments, if Morley told him of potential candidates he would comment on their suitability.[11]

When Gladstone retired, over naval expenditure, his successor, Lord Rosebery, declared that home rule could be implemented only when the 'predominant partner' was satisfied of its justice—that is, when there was an English majority in its favour. The East Wicklow Anti-Parnellite MP John Sweetman tried to persuade his colleagues to bring down the government but could find only one supporter.[12] Sweetman resigned his seat and defected to the Parnellites; he was later second president of Sinn Féin.

As Rosebery's majority was reduced by by-elections, defections, and rebellions, Parnellite MPs spent most of their time in Ireland, and a snap dissolution after losing a minor vote on the War Office led to a crushing Liberal defeat. Rosebery resigned the Liberal leadership; his successor, the irascible ultra-Protestant Sir William Harcourt, lacked enthusiasm for home rule and soon resigned in favour of the colourless Henry Campbell-Bannerman. Rosebery was widely seen as leader-in-waiting and spokesman for the Liberal imperialists—most prominently the front-benchers Asquith, Grey, and Haldane—who thought home rule a liability.[13]

The Liberal alliance seemed dead; parliamentary nationalists had little to put in its place. The Parnellites—increased to eleven at the 1895 election—experienced tensions between the separatism of many activists and the milder nationalism of some leaders. Redmond's remark during a debate on home rule at the Cambridge Union that separatism was not merely impossible but undesirable was quoted against him for the rest of his career.[14]

Some Parnellite members and officials of Dublin Corporation, such as 'Long John' Clancy and Parnell's former secretary Henry Campbell, were denounced for 'whiggery' and accused of being Freemasons.[15] Parnellite links with Cecil Rhodes, symbolised by the sinister Rhodes associate J. Rochfort Maguire, MP for West Clare 1892–5,[16] were incongruous, considering the fact that Parnellism also enjoyed the support of the separatist remnants of the IRB. The Parnellite *Irish Daily Independent* was both a centre of IRB activity[17] and a source of income for Parnellite leaders. J. L. Garvin, a Birkenhead Irishman and Parnellite activist, refused the job of British correspondent, because he was to do the work while an MP received most of the salary.[18] *United Ireland,* under the former MP Edmund Leamy, achieved a higher literary standard than the campaigning scandal-sheet of earlier days and propagated a cultural nationalism intended to offset the Parnellites' minority status,[19] but both papers were chronic loss-makers.

After the Liberal debacle, the nominal anti-Parnellite leader, Justin McCarthy,[20] stepped down, and the financial expert Thomas Sexton resigned to pursue a business career. William O'Brien responded to worsening Anglo-American relations by speaking wildly of when Fenianism sought American aid and suggesting that the Irish Party might decamp to Washington;[21] the Belfast separatist monthly *Shan Van Vocht,* edited by Alice Milligan and Ethna Carbery, hailed the prospect of Anglo-American war.[22] Douglas Hyde recalled the futility of past hopes for foreign aid and declared that the only hope was 'Sinn Féin amháin'—ourselves alone.[23]

O'Brien allowed himself to become bankrupt for refusing to pay legal costs to a Healyite, and he retired to County Mayo.[24] Two Healyite MPs, John Barry and John Morrogh (another Rhodes associate), resigned in protest at the infighting.[25]

Tim Healy and his followers, centred around his extensive network of relatives, wished to abandon the Liberal alliance, pursue independent opposition, and transfer power from party headquarters to constituency organisations, where Healy's clerical allies were powerful.[26] Critics argued that this would transform the party into a Westminster equivalent of the German Catholic Centre Party; the Healyite Cardinal Logue feared that Home Rule would lead to a republic and to French-style anti-clericalism.[27] Alternatively, Healyism might re-create the pre-Parnell situation, with MPs operating as vaguely nationalist adventurers nominated by local priests and notables, while dissatisfied young men fell into hopeless separatist conspiracies.

Frank Callanan has shown how Healy's position contravened the principles on which he excoriated Parnell during the split. Healy claimed that the party pledge was never meant to restrict MPs' actions outside Parliament; but when he originally drew up the pledge he took the stricter interpretation.[28] He denounced Dillonites for accepting money from Liberals, but during the struggle with Parnell he had privately asked Liberals to give financial assistance to the Irish Party.[29] Healy also attacked Dillonites for 'selling seats to the Liberals' by letting them take responsibility for four marginal Ulster seats, where the Irish Party could no longer afford the elaborate and expensive process of supervising the register and where a Protestant Liberal might get votes unavailable to a nationalist candidate.[30] After 1895 the North Tyrone marginal seat was represented by Liberals—irritating some nationalists, who saw North Tyrone MPs as ambitious lawyers using nationalist voters to obtain legal and judicial offices from which genuine nationalists excluded themselves.

The stronger anti-Parnellite faction was led by John Dillon, who believed in a centralised organisation dominated by the parliamentary party and aligned with the Liberals. The problems with this—apart from the Liberals' movement away from the nationalists—were that with Conservatives in power lesser concessions might be obtained by avoiding excessive commitment to the opposition, and that on some issues important sections of Irish society found Conservatives more congenial than

Liberals. This applied particularly to education, where the Catholic hierarchy praised Conservative support for Anglican and Catholic denominationalism against a Liberal preference for non-denominational state schools controlled by local authorities.[31]

There was also a tendency for sections of the higher clergy, especially in middle-class Dublin, for higher-status religious orders, whose schools produced servants of the state, and for the Catholic upper classes to defer to the social hierarchy surmounted by the Crown, as a source both of social graces and of material favours and because they saw this as enjoined by religion.[32] The capture of the St Stephen's Green constituency by a Catholic Unionist MP in 1892 and 1895, for example, reflected a local Catholic middle-class vote. Stauncher nationalists complained that teachers in 'snob' schools discouraged nationalism among pupils while 'respectable' Catholics, who despised the Irish Party and its clerical allies as vulgar demagogues showed no disposition to renounce advantages won by earlier 'demagogues' and revert to pre-emancipation days.[33]

Healy and his followers held that the Liberal alliance had died with the failure of the second Home Rule Bill and the retirement of Gladstone and that Irish MPs should do their best to obtain concessions from the existing (Conservative) government. Paradoxically, this brought them closer to the Parnellites' tactic of 'independent opposition'. In 1895–6 Healy joined Redmond in supporting the Recess Committee, set up by the liberal Unionist MP Sir Horace Plunkett to bring together nationalists and unionists in pursuing economic development; the committee's report led to the establishment of the Department of Agriculture and Technical Instruction, with Plunkett as its first vice-president.[34]

In 1896–8 Healy and Redmond again joined with Unionists in a protest campaign about the overtaxation of Ireland sparked by the report of the Childers Commission on Irish finance, set up by Gladstone as part of the preparations for home rule. The Dillonites held aloof from such contacts and clung to the project of a renewed Liberal alliance. Dillonites feared that such issues would distract from home rule, a belief reinforced by Unionist talk of 'killing home rule with kindness' through economic reform and by the virtual disappearance of Unionist support on the 'financial relations question' when the government made a few financial concessions to landlords. This was not simply revolutionary defeatism but fear that the party would dissolve unless tight divisions were maintained between supporters and opponents.

The opposition of Dillon and his allies to Plunkett's co-operative movement reflected the interests of the shopkeeping class, who played a vital role in the organisation of the Irish Party and whose children became professionals and benefited from local nationalist patronage. This was the class that Dillon joined by inheriting a shop in Ballaghderreen and that Unionist critics often attacked as an exploitative new aristocracy, the real beneficiaries of the Land War.

The Dillonites also feared that alliances between local Catholic and Protestant notables through the co-operatives and consultative bodies like the DATI's Council of Agriculture, with its mixture of elected and nominated representatives, might let the government manage Ireland without reference to the Irish Party. Clerics such as Bishop John Clancy of Elphin and the Jesuit Father Thomas Finlay particularly stimulated Dillon's anti-clerical suspicions.[35] Plunkett might be esteemed by some nationalists—Barry O'Brien thought he might lead Ireland if he were a nationalist[36]— but he could also be seen as a cunning Unionist manipulator.

Dillonism kept alive the concept of the party as proto-state but made it harder to compromise with unionism or with new social movements emerging within the nationalist community. The central problem of the Irish Party was that it was not an ordinary party. It was often compared to an army, depending on unconditional obedience; but could it maintain discipline with no prospect of victory and with its officers quarrelling?

The view that the Parnellian strategy of a tightly centralised party was only tolerable as a short-term emergency measure, which in the long run might make the party a self-selected oligarchy, was taken up by new cultural and political groups that emerged in the eighteen-nineties, distrusted by Dillon and his allies because they were independent. An extreme example is the complaint by Sinn Féin in the first decade of the twentieth century that they were never invited to national conventions of the Irish Party. Sinn Féin called home rulers 'unionists', opposed Irish Party candidates and denounced its supporters; but since the party claimed to represent nationalist Ireland as a whole and to receive its mandate from gatherings representing all nationalist organisations, the claim was not completely inconceivable.[37]

The fate of the *Freeman's Journal* can also be seen as the product of Dillonism. After backing Parnell in the belief that he would win, then switching sides after it was damaged by the Healyite *National Press,* the Dwyer Grays lost control to the party. The complaints of Healyites, a minority on the new board, reflected not just policy disputes but the belief that the paper should be run as a commercial proposition rather than a party mouthpiece.[38] The combination of party control, the whiggish reputation of its staff and the cheeseparing management of Sexton, who constantly cut costs to maintain dividends, fatally handicapped its response to new journalistic trends and led to its being superseded as the voice of conservative nationalism by Murphy's *Independent.*[39]

This political focus allowed the Dillonites, dedicated to maintaining a central parliamentary leadership relatively independent of local interests and clinging to the hope of achieving home rule through a renewal of the Liberal alliance, to defeat the Healyite call for a decentralised party dominated by the constituency organisations— which to a great extent meant the Catholic clergy and their nominees. Healy was a part-time leader, interested in his law practice as much as in his parliamentary duties.[40] The Healyites' reliance on priests and notables meant that they never created a professional organisation, despite the abortive People's Rights Association, or a mass base, except in parts of Ulster, where priests were more dominant and lay organisation weak.

In 1892–5 the parliamentary party was almost evenly divided, but by 1895 Healyites were driven from the executive.[41] The conflict was accompanied by ridicule and invective from Healy, much of which did permanent damage, and a general sense that MPs had been discredited. Subscriptions ebbed with political enthusiasm; organisation and finance were in a poor condition. The granting of seats to a wealthy Irish-Australian, J. M. Curran, and his son, T. B. Curran, in return for guaranteeing anti-Parnellite election expenses was a humiliating display of weakness.[42]

B efore considering the new movements and the revival of parliamentary politics after 1898, it is necessary to examine some tendencies in Irish union-ism to see how nationalists persuaded themselves that its disintegration was imminent.

After the lapse of the immediate home rule threat, Unionist leaders reverted to old-style amateur politics, while the economic and political decline of landlordism continued. Rents were revised downwards with falling prices under the Land Law (Ireland) Act (1881); most landlords accepted land purchase as the only way out and were primarily concerned with terms—though demands for compulsory purchase re-emerged among Ulster Protestant tenants. There was resentment at the British government's lack of respect for Irish landlords, who were seen as light-weights and a liability, and with attempts to conciliate sections of nationalist opinion with appointments such as that of T. P. Gill, a former MP criticised by the Parnell Commission, as Secretary of the DATI.

Two responses to this crisis of landlord unionism are symbolised by Lord Castletown and Lord Ashtown. Barnaby Fitzpatrick, second Viscount Castletown of Upper Ossory, was a former Liberal MP descended from an old Irish family, promin-ent in the Property Defence Association, which opposed the Plan of Campaign. He lived at Doneraile, County Cork, where his wife was the heiress to Viscount Doneraile. His co-operation with the parish priest (from 1895 the novelist P. A. Sheehan) in managing the affairs of the town could be seen as model paternalism or as blatant clerical co-operation with the powers that be. He was one of the most prominent Unionists to demand financial concessions from the government in 1896–7 after the Childers Commission on financial relations between Britain and Ireland supported claims that Ireland had been taxed beyond its ability to pay. This view was not shared by all Unionists and had greater appeal for landlords than for northern industrialists; but some landlords and landlord-oriented MPs, including Saunderson, Carson, and Lecky, made common cause with nationalism the issue.[43]

The campaign was hailed by the eccentric Standish O'Grady, a journalist and unsuccessful lawyer who combined hostility to commercial civilisation, nostalgia for a County Cork boyhood and an idealised aristocratic-heroic past with dreams of an Ireland reconciled to a military-agrarian British empire led by warrior-monarchs free from parliamentary intriguers.[44] He harked back to older 'Patriot' ideologies and forward to the alliance of lord and peasant against modernity suggested by Barrington Moore as the social base of fascism.

A speech by Lord Castletown that referred to re-enacting the Boston Tea Party unless Irish grievances were redressed led him to be hailed as a possible national leader; but the Unionist participants aimed only to pressure the government, which bought off landlords with concessions on de-rating. To nationalist commentators this proved that landlords' selfishness was incurable, while at the same time they claimed that unionism would disappear if the Childers Report were explained to the rank and file.[45]

The tax campaign influenced the conversion to nationalism of the Catholic unionist landowner Edward Martyn, first president of Sinn Féin. It provides the basis for two of his plays, *The Tale of a Town* and *The Placehunters,* which show unionists momentarily swayed by patriotism but restrained by social pressure and official patronage. When *The Tale of a Town* was staged in revised form—adding a Standish O'Grady figure—one critic called it 'the rise, fall and extinction of Lord Castletown.'[46]

For a time Lord Castletown was the most prominent unionist on the Executive Committee of the Gaelic League; he was also active in the industrial movement. These industrial and antiquarian activities were traditional pursuits of 'Patriot' aristo-crats but could be seen as amateurish and patronising dilettantism; the industrial movement, like the Gaelic League, was increasingly dominated by middle-class nationalists. Here, as elsewhere, Parnell with his industrial projects was a transitional figure. As last Chancellor of the Royal University of Ireland, Lord Castletown helped to create the National University of Ireland, in which he was advised by Canon Sheehan.[47] He was prominent in the devolutionist group of landlords after 1903 and by 1909 called himself a home-ruler. Love of ritual, and perhaps a desire to escape into fantasy from political disappointment and financial problems, found expression in the Freemasons (of which he was grand secretary) and in occultism.[48]

Frederick Trench, third Baron Ashtown, who had large estates in County Galway and other land in County Waterford, represented an agenda, widespread among the Irish ruling class in the first half of the nineteenth century, that saw the unremitting imposition of Protestantism and unrestricted property rights as the answer to Ireland's problems. He achieved notoriety as the editor of *Grievances from Ireland,* published from 1905 to 1910 to rival the Irish Unionist Association's *Notes from Ireland.* He saw nationalism and Catholicism as criminal conspiracies using concessions to advance concerted plans. When the Ancient Order of Hibernians became prominent in the Irish Party machine he called them the 'hidden power' that had directed rebellion and massacre since the seventeenth century.[49] His understanding of nationalism is encapsulated in his claim that commemorations of the Battle of Vinegar Hill really celebrated massacres of loyalists, as nobody would celebrate defeat.[50]

Lord Ashtown lamented the decline of paternalist relations between landlord and tenant and praised his harvest dinners as exemplifying the old spirit. He attended, rifle in hand, defying alleged threats.[51] When a bomb exploded at his Waterford residence in 1904, nationalists, and the police, believed he staged it.[52] His talk of social paternalism accompanied an unremitting defence of marketised agriculture and of grazing over tillage; he was made a target by anti-grazing agitations, which he interpreted as aimed at driving out loyal graziers once landlords were defeated.[53] Since *Grievances from Ireland* aimed at a cross-class Protestant readership, it disguised the extent of his pro-landlord views.[54] These appear in newspaper correspondence in which he declared that by installing the landlords in Ireland as a ruling garrison England made a contract it had no right to break and denounced land purchase as 'paying loyalists to leave the country.'[55]

Lord Ashtown was part of an ultra-Protestant sub-culture still preaching modernisation through Protestant evangelisation and speaking for groups affected by the breakdown of traditional structures of the Anglo-Irish ascendancy. In the eighteen-nineties this sub-culture was most visibly represented in Dublin by missionary groups, such as that headed by the former Catholic priest Thomas Connellan, publisher of a monthly called the *Catholic*.[56] Attempts by evangelical street-preachers to spread Protestantism were met with violence, sometimes orchestrated by priests. These and other social pressures on isolated Protestants encouraged evangelicals to believe that they were dealing with an organised tyranny of lies, while charitable work in Dublin slums by evangelicals who saw conversion as necessary for moral reform and for salvation was resented by Catholics as stealing souls by bribery.[57] The tendency of such missionaries to equate nationalism with priestly tyranny led some to include anti-nationalist propaganda in their missionary work; addressing Belfast audiences, Connellan attributed poverty to financial exactions by priests and nationalist politicians.[58]

Some evangelicals had the embarrassing habit of praising Sinn Féin's criticism of priests and of suggesting that denunciations of foreign rule should be applied to the 'foreign [i.e. Roman] Church'.[59] Griffith, attributing Irish divisions to British propaganda, claimed that these were British agents spreading religious division while fabricating accounts of mass conversions for credulous English subscribers.[60]

This might appear unpromising territory for conversions to nationalism, but the ultra-Protestant world view provided an idiom for populist protest, such as that by the journalist Lindsay Crawford and the Dublin tradesman Andrew Beattie, against the perceived incompetence of the Unionist elite and, in Dublin, for the decline of older ascendancy ties of patronage and the movement of the respectable classes from the nationalist-controlled city to the low-rated townships of Rathmines and Pembroke. This drew strength from the contemporary ultra-Protestant crusade led by Harcourt against Anglo-Catholic influence in the Church of England, while protests against ritualist practices in middle-class Anglican congregations provided populists with a rallying-point.[61] The populist critique of government and landlord collaboration with Catholic lay and clerical elites, exemplified by the Castletown-Sheehan partnership, often coincided with those made by advanced nationalists, leading to hopes that it might break down the elite manipulation seen by nationalists as central to unionism and convert Protestants to nationalism, just as populist unionists claimed that 'democratic unionism' could convert nationalists.

The continuing decline of landed unionism and the eventual defeat of southern unionism should not disguise the extent to which unionists in the eighteen-nineties could maintain a belief in eventual victory. Landlords and unionists enjoyed considerable social cachet, even in the eyes of ostensible opponents. In the heart of Dublin, Trinity College students flaunted loyalism and clashed with nationalist demonstrators; the college prided itself on its historical reputation, social standing and scholarly achievement and looked down on the Jesuit-run University College as a glorified secondary school. Even some Catholic professionals who demanded a Catholic university got their children into Trinity by finding priests willing to excuse them from the ban.[62]

Spectacle designed to surround the functionings of the state with awe was visible to a degree only dimly appreciable by later generations under a republic whose neglect of public ceremonial was a conscious reaction against the conspicuous displays of Viceroyalty. The state machine and its upper-class adherents reinforced social standing with patronage: minor jobs for favoured ex-policemen, ex-servicemen, and other hangers-on, custom for tradesmen in Dublin and provincial towns—though the sight of nationalist public authorities petitioning for barracks provoked separatist contempt. Just as nationalists despised unionism as a false consciousness manipulated by place-hunters, unionists saw nationalists as tools of demagogues and priests. This was not confined to Protestant unionists: many upper-class Catholic unionists distinguished between their personal religion and what they saw as the abuse of clerical power over the lower orders.

The business community and professions were dominated by unionists, especially when a Unionist government gave out jobs. The movement of the Protestant middle class to the townships south of the Grand Canal can be seen as a retreat to the ghetto, but at the time it could also be seen as a withdrawal of the respectable classes from corrupt and incompetent municipal administration and the rowdy populism of the city. In some ways this class were as far removed from the unionism of Lord Ashtown or Standish O'Grady as from the nationalism of Griffith or Moran: trusting in the power of the empire and the backwardness of nationalist Ireland, they engaged in wishful thinking about the demise of nationalism.[63]

Unionists were not the only group that saw politics in British terms. The eighteen-eighties and nineties saw an upsurge in trade union activity in both Britain and Ireland, aimed at recruiting unskilled labourers; and trades councils were formed in the larger towns in the late eighties. Some of those involved in England were Irish nationalists, the most prominent being the Georgist associates of Davitt, Edward McHugh, and the future nationalist MP Richard McGhee, who founded the

National Union of Dock Labourers in Liverpool.[64] Home rule propaganda in Britain compared land agitation to strikes and pointed out that one might be outlawed on the same principles as the other. Davitt pressed for the Irish Party to include labour representatives, and 1892 saw the election of two labour-nationalist anti-Parnellites, Eugene Crean, former president of Cork Trades Council, and Michael Austin.[65] Parnell also appealed to labour, and in 1892 William Field was elected for the working-class St Patrick's division of Dublin as a 'labour-Parnellite'. All three stood for a traditional view stressing Irish class solidarity against outside competition rather than the class conflict and desire for independent labour representation developing in the British movement.[66]

Independent labour organisation was another matter. Redmond denounced a County Dublin labourers' strike as an anti-Parnellite scheme by Davitt; Connolly recalled his statements as proof of the Irish Party's reactionary nature. Ironically, British advocates of an independent labour party were partly inspired by the prominence of the Irish Party under Parnell as an independent sectional party rather than an affiliate of the Liberal Party. The Irish Party maintained good relations with Labour Party MPs elected after 1906, annoying those like Connolly who advocated independent Irish socialist representation. Members of the United Irish League were allowed to join the British Labour Party on application.

Field, a well-known advocate of Irish industrial development, saw no conflict between claiming to represent labour and advocating a 'commercial party' representing business. Like many Liberals, he advocated the nationalisation of utilities and building land to reduce rents and service charges for businesses and residents, and he regularly voiced nationalist complaints that economic development was stifled by excessive transit charges and by the dominance in bodies like the Port and Docks Board and Chamber of Commerce (Field belonged to both) of unionist businessmen whose interests lay in importing and retailing rather than production. Field ran a sizable butcher's business in Blackrock, where he first came to prominence in the eighteen-seventies as a leader of the growing Catholic middle class in their challenge to Protestant control of the local council, and helped found the *Meat Trades Journal* and meat traders' organisations in Britain as well as Ireland. He became a prominent spokesman for the British meat trade, advocating Continental-style tariff protection. He remained sympathetic to organised labour for most of his parliamentary career; even Griffith and Connolly occasionally suggested that he should be asked to abandon the Irish Party for Sinn Féin or Labour. His Dublin reputation as a reformer was only partly diminished by personal eccentricity, resistance to the closure of unhygienic abbatoirs, alleged participation in price-fixing by Dublin butchers, and campaigning to replace the compulsory destruction of tubercular meat with Continental-style sale to the poor at reduced prices—the sort of pandering to vested interests that convinced many that the Irish Party was not a satisfactory vehicle for labour.[67]

Trades councils distanced themselves from Irish Party factions, though they sometimes participated in constituency selection conventions; this reflected not only British influence but fear of entanglement in factional disputes. Agricultural labourers' associations, more open to dominance by MPs, were excluded from the Irish Trades Union Congress after its first years. Field attended the first two ITUC conferences, representing a Leinster labourers' union.[68] The extension of the municipal franchise in 1899 saw the election of a labour group to Dublin Corporation, soon partially reabsorbed by existing factions.

Smaller radical groups, most famously the Irish Socialist Republican Party, appeared in the cities. Outspoken socialists like Cornelius Lyhane, driven from Cork in 1899 by the Catholic bishop,[69] and Frederick Ryan added to fears aroused in some quarters by the Liberal alliance, the spread of the British yellow press, and the appearance of rationalist publications on Dublin bookstalls.

Douglas Hyde, first president of the Gaelic League, was the home-educated son of a rural clergyman—though less attached to his irascible and hard-drinking father than to an Irish-speaking gamekeeper. He was a Protestant intellectual adrift in the decline of older social, religious and intellectual frameworks, yet he maintained a sense of separation from the self-segregating unionist metropolitan establishment.[70] The sources of the Irish revival were symbolised by his alliance with Eoin MacNeill, a professionally educated son of the middle class, the first Catholic in his civil service office after it moved from patronage to competitive examination, and a trained scholar wishing to combine modern scholarship with the beliefs of the Glens of Antrim just as he wished to see Dublin remade by the values of his childhood.[71] There was a long tradition of antiquarian interest in Irish and in small-scale bodies such as the Society for the Preservation of the Irish Language and the Gaelic Union. There was also a scholarly tradition with a strong ascendancy and elite element that tended to focus on written Irish and to see the spoken language as degenerate. This view, exemplified by the Gaelic League's *bête noire,* Professor Robert Atkinson of Trinity College, was not confined to unionist scholars but was shared by a veteran nationalist and founder-member of the Gaelic League, Thomas O'Neill Russell, who wanted a literary language based on the seventeenth-century writer Seathrún Céitinn.[72] Some nationalists, beginning with Davis, wrote of reviving Irish as a mark of Irish identity; a later exponent was William O'Brien, who after initial hostility[73] learnt Irish in prison and in 1892 spoke to the Cork Young Ireland Society in utopian terms about the language as the key to a worldwide spiritual revival.[74]

The fact that these tendencies now produced a mass movement reflects the crisis after the Parnell split. The intellectual framework laid down by the Young Irelanders and their disciples was outmoded by the passage of time and the social and political developments of the eighteen-eighties, while the political project that drove these developments was thrown into confusion by the split. The Gaelic League tried to find a new basis for nationality, uniting Parnellite and anti-Parnellite, Protestant and Catholic. The agencies that spread nineteenth-century nationalism, such as the railways and the press, were identified by Hyde as agencies of de-nationalisation; the political triumphs of O'Connell and Parnell were seen as superficial beside that of Anglicisation.[75] At a Gaelic League class in London, D. P. Moran realised that while reading nationalist literature and working in nationalist organisations he had been a West Briton, knowing nothing of Irish Ireland.[76]

While the Gaelic League's inspiration was nationalist, to avoid factional struggles it was affiliated to none of the nationalist parties; it also attracted some unionists, who saw language revival as non-political or who hoped that cultural revivalism might replace political nationalism. Denunciations by the Gaelic League of those who sought political autonomy through a 'Union of Hearts' while acquiescing in cultural Anglicisation could be incorporated in a separatist critique of the Irish Party, as in Father Peter Yorke's lecture of 1899, 'The Turn of the Tide', which accused parliamentarians of boycotting Irish in favour of 'the all-important task of making the political wheel go around, compared British Liberal talk of a 'Union of Hearts' to the betrayer's kiss of Judas, and hoped the language revival would realise Swift's wish to build a wall of brass around Ireland.[77]

The idea that political nationalism was superfluous or even harmful in com- parison with cultural revival could also be exploited by the tradition of 'patriotic' Irish Toryism, which claimed that Ireland's woes stemmed from British Liberal interference on behalf of nationalists and emphasised Irish distinctiveness to argue that the Irish were 'naturally' unsuited to British ideas of responsible government and were better off under paternal aristocratic rule. If the Welsh continued to use their own language without developing a political nationalism, might not the Irish revival co-exist with loyalty to the empire? (Griffith spoke darkly of aristocratic Gaelic Leaguers advocating 'a Welshified Ireland strumming a harp of Birmingham manufacture.')[78] Antiquarian unionists like Standish O'Grady could contrast pre- conquest Irish aristocrats with the plebeian levellers of contemporary nationalism and enquire what Red Hugh O'Donnell or Dónall O'Sullivan Beare would have thought of republicans and Land Leaguers. Such questions could prove embarrassing for those nationalists who bothered to address them. William Rooney suggested that eighteenth-century Irish poetry seemed Jacobite rather than republican because Jacobite collectors ignored republican songs.[79]

The threat of a unionist takeover receded after 1900 as the Gaelic League de- veloped mass membership and became equated with populist values through widely publicised clashes with Trinity dons over Irish in the schools and the involvement of Catholic priests at lower levels. Its branches fitted in to the nationalist tradition of local politico-literary societies, and it built up a constituency of self-improving urban white-collar workers who found in the league and in the rediscovery of the rural west a society that seemed relatively egalitarian and deeply rooted, in contrast with the social shows and restrictions of urban life. The idea of reviving Irish as a central nationalist objective gained widespread if often superficial support.

These developments brought new problems. Some sections of the higher clergy were hostile to the Gaelic League, from utilitarianism, snobbery, or a desire to control socialisation in provincial towns.[80] But it proved attractive to believers in a 'faith and fatherland' Irishness, who wished to downgrade rebellious and relatively secular nineteenth-century nationalism and dangerous outside influences in favour of a patriarchal rural past.[81] Ironically, their unionist counterparts, like O'Grady, shared the sentimental and idyllic view of the past. Clericalists found powerful spokesmen in Father Peadar Ó Laoghaire, whose novel *Séadna* marked a decisive victory for those who believed that written Irish should reflect the contemporary spoken language, the lexicographer Father Pádraig Ó Duinnín, and D. P. Moran's *Leader*. They were all identified with the faction spearheaded by the Keating Branch of the league in Dublin, whose cultural exclusivity later became identified with separatism.

Many of the Gaelic League's attitudes were anathema to separatists in the Fenian tradition, because its Gaelicism discounted the literature of the nineteenth-century Anglo-Irish separatist tradition, because some Gaelic Leaguers' view of Irishness as 'naturally' identified with Catholicism ran counter to Fenian tradition and to painful experiences of conflict with church authorities, and because its emphasis on cultural revival as superior to political activism contradicted the view, which nineteenth-century separatists shared with their parliamentarian rivals, that political participation was intrinsic to the life of a nation. (Gaelic Leaguers criticised Davis for implying in 'A Nation Once Again' that a nation was not really a nation without political institutions.) Both separatists and parliamentarians tried to annex the organisation for their own purposes, with some success; the league's leadership resisted the offer of a parliamentary seat for Hyde—a traditional party tactic in absorbing independent organisations—but had to take cognisance of party views and strike a balance between them and separatist activists.

T he last years of the decade saw a revival of political nationalism. Four factors stand out: the 1798 centenary; the Boer War; the extension of elected local government throughout Ireland, widening the franchise where it already existed; and the United Irish League under William O'Brien.

During the 1798 anniversary, parliamentarians and separatists competed to control commemorative events and the construction of monuments, to show strength and to recruit new activists. The monuments also challenged landlord and state control of public space, and their construction provided opportunities to weed out lukewarm nationalists. In Youghal, the Town Commissioners' decision not to replace a fountain donated by a landlord with a 1798 monument led to the return of rival nationalist candidates at the next local election.[82] In Dublin, separatists raised funds for a Wolfe Tone monument in St Stephen's Green, while Redmond planned a Parnell monument at the top of O'Connell Street.[83] Separatists denounced Redmond for hindering the completion of the Tone memorial, for exploiting Parnell's memory for his own political aggrandisement, and for commissioning the Irish-

American sculptor Augustus St Gaudens rather than an Irish artist. Redmond was not, however, the only obstacle to the Tone monument. The foundation stone laid by John O'Leary at St Stephen's Green became an embarrassment because of infighting and political mismanagement. Meanwhile the site of the proposed memorial was taken by a Unionist-sponsored monument to the Irishmen who fought in the British army during the Boer war, dubbed by separatists the 'Traitors' Gate'.[84] Separatists—and some parliamentarians, notably William Redmond—predicted that colonial tensions between France and Britain might bring war and a French invasion more successful than 1798.[85]

Such attitudes were hardly likely to promote Liberal-nationalist alignment, which was weakened further by war between Britain and the South African Boer republics. The Liberals split three ways: Rosebery, Asquith and the Liberal imperialists backed the war, a radical minority denounced it as aggression by jingoist imperialists and cosmopolitan financiers, while Campbell-Bannerman tried to maintain neutrality.[86]

British pro-Boers included many supporters of home rule, but few went as far as mainstream Irish nationalists. Irish Party papers rejoiced in British defeats and lamented the Boers' failure to seize the ports before British reinforcements landed. Resolutions congratulated Joseph Chamberlain for wrecking the British empire.[87] William O'Brien's *Irish People* published facetious verses about British setbacks,[88] and badges showing Paul Kruger, the president of Transvaal, became popular. Party activists were dismissed from the magistracy by the Dublin Castle authorities for exulting in Boer victories. Davitt resigned from Parliament in protest at the war and covered it as a journalist behind Boer lines. (A doubtful source claims that he participated in diplomatic intrigues aimed at French intervention.)[89]

Some responses anticipated the First World War. Emigration increased because of rumours that British losses would lead to conscription.[90] An anti-recruiting campaign got under way, drawing on older precedents and using Young Ireland and Fenian anti-recruiting ballads. Parliamentarians and separatists alike pointed out the disproportionate number of Irishmen in the British army, attributing this to British racial degeneracy. They needed only to cite British social-Darwinist literature on the deteriorating physique of recruits, radical complaints about hysterical jingoism, music-hall jeers at Kruger as a Bible-reading hypocrite, and Kipling's 'Absent-Minded Beggar' appealing for soldiers' abandoned mistresses and 'illegitimate' children.[91] Potential recruits were told that Irish soldiers were sent to the slaughter to protect British lives.[92] Joseph Devlin wrote a ballad accusing the British army of massacre and rape (reprinted by separatist opponents during the First World War).[93] Father P. F. Kavanagh, author of a 'faith and fatherland' history of the 1798 rising, asserted that every soldier who died fighting for Britain would go to Hell as a murderer.[94] Survivors would end in workhouses as a burden on the ratepayers.

Separatists accused parliamentarians of incompetent and half-hearted opposition to recruitment, pointing out that papers that denounced the war also carried recruiting advertisements, and said that ex-soldiers should be ostracised for ever.[95] The concept of neutrality entered separatist discourse. Maud Gonne founded an Irish Neutrality Association, and Terence MacSwiney noted as an argument against home rule that only complete separation would keep Ireland out of British wars.[96]

Nationalists seized on the fact that recruitment rates were lower in the Protestant north than in Dublin (because of a shortage of employment opportunities) as proof of the superficiality of Orange loyalties. A versifier remarked that

It is painfully apparent that the 'Chapters' black and red
Are content to fight, as usual, with words,

concluding that when Home Rule came

You may safely risk your very latest coin
That we ne'er shall see the warriors of 'Dyan, Number One'
Lining ditches on the pleasant banks of Boyne.[97]

The misfortunes of upper-class unionist reservists captured by the Boers (including the future Prime Minister of Northern Ireland, James Craig) provoked nationalist mirth.

The targets of this ridicule saw things differently. Alvin Jackson discusses the role of the Boer War in the political formation of the Ulster unionist elite that opposed the third Home Rule Bill;[98] and nationalists in the House of Commons cheering British defeats certainly provided material for propaganda.[99] Unionists claimed that these expressions of 'disloyalty' were superficial political gestures and that Irishmen in the British army—and the crowds and civic officials who welcomed Queen Victoria to Ireland in 1900—represented Irish attitudes. After a royal proclamation declared that in honour of the deeds of Irishmen in the British army they might wear shamrock—previously prohibited as a political emblem—on St Patrick's Day, Belfast unionists flaunted it as a symbol of loyalty, while nationalists went unadorned or pinned shamrock to Kruger badges.[100]

Unionists could point out that nationalist assistance to the Boers was limited to fund-raising by the Irish Transvaal Committee, composed of separatists and some MPs, and to the few Irish and Irish-Americans who joined volunteers of other nationalities in two 'Irish Brigades', fighting under John Blake, John MacBride, and Arthur Lynch.[101] Lynch, the Australian littérateur who commanded one of these units, later declared that if the Irish throughout the world sent so few volunteers, talk of fighting for freedom could not be taken seriously.[102] Lord Salisbury taunted that even with the British army tied down in South Africa there had been no serious disturbances in Ireland.[103] Moran compared nationalists 'screeching after the manly Boers' to Dublin Fusiliers who cheered Kruger while embarking to fight him. One motive for the Easter Rising was the fear that nationalism would die of ridicule if the First World War repeated the Boer War experience.

Pro-Boer resolutions and speeches received added force when they were made by members of the new county councils. In the eighteen-eighties Salisbury had declared, regarding Chamberlain's proposal of provincial councils, that elected Irish local government would be worse than home rule. An earlier Unionist scheme included nominated members (as on boards of guardians) to preserve landlord and unionist influence. The abandonment of this provision showed how little attention the Unionist government now paid to southern landlords.[104]

Some landlords hoped that local influence might give them a significant presence on the new councils, and this was reinforced when Redmond stated that in recognition of their local role unionists should have a fair share of the new councils—reflecting the British situation, where aristocrats often chaired local authorities. This revealed a personal conviction, as well as the advantage for Parnellites of retaining potential Unionist allies.[105]

Redmond's proposal met with little success, partly because of opposition from the United Irish League. The league had been founded by William O'Brien in County Mayo in 1398 in response to the near-famine of 1897–8 in the west and to bring about a reunification through a mass agrarian movement, and it came to dominate party organisation and local government. The UIL made local elections a test of national loyalties and said that concessions to landlords before the land question was settled showed weakness and prolonged the fight: returning landlords by election or co-option would let them dominate the new bodies, with the assistance of lukewarm nationalists.[106]

Outside north-eastern Ulster, the local elections produced extensive defeats of landlords, and those who succeeded, such as O'Conor Don in Roscommon and Lord Greville, first chairman of Westmeath County Council, were isolated by pro-Boer resolutions and the flying of the Green Flag (which the RIC removed by force) over courthouses where the councils met.[107] O'Conor Don's retort that such behaviour was inconsistent with willingness to take the oath of allegiance as magistrates merely illustrates the fact that the real issue was consolidation of the nationalist bloc.[108] Many remaining Unionists withdrew at the end of their first three-year terms in 1902; unionist propaganda emphasised the exclusion of these large property-holders and employers from local government.

Local government reform extended the patronage available to nationalists (and to unionists in Ulster), strengthened intermediate organisations at the expense of London-centred leadership in both unionist and nationalist parties, and in the long run gave nationalists at local level a reputation for jobbery and petty corruption (not entirely dispelled by comparisons with the corruption and patronage of the old landlord-controlled bodies) and bred discontent with dominant local factions.

The establishment of the non-political General Council of County Councils by the Wexford landowner and Home Rule MP Sir Thomas Esmonde led some government officials to fear, and some separatists to hope, that it might become an embryonic parliament.[109] However, Esmonde, who had been associated with Healy in the factional disputes of the eighteen-nineties, was distrusted by the United Irish League. The UIL leadership suspected him of wishing to create an assembly of notables that could rival the party and deal independently with the government. UIL representatives on the General Council passed a home rule resolution, over Esmonde's protests, causing unionist councils to withdraw.[110] Esmonde and John Sweetman, representing Meath County Council, maintained nominal pre-eminence until 1907, but the possibility that the General Council might rival Dublin Castle or the Irish Party had been eliminated—except from Sinn Féin propaganda.

The UIL aimed at the compulsory purchase of tenanted land and the division of grazing land among local smallholders, but it also tried to counter separatist exploitation of the 1798 centenary and to develop a popular movement to overcome factional divisions at local level and to force MPs to reunite, on O'Brien's terms. Landlords and graziers became targets of agitation led by O'Brien, Davitt (as MP for South Mayo), and a network of local activists and paid organisers—paid by O'Brien's wife, Sophie Raffalovich, whose family were prominent merchants in Odessa. UIL branches spread throughout Connacht, using boycott tactics to force local hold-outs to join. O'Brien established a weekly paper, the *Irish People*—named after the Fenian paper of the sixties and decorated with crossed pike-and-gun motifs—to function as *United Ireland* had in the eighties. He declared that the new league was the people's organisation and that the people, not politicians, should be its basis.[111] An elaborate representative structure linked branches through county and provincial directories to a National Directory. A court case in County Mayo in which a Parnellite and an anti-Parnellite were jointly tried and imprisoned for league activities symbolised unity. Parnellites such as Timothy Harrington and J. J. O'Kelly appeared on UIL platforms or wrote for the *Irish People*.

Redmond saw much of his base in the west eroded and his attempts at tactical alliance with Unionists defeated by the renewed land agitation, and he faced the prospect of being confined to an urban base uncomfortably reliant on separatist and radical support. Healy recognised that the UIL's aim of re-creating a strong centrally led movement based on mass agitation disrupted the prospect of an Ireland managed by brokerage between the British government and Catholic lay and clerical elites acting in the name of a quiescent populace. It was also clear that O'Brien's aim of purifying the parliamentary representation as part of a league-led reunification was primarily directed against Healy and his allies.

Despite the bitter memories of the split, Healy and Redmond had been pushed into tacit co-operation by hostility to Dillon, the need for allies, and the fact that William Martin Murphy was virtually the only potential purchaser available for the loss-making *Irish Independent*. They began a process of reunification among MPs, led from above, to counter the UIL threat growing up from below. Faced with the prospect of being isolated as the enemy of reunification, Dillon reluctantly joined the merger. As a gesture to Parnellites, Redmond was chosen as leader, despite Dillon's preference for the more biddable Harrington.[112] This reluctance stemmed from Redmond's links to Healy and his conservatism in nationalist eyes—embarrassingly demonstrated when he praised the bravery of Irishmen in the British army and spoke of the welcome Queen Victoria might expect on her coming visit[113]—but the Parnellite leader was too formidable to leave outside in alliance with Healy.

The events of the following months are often presented as a foolish revolt by Healy against the reunited Irish Party.[114] They were a determined purge of Healyites and other whiggish MPs, aimed at establishing dominance by O'Brien and the Dillonites, while Redmond tried to maintain a counterbalance. The *Irish People* always declared reunification unacceptable if it merely 'stereotyped the existing Parliamentary representation.'[115] As it proclaimed that Healyites must be driven from Parliament to avoid a return to the dissensions of the nineties, and turned a vote on allowing Murphy to supply electricity to Dublin into a loyalty test,[116] Redmond tried to lure Murphy back into Parliament by offering an unopposed return for North Mayo. The County Mayo UIL disregarded the deal; and these defeats sharpened Murphy's dislike for the party.[117]

Redmond was also involved in allowing J. L. Carew, defeated in College Green, Dublin, by the UIL-supported trade unionist J. P. Nannetti, to seize South Meath from John Howard Parnell through an electoral technicality.[118]

Healy's principal lieutenants were defeated, and Healy was never again a serious challenger for the leadership. In Cork city O'Brien personally unseated Healy's brother and confidant Maurice in a violent campaign during which the Healys' cousin, A. M. Sullivan, received head injuries and the *Cork Daily Herald,* owned by Healy's allies, the Morroghs, was destroyed by a boycott organised by the UIL.[119] In County Donegal, Bishop O'Donnell's support of the UIL forced the veteran T. D. Sullivan out of West Donegal without a contest, while the financial expert Arthur O'Connor was driven from his East Donegal seat to North Donegal—where the absentee T. B. Curran stepped down and O'Connor had the support of the Healyite Bishop of Derry, John Keyes O'Doherty—then defeated by a Derry solicitor, William O'Doherty, with O'Donnell openly intervening in Bishop O'Doherty's diocese.[120]

In Derry city the UIL denounced the whiggish MP Count Moore, a Tipperary Catholic landlord supported by Bishop O'Doherty and his clergy, who discouraged nationalist political organisation in the city, fearing it would antagonise Protestants and endanger clerical leadership,[121] and declared it better for Derry to have a Unionist MP than a rackrenting whig. A Unionist was elected, compounding the political damage suffered through Dillonite refusal to support Healyite campaigns about Derry Corporation.[122]

The purge was not universally successful, as the UIL had to come to terms with some minor Healyites and whigs. The UIL activist Laurence Ginnell failed to unseat the Healyite Hugh Kennedy in North Westmeath, while T. D. Sullivan's brother Dónal retained South Westmeath until his death in 1907. (This may reflect the bitterness of the Parnell split in the Meath diocese and the influence of the bishop, based in Mullingar.) Major J. E. Jameson, of the whiskey dynasty, was retained in

West Clare, despite clear imperialist sympathies, after pledging himself to the UIL. The Presbyterian distiller Sam Young was entrenched in East Cavan by his wealth and clericalist-Healyite strength in the Ulster borderland: he regularly praised Catholicism, so fervently as to rouse expectations of conversion. Esmonde remained in Parliament by moving from County Kerry to his native North Wexford, where he defeated Healy's brother Thomas. His victory came despite the protests of the Healyite councillor John Cummins and his uncle, the veteran land campaigner Canon Thomas Doyle of Ramsgrange, who declared that Redmond's denunciations of the Catholic clergy in the split—contrasted with Parnell's politeness—meant that no Catholic should have anything to do with him.[123]

Healy was challenged in North Louth by the UIL organiser Edmund Haviland-Burke. O'Brien held a rally in Dundalk, daring Healy to face his constituents. Healy unexpectedly appeared. Amid uproar and missile-throwing, the two spoke from the same platform; O'Brien characterised the crowd as the electors of North Louth telling Healy to quit, while Healy denounced them as a hired mob.[124] Healy's re-election can be attributed to his ability to concentrate on his own defence while his opponents fought many other campaigns, to clerical support, and to a personal following in Carlingford and Cooley that countered the anti-Healy vote centred in Dundalk. O'Brien's local supporters included lodges of the AOH; the *Irish People* published reports of AOH meetings.

Losses to unionism in County Derry and—more surprisingly—in Galway (due to a decay of local organisation under an absentee MP and a free-spending campaign by a prominent Catholic landlord) were offset by the recapture of St Stephen's Green and South Dublin, helped by hard-line Unionist revolts.[125] The Dublin seats were taken by prominent Catholic businessmen whose nationalism was lukewarm. James McCann in St Stephen's Green was a former Unionist who did not take the party whip but endeared himself to Irish-Irelanders by experiments in industrial development; J. J. Mooney, from a well-known Dublin family of publicans, whose brother was a prominent associate of Murphy, became a confidant of Redmond and one of the most right-wing party members. Nonetheless, their victories underlined southern unionist weakness.

UIL denunciations of Healyites in 1900 were reminiscent of those directed against the Irish Party by Sinn Féin in 1918. The Healyites were depicted as adventurers engaged in shady financial speculations and as place-hunting social climbers, with the attendance of Young, T. B. Curran and Carew at a garden party in Buckingham Palace attracting particular derision.[126] Florence O'Driscoll, a Healyite ex-MP who stood in Mid-Tipperary, had connections with Australian gold-mining stocks,[127] while the Morroghs had business connections with Rhodes, though their profits from de Beers went into a woollen mill at Blarney.[128]

With MPs unpaid and Irish members generally drawn from a lower social class than other nineteenth-century politicians, some lent their names to companies, often dubious ones.[129] The UIL-supported West Mayo MP, Dr Robert Ambrose, was involved in a company collapse some years previously;[130] and William O'Malley, member for Connemara, had several similar experiences.[131] O'Brien accused MPs of reviving the corruption and ineffectiveness of pre-Parnell politics while the country faced irreversible depopulation through emigration. The UIL defined itself against MPs and their London-centred perspective, just as populist revolts within unionism attacked aristocratic amateurism and Westminster-fixation.[132]

The factionalism of the eighteen-nineties was blamed on MPs' self-indulgence. Healyites who appealed to their voting record in the House of Commons were told that what counted was work among the people. O'Brien asked whether the nation belonged to MPs or to the people; this was to be a recurring Sinn Féin theme, though where Sinn Féin declared that parliamentary oligarchy could be prevented only by abstention, O'Brien claimed that UIL representative structures made MPs accountable. A recurrent theme of nationalists dissatisfied with parliamentarianism but unwilling to give it up was that MPs should be subordinated to a Dublin executive removed from the Westminster atmosphere. The UIL platform included commitments to such Irish-Ireland themes as language revival and industrial development. The *Irish People* had a companion journal aimed at young people, *St. Patrick's,* founded by O'Brien at the behest of a priest to rival 'corrupting' British journals; its youthful contributors included Brian O'Higgins, Peadar Kearney, Cahir Healy, and Terence MacSwiney.[133]

Philip Bull argues that the UIL could have forestalled the growth of Sinn Féin had O'Brien's intentions not been derailed as MPs came to dominate the UIL executive. He also argues that the South Mayo by-election of 1900 for Davitt's seat, where Griffith and Rooney ran the absent John MacBride against O'Brien's protégé John O'Donnell, marks a missed opportunity to conciliate the new generation of separatists.[134] Brian Maye presents the Irish Party as incompetents for rejecting Griffith's 'statesmanlike' suggestion that they should elect MacBride as a gesture of support for the Boers, then return O'Donnell after MacBride was unseated by Parliament.[135] The sincerity of this proposal has been exaggerated: when it was rejected, separatists denounced the parliamentarians as traitors and tools of England. Griffith even published claims that the financing of the UIL by O'Brien's wife reflected a 'Jewish plot' to prop up the British empire by undermining separatism and by damaging the French army through Dreyfus.[136] When the Irish Party later elected another leader of the Irish Brigade, Arthur Lynch, Griffith did not hail this expression of support for the Boers but denounced Lynch as a turncoat and told separatists not to support him.[137] Griffith regularly offered the Irish Party 'statesmanlike' advice and used their refusals to contrast his own 'disinterested wisdom' with their 'folly and corruption'.

The South Mayo by-election took place as the UIL was gathering momentum for the general election of 1900. To back down would have weakened its aura of invincibility and strengthened Healyite resistance. The MacBride candidacy represented an alliance between Healyites, graziers, and separatists fearing the re-emergence of a strong parliamentary movement.[138] Neither side emerged with credit. Griffith claimed that Davitt—absent in South Africa—supported him, while the UIL claimed that MacBride supported them.[139] O'Brien and the Sligo MP P. A. McHugh used mob violence and boycotted the MacBrides and other opponents.[140]

The wider view of the UIL as anticipating Sinn Féin ignores flaws visible to contemporary observers. Like the Land League, the UIL was an agrarian movement, based on western small farmers, which moderated its radicalism as it tried to attract more conservative groups. It could be captured by local elites who purged rank-and-file radicalism. In Enniskillen, for instance, a branch dominated by working-class members was disaffiliated after it criticised merchants who dominated nationalist politics in the town—notably Jeremiah Jordan MP and his successor, Patrick Crumley—for decorating shops with Union Jacks and subscribing to a military monument.[141] Its agrarian focus limited its appeal in urban areas; in Dublin it had significant numbers of activists only in the working-class Arran Quay ward—Field's base—and was seen as a tool of publicans.[142] There were well-publicised instances of UIL members operating as grabbers or graziers. When an Irish-American priest said that the UIL awaited the opportunity to rise up against England, Griffith snorted: 'If they ever do rise it will be for the purpose of grabbing their neighbours' farms.'[143]

It may be questioned how far the new MPs were an improvement on their predecessors. Some of the defeated, like the absentee Currans and the Kildare MP C. J. Engledew, a minor landowner who thought the Local Government Act too radical and the only nationalist MP to vote thanks to Kitchener after the battle of Omdurman,[144] were no loss; but T. D. Sullivan, who was actively pro-Boer and respected even by separatists, and the financial experts Maurice Healy and Arthur O'Connor were definite losses. While new MPs such as Conor O'Kelly, John O'Donnell, Tom O'Donnell and John Pius Boland represented a new generation, others, such as the veteran Sligo ex-Fenian and Land Leaguer John O'Dowd, came from the same generation and background as their predecessors. Some shared the growing conservatism of contemporaries who had already entered Parliament.

References to 'the squires of the Irish National Party'[145] and the image of the party as replicas of Redmond are mistaken, though it did contain a few members from landed backgrounds. Though his family background, the Protestantism of his mother and second wife and his education at Clongowes Wood certainly pre-disposed him towards accommodation with the older elites and the empire, Redmond himself was the son of a younger son, trained for the professions rather than land ownership. His nationalist politics were seen as dangerously radical by his mother and by the uncle from whom he eventually inherited a heavily mortgaged estate.[146] The party's MPs and activists were dominated by two categories. One was the established professional or tradesman with a local base, an element that became more predominant over time. This group grew more conservative as they aged, achieved professional success or inherited family businesses, and acquired family responsibilities. Such people could be drawn from the class of tradesmen and professionals who serviced Irish communities in British cities as well as from the towns and villages of Ireland. William M'Killop, elected for Sligo North in 1900, was a Glasgow restaurateur; the *United Irishman* noted that his Glasgow premises were decorated with Union Jacks to celebrate the relief of Mafeking.[147]

The second group were professional activists, who might have business experience or professional qualifications but concentrated on politics. David Sheehy, formerly a miller, was one example. The image of the small-town businessman who damages or loses his business by political involvement recurs in the literature of the period, sometimes symbolising self-sacrifice,[148] sometimes the irrelevance of politics to the welfare of Ireland.[149] The Irish MP in London supporting himself by journalism and the briefless barrister writing for the *Freeman's Journal* and serving as political organiser were counterparts of the socially marginal white-collar workers Tom Garvin identifies as the backbone of physical-force separatism.[150] This could be a stepping-stone to membership of the first group through inheritance, professional advancement or other means of acquiring status or part of a permanent Bohemian life-style, exemplified by T. P. O'Connor. J. L. Carew's social climbing was attributed to the ambitions of his new wife;[151] the contrast between the impoverished Dillon and O'Brien of the Land War and the wealthy married men of later years was a constant theme of critics.

In either form, this provided the basis for another contemporary stereotype of the Irish MP, invoked by conservatives and separatists alike: a needy and cynical adventurer, uttering sentiments he did not feel to make himself worth buying.[152] Someone like James Mullin, who raised himself from a labouring background in County Tyrone through Queen's College, Galway, to become a doctor and nationalist leader in Cardiff, might see his career as proof that anti-Irish prejudice was dying down and that it was possible to accommodate Irish identity on honourable terms within the British empire; others might see his movement from Fenianism to Davittite radicalism, sentimental republicanism and a justiceship of the peace, his criticism of the Gaelic League and abandonment of Catholicism for agnosticism as embodying parliamentarian apostasy.[153]

O'Brien's recruits, from the same background as their Healyite rivals, were exposed to similar criticisms. Healy taunted the UIL with the fact that its organisers included one thrice-convicted drunkard and one rejected police recruit, and called them ruffians fed on the thirty pieces of silver.[154] John O'Donnell was regularly accused of entering politics only after being rejected by the RIC, though he produced evidence disproving it. Griffith also accused him of wife-beating.[155] Edmund Haviland-Burke, who stood against Healy and was later returned for a midland

constituency, was an English-born former Liberal candidate for an English constituency, though he had also been a Protestant Home Rule Association activist in
the eighties and a prominent Parnellite activist in the nineties; Griffith regularly
denounced him as an Englishman and derided his claim of descent from Edmund
Burke, who had no direct descendants. (Haviland-Burke claimed collateral descent
through Burke's sister.)[156]

The urban intellectuals of the Irish-Ireland movements were generally scornful
of the UIL, because of its agrarian focus and its intolerance of debate. Its nominal
commitment to industrial development and to the Irish revival reflected existing
nationalist pieties (O'Brien claimed that the revival derived from *United Ireland*)
rather than later, more intense developments; the County Donegal Gaelic Leaguer
and UIL activist P. T. MacGinley complained that its campaigns were conducted
through English even in Irish-speaking areas.[157] Its representative mechanisms had
little ability to hold the leadership to account; since the national convention lasted
only a day or two, it was hard for delegates to concert action from the floor or to
debate matters adequately—though a widespread groundswell of opinion could
override the leadership. This top-down structure was partly inherent in the nature
of constitutionalist politics, since the Irish Party could plead they understood the
Westminster situation better than the rank and file, but it also reflected the personality of William O'Brien.

O'Brien, like other prominent nationalists, came from a provincial middle-class
family that combined resentment at the local gentry with awe at their social
standing and with compensatory claims to noble lineage.[158] O'Brien himself claimed
kinship with Edmund Burke through his mother's family, the Nagles. The eighteen-
sixties saw conflict between the parents on the one hand, disillusioned Young
Irelanders who had become supporters of the Liberal lawyer and Mallow MP
Edward Sullivan, who had prosecuted Fenians,[159] and O'Brien's older brother, a
Fenian, who rejected his mother's hope that he might become a priest and his
father's ambition of getting him an official position through political influence.[160]
This was interrupted by the family's financial collapse and transplantation to Cork;
the youthful William became a journalist through his facility with words and acted
as mainstay of the family after his father died, while his mother and siblings
slowly died from TB.[161]

O'Brien found solace in politics and religion. He was a devout Catholic with a
strong mystical streak, believing that without the hopes offered by religion life was
unbearable; Healy said he could always tell when he took O'Brien's coat by mistake
because he found *The Imitation of Christ* in the pocket.[162] Yet he briefly attended
Queen's College, despite the ecclesiastical ban, spent much of his career in
opposition to most Irish priests, wrote scathingly of clerical social and political pretensions, and was widely seen as anti-clerical. He found in the idiom of romantic
nationalism a means of identifying his emotional turmoil and social insecurity with
the economic decline and political oppression of his country yet was shrewd

enough to withdraw from the IRB when he realised it was inefficient and riddled with informers.[163]

In the eighteen-eighties O'Brien was seen as devoted utterly to the cause, alone in the world, living in a hotel room with his worldly goods contained in two suitcases, pouring out speeches and journalism, risking his life in prison; to unionists he was an obscene agitator, whose violations of journalistic decorum and use of his body as a political weapon aroused disgust. For separatists he was an impostor aping genuine martyrs. O'Donovan Rossa, driven by memories of the Famine dead and seeing in O'Brien's defiance of prison regulations (during short sentences for land agitation) a parody of his own life-or-death struggles in Milbank Penitentiary, denounced O'Brien's portrayal of separatists as drunken fantasists and predicted that he would eventually receive a government pension.[164] The austere O'Leary—whose house property in County Tipperary was affected by O'Brien's Plan of Campaign—remarked that complaints about unfair prison treatment were unmanly and that patriots should accept the natural consequence of rebellion.[165]

O'Brien's political style rested on self-dramatisation and a certain awareness of the extent to which this was political theatre. This self-awareness saved him for much of his career from the fate of Frank Hugh O'Donnell, a similar figure, who devoured his life in anachronistic visions of neo-aristocratic nationalism and pouring out diatribes against scapegoats for the failure of his dreams.[166] The later O'Brien also remained relatively receptive to some dissatisfactions and enthusiasms of younger nationalists; there was some validity in Griffith's comment that he retained the vigour and enthusiasm of a boy.

The other side of this enthusiasm was egotism, which led Davitt to nickname him 'the Czar'.[167] Moran called him 'the Screecher' (i.e. baby). While his intuitions were often shrewd, once he formed an opinion he clung to it as if he, and Ireland, could not survive its defeat. The structures of the UIL offered not a forum for consultation but the framework for Bonapartist appeals over the heads of the political elite, with the assumption that O'Brien knew what the people wanted and that structures that refused to endorse him could not represent 'the people'. Criticism was unthinkable: an enemy could not be simply mistaken. His symbolic language of all-or-nothing defiance can be justified as a political tactic, but his career was littered with embarrassing changes of course, in which demonised enemies became angels of light, and vice versa, and with the ruined lives of associates led to disaster by his recklessness.

He was perhaps the most powerful platform orator of his day, though as his career went on his characteristic tricks irritated many who in adolescence absorbed them uncritically; Irish-Irelander distrust of oratory reacted against O'Brien's sentimental Niagara as much as Redmond's polished classical style. Expressions of sympathy from separatists and Irish-Irelanders come from the last stage of his career, when his arrogant enthusiasm left him fighting the structures he himself created. The Irish-Ireland view of his zenith is encapsulated by Moran's portrayal of

'John Francis Xavier High Faluter' revelling in flattery as no more than his due, and intoxicating provincials with vacuous rhetoric as he declares that Ireland's fate depends on replacing their 'Tweedleite' [Healyite] MP with an equally corrupt 'Twaddleite'.[168]

The limits of debate within the UIL were manifest at the national convention after the general election of 1900. Redmond and his Parnellite allies wished to re-admit Healy to the party. O'Brien pre-empted this by arranging a resolution forbidding MPs to re-admit Healy. An orchestrated campaign saw numerous UIL branches pass resolutions demanding Healy's exclusion; when Harrington and Redmond's confidant Pat O'Brien, MP for Kilkenny city, advocated Healy's retention, the *Irish People* threatened them with expulsion.[169]

Healy decided that the decision of the convention—held in the first week of the parliamentary session to assert that Ireland's centre of gravity rested in Dublin rather than London—was a foregone conclusion and preferred to raise Irish questions in Parliament.[170] He also unexpectedly moved a by-election writ for North Monaghan, hoping to disrupt the arrangements for selecting candidates.

Harrington was shouted down at the convention, despite Redmond's attempts to secure him a hearing and his protest that if the Irish people could not tolerate debate they did not deserve freedom.[171] O'Brien called Healy a poisoned bullet that must be extracted immediately; an ally said that Healy had one hand on the nation's throat and another in its pocket.[172] Just before the vote, Redmond stated that although he observed impartiality as chairman and would accept the decision, he personally disagreed with the motion. On a show of hands, only a small minority opposed the motion. (Carew was also excluded.[173]) Healy declared: 'The Member for Cork has created two Irish Parties, of which I am one.'[174]

2

ELITES
1900–5

The reunification of the Irish Party produced a new wave of agitation and saw several MPs imprisoned, but at first it had little impact. The Unionist government had won a landslide victory in 1900, while the Liberals were divided, irritated by Irish support for the Boers and debating whether home rule should be definitely abandoned as a political liability. The Tories' Education Act, whose subsidies for denominational schools in England pleased the Catholic Church but antagonised the Nonconformists, who provided the core of Liberal support, left the party caught between further alienating the Liberals—and those party supporters, such as Davitt, who shared Liberal views on education—and antagonising the Catholic clergy and sections of the Irish community in Britain. Tim Healy soon picked up a few dissident MPs to join in embarrassing the party and relieving the pressure on the Chief Secretary.

Some of the problems that had beset the Plan of Campaign recurred on the de Freyne estate in County Roscommon, where the Irish Party was accused of recklessly leading tenants to eviction. For critics of the party it seemed that the United Irish League had simply provided an agrarian fig leaf to disguise the party's political bankruptcy and that the field would soon be open for rival policies. D. P. Moran combined cultural revivalism, criticism of the party's anti-intellectualism and authoritarianism and the politics of Catholic grievance to provide a rationale for a populist version of the traditional Catholic 'whiggery' that placed Catholic middle-class interests above political nationalism. Arthur Griffith drew on the ideology of Young Ireland and on artisan traditions of self-help and anti-deferentialism to combine a re-invented separatism with the Parnellite legacy and the 'Hungarian policy' as the course to be taken by a new Parnell when the party finally reverted to corruption and chaos.

The agrarian agitation was, however, making it harder for the British government to manage Ireland, especially as the Ulster unionist bloc was facing its own internal challenges from a tenant farmers' revolt under T. W. Russell and a populist

Protestant movement denouncing the unionist leadership as effete aristocrats and calling for a democratic unionism more responsive to working-class concerns. Optimistic nationalists saw these groups as vindicating the long-standing nationalist view of unionism as composed of landlord manipulators and plebeian dupes, and as a sign of the impending conversion of unionist dissidents to nationalism. Moreover, the government was facing fiscal problems, which led to a devastating internal dispute over tariff reform, while the landlords, facing falling agricultural prices and consequent rent reductions, wished to sell if they could obtain the right terms.

In 1902 the Chief Secretary for Ireland, George Wyndham, gave his backing to a proposal for a conference between representatives of landlords and tenants to agree the terms of a Land Act. When the conference led to agreement that made possible the passing of the Irish Land Act (1903), with the difference between land-lords' and tenants' demands made up by a government subsidy, Wyndham saw himself as facing a historic opportunity to settle Ireland. On the nationalist side, William O'Brien similarly decided that by working together with moderate union-ists, such as those who represented the landlord interest at the Land Conference, it might be possible to divide the unionist bloc and eventually obtain Irish autonomy by consent.

For other nationalists, principally John Dillon and Michael Davitt, the Irish Land Act represented the rescue of the landlords at public expense and seemed to threaten home rule by defusing agrarian discontent and replacing a cohesive party-directed agitation with groups of notables doing deals on specific issues. Faced with the prospect of a new split, Redmond refused O'Brien's demand that Dillon and his allies be disciplined. O'Brien then fatally weakened his position by resigning from the party and the UIL, in the belief that he was indispensable; instead the architect of the UIL found himself reduced to the leadership of a splinter group in Cork. Meanwhile, Wyndham's hopes of buying support with further reform measures were blocked by financial constraints and opposition from unionist hard-liners.

The Irish Land Act, which defused the Protestant tenant farmers' revolt, and the increasing weakness of the Unionist government helped a more aggressive leadership dominated by industrialists and professionals centred on Belfast to consolidate Ulster unionism around the constitutional issue. Wyndham was finally brought down by his incautious contacts with a group of moderate unionist veterans of the Land Conference who advocated a limited form of devolution.

By 1905 the possibility that the Irish Party might gain some form of self-government by alliance with the resurgent Liberals had been reawakened. Deal-making Catholic notables and middle-class seekers of patronage deserted the dying Unionist government and posed as home-rulers. Young professionals who had previously hearkened to Moran or Griffith decided that support for the party was a necessity of practical politics and turned to such ginger groups as the Young Ireland Branch of the UIL. A new political star was emerging, in the shape of the northern party activist Joe Devlin, who combined organisational skills with a mixture of populist Catholicism and advocacy of social reform. Moran himself spoke more favourably of the party.

Nonetheless, sources of trouble remained. The embittered O'Brien, with great financial resources and a strong electoral base in Cork, was forging alliances with Healy and the unionist devolutionists. Griffith was assembling the disparate separatist clubs into a new alliance called Sinn Féin, despite divisions between republicans and those prepared to accept Griffith's proposed 'dual monarchy'. The significance of the newly consolidated and more Ulster-centred form of unionism was grasped only by a few nationalists, such as Moran's associate Arthur Clery, who argued that home rule could be obtained only by partition.

The new Parliament saw a recurrence of land agitation, with the de Freyne estate in County Roscommon attracting particular attention, and the imprisonment of several MPs and local agrarian leaders. The Unionist government had an overwhelming majority. Lord Rosebery seemed bound for political revival by voicing the Liberal right's dislike of 'unpatriotic' pro-Boer colleagues and resentment that the leadership clung to outdated policies, including home rule.[1] The Irish Party in Parliament organised obstruction reminiscent of the eighteen-eighties; several members were suspended.

The ultimate defiance came in November 1901, when the seat for Galway city fell vacant. Horace Plunkett was the Unionist candidate. The Irish Party nominated Colonel Arthur Lynch; some local activists had wished to nominate Kruger.[2] Lynch was elected, with clerical influence used as aggressively for him as against his Parnellite candidacy in 1892.[3] Griffith ridiculed Lynch's conversion to constitutional nationalism, declaring him a pale shadow of MacBride; Griffith's future ally Edward Martyn campaigned for Plunkett.[4]

In Ulster the Liberal Unionist MP and former junior minister T. W. Russell led a Protestant farmers' agitation in favour of compulsory purchase. Russell capitalised on the dissipation of the home rule threat and Presbyterian resentment of landlord and Anglican dominance. He blamed the failures of the Union on selfish land-lordism: if the land question were solved and a democratic Unionist leadership created, nationalism would disintegrate. Russellites fought by-elections against official Unionists, winning two through nationalist tactical voting and the support of a significant minority of Protestant voters.[5]

Russellism overlapped a second dissident movement reaching urban Protestants less responsive to agrarianism. In Dublin the leading figure was Lindsay Crawford, editor of the *Irish Protestant,* who was influenced by Michael MacCarthy, a former Catholic and nationalist who attributed Ireland's woes to Catholic superstition and priestly extortion.[6] Crawford attributed unionist weakness to governmental collaboration with the Catholic clergy and their political hirelings; a democratic unionism addressing democratic nationalists resentful of clerical financial, educational and political mismanagement could revive the Union. At one point six of twelve Dublin Corporation Unionists supported Crawford.[7] In Belfast the movement was led by the street-preachers Arthur Trew and T. H. Sloan. When William Johnston of Ballykilbeg died in 1902, his South Belfast seat was taken by Sloan in a by-election—infuriating Trew, who was in jail for public order offences. Sloanite anti-Catholic rhetoric and rowdy behaviour was cited by the Irish People as proof that Orangeism was degenerating from Johnston's sincere fanaticism to blasphemous paganism.[8]

Fights between supporters of 'godly Sloan' and 'angelic Trew' amused D. P. Moran. Sloan, already suspended from the Orange Order after heckling Edward Saunderson at a demonstration, organised an Independent Orange Order, with Crawford as grand master. Russellites expelled from the official order formed rural lodges.

Nationalists saw 'democratic' unionists as vindicating nationalist interpretations of unionism as a landlord conspiracy and a sign that large-scale conversion to nationalism was imminent. While many nationalists endorsed some 'democratic' unionist criticisms of 'whig' Catholic lay and clerical elites, they expressed 'democratic' nationalism through UIL-style mass mobilisation or separatism. Michael MacCarthy was seen—even by the relatively anti-clerical Griffith—as a venal renegade inflaming Protestant prejudices.[9] His description of himself as 'Catholic', to make the unwary think that he still followed the Roman church, roused particular scorn.[10]

While some associates of Russell and Crawford had nationalist sympathies—notably the Russellite Richard Lyttle, non-subscribing Presbyterian minister of Moneyrea, County Down, a pro-Boer, Gaelic Leaguer, and friend of Alice Milligan[11]—and both ended as supporters of nationalism, few took their search for 'democracy' to this conclusion. Their importance lay in provoking a new, more aggressively populist Ulster unionism and in encouraging nationalists to underestimate unionist strength.

With the Irish Party reunited, parliamentary obstruction and land agitation reviving, unionism divided, and many 'whig' MPs defeated or silenced, the British government's task of managing Ireland through associates other than the Irish Party became more difficult. However, tensions between the politics of Catholic grievance and nationalism remained, and Wyndham sought new collaborators.

The Catholic Bishop of Elphin, Dr John Clancy, denounced the de Freyne agitation as the work of reckless 'strolling agitators' leading tenants to destruction.[12] This reflected painful memories of the fate of evicted Plan of Campaign tenants, and episcopal preference for managing disputes by mediation. Clancy, known for co-operation with Plunkett, regularly mediated in trade disputes in County Sligo; shortly before his death in 1911 he encountered the same impasse when Larkinism produced a strike where old rules did not apply.[13]

Clancy was also allegedly influenced by the de Freynes' Catholicism and the Maynooth trustees' mortgage on the estate[14]—an unfortunate commentary on claims that Ireland's problems would be solved if the ruling class were Catholics guided by priests.[15] Such claims occur even in the populist novels of Canon Joseph Guinan of County Longford. This novelist-priest, overshadowed by his more intellectual counterpart Canon Sheehan, is remembered for invocations of the benevolent 'soggarth aroon' presiding over his impoverished flock, and denunciations of Land War evictions. He gives more concrete descriptions of poverty than Sheehan, and he is also more anti-Protestant—County Longford lay far enough north to have an Orange presence—but he suspected the Land League as materialistic, demagogic, and a source of lay political rivals to local priestly authority.[16] In one novel a land-lord converts to Catholicism, and Guinan declares that had others done so, recent problems would never have arisen.[17] Another portrays an absentee landlord as well-meaning but destroyed by lack of moral guidance.[18]

Catholic priests and religious orders managed numerous national schools, government-financed but Catholic in all but name. This was criticised by nationalists and unionists on grounds of managerial power over teachers, who were dismissible at will, the tolerance of poor-quality teaching and building conditions, of religious teachers restricting opportunities for lay professionals,[19] and claims that schools overemphasised religion and 'genteel' subjects. Gaelic Leaguers attributed this to West Britonism, claiming that a curriculum expressing Irish identity would encourage economic initiative and self-confident religious faith.[20]

Catholic activists recalled French anti-clericals laicising schools and making schoolteachers missionaries of secularism. It remained to be seen whether such dangers might come from anti-clerical nationalist politicians or the government; Walter Starkie, a Catholic Trinity graduate who headed the Board of National Education amid Gaelic League criticism, provoked furious clerical responses by criticising managers.[21]

Catholic clerics who organised and administered local industries with govern-ment support were cited in defence of the Catholic church against charges of hindering economic development.[22] The hero of Canon Sheehan's novel The New Curate, who starts a shirt factory and a fishing industry with government loans,[23] and the priest in Guinan's The Island Parish, who orders parishioners to remove pigs from their houses and notifies the sanitary inspector if they refuse,[24] are fictional exemplars of this civilising mission, linked to advocacy of a decentralised rural civilisation.

Clerical direction could be authoritarian and unaccountable. In a celebrated example, Bishop Clancy received a grant to establish a furniture factory in County Sligo. The factory collapsed through mismanagement,[25] and local investors recovered their money only with help from Arthur Jackson, manager of Pollexfen and Company, owned by W. B. Yeats's mother's family. When Moran attacked Yeats by reference to his relatives' employment practices, Griffith published a letter defending 'our Protestant Good Samaritan'.[26]

Populist unionists called the Congested Districts Board a clerical slush fund, noting clusters of grants in areas such as Kiltimagh, whose parish priest, a political ally of Dillon, sat on the board.[27] The nationalist Church of Ireland novelist James Hannay, who claimed that an autonomous Ireland might allow the Protestant upper classes more influence and be less susceptible to clerical pressure, depicted a Protestant-owned woollen mill undercut by a convent-operated rival receiving government grants, employing sectarian whispering campaigns and paying starvation wages while trumpeting its 'benevolence'.[28]

In Belfast, Bishop Henry Henry of Down and Connor organised Catholic representation on Belfast Corporation around a clerically directed middle-class Catholic Association, playing down nationalism to lobby for Catholic interests within the system. This was challenged by the local UIL, led by Joseph Devlin and his weekly *Northern Star,* which combined appeals to nationalism and social reform and denounced the association as a self-serving whig elite. Most of the Catholic hierarchy saw Henry's behaviour as reckless. The conflict lasted several years and concluded with the absorption of the Catholic Association, on Devlin's terms.[29]

Devlin, MP for North Kilkenny in 1904, the only figure from the younger generation to enter the inner leadership of the Irish Party, was widely seen as eventual heir-apparent. He appealed to Belfast workers by presenting himself as the defender of labour against the unionist 'millocracy' and by spending some of his increasing wealth on charitable activities, such as seaside excursions for slum children and a holiday home for weary mill-girls.[30] As grand master from 1904, he made the Board of Erin a major party auxiliary, officered by associates such as John Dillon Nugent and J. T. Donovan.

Devlin's humble origins were mocked by snobbish opponents and contributed to his tendency to defer to Redmond and Dillon, with severe implications over partition. His populism was criticised as intolerant of debate. The AOH, as a Catholic fraternal network, acquired a reputation for sectarianism and corruption, encouraging accusations that a home rule Parliament would resemble Tammany Hall. Devlin's alliance with Catholic business elements led to tensions with his claim to represent working-class interests, producing charges of hypocrisy from trade union critics, while even nationalists far removed from Henry's whiggery invoked his memory to present Devlin as an anti-clerical, hypocritically professing Catholicism. Henry's defeat showed the danger of episcopal *Honoratiorenpolitik* or patronage politics without reference to the political sentiments of their flock, but also that suspicions of anti-clericalism were hard to dissipate.

The UIL victory in 1900 was deceptive. The purge of unreliable MPs was incomplete, because the snap election did not give enough time for the UIL to spread, and its potential was limited outside its western heartland.[31] Some recruits proved unreliable. William O'Doherty, the MP for North Donegal, sided with Healy and defied party boycotts of state ceremonies. When St Eunan's Cathedral opened in Letterkenny in 1901, the decorations included Union Jacks supplied by

O'Doherty, and others flown on the house of the East Donegal MP, Edward McFadden. The failure of bishop and populace to protest annoyed separatists.[32]

Dr E. C. Thompson, a Unionist defector, became MP for North Monaghan in a by-election; a rival candidate withdrew when O'Brien called him a crypto-Healyite.[33] O'Brien soon accepted that the displaced candidate was not a Healyite;[34] Thompson allied himself with Healy.[35]

Even after 1900 many new recruits were problematic, because their ability to support themselves financially led the party to overlook shortcomings or because they were chosen for old friendships and long service rather than ability. Arthur Lynch's successor in Galway (after he recklessly returned and was convicted of high treason) was Christopher Devlin, chief Irish organiser of a Canadian government emigration scheme denounced by nationalists. O'Brien claimed that Devlin 'gave up his evil trade'; in fact he delegated it to a deputy.[36] The veteran Parnellite 'Long John' O'Connor was returned for North Kildare in 1902 with help from Redmond. Redmond then discovered that O'Connor had an estranged wife suing for maintenance; O'Connor intended to divorce her for adultery, she intended to cite his adultery. Redmond was aggrieved that O'Connor concealed this when seeking nomination, but the scandal was hushed up, and O'Connor remained an MP until 1918.[37] One of the party's most prominent figures, T. P. O'Connor, had an estranged American wife who regularly threatened publicity unless her allowance was paid,[38] and his long-standing interest in Greek affairs was inspired by a Greek mistress.[39] His contributions to *Reynolds's News*—a radical paper supporting home rule, notorious for irreligion, 'daring' fiction, and birth-control advertisements—provoked sarcasm about O'Connor as Catholic statesman and the moral authority he wielded against Parnell.[40]

Healy gathered new malcontents. Four MPs—Sam Young, E. C. Thompson, William O'Doherty, and Major J. E. Jameson—attended the coronation of King Edward VII, despite party orders;[41] and the erratic South Leitrim MP and Roscommon newspaper proprietor Jasper Tully was expelled after quarrelling with rivals.[42] None had a strong electoral base except Young.[43] Another Healy ally, the veteran North Galway MP Colonel John Philip Nolan, lost the party whip after embarrassing disclosures about the treatment of tenants. Jameson took the Conservative whip after 1903.

Despite a few Healy-inclined MPs and pockets of support in south and west Ulster—especially in dioceses with Healyite bishops—there was no chance of serious revival. Even a cynical alliance between John Howard Parnell and Healyites could not defeat the UIL organiser David Sheehy in the South Meath by-election in 1902.[44] Nevertheless, dissidents exploited tensions between party and bishops, and weakened the party's claims to speak for nationalist Ireland.

In 1902 Wyndham introduced an abortive Land Purchase Bill, supported by Healy; the party rejected it and withdrew temporarily from the House of Commons in protest. Their absence, coinciding with an Education Bill supported by English Catholics but opposed by Nonconformist Liberals, irritated the bishops; Healy gained by keeping his group at Westminster to support the bill.[45]

The limitations of the land campaign, endemic factionalism and the gap between nationalist ideology and the actual collaboration of large sections of Catholic lay and clerical social elites with the old regime gave scope for critics. The strongest criticisms were not electoral but journalistic, reflecting the advanced-nationalist self-image, contrasting principled self-education through the printed word and discussion with unprincipled pragmatism and volatile rhetoric. Their primary audience was among groups outside existing patronage networks: young white-collar workers in the towns, factions out of favour with local bosses, and small businessmen and tradesmen resenting competition from imports and seeing professionals, transport companies, importing agencies and monster shops like Clery's (controlled by William Martin Murphy) as parasites.

But resentment was not confined to these circles. The most conservative Catholic whig might complain that Protestant associates denied him due recognition. John Mallon, the leading political detective of the Dublin Metropolitan Police, complained that his role in solving the Phoenix Park murders was not properly recognised, and gained promotion by appealing 'as a Catholic and Nationalist' to Irish Party leaders whom he spied on.[46] Priests and prelates who deferred to the Crown and collaborated with Dublin Castle or local landlords feared and resented a Britishness identified with Protestant or secular distrust of clerical power. Might British popular culture—the increasing circulation of British papers, and risqué plays in Dublin theatres—undermine Irish Catholicism? Might social, political and economic dominance by an increasingly secularised Protestant upper and pro-fessional class encourage Catholic professionals to dilute faith for the sake of advancement? (Both Guinan and Sheehan portray ambitious Catholics becoming Freemasons.)[47]

The religious commitment of the Catholic population was underestimated by their pastors almost as much as by Protestant evangelists. Even some priests with deferential tendencies saw a Catholicised Irish identity as a barrier against secular-isation and hoped that the Irish Party, rather than just 'whig' professionals, might become the nucleus of the hoped-for Catholic governing class. Guinan's *Curate of Kilcloon* delivers an impassioned speech (in English) contrasting ascetic Aran Islanders with degenerate West Britons.[48] *The Moores of Glynn* contrasts Father Eugene O'Growney, the Gaelic League pioneer, with a disreputable seoinín and provides an origin-myth for a future home rule Ireland by depicting the devout son of a big farmer working to support his family after eviction, buying an Orange-owned farm and becoming a Home Rule MP.[49] After all, the Catholic clergy were recruited from farming classes predisposed towards nationalism; younger and more enthusiastic clergy dreamed of an exemplary Catholic Ireland through alliance with nationalism—whether constitutionalist or separatist.

Nationalist critiques of the Irish Party's agrarianism combined neo-traditionalist and modernist elements. Some were more influenced by the Fenian tradition, which had anti-clerical elements and emphasised political participation, others by

Catholic or culturalist ideas that played down political participation and linked faith and fatherland. Most invoked as origin-myth the virtuous small peasant, contrasted with the snobbish bourgeoisie—rural or urban, Catholic or Protestant; some wanted an industrialised Ireland, others a decentralised rural civilisation supported but not dominated by industry. All agreed that the Irish Party and 'whigs' neglected cultural and social problems.

In 1900–5 the two most prominent voices of the urban nationalist critique of UIL agrarianism, its equation of debate with disloyalty and its insistence that civil society must be constrained for the distant prospect of home rule, came from weekly papers. In the *United Irishman,* Arthur Griffith restated John Mitchel's separatism in terms of Parnellism and artisan traditions of self-help; in the *Leader,* D. P. Moran harnessed cultural nationalism to an aggressive form of Catholic-whig nationalism for younger Catholic professionals, more numerous and confident and less deferential than their predecessors.

Griffith's paper succeeded the monthly *Shan Van Vocht,* run from Belfast by Alice Milligan and Anna Johnston from 1896 to 1900. The Belfast monthly was an extension of the manuscript journals of the separatist clubs (some of whose articles it printed).[50] It helped to maintain the club network and to attract recruits such as Bulmer Hobson,[51] as did Milligan's and Johnston's visits to provincial towns to lecture and give slide shows on Irish history.[52]

Unlike the *Shan Van Vocht,* primarily literary and historical, the weekly *United Irishman* commented extensively on events, filling a gap opened by the demise of *United Ireland* and the rightward movement of the *Independent.* It retained a strong didactic element, expressed in Griffith's fulfilment of Davis's project of an anthology of ballads (with commentary) telling Ireland's history, interminable lists of place-names containing a reference to trees, showing the extent of Irish woodland before English ravaging, and descriptions of Dublin stonework proving Portland stone inferior to Irish limestone. Such anti-commercial features were subsidised by advertisements from businesses addressing readers committed to buying Irish goods, and contributions from clubs, the IRB, and individual patrons. The clubs were not purely pedagogical: 'national pilgrimages' to historic sites were also social outings, and separatism was related to bicycle excursions in William Bulfin's *Rambles in Eirinn,* serialised by Griffith.[53]

The link between Griffith's activities and the pastimes of the poor was visible in his defence of working-class men who swam without bathing-costumes (which they could not afford) in areas of Dublin Bay, such as Ringsend, where their presence affronted middle-class sensibilities.[54] (Griffith himself regularly swam at the Forty Foot.) He also defended the GAA against Catholic and Protestant middle-class sab-batarians who condemned working men enjoying themselves on their one free day.[55] Not all pastimes were defended: Griffith denounced the prurience and jingoism of music-halls and the genteel West Britonism of 'respectable' musical entertainments. He attributed both to Anglicisation, and advocated Gaelic League concerts and céilithe.[56]

Griffith was assisted by William Rooney, son of a Fenian and Land War prisoner.[57] Rooney, a low-paid clerk since his early teens, devoted his spare time to political and cultural activity until his death at twenty-nine from TB and overwork. His total commitment and uncompromising separatist statements in Davisian prose and verse were deeply influential. Griffith called him the finest man he ever hoped to know, published selections of his writings, and mourned him as a second Davis.[58] MacSwiney modelled himself on Rooney;[59] the young Brian O'Higgins made a pilgrimage to his grave.[60] Griffith's later republican critics appealed to Rooney's memory.[61]

Griffith modelled himself on Mitchel, 'the greatest man in Irish history.'[62] He absorbed the patriotic literature of the late eighteenth and nineteenth centuries in the National Library, and reprinted voluminous extracts. His favourite Young Ireland poet was the working-class radical Jean de Jean Fraser.[63] For Griffith, eighteenth-century estimates of Ireland's natural resources, Mitchel's denunciations of British government policy in the eighteen-forties and satires on legal place-hunters from the first Gladstone government remained valid. His contempt for British political and economic liberalism was reinforced by poverty experienced in Dublin, by seeing the raw edge of British imperialism in South Africa (where he met Cape troopers who boasted of massacre and rape in Matabeleland and saw ruthless exploitation of workers by mine-owners),[64] and by the detectives who spied on him[65] and, under the Conservatives, suppressed issues of nationalist papers insulting to the Crown and its servants.[66] Nineteenth-century British liberals had pointed to a press free from prior suppression and to the absence of Continental-style political secret police and centralised gendarmerie—such as the RIC—as essential to freedom.[67]

Griffith maintained the attitudes and political traditions of nineteenth-century Dublin artisans. His protectionism was justified by reference to Friedrich List and the American economist Henry Carey (son of a United Irishman)[68] but derived from traditional resistance by the trades to importing goods that could be supplied locally. He attacked firms and local authorities that accepted cheaper tenders from overseas firms, claiming that the extra cost was offset by keeping money in the local economy.[69] When Griffith's paper suppliers subsidised exports by charging Irish customers higher prices, he used Swedish paper until they cut prices.[70]

He praised the Continental model of protectionism and an interventionist state, and said Ireland must establish direct contact with the Continent rather than seeing it through the distorting lens of the British press. He described the situation in small European states to deny claims that 'little Ireland' could not survive by itself.[71]

Griffith drew from Mitchel a hostility to individualist and utilitarian political economy. He called Adam Smith a conscious liar, plotting world conquest by England by persuading other countries to open their markets.[72] He jeered that liberal 'Stone Age Economists' believed that 'Adam Smith was the first man,'[73] and claimed that Francis Bacon, 'Father of the Utilitarian Lie', made Shakespeare's Merrie England 'the land of damned souls it is today.'[74] Population, not trade, was the measure of national wealth; a unionist who objected that this implied that China was the wealthiest country in the world was dismissed out of hand.

Griffith set against 'enlightened self-interest' a classical republican ethos of self-sacrifice for the nation, emphasising virtue, equality and political participation and distrusting commercialism as leading to corruption and the enslavement of a degraded and dependent populace by a tyrannical elite and its mercenaries. He did not oppose economic development—he excoriated the well-off who urged the poor to accept poverty as God's will[75]—but believed it could come only from a strong state, and that any sacrifice was justified in creating a national state; he therefore praised Davis for maintaining against O'Connell that it was better for the Irish to live in rags on potatoes than to be Anglicised.[76] For Griffith, individual rights were inseparable from duty to the nation. He himself turned down well-paid newspaper jobs, lived in poverty, and delayed marriage for fifteen years, resisting the pull of the generational cycle that tamed so many radicals.[77] Those who refused total allegiance to Ireland (as defined by Griffith) forfeited any moral standing; he subjected them to unlimited abuse and slander,[78] based on a code of honour that presented separatism as an absolute value and equated compromise with self-annihilation or prostitution. 'Respectable' shopkeepers and professionals who served Dublin Castle and ignored the slums were no better than women consorting with soldiers in O'Connell Street. If Ireland achieved prosperity by incorporation in Britain, 'the decent nations of the world would draw their skirts from the harlot Erin as she passed.'[79] He thought that Scotland and Wales had made this choice and told pan-Celts that until they dissociated themselves from England they too were 'the enemy'. He befriended Scottish nationalists such as William Gillies and Ruairidh Erskine of Mar.[80]

Griffith believed that an independent Irish state would increase the standard of living by a systematic development of natural resources concealed and suppressed by Britain. He claimed that John Boyd Dunlop, the inventor of the pneumatic tyre, was induced by British vested interests to leave Ireland,[81] and that coal deposits in Counties Antrim and Tyrone went unworked because the Londonderrys safeguarded their Durham coal interests.[82] The national economy should be as self-contained as possible, and large areas of the citizen's life protected from the market; urban workers should be given inalienable housing.[83] He distrusted foreign investment but suggested that Irish-American capitalists could help develop Ireland, if strictly subordinated to Irish authorities.[84] He denied émigrés any share in determining Ireland's destiny, though he agreed that those loyal to the Irish cause could help the leadership at home.[85] This covered his American IRB sponsors; the prime targets of his censure were Irish Party MPs domiciled in England.

Griffith equated emigration with suicide. Cartoons show the Devil dressed as Uncle Sam scattering prepaid tickets across Ireland, or emigrants crowding off a pier into the jaws of a skull.[86] He saw emigrants—as did many nationalists—as rushing to moral and economic ruin, deceived by fallacious reports of prosperity overseas.

He asserted that the depopulation of Ireland was orchestrated by Britain, as evidenced by Canadian campaigns to attract Irish settlers, and that an Irish government should ban emigration.[87]

Before 1906, Griffith maintained contacts with British radicals and notably with *Reynolds's News,* which he praised for raising issues, such as the suppression of separatist newspapers, that Irish dailies and the Irish Party dared not take up.[88] (This contact may have been through H. M. Kennedy, the Irish-born Anglican vicar of Plumpton in Cumbria, a member of the Social Democratic Federation and the National Democratic League.)[89]

Griffith took the Parnellite-separatist view of the 'British democracy' as moral degenerates and anti-Irish jingoistic bigots manipulated by a crafty oligarchy.[90] Davittite hopes of rousing them against a common enemy were utterly misplaced. Griffith disliked Davitt, because of his role in the Parnell split, his faith in the 'British democracy' and his perceived betrayal of his IRB oath, though after Davitt's death he was invoked as a touchstone of antique virtue betrayed by the Irish Party.[91] The idea that Irish workers should prefer British workers to Irish employers was naïve (the British put national solidarity first) and treasonable. The Liberal Party was a branch of the oligarchy, less honest than the Tories; he recalled the anti-Irish records of Gladstonian 'friends of Ireland'.[92] Readers debated whether Cromwell was as bad as he was painted; some thought his open enmity preferable to hypocritical whig friendship. A letter 'from Cromwell in Hell' praised the *Leader* and applauded David Sheehy's by-election victory. Griffith called Cromwell the original Nonconformist British democrat.[93]

Griffith argued that Continental states were freer than Britain, where the executive held absolute power and where state and people refused to recognise mutual responsibility. Irish loyalism, Catholic and Anglican, contained elements of divine-right deferentialism; refusal to recognise an Irish home rule majority was defended by A. V. Dicey's reference to theories of the absolute supremacy of Parliament and its right to assert the interests of the British majority against the will of Ireland, and emergency legislation justified by classical imperialist exhortations to uphold law against anarchy, irrespective of consent. Griffith praised Continental conscription as producing citizen armies, preferable to British mercenaries,[94] commented on British denunciations of Tsarist oppression that Finnish and Polish populations grew while Ireland declined, and argued that, though imperialism was wrong, the French variety showed a misguided sense of responsibility, while British imperialism was sheer exploitation.[95] After supporting Dreyfus, because he thought anti-Dreyfusards weakened France against Britain, Griffith turned anti-Dreyfusard because the British supported him.[96] Distrust of the British press ('a wall of paper around Ireland') and an awareness of the methods of empire in Africa combined with anti-liberal preconceptions to discount reported misdeeds of Britain's enemies.

Like many professional unmaskers, Griffith's scepticism shaded into paranoia, and he was susceptible to demented cranks. Frank Hugh O'Donnell gave him three articles a week as 'Llenodo', 'Red Hand' and 'The Foreign Secretary', until he appeared at a UIL convention to praise William O'Brien; when this attempted political come-back failed, O'Donnell denounced the party as degenerates in an unsuccessful attempt to reingratiate himself with separatists,[97] and O'Brien became 'a spouter ... with Ghetto shekels paid.' Griffith also regularly published letters from a retired British army officer, Colonel Warburton, accusing successive governments of preventing the development of Irish bogs; Plunkett was a particular target of his invective. Warburton's rage arose from resentment at contempt from more prestigious regiments while serving in the Royal Engineers, and guilt at his own participation in atrocities against the Maori.[98]

O'Donnell encouraged Griffith's anti-Semitism, which derived from seeing 'cosmopolitan' Jews as supporters of the British empire, a view reinforced by memories of 'the Jew D'Israeli'[99] and the Jewish origins of many pro-British South African 'randlords', and by Dublin prejudice against Jews as traders and sources of cheap immigrant labour.[100]

Anti-Semitism in early twentieth-century Ireland was not confined to separatists. Religious anti-Semitism derived from French Catholic sources—some Protestant populists cited links between anti-Semitism and Catholicism and publicised the Limerick pogrom as proof of what religious minorities could expect from home rule;[101] and while some party leaders held enlightened views, including Davitt, Redmond (who offered a parliamentary nomination to Jacob Elyan, a prominent Dublin Jew and associate of William Field), and O'Brien, MPs such as Eugene Crean and the mayor of Limerick, Michael Joyce, were openly anti-Semitic.[102] Griffith's anti-Semitism should not be exaggerated—he does not express physical repulsion at Jews in the manner of O'Donnell and Moran, and he maintained friendships with individual Jews[103]—but it is intrinsic to his world view. It rested less on specific hatred for Jews than on nationalist dislike of any commercially advanced minority. Griffith saw the Armenian massacres denounced by British Liberals as exaggerated reports of killings of Armenian usurers by oppressed Turkish peasants.[104] His support for Zionism rested on intellectual affinity: like Sinn Féin, it glorified armed citizenship and physical labour against aristocratic leisure and capitalist commercialism. He believed that the world was as a matter of fact founded on integral nationalism, and that minorities dazzled by liberal universalism faced extermination.

Griffith voiced producerist hostility to old-style governmental and aristocratic patronage: regular complaints concerned hiring military bands rather than local voluntary bands—often a locus of nationalist activity—and the use of soldiers for jobs that could be done by civilians, which Griffith claimed encouraged poverty and hence recruitment. He opposed preferential treatment for former soldiers and policemen, told local authorities to exclude them from jobs, and described the appointment of former policemen as school attendance officers as sending government spies into people's houses.[105] He was opposed to commercial society and its associated mass culture, seen as turning creative participants into passive recipients, demoralised and enslaved. He regularly exposed dubious stock-market speculation, fraudulent patent medicines, jingoist propaganda, and similar features of the mass-market press.[106]

Griffith thought self-command essential to civic virtue and believed that immoral or sentimental literature and drama, and the commercial press in general, encouraged dependence. Soccer and other foreign sports were seen as snobbish pretensions of middle-class West Britons or as commercialised pastimes of the degraded English lower classes—unlike patriotic GAA amateurism—and endangered national virtue through socialisation with anti-national elements. The drink trade was identified as a source of male self-indulgence and family misery, a rival to separatist clubs, the focus—through publicans' local contacts—for Irish Party activism, and a source of income for unionist brewers and distillers and (through taxes) the British government. Catholic and Irish-Ireland activists 'named and shamed' publicans who remained open on St Patrick's Day[107] and campaigned for the restriction of opening hours and licences.

Griffith saw William Martin Murphy as embodying cosmopolitan commercialism. After Murphy bought the bankrupt *Irish Independent* it adopted techniques from British popular journalism, and began overhauling the *Freeman's Journal.* Clery's symbolised glamorous imports, the antithesis of small traders prominent in Dublin Sinn Féin. Much of Murphy's railway investment went overseas. When Murphy announced an International Exhibition in Dublin modelled on that of William Dargan in the eighteen-fifties, Griffith claimed that Dargan's exhibition retarded development by promoting imports and counteracting Young Ireland's encouragement of Irish industries.[108] A public meeting promoting the exhibition was invaded by Irish-Irelanders led by Griffith, Maud Gonne, and Eoin MacNeill; they were beaten by the DMP, and MacNeill nearly lost his job.[109] Irish-Irelanders organised a rival National Exhibition and proclaimed a boycott; but when the International Exhibition opened in 1907, hailed as proof of prosperity and reconciliation with the empire, its glamour proved attractive. It was opened by King Edward VII, who offered Murphy a knighthood, which he turned down because of the absence of home rule.[110] Despite the Irish Party's support for the boycott, many clerics and some MPs organised excursions; Terence MacSwiney even found that separatist friends wanted to visit it.[111]

Griffith's literary tastes were broad by the standards of his milieu. He thought the best living Irish writers were Yeats, Standish O'Grady, and the three Georges—Shaw, Russell, and Moore.[112] (He later quarrelled with Yeats and denounced Moore and Shaw for not settling in Ireland.) He published contemporary minor poets and playwrights, mostly protégés of Russell. In the early years of the *United Irishman,* Frank Fay was drama critic.[113] Griffith supported creative literature as part of self-determination but believed that artistic integrity was inseparable from nation-building. Since only nationalism truly expressed Irish identity, any true writer must be a nationalist (he claimed that honest unionists, such as Le Fanu and Lever, ended as nationalists);[114] writers who exempted themselves from the Davisite patriotic literary model would finally sell themselves to a British commercial public or to aristocratic and state patronage.

Griffith's definition of Irish nationality was historical rather than racial or religious. Irishness could not be equated with language: 'a man might speak Irish as well as Diarmuid MacMurrough, Niall Garbh O'Donnell, Owen O'Connolly, or Murrough of the Burnings and be a traitor to Ireland.'[115] He took an interest in Irish scholarship—especially when it was politically usable, such as Whitley Stokes's demolition of Robert Atkinson[116]—and published summaries of Middle Irish sagas, but he distrusted the critical attitudes of scholars like MacNeill. Griffith believed in an immemorial high-kingship as a precedent for Irish statehood—though he held that the ancient Irish constitution was irrevocably dissolved by Brian Bórú, and the Irish were not bound to it.[117] He was reluctant to accept criticism of accounts of pre-Christian Ireland and declared that round towers were pagan monuments, in defiance of scholarly consensus,[118] because significant traces of a pre-Christian past hindered the equation of Irishness with Catholicism. 'Cuchulain, not Patrick, was the founder of Irish civilisation.'[119] Griffith accepted the Catholicism of the early Irish church; as a Parnellite he attributed to it flaws of its contemporary successor. He praised the sixth-century high king Diarmaid mac Cearrbheoil, whose attempts to extend authority over provincial kings and refusal to recognise ecclesiastical immunities brought him into conflict with the church. Griffith presents Diarmaid as a proto-Parnell who would have united Ireland had he not been destroyed by narrow-minded priests valuing their own privileges above the national interest.[120]

In the eighteen-nineties Griffith and Rooney defended compulsory education against Archbishop Walsh.[121] Griffith criticised Rev. Denis Hallinan of Newcastle, County Limerick, for denouncing Carnegie libraries for being non-sectarian.[122] He condemned extortionate charges at Glasnevin cemetery—a 'charity' run by priests and Catholic professionals—and called for municipalisation.[123] He criticised 'Castle Catholic' priests and Catholic institutions that sought official or landlord patronage. He advocated boycotts of Catholic charitable fund-raising events opened by the Lord Lieutenant.[124] He criticised priests who preferred cheap imported religious artefacts to products of Irish craftsmen lacking 'that spiritual quality instilled by a German Jew or atheist paid at so many marks an hour.' (He was equally critical of Protestant clerics importing organs and stained glass.)[125] Unless clerics devoted less time and money to elaborate churches and more attention to the country's welfare, congregations would vanish through emigration.

Griffith's IRB connections and his defence of the French Republic against Catholic denunciations, seen as English-inspired attempts to alienate Ireland from an ally, led Catholic activists to see him and his associates as enemies of religion. In 1906 the United Irishman went bankrupt after a Limerick priest sued it for criticising his attitude to a Gaelic League feis; Hallinan was a prosecution witness. Griffith transferred its assets away from the limited liability company controlling it and re-started it as *Sinn Féin*. He justified this by arguing that the court showed politically inspired bias.[126]

Griffith published articles by Frederick Ryan, the most outspoken socialist and agnostic in Dublin, including criticisms of Griffith's opportunist use of religious issues to whip up populist Catholic resentment against collaboration with the administration;[127] for Griffith also appealed to those, like Mary Butler, who despised compromise in religion or politics and thought Catholicism and Sinn Féin natural allies, upholding essentialism against utilitarianism and sceptical commercial modernity.[128] Ryan irritated 'faith and fatherland' contributors. When he denied that Chinese beliefs were inferior to Christianity and denounced Hell as monstrous, Father P. F. Kavanagh protested. Griffith replied that he disagreed with Ryan.[129]

Griffith's fear of the fragmenting of nationalist movements by local priests and notables made him as centralist as Dillon. He claimed that the GAA was ruined by parliamentarian-inspired devolution of authority from executive to county boards.[130] He backed the Gaelic League executive against Munster dissidents, denounced as clerical catspaws. His centralism produced sympathy for advocates of an archaic standard language; he published denunciations of Gaeltacht Irish as 'corrupt' and claims that Munster Irish was promoted by a British conspiracy to fragment the language.[131] He denounced the Gaelic League's non-political attitude, claiming that the league derived popularity from Irish hostility towards Britain; he demanded courses in Irish history accompanying Irish classes.[132]

He opposed a separate Catholic university as benefiting only upper-class Castle Catholics and perpetuating sectarian divisions. Griffith wanted Trinity College reformed as a single national university, creating a unified elite; he opposed independent universities in Cork and Belfast. The university should offer extensive scholarships and imitate meritocratic Scottish and Continental universities rather than Oxford and Cambridge.[133] Similarly, he wanted local authority posts awarded by competitive examination, to create an embryonic 'National Civil Service'.[134] The curriculum would include elements, such as Irish and Irish history, reflecting Irish nationality, as defined by Griffith.

The Sinn Féin movement developed from campaigns against members of Dublin Corporation who supported a loyal address to Queen Victoria in 1900. The role of Dublin Castle patronage, social snobbery and title-hunting in rallying support for the address and of pressure by employers to support the visit linked British rule, corruption, and petty tyranny. The *United Irishman* orchestrated opposition to councillors who supported the address as they sought re-election, co-operating with more nationalistic elements in the Irish Party and with radical labour activists, including Connolly. (Joyce's 'Ivy Day in the Committee Room' involves a contest between a pro-address publican supported by Unionists and a labour-Sinn Féin candidate.)[135]

The royal visit of 1900 renewed attempts to cultivate attachment to the Crown in Ireland; these gathered pace with the accession of King Edward VII. Rumour presented the King as a friend to Ireland, even as a secret Catholic. (Orangemen called him 'Popish Ned', and Thomas Connellan compared him to Charles II.)[136]

Griffith denounced professing nationalists who joined the royalist cult, merchants in garrison towns who decorated shops for the coronation, and councillors who praised royal intentions. Ultra-Protestant opposition, which frustrated proposals to remove a coronation declaration insulting Catholic doctrines, played into Griffith's hands. He published the text repeatedly, enquired why the police tore down posters reprinting a royal statement, noted the Christian charity of clerical dignitaries hailing someone who insulted their beliefs, and contrasted silence on King Edward's adulteries with denunciations of Parnell.[137]

The dual monarchism advocated by *The Resurrection of Hungary* appeared in this context. Griffith may later have seen it as desirable for its own sake, but at first he made his republicanism clear: he praised Norwegians for securing independence from Sweden without bloodshed, but when they chose a king he reprinted Beranger's satirical verse on the Belgian decision to become a monarchy. At the same time he declared the crucial distinction between this situation and Ireland's. Norway freely chose a state official; the Irish were forced subjects, and participants in deferential displays hailed their degradation.[138] The Irish Party refused to attend the coronation, on grounds stated by Parnell in the eighteen-eighties: the Irish could not pay tribute while their stated will was overridden. At the same time, home rule was presented to British audiences as reform of the Union, not nullification, and unionists and Catholic whigs argued that refusal to recognise the Crown implied separatism.

The Resurrection of Hungary capitalised on this tension, meeting the claim that the only alternative to the Irish Party was hopeless insurrection while proclaiming Sinn Féin a truer heir to Parnell than the party. Griffith advanced abstention based on non-recognition of the Union, periodically advocated by figures like the Young Irelanders, supported by vigorous agitation as the only means of achieving self-government. His argument that Flood's Renunciation Act (1783) constituted fundamental law unalterable by subsequent British Parliaments clashed with accepted definitions of parliamentary sovereignty and was seen as the weakest point in his argument.[139] He exalted Flood rather than Grattan, whom he denounced as a naïve and incompetent constitutionalist windbag.[140]

Griffith argued that majority support for the Irish Party did not involve consent to the Union, because the majority believed the party separatist at heart. Achievements attributed to parliamentary agitation derived from popular resistance; whiggery—a corrupt, self-serving elite remote from the population, concealing powerlessness before a British majority by mystifications about high politics—inevitably derived from representation at Westminster. Parnell could have triumphed by withdrawing from Parliament in 1882; instead he tried to use Parliament in the hope of speedy victory. When his followers were corrupted and turned against him, he tried, too late, to revive the successful tactics of the early eighties.[141]

Nationalists should withdraw from Parliament—from the whole Crown apparatus of deference and corruption, such as courts and police force—and administer themselves through local authorities and a reconvened Irish Parliament. Anti-recruiting campaigns against police and army would be directed by Irish authorities. 'Voluntary protection' through the encouragement of industry and non-importation campaigns and confining official contracts to Irish goods and labour would bring economic revival; money once wasted on MPs would pay Irish consuls overseas to promote trade. With local collaboration withdrawn, and pressured by foreign powers, Britain would come to terms—from frank self-interest rather than a hypocritical 'Union of Hearts'—as Austria had come to terms with Hungary in 1866–7. A self-governing Ireland, linked to Britain only by a shared monarch with separate Crowns, would regain the prosperity enjoyed under Grattan's Parliament and the population lost since the Famine, until Britain could not prevent total secession.

The Resurrection of Hungary sold well[142] and was seen by critics as different as Frederick Ryan,[143] Tom Kettle[144] and Standish O'Grady[145] as a major contribution to Irish political literature. Unionist plaudits had ulterior motives: they saw it as revealing 'true' motives behind parliamentarian 'loyalty'.[146] Criticism focused on the literary form of the book. It was compared to a fairy tale or a second-rate romantic novel. Though some, including Griffith himself, treated it as a handbook to be read literally, it is a political satire full of facetious contemporary references.[147]

Critics noted the difficulty of boycotting the government without handing over administration to whigs and loyalists. Griffith replied that recalcitrants would be controlled by public opinion, as in the Land War. To the charge that he presented an obsolete constitution as perpetually binding, Griffith said that the Renunciation Act merely proved British claims to rule Ireland contradictory in their own terms: once the Irish people regained the constitution of 1782 they could alter it.[148] There were contradictions between principled non-recognition and the detailed strategy proposed. If the Union was illegitimate, was the act establishing county councils invalid? If the government was illegitimate, why did Sinn Féiners pay tax? Did wholesale delegitimation of *de facto* authority amount to legitimism detached from real life?—the view of D. P. Moran, observing neo-Jacobite eccentrics on the Sinn Féin right. Might glorifying non-co-operation produce anarchy?

Frederick Ryan criticised Griffith's opportunist praise of protests involving non-recognition of government authority over particular issues. One such was a concerted refusal by wine-growers in the south of France, led by Marcellin Albert, to pay tax until the government compensated them for vines destroyed by disease. Another was the symbolic refusal of British Nonconformists to pay rates to local authorities that subsidised denominational schools. Ryan saw such gestures as examples of Sinn Féin tactics in action. He argued that if every discontented minority adopted this tactic, government would become impossible.[149] Griffith answered that every weapon must be grasped. Sinn Féiners were not bound to abstention from local authorities, which they could control—unlike the House of Commons.

Ireland's rights could be asserted only with majority support, and so tax must be paid when concerted non-payment was impossible. It is also notable that in 1913 Griffith failed to see any contradiction between his denunciations of Larkin as a wrecker and his earlier support for Marcellin Albert.

Ryan assumed that rational argument would inevitably produce majority support: disrespect for majority rule was therefore profoundly illiberal. Griffith's view of the non-Sinn Féin majority as dupes misled by knaves was a variant of the Parnellite argument that they were not bound by the decision of the majority of nationalists, because the majority were not really nationalists; likewise his argument (in itself perfectly understandable, and shared in a milder form by most nationalists) that the Union was not binding because it was imposed and maintained by fraud or force and that those who acquiesced in it connived in their own enslavement. Critics saw that such views might in other hands develop into a claim to resist a compromise supported by the majority, on the grounds that the majority had no right to compromise its freedom.

Griffith cannot be held responsible for the minority who in 1922 denounced his acceptance of the Treaty on the grounds that a majority of the living had no right to disown the dead generations, or the still smaller minority who for decades after 1922 claimed that the results of the 1918 and 1920 elections entitled them to disregard every election since as invalid; but Ryan and Moran had detected the possibility that the tactics Griffith devised for asserting popular power against party bosses and collaborationist elites might under certain circumstances be perverted in this manner. Some of these implications emerged after 1906 as Griffith, reacting against the revived alliance of the Liberals and the Irish Party, emphasised values Sinn Féin shared with Tories; others appeared after 1922 when republican legitimists, denying that majorities conferred even *de facto* legitimacy, adopted attitudes that Griffith's critics warned against and Griffith discounted.

Griffith presents the 'Hungarian policy' as suitable for a Deák or a Parnell, genuinely thinking it a final solution but allowing it to be taken further. Aspiring to be Parnell and knowing he was not, Griffith conferred the leadership of Sinn Féin on the misogynist landowner Edward Martyn and the cranky former MP John Sweetman, politically to the right of the Sinn Féin membership, and they paid for the publication of *The Resurrection of Hungary* in book form. Sinn Féin's centre of political gravity lay elsewhere.

Sinn Féin appeared as an organised Dublin Corporation group in January 1904,[150] and consolidated itself as the main opposition force in 1906 when five Irish Party councillors (including Tom Kelly, later leader of the group) defected to join four elected Sinn Féiners under Walter Cole. Sinn Féin spoke for small traders and skilled workers, demanding reduced rates, greater efficiency, and contracts for local firms. Some leading members of the small-business Industrial Development Associations in provincial towns—notably J. L. Fawsitt, E. J. Riordan, and Elisabeth Somers, who wrote for Sinn Féin papers as 'Lasairfhíona'—were sympathisers; Sinn

Féin activists helped with IDA propaganda, and Griffith, with some exaggeration, claimed credit for the whole movement. Sinn Féin, like the Irish Party, also co-operated with labour representatives. It saw politics as a struggle between the general good and sectional interests; it saw no contradiction between demands for reduced expenditure and for workers' housing, because it believed that housing could be provided cheaply in the suburbs if publicans and slum-owners did not insist on expensive inner-city schemes.[151]

Outside Dublin, Sinn Féin representation was scattered. Councillors were elected in Castleisland, County Kerry (which had a Sinn Féin parish priest);[152] there was one on Cork Corporation;[153] and there were representatives in Oldcastle, Thomastown, and Kinsale.[154] A Sinn Féin presence emerged in north and east Galway, particularly around Loughrea and Tuam,[155] in County Wexford, and in Roscommon;[156] a branch in Carron, County Clare, joined the local UIL in cattle-drives;[157] and in the traditional AOH heartland of north-west and south Ulster the separatist Irish-American Alliance faction of the AOH—led by Seumas MacManus, widower of Anna Johnston—operated Sinn Féin branches.[158]

D. P. Moran's weekly, the *Leader*, which appeared in September 1900, appealed to the same constituency as Griffith. It too denounced British mass culture as corrupting and degenerate, ridiculed snobberies and West Britonisms among the Catholic bourgeoisie, criticised the Irish Party as hypocritical and in-effective, and called for self-reliance and a producerist ethos driven by pride in Irish distinctiveness. Like Griffith, it patrolled the frontiers of Irish Ireland, inveighing against those who played soccer or sang music-hall songs as flabby and backboneless.

Griffith welcomed Moran's paper, but they soon quarrelled. Griffith denounced 'D. P. Hooligan, editor of *The Oracle*,' then ignored him, while Moran ridiculed 'tin-pikers' and 'the Green Hungarian Band'. Oliver St John Gogarty recalled mockery from 'a more popular and vulgar periodical' hindering Sinn Féin;[159] while James Hannay suggested that provincial newsagents could tell Irish Party supporters from separatists by seeing who took the *Leader* and who the *United Irishman*.[160]

Griffith grew up in the traditional artisan milieu of Dublin. His attitudes were shaped by local separatist traditions and developed through his study of nineteenth-century separatist literature. Moran's family had separatist traditions (an elder brother worked with O'Donovan Rossa) but were more middle-class: they sent Moran and a brother to Castleknock College, a Catholic boarding-school.[161] Griffith's nationalism, despite authoritarian elements, was egalitarian; Moran thought snobbery was inevitable and that nationalists should exploit it. As a boy, Moran acquired from nineteenth-century literature 'a sound National education outside school hours,' an emotional sense of Ireland's past greatness and British treachery, and a belief that Ireland could win freedom if determined to fight. He saw no contradiction in also feeling provincial Ireland intolerably restrictive and in seeking escape. In 1888 he went to London as a journalist. He was awestruck by the city's economic and military might, and reassessed youthful beliefs that because Ireland nearly won in 1798 it could defeat Britain in a re-match.[162]

In fact Moran was overimpressed: Griffith, who read Ivan Bloch's books arguing that new technology had shifted the balance of advantages towards defenders in modern warfare, had a stronger sense of the potential of guerrilla warfare, of likely British involvement in European war, and the extent to which British rule in Ireland increasingly depended on co-operation from sections of the Catholic community.[163] Moran came to see those who advocated physical force and those who took parliamentary rhetoric seriously as suffering delayed adolescence.

Moran's memories of London were not all unpleasant. He was impressed by the relative tolerance for political debate, compared with Irish insistence on political conformity. Nonetheless he felt distinctively Irish and unwilling to be assimilated; and when the Gaelic League provided a new rationale, he returned to Ireland to make a career.

He had been a Parnellite in the early eighteen-nineties and, as critics recalled, anti-clerical,[164] but this gave way to a sense of Catholicism as underpinning Irish identity. University College Jesuits encouraged Moran to counter the anti-clericalism of Griffith.[165] Father Thomas Finlay published Moran's political credo, 'The principles of Irish Ireland', in the *New Ireland Review* in 1898–9. The Finlay-Moran alliance was noted by Thomas Connellan, who remarked that Plunkett might return from travel abroad to discover Moran ensconced in the Department of Agriculture and Technical Instruction. At the same time Moran was outspokenly critical of 'West British' clerically run secondary schools—including Castleknock—and similar social attitudes among sections of the clergy. This reflected generational change within the Catholic professional class. Catholic colleges functioned as much to supply Catholic professionals to Britain and the empire as to replenish the Catholic professional classes in Ireland; but as unionist and Protestant dominance of the professions and civil service diminished and the Catholic professional sub-culture grew in strength and confidence, expectations rose. Catholic colleges formed old boys' associations and published magazines; University College revived its Literary and Historical Society and produced dining-clubs whose members looked forward to ruling Ireland under home rule.[166] Some achieved that ambition under the Irish Free State.

Catholic social networks at national level were growing; but in the early twentieth century, Catholic graduates and ambitious white-collar workers who stayed in Ireland were caught between residual Protestant and Castle Catholic influence at national level and local patronage rings.[167] Moran provided one outlet for resentment, with campaigns illustrating Protestant dominance in the higher civil service, railways, and banks.[168] Unionist populists suggested that this attention should be directed to competition by clerics against educated lay Catholics; Griffith argued that discrimination was not against Catholics but against nationalists and that boycotting Protestant-run industries divided Catholics and Protestants to benefit Britain. Catholics appointed as a result of such campaigns were incompetents who gave Catholics a bad name; the real problem was the orientation of Catholic education towards the professions.[169]

Moran's emphasis on Catholic self-help and struggle for the heights of the economy voiced the concerns of his generation under Tory rule. It was partly marginalised as home rule returned to the agenda but anticipated the role of the Ancient Order of Hibernians in the later years of the Irish Party and resonated through Catholic Action into the nineteen-fifties. In this sense Griffith correctly identified Moran as the heir of nineteenth-century Catholic whigs. Moran admired O'Connell and compared his economic campaigns to those of the Liberator, though his O'Connell was the Catholic leader rather than the radical utilitarian. Frank Callanan is also correct in seeing him as an heir of the Healyite project.[170] Moran harnessed Irish revivalism and its critique of nineteenth-century nationalism to the view that the central struggle was not between Britain and Ireland but between Catholic and Protestant, that total separation was impossible—perhaps undesirable—and that the Catholic community should assert itself economically and culturally until it was strong enough to force Britain to accept a Catholic elite as managers of an autonomous Ireland linked to Britain in external affairs. The nearest equivalent might be Québec, cited by unionists who claimed that Québec's Protestant Anglophones were mistreated by an authoritarian clericalist government.

Moran's closest political relationship was with the Catholic Association, founded in Dublin in 1902 and intended, like its Belfast counterpart, to be an organisation led by Catholic notables promoting Catholic advancement while relegating the national question to a secondary position.[171] It was strongest in the unionist-dominated middle-class townships of Rathmines and Pembroke, where Moran lived. A prominent member was the apothecary J. C. MacWalter, a supporter of the Keating Branch of the Gaelic League and a member of Dublin Corporation, whom Griffith regularly denounced as a whig and seller of dubious patent medicines.[172]

The handbook of the Catholic Association was developed by the Jesuit Peter Finlay (brother of Father Tom Finlay), from articles in the *Leader*. He spoke of an umbrella organisation defending Catholic interests and providing social and economic networks like the Protestant YMCA.[173] The association was distrusted by the Irish Party. While its documenting of anti-Catholic discrimination in railway companies and banks was generally accepted as accurate, its calls for boycotts of discriminatory Protestant firms were criticised and provoked Protestant reaction. Archbishop Walsh denounced it after Protestant businessmen began a counter-boycott of Catholic charities.[174] A low-key successor, the Catholic Defence Society, was established under tighter clerical supervision; a few years later its role as Catholic network and umbrella organisation was taken up by the Ancient Order of Hibernians.[175]

In the early years of the *Leader*, Moran distanced himself from the Irish Party. He saw O'Brien as a mad dictator and Dillon as a 'political fossil' and thought Ireland might do best with a Redmond-Healy leadership. He even endorsed Plunkett in Dublin South in 1900 and in the Galway city by-election, claiming that he did more good for Ireland than 'green' rhetoricians.[176] This was probably encouraged by Finlay. Moran later turned on Plunkett over *Ireland in the New Century*.

Griffith's denunciations of the *Leader* began when James Stephens, founder of the IRB, died and Moran commented that Fenianism and the nineteenth-century separatist tradition were outmoded by the Irish revival. 'Bodenstown will be forgotten when Ireland comes into her own.'[177] When King Edward VII visited Ireland in 1903, Moran took a position to the right of the Irish Party—though distancing himself from loyal-address 'flunkeys'. He argued that since the Irish Party accepted the Crown, refusal to formally recognise it before home rule was granted simply provided unionist propaganda. He proposed that nationalists present addresses offering loyalty if their grievances were redressed.[178] Griffith commented that this 'Collar the King Policy' was ur workable (the King would only receive non-contentious addresses) and immoral, because it assumed that victory and time legitimised usurpation.[179] *The Resurrection of Hungary* attributes the 'Collar the King' policy to 'jellyfish'.[180]

Griffith believed that the eighteenth and nineteenth centuries provided unchanging terms of reference; Moran was aggressively contemporary. He attacked local authorities that gave contracts to non-Irish firms but criticised Griffith's protectionism and argued that customers would only buy Irish products that were 'as good and cheap' as competitors. (Griffith called this no protection at all, and those who proposed it traitors.)[181] Moran said that much blame for industrial failure lay with businessmen who failed to publicise their wares effectively; they should adopt 'modern methods of publicity', particularly advertising in the *Leader*. He published regular articles on individual firms to inform readers—and advertisers. Griffith sneered at claims that 'Ireland can be saved by advertising.'

Moran displayed no interest in the content of Irish culture: it served only as a mark of difference from England and a means of asserting Irish moral superiority. He equated 'Gael' with 'Catholic'. ('Ireland for the Italians,' remarked Griffith.)[182] The *Leader's* main contribution to the revival lay in attracting recruits to the Gaelic League, Father Peadar Ó Laoghaire's articles in Irish as introductory texts for learners, and the attempts of Father Pádraig Ó Duinnín, the lexicographer, to develop the literary language by using it for articles on contemporary world events.[183] Moran's alliance with the Munster faction attracted Griffith's censure. In his satirical extravaganza *The Conspirators*, D. P. Hooligan is an incompetent assassin hired by the Man in the Mask (Finlay) to remove Hyde and bring about a clericalist take-over of the Gaelic League. Hooligan and the Mask conspire with the league's arch-enemies, the Trinity dons J. P. Mahaffy and Anthony Traill.[184]

Griffith went as far as to suggest that Moran was a British agent, stirring up sectarian feeling to justify unionist propaganda. This, like his accusations against the Irish Church Missions, allowed him to avoid admitting that Catholics and Protestants might generate sectarian hatred themselves. Hooligan is portrayed as a native converted to loyalty by 'Reverend Mr. Rawlhiston of the Irish Church Missions.'[185] This is T. W. Rolleston, whose conversion from home rule to imperialism was regularly denounced by Griffith. John O'Leary complained that Rolleston was entitled to change his views, however mistakenly, without having his good faith denied.[186]

Moran was distinguished from older whigs by the absence of deference to the British Crown (though his clerical and middle-class readers aspired to receive deference themselves); his 'Collar the King' policy was outspokenly based on expediency rather than the view that the social hierarchy mirrored the Court of Heaven and that the British Crown was a bulwark against godless republicanism.[187] His allegiance to the producerist and developmental ethos of the small business-man, as against importer and professional, also marks him off from the image of the deferential Irish whig; and although his sectarianism and his association with Catholic job-hunters make him in some respects less sympathetic than Griffith, he was perhaps more modern. His insistence that nationalism must recognise vast social and economic changes since the eighteenth century contrasts with Griffith's fundamentalist citations of Young Ireland; even his insistence that most Protestants did not subscribe to the nationalist version of Irishness can be seen as facing what Griffith—and most nationalists—evaded. Moran was the fox to Griffith's hedgehog; he lost out to Griffith in historical reputation because, while he knew many things, Griffith centred his life on one thing Moran did not take into account: the extent of nationalist discontent with the British state, and the ability of a determined minority in time of crisis to channel these discontents into a nationalist project more radical than seemed possible in 1900.

Moran's contributors were a mixture of provincial clerics and young Dubliners who fancied themselves as Catholic intellectuals. There was some tension between them: Dublin laymen were less sanguine than rural clerics about maintaining the social and intellectual control possible in a rural parish, and more aware of the need to articulate and defend their beliefs. Several Dublin contributors—notably Arthur Clery, Hugh Kennedy, Richard Hazleton, and Louis Walsh—had links to University College and overlapped with the 'ginger group' of young party activists around Tom Kettle that wrote for the Jesuits' *New Ireland Review,* produced the short-lived weekly *Nationist* in 1905, and formed the Young Ireland Branch of the United Irish League in 1906.[188] Kettle disliked the name-calling and bullying of 'blackthorn-stick-in-waiting' Moran and devised the *Nationist* as a rival to the *Leader.* Its demise (caused by insufficient financial backing and clerical suspicion) indicated problems facing its highbrow form of Christian democracy.[189]

Kettle and the YIBs, aspiring to be the governing class in a future home-rule Ireland, wished to remedy the Irish Party's perceived lack of interest in the new cultural movements. In general the party distrusted the new movements, though there were exceptions: John Pius Boland and Thomas O'Donnell, elected for County Kerry seats in 1900, were Irish revivalists and industrial activists, with Boland promoting Irish trade-marks and the production of fuller information on Ireland's economic performance;[190] Field was prominent in the industrial movement since the eighteen-eighties; Hugh Law, elected for West Donegal in 1902, was a friend of George Russell, associated with the co-operative movement and attacked for criticising literary censorship;[191] Stephen Gwynn was one of the founders of the Dublin publishing house of Maunsel.

Kettle and some associates wished to assert claims to political and intellectual leadership against old-style Catholic whiggery and Protestant privilege—to combine the political achievements of the Irish Party with the latest Continental thought. To a sceptical contemporary like James Joyce, their university milieu resembled a tightly controlled provincial day-school.[192] Christian democracy was suspect also in official Catholic circles, especially when some YIBs abandoned Catholicism and criticised former associates for intellectual bad faith in claiming that it could be reconciled with modernity. Kettle had periods of doubt and melancholia, imperfectly disguised by affecting breezy Chestertonian confidence; one friend recalled his delight in skirting the verge of unbelief.[193] Many party activists saw YIBs as arrogant and pretentious youngsters.

The obstacles facing the YIBs were not purely intellectual. They emerged from college into the older milieu of briefless barristers and journalists around the party machine. Some entered Parliament (including Kettle, Hazleton, and E. J. Kelly, scion of a prominent County Donegal family, MP for East Donegal from 1910) but found themselves frustrated by the persistence of older leaders. As Liberal reforms after 1906 increased professional opportunities, some YIBs benefited—with Kettle appointed first professor of national economics in University College—and, like older activists, were denounced as job-hunters.

Griffith, incensed by anyone claiming advanced ideas without supporting Sinn Féin, repeatedly accused Kettle of bad faith—with all the more impact because Kettle, like J. J. Horgan, had flirted with Sinn Féin and had harboured nostalgia for the days of Parnell and the heroic simplicities of advanced nationalism, while feeling that the Irish Party offered the only way forward.[194] The stereotype of YIB place-hunters became entrenched in separatist memory. P. S. O'Hegarty said that the party in latter days attracted no able young men except Hazleton and Kettle: 'In one case the motives were thought to be mixed; in the other they were known to be ambition.'[195] W. J. Brennan-Whitmore many years later declared it impossible that Rory O'Connor, a former member of the notorious YIB, could have helped Joseph Plunkett plan the Easter Rising; but Plunkett and MacDonagh were former YIBs.[196] YIB criticisms of Irish Party structures and strategy often resembled those of separatists; political frustration could become separatism. Eoin MacNeill, never a YIB, inhabited the same sub-culture, and his mixture of separatist sentiment with pragmatic acceptance of the party's political leadership, distrust of excessive closeness to the Liberals and articulation of Christian democrat ideology in reaction to continuing whig and Protestant privileges retarding his advancement is reminiscent of some YIBs.[197]

One other feature of the Young Ireland Branch deserves mention. It was the only branch of the United Irish League that admitted women, notably Hanna Sheehy-Skeffington. This period saw the emergence of significant numbers of educated Catholic women professionals, facing not only the obstacles experienced by male contemporaries but also discrimination. While women participated in past nationalist movements—as early as Young Ireland the rhetoric of classical citizen-ship was used to oppose genteel ideals of female passivity and to justify women's political participation—this period saw the first significant Catholic involvement in the women's suffrage movement, founded decades earlier by middle-class Protestant women who saw it as an extension of social work. Here was another new cultural movement, derided by conservative elements of the Irish Party as a pretentious minority, providing recruits for a separatist movement more receptive to the need for support.[198]

N ot even the leaders of the Irish Party could ignore the limits of agrarianism as the basis for a lasting movement. O'Brien, seeing UIL organisation decay-ing in the west as it moved away from its agrarian roots, wished to commit the party to a full-scale land campaign but was overruled. Other leaders believed the party had insufficient resources to sustain such a campaign and that the large-scale imprisonment of leaders and organisers would see the disintegration of party discipline.[199] When Captain John Shawe-Taylor issued an appeal for landlord and tenant representatives to discuss the land question, O'Brien was discontented and prepared for new ideas. Appeals for a round-table conference had been made by marginal figures such as the County Kerry landlord Lindsay Talbot-Crosbie and Dr Edward Thompson and were denounced by UIL leaders, including O'Brien, who called conciliating landlords a betrayal of tenants and suggested that such appeals should be addressed to hard-line landlords.[200] What marked out Shawe-Taylor's appeal was that Wyndham promptly endorsed it, and a group of moderate landlords came forward, balloted fellow-landlords, and received a mandate for negotiations. Several were active opponents of the land campaigns of the eighteen-eighties. Lord Dunraven and Lord Castletown subscribed to Smith-Barry's Property Defence Association (Dunraven was Smith-Barry's brother-in-law). Another member, the County Monaghan landlord Lord Rossmore, was dismissed from the magistracy in 1883 for staging an Orange demonstration close to a Land League meeting.

The conference between four landlords (Lord Dunraven, Lord Mayo, Colonel William Hutcheson-Poe, and Colonel Sir Nugent Everard) and four tenant represen-tatives (Redmond, O'Brien, Harrington, and T. W. Russell) worked out a scheme based on the government paying the difference between the price offered by tenants and that demanded by landlords. In fact Redmond had proposed a settlement on these lines in 1900.[201] This was the basis for the Irish Land Act (1903). Wyndham and Dunraven were impressed by O'Brien.[202]

As the act progressed through Parliament, O'Brien became convinced that the conference method could bring other social reforms and secure unionist consent for limited self-government, developing into full home rule. Meanwhile a royal visit presented King Edward as the patron of Irish settlement. It was later claimed, in an exercise in image-building, that the King encouraged further conciliatory measures and lent his name for private use in later initiatives. Redmond's respect for the King amounted almost to naïve monarchism; for the rest of his life O'Brien believed in royal good will.[203]

The Irish Party refrained from participation in the welcome, despite some exuberant local representatives.[204] Tim McCarthy, editor of the *Irish People,* went to jail for denouncing the visit.[205] Sinn Féin, claiming credit for forcing the party to oppose the visit, moved to exploit the situation; and Griffith denounced the Land Conference as a landlord swindle.[206] A Sinn Féin delegation led by Maud Gonne confronted the lord mayor of Dublin, Harrington, during a public meeting demanding commitment against a loyal address; disorder ensued.[207] A corporation faction led by Alderman W. F. Cotton proposed an address but was defeated by Sinn Féiners and Irish Party radicals led by J. H. Hutchinson, who succeeded Harrington as mayor and engaged in tacit co-operation with Sinn Féin. The bishops greeted King Edward at Maynooth in a room decked with his racing colours.

Drunk with praise for his triumph, Wyndham turned down transfer to another government post, claiming that he could transform Ireland.[208] Police expenditure was cut back, on the grounds that land settlement would reduce disaffection. This was to affect the efficiency of the Special Branch, with results apparent in 1916.[209]

It is not clear how far Wyndham had a coherent plan, as distinct from fantasies of triumph. Shawe-Taylor went north with letters of introduction from the Duke of Connaught, the king's brother and commander-in-chief of the forces in Ireland, to sound Ulster unionists on the university question.[210] Lord Dunraven, his associates and Wyndham's Under-Secretary, Sir Antony MacDonnell (an Indian administrator from a County Mayo Catholic gentry family, brother of a nationalist MP, and thought to have home rule sympathies), contemplated reform of the Irish administration, with limited functions devolved to a partly elected, partly nominated body. Wyndham probably knew of these conversations but maintained a certain distance.[211]

The core group numbered about thirty landlords. Dunraven and Castletown were associated with the financial adventurer Moreton Frewen in failed cattle-raising schemes in the American west; Horace Plunkett developed an enduring dislike for Frewen after clearing up the consequences. Plunkett also detested Dunraven. *Ireland in the New Century* criticises Wyndham's policy as opportunist concession at the expense of long-term character-building through self-help.[212]

Frewen, younger son of a Sussex landed family, married a daughter of the American financier Leonard Jerome. Her sisters married Lord Randolph Churchill and Sir John Leslie of County Monaghan. Frewen used contacts among the Tory gentry to enlist investors—including his wife, children, and relatives—in reckless schemes. Business partners included Lord Dunraven and Lord Dudley, Lord Lieutenant 1902–5, who identified with the devolution scheme drawn up by MacDonnell and Dunraven. Frewen moved on the fringes of British politics, drumming up financial support (sometimes through blackmail) and trying to persuade the gentry that bimetallism and imperial federation would save their caste. He befriended Tim Healy by mutual attraction of mavericks and buccaneers, and was drawn further into Irish affairs by inheriting small Irish properties.[213]

Lord Dunraven's family were seen as model landlords. Their County Limerick estate was not their main source of income: they acquired Welsh coal mines and slate quarries through marriage. He had talent but limited achievements; associated with Lord Randolph Churchill, he resigned a junior ministry when Churchill resigned as Chancellor of the Exchequer.[214]

The group had their own Irish patriotism. Dunraven, Castletown and Everard were industrial revivalists. Everard wrote on tobacco-growing for Sinn Féin's 1908 Irish yearbook. Lord Dunraven had also tried to develop Irish tobacco. Castletown resigned from the Gaelic League executive in 1900 after his 'pan-Celtic' faction was defeated by nationalist-minded Gaelic Leaguers, diminishing unionist support for the league. Castletown continued as patron of the league in County Laois. He experimented with forestry and timber-processing.[215] Dunraven and Everard were among the few landlords to win election to county councils in 1899; Everard survived on Meath County Council until 1920.[216]

They also shared the military and imperial traditions of their caste. Castletown, Dunraven, Shawe-Taylor and Hutcheson-Poe served in imperial campaigns; Hutcheson-Poe lost a leg in Sudan; Dunraven's health was affected by illness contracted in South Africa. They were disgusted at nationalist denunciations of the Boer War.[217] They had not attained the power and recognition that their upbringing, social position and talents led them to expect—partly because of personal failings; a sympathetic observer called Castletown 'an ass with no backbone' and Dunraven 'eaten up with vanity.'[218] They thought landlords conceded leadership too easily and, once extracted from the land system, might regain influence and reconcile Irish patriotism with the empire.[219]

They were untypical of their caste in trying to come to terms with nationalism Some followed years later, seeing home rule as inevitable or seeking a moderate alternative to Sinn Féin after 1916. Most continued in doomed and myopic intransigence or reconciled themselves to emigration or social isolation. The Dunraven group never came to terms with the mass politics driving Irish nationalism and Ulster unionism. Their project, had it ever come into existence, would have fallen foul of the social, economic and religious rivalries that drove Moran and Griffith;

but it combined with O'Brien's romantic nationalism and Healy's opportunism to produce one of the most sustained and extensive attempts at unionist-nationalist co-operation in the twentieth century.

O'Brien declared for 'Conference plus business' and by personal magnetism and wire-pulling got the parliamentary party and UIL National Directory to endorse it.[220] He opened the *Irish People* to moderate unionists; Dunraven contributed a lengthy article, though references to the Boer War were toned down. O'Brien had tacit support from Redmond, but the pressures exerted for the new policy exposed latent hostility accumulating since the conference.[221]

Only Davitt and Patrick White, MP for North Meath, a maverick with Sinn Féin sympathies but no political weight had opposed the Irish Land Act before it was passed. Now the former MP and financial expert Thomas Sexton, manager of the *Freeman's Journal,* campaigned against its financial provisions, and it was known that Dillon disapproved of it.[222] He feared that if farmers got their land they would lose interest in politics; the centralised Irish Party partially reconstituted in 1900 would disintegrate, and Ireland would revert—as almost happened in the eighteen-nineties—to the political system of his youth, with parliamentary politics monopolised by whigs and place-hunters and honest nationalists driven into bitter, desperate and disorganised physical force. This fear was reinforced by Sinn Féin's campaign on the act—though Griffith seized on Dillon's reaction to prove the party self-confessed incompetents.

Dillon and his allies knew of Wyndham's intrigues. Dillon's friend John Muldoon, a lawyer and party activist, wrote of Wyndham's encouragement of 'every perjured traitor' who broke with the party, and claimed that William O'Doherty was his paid agent.[223] Harrington was offered knighthood or a colonial governorship to support a loyal address.[224] A conciliationist policy would encourage place-hunting by ending the traditional distance between party and administration; it would cut off recruitment to the party machine and American contributions vital to party finances; it would tie the party to a declining Tory government and endanger relations with natural Liberal allies; it might bind the party to an unaccountable administrative machine more reminiscent of the nominated councils advising the Indian administration than Gladstonian home rule.

O'Brien recalled the 'independent opposition' principle: that the party had no 'natural allies' and should take what it could get. He believed it possible to arouse popular enthusiasm by further reforms. He ridiculed the idea that nationality was 'famine-sickness'.[225] He thought that a successful exercise of responsibility would prove Irish capacity for self-government and that the situation offered a unique chance of splitting the unionist bloc and removing Irish and British Protestant fears—the most formidable barrier to home rule. He was encouraged in this by optimism about independent orangeism and Russellism.[226] He trusted in personal charisma to maintain support, as it had won support from UIL activists not normally disposed to compromise.

O'Brien brushed Dillon's views aside in floods of euphoric rhetoric. Dillon refused to admit there was anything to be said for O'Brien's hopes. He thought O'Brien had succumbed to flattery or gone mad; O'Brien thought Dillon's temperamental sympathy for English radicalism had led him to mistake it for Irish nationalism. Their political partnership, strained since O'Brien moved away from Parliament in 1896, broke for ever. Dillon publicly denounced the new policy; O'Brien told Redmond to discipline him. Healy and Frewen approached Redmond with an offer from a syndicate to buy up the *Freeman's Journal* on behalf of Redmond, Healy, and O'Brien.[227]

Redmond refused to act against Dillon. The East Mayo MP was financially independent, and his expulsion would provoke a nationwide split. Dillon had the support of Davitt, of Devlin's Belfast machine (Devlin told Dillon it would provide a secure base in the coming dispute),[228] of the Irish organisation in Britain, led by T. P. O'Connor, traditionally more radical than the Irish at home[229] (though some individuals sympathised with O'Brien), and of younger intellectuals and Irish-Irelanders, who saw the conciliation policy as restoring 'feudalistic influences'.[230] The Sheehy-Skeffingtons opposed O'Brien, as they opposed proposals to introduce minority safeguards into the third Home Rule Bill, on the grounds that democracy rested on faith that the majority could be persuaded by reason to act justly; minority safe-guards, and any impediment to majority will, concealed selfish class interests.

A revolt led by Dillon could mobilise discontent concealed by O'Brien's machine and its flood of resolutions. Landlords demanding high prices were affecting atti-tudes to the act. Redmond himself faced accusations of demanding extortionate prices from tenants on his family estate, inherited the previous year and run by trustees because of financial encumbrances; nor can he have relished dependence on O'Brien, whom he found personally distasteful, and shadowy financiers.

O'Brien retained personal prestige and dominated the UIL machine. In a strug-gle within the organisation he could attract many old Parnellites who survived the split through unionist support and admirers of O'Brien as the architect of national unity, whether they understood his policy or not. O'Brien was unwilling to struggle within the organisation; his personality and style of leadership precluded it. Equating his views with 'the people', he took UIL resolutions as the voice of the people, though he himself orchestrated them. When his control of the UIL was challenged he resigned; confident that no other policy was possible, he believed the organisation would collapse, and he would rebuild it to his own specifications.

On 4 November 1903 O'Brien told Redmond he was leaving Parliament and the UIL Directory, closing the *Irish People,* and withdrawing from public life. Even close allies were not consulted. Tim McCarthy, editor of the *Irish People,* learnt of its demise on 5 November, the day before the news became public.[231] Despite appeals from friends and allies,[232] O'Brien refused to reconsider. His resignation left Redmond dependent on Dillon. Thrown into confusion, the party and UIL rallied to unity. While O'Brien assured Lord Dunraven that 'the masses of the people are touchingly faithful,[233] the balance of opinion among nationalist activists and opinion-formers shifted irrevocably against him. He mistook personal sympathy for support for his policy, which could be maintained without his presence.

Most provincial newspapers that supported O'Brien rapidly turned against him or shifted to neutrality.[234] Within a few years Tim McCarthy, as editor of the Belfast *Irish News*, was one of O'Brien's bitterest critics. MPs like William Lundon (Limerick East), David Sheehy and Thomas J. Condon (Tipperary South), who wrote to O'Brien on his resignation assuring him of their loyalty, became supporters of Dillon and opponents of O'Brien.[235] Others, like Conor O'Kelly (North Mayo) and Thomas O'Donnell (West Kerry), wavered opportunistically. Some—notably Timothy Harrington, Jeremiah MacVeagh, Edward Barry (South Cork), and Edmund Haviland-Burke MP (Offaly)[236]—continued to hope for O'Brien's return. But among MPs only John O'Donnell, still secretary of the UIL, doubts overridden by personal loyalty,[237] Eugene Crean (MP for South-East Cork, former lord mayor and trade union official) and the old Fenian James Gilhooly (South-West Cork) followed O'Brien to the bitter end. He had some support in County Mayo, bolstered by his residence in Westport and O'Donnell's influence. O'Brienites controlled the Cork UIL and were strong in County Limerick, with individual supporters elsewhere. He obstructed party attempts to organise in County Cork and west Mayo by threatening open opposition.[238] His supporters on Cork Corporation allied themselves with 'whigs' who had supported a loyal address in 1900, led by the wine merchant Augustine Roche.

Despite claims that he was 'effacing himself' and leaving opponents a 'fair field', O'Brien maintained contact with remaining sympathisers and issued public letters and pamphlets.[239] 'William O'Brien's silence' became proverbial among facetious opponents. John O'Donnell tried to use his position as secretary of the UIL to orchestrate calls for O'Brien's return; the maverick Laurence Ginnell, who assisted O'Donnell in the league office and was on bad terms with him, kept Dillon and Muldoon informed.[240]

On 10 August 1904 Cork and Limerick delegations to the UIL Directory proposed a resolution reaffirming 'conciliation'. It was defeated by fifty votes to twelve; six Cork delegates resigned, and O'Donnell was replaced as secretary by Devlin.[241] O'Donnell bought the machinery of the *Irish People,* moved to Galway, and there set up the *Connaught Champion.* It was widely believed to be subsidised by O'Brien; this was not so at first, though O'Donnell accepted outside help by 1907.[242]

While O'Brien denounced UIL subservience to the Irish Party, Jasper Tully moved the writ for O'Brien's Cork seat, left vacant to avoid conflict.[243] O'Brien's Cork supporters nominated him without asking him to take the party pledge, and Redmond acquiesced in his unopposed return. O'Brien accepted election (announcing that he would not go to Westminster). He was influenced by news that the Dunraven group were forming an Irish Reform Association to press for devolution.

The Cork by-election of 1904 brought O'Brien the ally whose organisational skills and social programme secured his County Cork base. D. D. Sheehan was born in 1873. His parents were tenant farmers; he had vivid recollections of their eviction during the Land War. He was active intermittently from 1889 in organising agricultural labourers, who were numerous in Munster, notoriously ill-paid and ill-housed, and benefited little from the Land War. He spent some years in London as a journalist; he became editor of the *Southern Star* and acquired a leading position in the Land and Labour Association, founded in 1894 by the Clonmel solicitor J. J. O'Shee (MP for West Waterford from 1895) to campaign for the granting of smallholdings to labourers. Irish Party leaders—including O'Brien—suspected this independent organisation; but in 1901 Sheehan was elected MP for Mid-Cork, where labourers were particularly numerous, after defeating the official UIL candidate at the selection convention.[244] Sheehan had been a Parnellite and at O'Brien's secession inclined towards Redmond; but discontent with the party machine, and O'Brien's willingness to agitate for labourers' grievances as a matter for the conference, drew him to O'Brien. Sheehan's talents were placed at O'Brien's service, despite personal instability producing occasional drinking-bouts;[245] O'Brien looked on him with the warmth reserved for faithful collaborators.[246]

Wyndham's plans for the settlement of the university question were blocked by opposition from Ulster unionists and Trinity College. Official Ulster unionism responded to the Independent Orange Order and T. W. Russell by developing a more aggressive rhetoric, revamping its organisation—leading to the creation of the Ulster Unionist Council—and becoming more critical of the Dublin Castle administration, though criticisms were at first directed at MacDonnell rather than Wyndham.[247] The significance of these developments passed unnoticed by the Dunravenites in their aristocratic intrigues and by O'Brien, who—like most nationalists—failed to realise that mass politicisation that gave nationalists near-monopoly in most of Ireland produced among Ulster Protestants mass unionism as determined as its nationalist counterpart. The deposing of Rossmore as county grand master of the Monaghan Orange Order in favour of a local solicitor, Michael Knight,[248] was symptomatic of the new developments.

Land Bill finances, based on optimistic forecasts, were disrupted by declining values of government stock affecting land stock issued under the bill. Wyndham knew that finance might be insufficient but gambled that improved Irish conditions would become so obvious that resistance to more payment would be negligible.[249] Overall government spending had reached limits only sustainable by tariffs (advocated by Chamberlain) or extended direct taxation (as the Liberals undertook after 1906). A Labourers' Bill introduced by Wyndham was watered down until it was unacceptable to nationalists, then withdrawn.

Wyndham's health deteriorated as he resorted to alcohol and 'violent physical exercise'.[250] His crack-up mirrored the decline of the government, torn apart by the efforts of Chamberlain to offset the perceived weakness of its aristocratic leadership by mobilising popular enthusiasm for 'national efficiency' based around protection and imperial preference. With Chamberlain and free trade opponents resigning from the Cabinet, Liberals united around traditional commitment to free trade and mobilising Nonconformist support over education; and with defections and by-election losses eroding the government's majority, a Liberal government seemed closer than ever—removing a major argument for doing deals with Tories. Some tariff reformers argued that protectionism might underpin the Union by raising Irish agricultural prices; individual nationalists made sympathetic noises (notably George Noble Plunkett, Count Plunkett, who chaired the Dublin branch of the Chamberlainite Fiscal Reform Association);[251] and Griffith echoed Chamberlainite critiques of free trade as corruptly sustained by cosmopolitan banking and shipping interests and cited tariff reform as proof that even the British were recognising the fallacy of liberal economics, but there were few takers. Both Griffith and Moran argued that Irish industries would lose more from British competition than Irish farmers gained—especially since it seemed that agriculture might be exempted from tariffs to accommodate dominion farmers and British consumers.[252]

The opportunists of the Irish bar were already trimming in hope of preferment. Several previously 'liberal unionist' lawyers developed patriotic and religious feelings. When the St Stephen's Green division fell vacant in 1904, the leaders of the Irish Party were besieged by place-hunters—including Plunkett.[253] The party considered nominating the son of the dead MP but preferred to use his Meath influence against Patrick White at the general election. Redmond offered the seat to the retired general Sir William Butler—disliked by Dillon as too 'loyalist'—and to Douglas Hyde; both turned it down.[254]

The wealthy stockbroker Laurence Waldron, a former Unionist, was elected as a party-backed independent. His victory was assisted by continuing Unionist problems with ultra-Protestant dissidents. Michael MacCarthy stood in protest at government flirtation with a Catholic university and won support from working-class unionists and endorsement from Saunderson. Though he withdrew for lack of funds, his anti-Catholic speeches alienated Catholic whigs; and his departure to become a Protestant lecturer in Britain hardly consoled unionist leaders.[255]

O'Brien hoped to revive conciliation by a conference on the labourers' question to overcome the defects of the 1904 bill as the Land Conference remodelled the Land Bill of 1902. He argued that the Irish Party was well placed to extract concessions because of the precarious position of the government. A successful conference might also give O'Brien the undivided allegiance of the Land and Labour Association, for though distrusted by party leaders, O'Shee remained loyal to Redmond, supported by the organisation in Counties Waterford and Tipperary. Sheehan held Cork; Kerry and Limerick were divided. (The organisation had barely spread outside Munster.) Lord Dunraven wrote to Redmond proposing a conference, while O'Brien asked Wyndham to receive a labourers' delegation.[256] Canon Quinn of Newry gave notice of a motion at the UIL Directory meeting of 24 January 1905 calling for such a conference; O'Brien arranged for the Cork and Limerick UIL to send delegates and canvassed sympathetic Directory members, while refusing to go himself. Harrington pledged support but predicted defeat:

Had you remained within the organisation and fought the battle within, the struggle would have been an easy one ... But now it is all the other way ... Men who were ready to worship you in your presence and who know still in their hearts that you are right have nothing better than a sneer for you in your absence ... Do not look for anything to the meeting of the Directory if you cannot see your way to be present there. The policy is not merely to redouble the attack on the landlords, but to single out for special attack every one of them whose name was ever mentioned in connexion with the policy of conciliation.[257]

Redmond repudiated Lord Dunraven's proposal, announced that Canon Quinn (apparently motivated by personal rather than ideological sympathy for O'Brien)[258] had withdrawn the motion, and ruled further discussion out of order, despite protests by Harrington and O'Brienites.[259] Wyndham told O'Brien that while he wanted to solve the labourers' question, financial problems prevented any action.[260] O'Brien talked of resigning but was dissuaded.[261]

When the Irish Reform Association published its scheme, Wyndham denounced it. MacDonnell, unwilling to be a scapegoat, let it be known that he informed Wyndham.[262] In May, Ulster unionists renewed parliamentary attacks; the party leadership facilitated the onslaught while allowing the Ulstermen to take the lead.[263] John O'Donnell tried to persuade Redmond that attacks on Wyndham were aimed at his leadership; the erratic South Kildare MP Denis Kilbride horrified Dillon and Muldoon by incorporating an anti-Redmond diatribe in a speech attacking Wyndham.[264]

Wyndham resigned. His successor, Walter Long, pursued tighter law enforcement, partisan unionist appointments (previous Tory chief secretaries tried to preserve some appearance of merit), and hard-line unionism.[265] The Gaelic League was made a target by the withdrawal of government grants for teaching Irish and the prosecution of owners of carts—including the Sinn Féin alderman Walter Cole—for failing to display their name 'legibly' on their carts (Irish-language names being declared 'illegible').[266] MacDonnell was confined to a subordinate role; the government announced plans to re-draw constituency boundaries and to reduce the number of Irish MPs by twenty, to give the same representation by population as the rest of the United Kingdom. The Irish Party frustrated this with procedural tactics devised by the Protestant Nationalist MP for South Donegal, J. G. Swift MacNeill, who possessed legal expertise and an encyclopaedic knowledge of parliamentary rules.[267]

Some old associates, like the Doris brothers of the *Mayo News*, hoped O'Brien might now rejoin the official Irish Party.[268] Instead he grew more bitter against the party, which he blamed for Wyndham's frustration and deposing. He believed Wyndham and the Tory leadership would have supported devolution had the party cultivated them. He refused to recognise financial and political constraints on Wyndham and derided the idea that Ulster unionists, 'eight Orangemen', toppled him.

One of Moran's principal contributors drew different conclusions. Arthur Clery, a prominent member of the Kettle-Joyce generation at University College, advocated partition, horrifying MacNeill, who could hardly believe he was serious.[269] Clery pointed out that by most arguments used by nationalists, Ulster Protestants were a separate nationality. They had a distinct territory, continuous history, culture and traditions; they freely chose representatives pledged against inclusion in a home-rule Ireland. Clery argued that nationalists should concentrate on obtaining a border leaving as few Catholics as possible in the north. He gave detailed proposals based on parish boundaries.[270]

This extension of the definition of Irishness derived from awareness of the intensity of Ulster unionist feeling, acting upon preoccupation with the problems of Catholic graduates. If O'Brien believed home rule could come through historic compromise with unionist elites, Clery advocated partition in part from fear that such a deal would preserve existing structures of privilege.

The party leadership split the Land and Labour Association, fearing that Sheehan would create paper branches to deselect MPs.[271] Redmond loyalists dis-affiliated Sheehanite branches *en masse*; and O'Shee's LLA became the only labourers' organisation recognised by the party. Sheehan retained control in Counties Cork and Kerry, with some outposts elsewhere (including south Wexford, under John Cummins), and some people within the official LLA favoured reunification; but prospects of expansion were curtailed.

In June 1905 the second Cork city MP, the precariously neutral J. F. X. O'Brien, died. O'Brien put forward Augustine Roche, unpledged. The party did not oppose Roche, but O'Brien's action crystallised the realisation that O'Brien might have to be fought like Healy.[272] In September the *Irish People* reappeared, edited by John Herlihy. Its second issue contained a manifesto from the Irish Reform Association calling for a new conference to deal with the west and the evicted tenants, to pro-pose a Labourers' Bill, improve the finances of the Wyndham act, and resist reduced Irish representation. O'Brien called on the party to confer with the Reform Association, the LLA, the General Council of County Councils, the Russellites, and the Independent Orange Order. Dillon described this as subordinating the party to Dunraven, Sloan, T. W. Russell, and Healy.[273]

O'Brien co-operated with the campaign by Sir Bertram Windle, president of Queen's College, Cork, for an independent Munster university. This tied in with Dunraven's scheme, encouraged by the appointment of Lord Castletown as chan-cellor of the Royal University, to settle the university question by making the Catholic University a college equal to Trinity within the University of Dublin.[274]

O'Brien and Sheehan consolidated support in County Cork by establishing an Advisory Committee to mediate between landlords and tenants on purchase terms, not ruling out agitation if the landlord was obstinate. (O'Brien complained to Lord Dunraven that most landlords held out for the highest price without seeing the opportunity to secure their future, but he blamed the party for sabotaging the act

rather than organising farmers to work out terms.) The Advisory Committee produced a higher take-up of land purchase than in any other county; O'Brien claimed
it secured lower prices for County Cork than elsewhere. The committee also served
as the nucleus of a political organisation under O'Brien's control.[275] He hoped it
would produce 'a broad, powerful movement too strong for the party,' but plans for
similar committees in Counties Limerick and Mayo came to nothing. John O'Donnell
claimed that Conor O'Kelly betrayed plans for a County Mayo committee to Dillon.[276]

O'Donnell used more traditional methods to bolster support. In October 1905
he was briefly imprisoned for agrarian agitation. The appearance of Healy as
defence counsel showed that O'Brien had acquired another ally.[277] Healy always
combined distaste with slightly contemptuous affection for O'Brien, dating from
their co-operation on *United Ireland*.[278]

In August 1905, when Frewen presented himself as go-between, Healy said
that the way O'Brien stood by his commitments to Wyndham erased any grievances
he might have against him. The coming general election would sweep away the
mavericks with whom Healy collaborated, and North Louth was not particularly
safe. Alliance with O'Brien offered Healy new opportunities to gratify his amused
quasi-nihilistic exultation in his talents for creation or destruction. He said that
O'Brien genuinely believed in the 'voice of the people' and aggregate assemblies. '*Ich
nichts* [I don't].'[279]

Frewen found O'Brien responsive, though at first wary of private contact with
Healy.[280] Co-operation offered O'Brien support in Parliament, an additional bridgehead outside County Cork, possible residual Healyite support in Ulster and north
Leinster, perhaps the clerical support O'Brien notoriously lacked. It might also
bring the *Irish Independent*. But Murphy proved too shrewd to damage his newspaper by an unpopular political stance. While the *Independent* was generally critical
of the Irish Party, Murphy only occasionally intervened to tilt it towards O'Brien and
Healy and told them to blame its editor, T. R. Harrington.[281]

The support of another first-rank nationalist might encourage landlords to
take the conciliation movement seriously and counter charges that O'Brien was a
unionist puppet.

> Enormous as will be the effect of our co-operation, we must take care that our
> side shall be easily first in weight of metal. Between us two, I flatter myself the
> lords will meet their match, and our own people will realise that it is not we
> who are playing second fiddle ... without you I should really have to 'bear the
> battle on my single shield.'[282]

Urging Redmond to strike Healy at the 1906 general election, Dillon wrote that
if Healy were defeated, O'Brien carried little weight in Parliament, but Healy and
O'Brien together were formidable.[283]

Fearing large-scale conflict, George Crosbie, proprietor of the *Cork Examiner,*
and other moderates mediated between O'Brien and Redmond and secured an

agreement to avoid contests at the general election.[284] Healy was unopposed in North Louth, with plans to run a party candidate abandoned because of a public announcement by Cardinal Logue that the constituency should be spared a con-test—cited by anti-clericals as proof of party subservience to the church.[285] An attempt by south Mayo priests to oppose John O'Donnell was squashed by O'Brien's threat to abandon the pact and by the intervention of Archbishop Healy of Tuam, an ultra-conservative sympathetic to O'Brien; he had opposed the Plan of Campaign, quarrelled with Davitt over prices demanded from tenants of church lands, and publicly toasted the King as *de jure* monarch.[286]

In East Kerry, Eugene O'Sullivan, a solicitor linked with Sheehan's LLA, almost defeated the sitting MP, John Murphy, pursuing an old feud between the Murphy and O'Sullivan families. Murphy, the nominal 'Redmondite', had engaged in anti-Redmond intrigues with Ulster Healyites in 1904.[287]

Sinn Féin decided not to stand candidates, declaring that it would let the Irish Party prove its futility. Devlin's capture of West Belfast (held by Unionists since 1892) was a triumph, achieved by means of a vote-splitting Liberal Unionist and tactical voting by Independent Orangemen and Labour in return for nationalist support for Sloan and the Labour candidate, William Walker, in North Belfast; and the return of Hazleton and Kettle in by-elections soon afterwards provided a YIB parliamentary presence. The party's setback came in South Dublin, where J. J. Mooney had been appealing desperately for the cash-starved party to help pay to maintain nationalist organisation against well-funded Unionist opposition.[288] The Unionist vote united to return Long; Mooney did not return to Parliament until 1909, when he was elected for Newry.

Party control over local organisations remained patchy. The central leadership had not regained the control it exercised in Parnell's time. The Bristol UIL leader John Valentine, perhaps too much inclined to place British audiences before the need to maintain local support, lamented retrospectively:

> In this work John Redmond showed his weakness. He spoke more than once
> of the necessity for suitable men, but seemed afraid of alienating supporters
> and left matters to local people, who put forward, say a farmer or a dealer who
> had been prominent in cattle driving ... Thus the once great Irish Party ulti-
> mately had very few men who could assist Ireland's cause on the platform.[289]

Ambiguity about which organisations could attend conventions and how representatives should be chosen helped the leadership to influence decisions but could also lead to embarrassing reactions, as with Devlin's unsuccessful attempt to impose J. T. Donovan in North Monaghan in 1907 against a strong local candidate, J. C. R. Lardner.[290] Redmond's reluctance to commit himself to all-out opposition to Arthur Lynch in the convention for the West Clare by-election of 1909 was recalled by the unsuccessful candidate, Valentine, as indecision but also reflects reluctance to risk an outright, probably violent and possibly successful rebellion at the polls.[291]

In some instances factional disputes produced embarrassing dissension, even violence, publicised as proof of nationalist incapacity for self-government. Moran retorted that the convention was the equivalent of a parliamentary election by open vote, and under these circumstances most conventions went surprisingly well. The parallel with elections extended to canvassing and election addresses in local papers; more local studies would further modify images of a centrally directed monolith.[292] The Irish Party was a loose network at local rather than parliamentary level, centred on nuclei based around the individual leaders, each of whom had an inner core of confidants and an outer ring of followers, and held together by the reserved, respectful and mildly suspicious relationship between Redmond and Dillon. There was also an outer cloud of malcontents, whom O'Brien and Healy hoped to pull away into their own orbits.

1906 saw some striking convention reverses for the leadership. Plans to deselect Patrick White in favour of Sir Walter Nugent or Stephen Gwynn collapsed.[293] Dillon's ally Muldoon, who briefly represented North Donegal after the death of William O'Doherty in 1905, was deselected by the Healyite bishop and priests in favour of Philip O'Doherty, a Derry solicitor. An attempt to insert Muldoon in Devlin's North Kilkenny seat was defeated by an old Fenian, Michael Meagher.[294] Both O'Doherty and Meagher troubled the party leadership; Muldoon did not return to Parliament until 1909.

Sloan survived in South Belfast but repudiated the devolutionist views of Crawford, who soon proceeded via liberalism to nationalism. Nationalist hopes that Walker—a supporter of the Union who annoyed Catholics by supporting ultra-Protestant lobbyists during a by-election in 1905—might complete a 'three-leafed shamrock' of non-unionist Belfast MPs were disappointed. The Irish Land Act weakened T. W. Russell's protest vote; and the Unionist debacle increased the influence of the Ulster MPs within the shrunken Conservative party. It was not only nationalist Ireland that was moving from *Honoratiorenpolitik* to mass mobilisation around the constitutional issue.

3

LIBERAL ALLIANCE
1906–9

The significance of the Liberal landslide of 1906 for nationalists should not be overestimated. To prevent unionists deploying the home rule issue, the Liberals had expressly ruled out the introduction of home rule in the new Parliament, while pledging themselves to a limited measure of devolution, presented as 'administrative reform'. Many leading Liberals were known to regard home rule as an electoral liability, to be played down as much as possible; a few were openly opposed.

Much Liberal support derived from Nonconformists, whose attacks on state support for denominational education had strong anti-Catholic overtones and produced tensions between the Irish Party and the Catholic hierarchies of Ireland and Britain—both because the bishops' demands undermined the party's general preference for a Liberal alliance and because the activities of the Irish supporters of non-denominational education, encouraged by the English situation, increased episcopal suspicion of concealed anti-clericalism within the party. Liberal free trade beliefs also led to abortive proposals to admit Canadian cattle, which would have reduced prices for Irish cattle-farmers.

This situation was exploited by William O'Brien, who continued to advocate his conciliationist agenda and to create tension within the party over the activities of the small group of MPs who supported him, and by Arthur Griffith, whose attacks on Liberal universalism as hypocritical and destructive led him to move steadily to the right. At the same time Griffith was challenged by a group allied with the reviving IRB who wished Sinn Féin to replace its dual-monarchy 'Hungarian policy' with explicit republicanism. Both O'Brien and Sinn Féin were strengthened by the collapse in 1907 of the Irish Council Bill—brought in by the Liberals in fulfilment of their devolution pledge—which was rejected after a grass-roots upsurge of hostility among Irish Party members. Several activists defected to Sinn Féin, while O'Brien embarked on a 'unity' campaign aimed at mobilising his sympathisers within the party. The party managed to contain these revolts; O'Brien and his allies were re-admitted to membership, while Sinn Féin was defeated in the hard-fought Leitrim by-election and subsequently overstretched its resources by starting a short-lived daily paper on insufficient capital.

The Irish Party managed to obtain concessions from the British government, though these were often double-edged. The creation of the National University of Ireland led to a divisive controversy about making Irish a required subject for matriculation; the acquisition of government positions by party sympathisers led to accusations of corruption; and a new Land Bill led to a renewed revolt by O'Brien, who claimed that it would in fact hinder land purchase by making landlords reluctant to sell. The party also managed to associate itself with land agitation, calling for the division of cattle ranches among smallholders (despite embarrassing disclosures about the ranching interests of prominent party activists); while the appearance of the Ancient Order of Hibernians as a major organisation, under the leadership of Joe Devlin, strengthened the party's grass roots but led to accusations of sectarianism and jobbery by some party members as well as by dissidents and unionists. The O'Brienite members—led by Tim Healy after O'Brien's temporary retirement—joined with Sinn Féin and unionists in attacking party support for the 'people's budget', some of whose tax provisions were unpopular in Ireland; this led to a revival within Sinn Féin of the divisions between dual-monarchists and republicans after Griffith considered a tactical alliance with the O'Brienites. The dissolution of Parliament saw the Irish Party actively preparing to purge dissident MPs at the forthcoming general election.

A Liberal government opened the prospect of greater influence by the Irish Party over the Irish administration, but this was not straightforward. The landslide owed as much to Conservative divisions over tariff reform and education as to Liberal merits. Lord Rosebery, the former Prime Minister, self-destructed politically through repeated public indecision, but other Liberal Imperialists held important government positions. To prevent home rule reopening Liberal splits, Campbell-Bannerman pledged not to introduce it in the new Parliament—though the new Chief Secretary for Ireland, James Bryce, took up a proposal by Antony MacDonnell (retained as Under-Secretary) to present a new devolutionary reform of the Irish administration.

The need for administrative reform was generally recognised—even the Chief Secretary did not know how many boards were responsible to him—but Unionists were reluctant to accept that the Irish administration had serious weaknesses, for fear of giving political capital to home-rulers, while home-rulers suspected administrative reform as a potential substitute for home rule.[1]

The Irish Party was dubious about the retention of MacDonnell. When Bryce gave two O'Brienites posts in the Land Commission, the party leadership were furious,[2] and O'Brien received letters from office-seekers.[3] The retention of Horace Plunkett as head of the Department of Agriculture and Technical Instruction also provoked misgivings by the party, from personal and commercial hostility to Plunkett and from fear that unionist notables might still dominate the Dublin Castle administration. After promising a devolved Irish Council and settlement of the university question, Bryce became ambassador to Washington, leaving his successor—and MacDonnell—to work out the details.

Some Liberal candidates, including Russellites in Ulster, pledged themselves against home rule.[4] Russellite MPs in East Down and Fermanagh were defeated by unionists. Russell held South Tyrone, and R. G. Glendinning gained North Antrim, helped by Catholic tactical voting. After some uncertainty about whether they would sit in opposition as Liberal Unionists, they declared themselves government supporters.

T. C. Agar-Robartes, a Liberal imperialist candidate in Cornwall, pledged himself against home rule and any form of devolution. When he was unseated on petition in a partisan decision by a Tory judge, John Redmond and his close associate Pat O'Brien joined the Liberal outcry. Griffith seized this opportunity to accuse the Irish Party of subservience to the Liberals.[5] He used public awareness of the Liberal imperialist presence in the Cabinet to claim that the decision to exclude home rule resulted from an internal Liberal dispute, in which the Irish Party ensured the defeat of Gladstonians by failing to support them.[6] He also capitalised on exaggerated claims by the party about the Irish vote in Britain, declaring that if the party could influence a hundred British seats they should have thrown them to the Tories to give themselves the balance of power.[7] These accusations portrayed the Irish Party as incompetent weaklings, lacking the political acumen of Parnell or (by implication) Griffith.

The election was followed by cattle-driving in the midlands and the west, in which graziers' cattle were driven off their land by crowds trying to force them to give up land for division into smallholdings. The campaign was led by MPs and activists on the fringe of the Irish Party, with some separatist involvement. The most active cattle-driver, Laurence Ginnell, newly elected MP for North Westmeath, took advantage of incautious remarks by individual Liberals to claim that the British government secretly favoured cattle-driving to justify concessions.[8] The government was politically handicapped by the need to show that a sympathetic approach could keep Ireland quiet without emergency legislation, and Tories cited cattle-driving as proof of Irish lawlessness and Liberal incompetence.

The perception of cattle-driving as a product of the Liberals' political situation was not confined to Tories. When the jingoistic play *An Englishman's Home,* depicting Germans invading a complacent Liberal Britain negligent of military preparedness, was booed off the Dublin stage by separatists who cheered the invaders,[9] a conservative nationalist, J. J. O'Toole, argued that a German invasion might see the Irish, like Poles in East Prussia, subjugated by German settlers (an idea revived by wartime propagandists) and that it was in Ireland's interests to support the British against invaders. This annoyed separatist-inclined readers. One declared that German settlers could be defied by cattle-driving; O'Toole retorted that everyone knew that a Tory government would have stopped the cattle-drivers, and if Tories could do it, Germans could.[10]

Hostilities between O'Brien and the party resumed. The new Liberal government decided that free trade principles dictated a relaxation of quarantine restrictions on Canadian store cattle, which would affect cattle prices for Irish farmers. The party hesitated, reluctant to embarrass the new government and influenced by hostility towards graziers. Michael Davitt favoured the proposal; John Dillon speculated that it was inevitable and would be an appropriate punishment for tenants who paid high prices under the Wyndham act. This allowed O'Brienites to seize the initiative in attacking the proposal and to claim credit when the party was galvanised and the government backed down.[11] The president of the South of Ireland Cattle Traders' Association, M. J. Nagle, was outspokenly O'Brienite.[12] When Bryce succeeded in having the Labourers (Ireland) Act (1906) passed, both Sheehanite and O'Shee Land and Labour Associations claimed credit. (County Cork labourers called cottages built under the act 'Sheehan's cottages'.)

In the autumn of 1906 D. D. Sheehan and John O'Donnell were expelled from the party. Sheehan was re-elected without opposition and demanded re-admission, claiming that his constituents had vindicated him. In October, Lord Dunraven and O'Brien reconvened the Land Conference to discuss the plight of several thousand families evicted during various land campaigns. Redmond refused to attend, and though Timothy Harrington defied the party leadership to attend, it could achieve nothing without party support and the government backing that existed in 1903. Harrington's defiance of party orders not to attend was a slight coup, but Harrington was alienated from the party leadership and was seen—to some extent unfairly—as having behaved equivocally as lord mayor of Dublin during the debates in 1903 and 1904 on addresses to the King. (He had business links to the leader of the loyal addressers, Alderman W. F. Cotton.) He still played a prominent role in the party's Dublin organisation but was isolated from the leadership, and his health was declining as he developed a heart condition.[13]

John Shawe-Taylor impulsively contested a by-election in Galway city. O'Brien thought this ill-advised and did not openly endorse him. The election was marked by the usual rioting; Dillon contrasted the drunken behaviour of some Shawe-Taylor supporters with his talk of temperance reform, claimed that Shawe-Taylor's candidacy had been agreed at O'Brien's conference, and declared that no man with 'the black blood of Clan Cromwell' could be a genuine nationalist.[14] This was particularly inappropriate, as the successful party candidate was Stephen Gwynn, a Protestant man of letters, grandson of William Smith O'Brien and member of a well-known clerical dynasty. O'Brien mistakenly believed that Gwynn had formerly been associated with the Reform Association; he denounced him as a tame Protestant who saw the need for reconciliation but reneged to achieve political prominence as a powerless token.[15]

O'Brien sued the *Freeman's Journal* for libel at the spring assizes in Limerick, where he expected a more favourable hearing than in Dublin, after the paper alleged that he had rendered unnatural services to insatiable landlordism and conspired to sell fifteen nationalist seats to a crypto-unionist centre party. O'Brien's counsel, Tim Healy and J. H. Campbell, took advantage of cross-examination to bring out divisions between Redmond and the critics of the Land Conference, while the defence concentrated on O'Brien's habitual verbal ferocity towards his opponents, particularly Healy. The jury found the allegations libellous, but O'Brien was awarded only a farthing in damages. O'Brien publicised the verdict (though not the damages) for years afterwards, and the case further poisoned relations between the party leadership and the hypersensitive Thomas Sexton, who believed the *Freeman's Journal* did not get enough support.[16]

A major issue in the Liberal revival was Nonconformist opposition to Balfour's Education Bill in 1902 for subsidising Catholic and Anglican church schools— 'Rome on the rates.' Popular novelists like the Methodist minister Joseph Hocking and Harold Begbie described the spread of self-indulgent religious ritualism among a decadent aristocracy as leading to Jesuit plots against British liberties and declared that the Roman danger could only be averted by treating the Church of England as the Church of Rome was then treated in France and imposing a universal state system based on 'non-sectarian' religious teaching—that is, evangelical beliefs to the exclusion of Catholic and high Anglican interpretations. This created strange alliances. High Anglican Tories endorsed Catholic complaints that the abolition of the French concordat threatened all religion, and accused the Irish Party of shameful disloyalty to the church and abandonment of the poor Irish in Britain,[17] while some Irish ultra-Protestants declared that a Liberal government could not be worse than effete aristocratic temporisers, hailed French anti-clericals (who shared their preoccupation with priestly avarice and breaches of celibacy) as preparing for the spread of Protestantism, and dismayed Church of England allies by supporting the Education Bill introduced by the Liberal minister Augustine Birrell.[18]

The Irish Party could point out that Catholic schools in Britain, mostly built by the sacrifices of poor immigrants, were in urban areas where alternative schools were readily available, whereas the principal Nonconformist grievance concerned the use of Anglican schools for proselytism in many rural areas where they enjoyed a monopoly. In this way they exerted some influence on the issue, but their organisation and activists in Britain came under pressure from the clergy and Catholic campaign groups who accused them of going too far in compromising. Since these lobbyists were led by notables such as the Duke of Norfolk, widely disliked for hostility to home rule, this would not have been too important except for possible effects on Irish Catholic opinion.[19] It was a relief when the House of Lords killed the Education Bill, but also an embarrassment, as it presented the Tories as defenders of Catholic education. A worse embarrassment was the appointment of Birrell to succeed Bryce, leaving the university question and the Irish Council Bill, which might give elected politicians some control of Irish education, to the architect of the Education Bill.

The Education Bill did not apply to Ireland but revived perennial clerical fears that similar legislation might be attempted by British Liberals or anti-clerical Irish politicians. These fears were stimulated when Davitt engaged in newspaper contro-versy with Bishop Edward Thomas O'Dwyer soon after the election. Davitt had recently published an article depicting an Irish Parliament of 1910 in which radical democrats achieved state control of education despite opposition from place-hunting conservatives led by Redmond and O'Brien.[20] He declared his well-known belief in non-sectarian education, criticised the clergy for placing their interests above those of the people, and declared that democracy was coming whether they liked it or not.[21] He planned a campaign on the issue and recruited collaborators such as Francis Sheehy-Skeffington and P. D. Kenny.

Davitt's death on 31 May 1906 saved the Irish Party from considerable embarrassment. Sheehy-Skeffington and Frederick Ryan carried on the campaign in the short-lived *National Democrat* and in Sheehy-Skeffington's life of Davitt.[22] In accordance with Davitt's line on the common interest of the Irish and the British democracy, they maintained critical support for the Irish Party and the Liberal alliance. This was hardly an unmixed blessing: Griffith commented on the incon-gruity of a party supported by the *National Democrat* and Devlin's *Northern Star* denouncing him as anti-clerical.[23]

The difficulties of anti-clericalism were displayed more noticeably in the *Irish Peasant,* started in 1903 by James McCann MP, a stockbroker who decided to devote his fortune to industrial development. He bought canal shares and argued that revived canals could boost agriculture and industry and bring down freight rates by competing with the near-monopoly of the railways.[24] To provide increased canal traffic, McCann invested in Navan, where he bought land and leased it for tillage only and established a bacon factory and a sawmill. He founded the *Irish Peasant* to educate the local population for economic development, and installed P. D. Kenny as editor.

Kenny came from a small-farming background near Aghamore, County Mayo. He went to Lancashire as a labourer in his teens, obtained an education, worked as a journalist, and put himself through university, where he studied economics. He returned home in 1901 after inheriting the family smallholding and raised money to develop it by writing articles on social and economic problems, dismaying his neighbours by denouncing them as superstitious and inefficient drunkards. His experience instilled in him a resentment of the failure of the education system to develop the abilities of poor but intelligent children like himself, and dislike of the clergy and the United Irish League as hostile to new ideas and enforcing conformity.[25]

McCann was in good standing with the church—he was investment adviser to many Catholic institutions, though some claimed he had qualms of conscience about this[26]—and his projects could be seen as examples of the localised paternal development advocated by Catholic activists. Kenny's *Economics for Irishmen* was serialised in the Dominican monthly *Irish Rosary,* though a chapter added to the book on the economic limitations of the clergy irritated its former sponsors.[27] When McCann died in 1904, Kenny wrote a tribute in the same journal. McCann's death removed a restraint and a protective influence, and Kenny expressed controversial views more openly. Local priests organised whispering campaigns against the paper. At the beginning of 1906 the McCann family replaced Kenny with William P. Ryan, a Gaelic Leaguer from County Tipperary who spent many years as a journalist in London and published novels in Irish and English. Kenny was retained as a columnist.

The change of editorship made less difference than had been expected. Ryan was more devout than Kenny (at one time he wrote pseudonymous sectarian attacks on Yeats for the *Leader*) but was influenced by Catholic modernism, mediated through priest-intellectuals involved in the Celtic revival and Irish-Ireland movements, such as Father Jeremiah O'Donovan (who later left the priesthood and became an anti-clerical novelist) and Father Walter MacDonald of Maynooth. The modernist image of revelation as progressive rather than definitive appealed to Ryan's dislike of arbitrary power, his desire for social justice, and his belief in progress through free debate by autonomous intellectuals rather than pronouncements by a fixed hierarchy. The paper argued that lay control of education was compatible with Catholicism. The Gaelic League was hailed as a model of democratic education, and the Portarlington branch was defended in its struggle with the parish priest.[28]

The *Irish Peasant* displayed sympathy with Sinn Féin as a grass-roots movement opposing the hierarchical structure of the Irish Party. This produced tensions between Kenny's Davittite line that Ireland's interest lay with the 'British democracy' and those who saw Britain as a model to be avoided and thought Ireland could develop a de-centralised rural civilisation rather than imitating 'degraded' industrial Lancashire.[29]

At the end of 1906 Cardinal Michael Logue informed the McCann family that unless the *Irish Peasant* was closed he would denounce it. Given the McCanns' business interests and their religious beliefs, they had no option but to comply.[30] Ryan protested and announced his intention of appealing to Rome. He bought the title from the McCanns and moved to Dublin, where he re-established the paper as the *Peasant.* Kenny did not join the new paper; he quarrelled with Ryan and, after flirting briefly with the *National Democrat,*[31] adopted a liberal unionist position and wrote anti-clerical articles in the London unionist press. Moran bracketed 'Pat the Papist' with 'Mike [MacCarthy] the Catholic' as anti-Catholic mercenaries. Many criticisms Pat now delivered were already present in his earlier writing; the *National Democrat* lamented that this made it easier to portray critics of clerical influence as crypto-unionists.[32]

Kenny's defection did not end the divide in the *Peasant* between radical social reformers sympathetic to British counterparts and separatist purists. Social reformers were represented by Ryan, who, under the influence of George Russell, abandoned Catholicism for theosophy and developed pantheistic fantasies about ancient Celtic wisdom creating a socialist millennium,[33] and Frederick Ryan, who adopted the *Peasant and Nation* (as it became) as his principal outlet after the demise of the *National Democrat*.

G riffith denounced the suppression of the *Irish Peasant* and the studious avoidance of the subject by the Irish Party press,[34] but the separatism in the *Peasant and Nation* derived from his republican critics, centred at first in Belfast around the resurgent IRB. For much of the eighteen-eighties and nineties the IRB had declined; a generation of activists had gone into the Irish Party, its most prominent figures were dead or aging, and it had little in the way of a political agenda except amnesty agitation, the Parnellite alliance, and general commitment to a republic. By the turn of the century it was reduced to a secret body operating within the club network and scattered old men recruiting disciples locally—such as Louis Smith, an 1867 veteran in Magherafelt.[35]

Griffith helped to revive separatism, but despite IRB membership as a young man he was doubtful about secret societies. He knew enough about the last days of the Invincibles, who briefly survived the hanging of the Phoenix Park murderers before disintegrating through factional disputes and suspicions about informers, to see the dangers facing militaristic secret societies without a clear political agenda: he preferred the open defiance and long-term preparation characteristic of Young Ireland. Younger separatists who had not experienced the triumphs of the eighteen-eighties and who judged politics only by the faction-fighting of the Parnell split were impatient with his attempts to re-invent Parnellism, and they found in the IRB a nucleus for supporters of pure and simple republicanism.

From the start some Sinn Féiners, such as Alice Milligan and Terence MacSwiney, tried to organise republican opposition to the dual-monarchy policy.[36] In 1906 a group of young separatists who had taken over the Belfast IRB founded the Dungannon Clubs (subsequently merged with Cumann na nGaedheal) as a republican rival to Sinn Féin. This group, which included Denis McCullough, Bulmer Hobson, Dr Patrick McCartan (whose organising activities in east Tyrone met considerable opposition from the AOH and local clergy),[37] and P. S. O'Hegarty (a native of County Cork working as a civil servant in London), included some sympathetic veterans such as Tom Clarke; it also published a weekly paper in Belfast, the *Republic*.

Griffith looked on the new group with scepticism, especially when Hobson undertook fund-raising visits to the United States without his endorsement and when it showed signs of wishing to challenge his leadership of Sinn Féin. The merger of the *Republic* with the *Peasant* in 1907 marked the advance of the Belfast group into Dublin to displace the IRB leadership under F. J. Allen and to challenge Griffith at his strongest point.[38]

Sinn Féin was still growing in Dublin. Dillon told Redmond that Sinn Féin was dangerous but would probably come to nothing for lack of leadership. He blamed Harrington—whose own Corporation seat fell to Sinn Féin in 1908—for letting the Dublin organisation decay.[39] In late 1906 Richard Hazleton privately wrote that he would advise William Field to stand in South Dublin at the next election were it not that no other candidate could hold the St Patrick's division against Sinn Féin;[40] Griffith tabulated local election results in the division to show Sinn Féin strength, and when Field personally campaigned for Irish Party candidates in early 1908 but failed to reverse the swing to Sinn Féin, Griffith called on him to resign and face his constituents.[41]

The republicans shared with the radicals a distrust of Griffith's developing strategy. As the alliance between the Liberals and the Irish Party grew stronger, he moved to the right to challenge it, and his principal target became Liberal universalism rather than Tory deferentialism. This extended to socialist universalism—though he also capitalised on Irish working-class resentment of Irish Party preference for Liberals over Labour. Griffith ridiculed the idea of trade union solidarity between British and Irish workers and attacked Larkin as a British agent destroying Irish industry for the benefit of those perpetual allies, the British worker and employer.[42] State socialism was as alien to Griffith's producerist emphasis on self-reliance as old-style aristocratic patronage. While emphasising his support for a developmental state, he denounced socialism and expansion of the state's role in welfare as demoralising and leading to slavery and overtaxation.[43]

Griffith's illiberalism was enhanced by the diplomatic rapprochement between France and Britain, which he lamented as the seduction of the naïve French by the wily British.[44] As Germany replaced France as Britain's main potential enemy, Griffith played down French republican values and exalted the statesmanship of the Kaiser.[45] When German social democrats lost seats in a Reichstag election fought over naval expenditure, Griffith rejoiced in the defeat of woolly-minded dupes of British pacifist propaganda. Sheehy-Skeffington protested that Griffith sounded like a spokesman of the German Navy League; Griffith replied that if he were a German he would join it.[46] He declared that peace created cheats and effeminates, while war encouraged morality.[47] A free Ireland should not tolerate pacifists.[48]

His belief in strong leadership became more pronounced. He hailed Bismarck for pursuing his country's interests despite pettifogging parliamentarians, described the French Revolution as the work of foolish theorists, and called Bonaparte the true saviour of France.[49]

Frederick Ryan discovered that Griffith would no longer print his articles for fear of alienating conservative supporters.[50] Both he and W. P. Ryan attributed Griffith's changing attitudes to the influence of conservative patrons, such as John Sweetman, and criticised Griffith as an apologist for capitalism.[51] This critique, taken up by Larkinites, is unfair in questioning Griffith's good faith and playing down his divergences from standard liberal capitalism, but it illustrates problems that Griffith evaded to present a stark distinction between the hell of colonialism and the paradise following political and economic independence. After a brief exchange with Frederick Ryan,[52] Griffith ignored these criticisms, except to attribute them to Dublin Castle.[53]

The *Peasant and Nation* survived until 1910, when W. P. Ryan went to London to work on the *Daily Herald* and the purists founded a monthly paper, *Irish Freedom*. Frederick Ryan joined the Young Ireland Branch of the UIL, under the influence of the Sheehy-Skeffingtons, believing self-government necessary for social reform. He then left Ireland to work on an Egyptian nationalist paper. He died in England in 1913.[54]

Ryan's death provoked a controversy very revealing about the determination of Griffith to exclude from nationalism any possible justification of the Liberal alliance. Griffith called his old friend a sincere though muddled philanthropist, who might have made a good nationalist had he not deserted his national duty to pursue a delusion.

> Progress, the Brotherhood of Man, and all the other cants which English Radicalism exudes with a gurgle in its throat seemed real things to Frederick Ryan. He believed in them with a fervour that astonished those to whom they were merely strings [with which] to pull the stupid population.[55]

Francis Sheehy-Skeffington defended Ryan's nationalist credentials, denying that the true nationalist must regard class politics and the affairs of other nations as irrelevant to the task of Irish liberation. He quoted Ryan:

> I claim also to be a lover of Ireland. By Ireland I do not mean any 'eternal' or 'mystic' entity or any 'nationality' divorced from the real life of the people ... I mean the peasants in the fields, the workers in the factories, the teachers in the schools, the professors in the colleges, and all others who labour in Ireland and desire ... to create in Ireland a people healthy, educated, cultured in the best sense, with sufficient material comfort, developing their minds and their bodies to the end of maximising life, sensitive to intellectual and moral values, and conducting their national life on lines of justice, and freedom, and good faith ... I stand for Irish independence because by it alone can we obtain the machinery to produce this.[56]

Griffith retorted that this proved his point: Ryan was not a nationalist, precisely because he held the utilitarian view

> that a nation was nothing more than a collection of human beings, and that the interests of the nation were no more than the interests of the said human

beings—a body without a soul … When we say we love Ireland we do not mean by Ireland the peasants in the fields, the workers in the factories, the teachers in the schools, the professors in the colleges—we mean the soul into which we were born and which was born into us … the Ireland that goes back to Emhain Macha˙… The man who declared he wanted National freedom in order to promote social reform, did not know the meaning of the nation.[57]

As the Irish Council Bill was prepared, its prospects were freely debated and expectations diminished. This can be charted in Arthur Clery's articles in the *Leader* and the *New Ireland Review.* Clery argued that the bill was worth having only if it gave the Irish Party substantial control over the Irish administration, rather than a quasi-legislature with merely advisory functions and a large nominated element. He even suggested that the Irish Party should try to substitute for the proposed legislature a directly elected Chief Secretary, like the President of the United States. A sham legislature giving responsibility without power and encouraging disruption by confusing the central issue of home rule with disputes about what policies should be followed in its limited areas of jurisdiction would be worse than useless.[58]

O'Brien left Ireland early in 1907 to convalesce on the Mediterranean. He had seen the draft Irish Council Bill privately some months earlier, though the government did not accept the amendments he suggested. He felt no need to be present for the voting on the bill, as he assumed it would pass. When the bill appeared the *Irish People* declared that the party could have got better terms by supporting Lord Dunraven in 1904. Griffith took the same line—though he also denounced Dunraven and the Irish Land Act (1903)—calling the Irish Council Bill even worse than Chamberlain's devolution scheme, which Parnell rejected.[59]

Healy attacked the bill on clericalist grounds.[60] The Catholic hierarchy dreaded it as a step towards lay control of education; some separatist-inclined cultural nationalists, notably Pearse, supported the bill in the hope of a more nationalist education system; and Moran advised its acceptance as a first instalment.[61]

Unknown to O'Brien and his associates, Dillon and Redmond were dissatisfied with the bill. They considered it an elaborate administrative scheme with no sense of political reality—a charge often made against MacDonnell's experiments: his Indian experience encouraged him to think of enlightened administrators imposing reforms on a passive population. Its large nominated element was more reminiscent of the Council of Agriculture presided over by the hated Plunkett—or even the nominated central and provincial councils that advised the government of India—than Gladstonian home rule, or even the legislation establishing the county councils, where proposals for a nominated element were dropped. They feared it aimed at submerging the party in a non-political administration of moderate businessmen, professionals, and landlords,[62] that it would be unacceptable to party activists and would prove unworkable.

Only in retrospect was another advantage claimed for it: that it would have been implemented on an all-Ireland basis—if it got through the House of Lords, which is unlikely. Although the government increased the elected element, Redmond gave the bill a lukewarm welcome and stressed that he needed a mandate from a special convention of the UIL. Grass-roots opinion within the organisation revealed hostility to the bill,[63] encouraged by the lukewarm attitude of the leadership but also reflecting the long campaign against the Dunravenite proposals. Redmond duly moved its rejection at the convention, and the government withdrew it.[64]

Despite accumulating discontent with the Irish Council Bill, its rejection shocked Irish opinion and strengthened Sinn Féin. If the Irish Party leaders supported the bill and rejected it only because of grass-roots pressure, they were incompetent; if they opposed it all along and the government would not offer better terms, what use was the Liberal alliance? Several provincial papers—notably the *Kerryman, Meath Chronicle,* and *Kilkenny People*—suggested that the government's betrayal left the field open for abstentionism,[65] and prominent activists defected to Sinn Féin. The most prominent were Sir Thomas Esmonde, MP for North Wexford, chief whip of the Irish Party and chairman of the General Council of County Councils (and also a shareholder in the *Enniscorthy Echo,* which its proprietor, William Sears, and columnist Seán Etchingham made one of the few openly pro-Sinn Féin local papers); James O'Mara, MP for South Kilkenny (who resigned and did not seek re-election); C. J. Dolan, MP for North Leitrim; and William Ganly, chairman of North Longford UIL. The MPs Patrick White, Tom Kettle and Tom O'Donnell wanted stronger opposition to the government—White suggested abstention—but stayed with the party.[66]

This opportunity united the rival separatist factions for the time being. The Irish Unionist Alliance already quoted Griffith and the *Republic* to show that nationalist opinion was more anti-British than Liberals and Redmondites maintained and that concessions only gave an implacable enemy new weapons. Now the British press took notice of the existence of Sinn Féin, printing accounts, often hilariously garbled, of its beliefs and origins and seeing it as a serious threat to the Irish Party.[67]

The party moved to contain the split. Redmond reaffirmed the Liberal alliance, declaring to British audiences that the Irish Party would get home rule by helping the Liberals curb the House of Lords; Griffith replied that, short of a revolution, the British people would do no such thing.[68] (This was the line Redmond took in 1894 when denouncing Dillon's trust in the Liberal alliance.)[69] Gwynn and Kettle published rebuttals of Sinn Féin.[70] Griffith denounced Kettle as a renegade Sinn Féin sympathiser who joined the Irish Party for corrupt motives, under the influence of drink, provoking a Kettle-Griffith controversy over whether Parnell would have supported Sinn Féin.[71]

Reorganisation was undertaken in rebel constituencies. Redmond toured County Wexford to muster support against Esmonde,[72] and Ganly's supporters in County Longford came under pressure.[73] The struggle focused on County Leitrim, where several UIL branches seceded with Dolan and joined Sinn Féin. Dolan declared that he would prepare the ground for a contest when the electors were educated on the situation. A local paper, the *Leitrim Guardian,* was established to help the educative process.[74] Subscribers to Dolan's fund included Robert Barton, a future Treaty negotiator, who gave £50.[75]

The party moved to deprive its opponents of administrative influence. Esmonde was deposed as chairman of the General Council of County Councils; the vice-chairman, John Sweetman (a former MP, one of Griffith's financial backers, founding vice-president of Sinn Féin and second president after Edward Martyn resigned in 1908) was also deposed and was defeated for re-election to Meath County Council, though he returned to the county council some time later.[76]

The fate of the Irish Council Bill marked the end for MacDonnell's devolution schemes, and he resigned as Under-Secretary soon afterwards. He received a peerage, and intervened in the debates on the third Home Rule Bill to support the measure and to demand more generous home rule finance. The Under-Secretaryship went to the Ulster Liberal J. B. Dougherty.

Another Ulster Liberal, T. W. Russell, succeeded Plunkett as head of the Department of Agriculture and Technical Instruction. Plunkett's position became untenable through party pressure on the administration and on the Council of Agriculture through county councillors. He had retained a majority on the council through nominated members and a minority of elected representatives; Griffith therefore declared that the Irish Party had committed the unforgivable sin of appealing to the British government for help against a fellow-Irishman and suppressing the will of the nearest equivalent to an Irish legislature in existence. The *National Democrat* retorted that it was hardly surprising that his own nominees supported Plunkett.[77]

The fate of MacDonnell and Plunkett illustrates the issue of place-hunting, a perennial accusation against nationalist politicians in a whig alliance. The civil service was suspected (with good reason) of unionist and Protestant bias. Nationalists regularly complained that well-intentioned Chief Secretaries were mis-led or frustrated by the civil service. Catholics and nationalists had infiltrated the lower ranks since the institution of competitive examinations but, apart from the Chief Secretaryship of Morley in 1892–5, made little impact on the higher echelons before the Liberal election victory of 1906.[78] The 'Morley magistrates' provided the first significant nationalist presence on a local bench traditionally dominated by landlords but were mocked for snobbish pride in the title, excessive willingness to support new drink licences, and ignorance of the law—though landlord magistrates also lacked legal expertise, which was supplied by the presiding magistrate.

The tension between the desire to bring Catholic and nationalist influence into a biased administration and the jobbery and political compromise this entailed was a prominent issue between O'Connell and the Young Irelanders, who claimed that the whig alliance enriched a few job-hunters without benefiting the people and that, by pursuing specifically Catholic interests and reinforcing party divisions, it hindered the task of winning Irish Protestants and Tories to recognise the national interest.[79] The 'Independent Irish Party' of the eighteen-fifties pledged itself to pursue independent opposition and refuse office. Its destruction by the unscrupulous place-hunters John Sadleir and William Keogh—the 'Pope's Brass Band'—entered nationalist memory, and the home rule party bound MPs not merely against taking office but against soliciting any favour from the government. As part of the anti-Healy campaign, Swift MacNeill compared Healyites to the Brass Band;[80] Matthias McDonnell Bodkin, a former MP and a leader-writer for the *Freeman's Journal,* denounced the acceptance of an English judgeship by the Healyite former MP Arthur O'Connor as incompatible with the pledge.[81] This became harder to maintain when the Irish Party found itself exercising some responsibilities of power—advising a Liberal administration or running local government—while continuing activities that helped maintain popular support but brought conflict with an administration they could advise but not control.

Soon after Bryce's arrival, Dillon and Redmond pressed—with limited success—for the replacement of several pro-landlord assistant land commissioners.[82] This might not violate the letter of the pledge but it certainly breached its spirit. Once more local nationalists became justices of the peace, and were sneered at for snobbish pride.[83]

Griffith called the Local Government Board the fountainhead of corruption in Ireland.[84] Its archives were destroyed during the War of Independence but its union-ist president, Sir Henry Robinson, claimed that under the Liberal government many nationalist MPs—especially younger men and those associated with the AOH—did write to him in favour of candidates, usually equivocating about the pledge: 'If my pledge did not forbid it I would be happy to recommend X.' He also stated that some veteran members, such as Redmond, Dillon, Esmonde, and Healy, never approached him in this way.[85] Healy probably relied on personal contact with political friends; he approached Wyndham in this way and during an election petition admitted approaching Birrell in favour of an applicant from County Louth (carefully implicat-ing the South Louth MP, Joseph Nolan).[86] Redmond also intervened occasionally; correspondence with a supporter in County Limerick in 1906 shows him using the formula 'If it were not for my pledge ...' When the Limerick city MP Michael Joyce suggested that Redmond should intervene directly, Redmond replied that this would dishonour the party and himself.[87] Clearly he found equivocation stressful and prob-ably rarely intervened, which would explain Robinson's impression that he never did.

Suspicions of corruption were not confined to nationalists. Jeremiah MacVeagh pointed out that Presbyterians as well as Catholics were underrepresented in administrative positions.[88] Past persecution of Presbyterians was recalled to offset unionist predictions of Catholic tyranny under home rule, and appeals were made to traditional Presbyterian liberalism and distrust of aristocratic leadership. Some

Ulster Presbyterians responded, notably J. B. Armour (minister of the First Presbyterian Church, Ballymoney) and his friends W. H. Dodd (Liberal MP for North Tyrone before becoming a judge in 1907) and Sir J. B. Dougherty (former Presbyterian minister and professor at Magee College, Assistant Under-Secretary 1895–1908 and Under-Secretary 1908–14).[89]

Armour was a Liberal Unionist at the time of Gladstone's first Home Rule Bill. His change of allegiance in the late eighteen-eighties was inspired by resentment of landlord and episcopalian domination of the unionist coalition, and he spoke against resolutions opposing home rule at the Presbyterian general assemblies of 1893 and 1912. He served as chaplain to Lord Aberdeen and in private was scathing about Presbyterian unionists who despised the devout Presbyterian Aberdeen.[90]

Another prominent home-rule Liberal was Lord Pirrie, proprietor of Harland and Wolff, whose support was publicised to answer charges that home rule would destroy Ulster business confidence. With his eccentric relatives, business subordinates and political allies A. M. Carlisle and A. P. Wilson (who used the pen-name 'An Ulster Imperialist' and entertained visitors to Belfast looking for the Liberal viewpoint),[91] Pirrie subsidised the Liberal newspaper *Ulster Guardian*.[92]

After the Irish Council Bill, lists appeared of party supporters and their Liberal associates who received government jobs—mostly members of the staff of activists, journalists and lawyers associated with the *Freeman's Journal*. A prominent example was Matthias Bodkin, made a judge in 1908 despite dubious legal qualifications and derisive references to his attack on O'Connor.[93]

> I give you the boys of the *Freeman,*
> Where rallied another Brass Band
> To fight on the Floor of the House, boys,
> And drive out Sinn Féin from the land …
> The Sham Squireens are ready whenever
> The Castle shall give them the sign
> To abandon the Prince's Street inkpot
> And don the judicial ermine.[94]

It was widely agreed that there were too many Irish judgeships. Their salaries and pensions were exorbitant in comparison with earnings at the bar, and judicial promotion reflected party allegiances. Nationalists and populist unionists accused lawyer-politicians among Irish unionist MPs of greater zeal for legal advancement than for the Union. 'Ulster Unionism is not a party,' Kettle sneered, 'it is merely an appetite.'[95] Unionists, O'Brienites and Sinn Féiners applied similar accusations to the Irish Party. In 1907, when W. H. Dodd was raised to the bench, the national Sinn Féin leaders tried to boycott the ensuing North Tyrone by-election in protest against place-hunting but found that local nationalists refused to hand the seat to the Unionists. (The Liberal majority fell by two; Moran facetiously suggested that one Sinn Féiner voted Unionist.)[96]

Criticism of the operation of the pledge was not confined to O'Brien and Sinn Féin. Moran criticised it as 'a very green and foolish rule,' widely evaded but taken seriously enough to deter committed nationalists, so that the best jobs were reserved for place-hunters, lukewarm nationalists, and Protestant Liberals. This type of appointee in turn reinforced the impression that the party was becoming a patronage machine for whig opportunists.

Other problems arose when party activities involved direct conflict with the law, as when MPs and activists were tried for cattle-driving and other types of agitation, sometimes by judges nominated by the party.[97] Dodd acquired a reputation for harsh sentencing in such cases.

For many Irish-Ireland critics the corruptions of the Liberal alliance were symbolised by the new Lord Lieutenant, the Earl of Aberdeen, and his wife. Their long-standing interest in Irish industrial development, acquired in the Viceregal Lodge during Gladstone's first home rule administration, was genuine but patronising, and Lady Aberdeen's activities on behalf of her Women's National Health Association— which continued long after her husband's retirement as Viceroy—often involved wire-pulling and the advancement of protégés. The obvious dominance of Lady Aberdeen was satirised, as was their perceived meanness. The Aberdeens responded to a Unionist boycott of Castle functions by inviting provincial notables and upper-middle-class Dublin nationalists of presentable social standing. They toured the country attending local charitable functions; the snobbery and social pretensions of those who received them attracted unfavourable comment. Moran mocked nationalists who caught 'the viceregal microbe' of snobbery and suggested that a friendly Lord Lieutenant was more dangerous to nationalist principle than a hostile one.[98] Separatists called the anti-TB campaign a plot to destroy Irish trade by implying that Irish goods were infected.[99] As part of his campaign against aristocratic charity and patronage as corrupt and demoralising rituals of subservience, Griffith attacked Lady Aberdeen for using Scottish labour and materials to build Peamount Sanatorium at Newcastle, County Dublin;[100] tuberculosis could not be cured by 'concentration camps for consumptives,'[101] because it derived from airborne dirt, slum conditions, and the deterioration of the Irish climate due to deafforestation (by the British).[102]

This view was not unique to Griffith: O'Brienites later adopted it as part of a campaign for state-financed housing.[103] Griffith published letters by anti-vaccinationists accusing doctors of inventing this useless and harmful practice to make money by 'curing' diseases deriving from poverty.[104] Brian O'Higgins, who also believed that Britain planned a new famine, wrote a satirical ditty ridiculing microbes.[105]

Party leaders and MPs saw the potential political liabilities of social contacts with the administration. As in 1892–5, they refused to visit the Viceregal Lodge, the Chief Secretary's residence, or Dublin Castle, even on business. Even Stephen Gwynn, who co-operated with Lady Aberdeen in philanthropic work, refused to visit the Viceregal Lodge, saying that it was particularly important that MPs of ascendancy origin should not suggest pretensions to social superiority.[106]

O'Brien was amazed at the rejection of the Irish Council Bill. Unaware of events behind the scenes, he assumed that Redmond and Dillon favoured the bill but had abandoned it from cowardice—an idea encouraged by Dillon's inability to attend the convention because of his wife's sudden death. O'Brien refused to accept that the bill was unpopular, partly because of association with his alleged intrigues and the tactless and abusive tone of the *Irish People's* advocacy of 'conciliation', involving such methods as the publication of his alleged diaries containing 'private' criticisms of Dillon and other opponents. He attributed its rejection to the Board of Erin, which now became a major target of his attacks.[107]

The AOH derived from secret Catholic agrarian societies active in Ulster, north Connacht and north Leinster during the nineteenth century. Its members wore green sashes and carried banners in processions similar in style to those of the Orange Order. In 1904 it was reorganised as the Ancient Order of Hibernians (Board of Erin), under the presidency of Joe Devlin, with John Dillon Nugent (from Keady, County Armagh, living in Dublin) as secretary. A smaller, separatist-inclined faction broke away and received official recognition from the American AOH when its leadership was held by separatists, calling itself the Ancient Order of Hibernians (Irish-American Alliance).[108]

By 1907 the Board of Erin was visibly growing in strength. It first made its presence felt in Dublin during a large demonstration by Catholic groups in the Phoenix Park against anti-clerical legislation in France.[109] Sinn Féin attacked the demonstration as an attempt to form a job-hunting Catholic party; Walter Cole, a Sinn Féin alderman on Dublin Corporation, opposed a resolution in support of the demonstration as an interference in French internal affairs calculated to breed division between the Irish people and a natural ally.[110] (This may reflect opportunism: Moran pointed out that Griffith's ally Edward Martyn chaired the original Catholic Association.)[111] Accusations of 'Garibaldianism' were flung around, and Griffith noted that some organisers spoke of stamping out Sinn Féin, together with the *Peasant* and the *National Democrat,* as anti-clerical.[112] At the next corporation election, Cole was defeated by an Irish Party candidate.[113]

O'Brien referred to the decline of UIL membership and subscriptions to the Irish Party as evidence of political bankruptcy caused by failure to adopt the only viable policy. (In fact the decline of the UIL began before O'Brien's resignation and reflected the absence of large-scale agrarian agitation.) He claimed that the party survived only because its newspapers suppressed and misrepresented his views, its funds were replenished by American money solicited under false pretences, and its organisation was taken over by a job-hunting sectarian secret society that would have excluded the great Protestant patriots of the past.[114]

O'Brien's critique of the AOH is not invalidated by personal inconsistencies. He accepted AOH help in North Louth in 1900 and from 1907 co-operated with the breakaway Irish-American Alliance.[115] (Healy's County Louth supporters included an AOH splinter group.)[116] At local level many O'Brienites were involved in Catholic societies similar to the AOH: in 1910 O'Brienites in Cork protested when their supporters were expelled *en masse* from the Catholic Young Men's Society by the AOH-Redmondite majority,[117] and in 1914 O'Brienites in Bantry walked out of a local confraternity Mass when a preacher accused O'Brien of anti-clericalism.[118] O'Brien and Healy also tried to capitalise on the fact that significant elements of the church distrusted the AOH as lay-controlled and a secret society. Its principal patron was the party's chief episcopal ally, Bishop O'Donnell of Raphoe, who revised its rules and rituals to exclude anything unacceptable to the church; but its social activities at local level brought conflict with priests who resented it as a rival to clerically controlled amusements and complained if Hibernians refused to allow priestly supervision of dances and similar events.[119] Cardinal Logue publicly denounced Hibernians in County Tyrone for fostering unacceptable behaviour and intimidating those who refused to join the order; this was standard behaviour among rural nationalist organisations but may also reflect a reaction to the vocal Sinn Féin presence in East Tyrone.[120]

O'Brien's position was strengthened by the upheavals following the Irish Council Bill. He contacted Esmonde, who received support from the County Wexford O'Brienite councillor John Cummins and gave financial help to John O'Donnell's paper.[121] The *Irish People* praised Sinn Féin as honest youngsters, sickened by Devlinite thuggery and corruption, who could be won over by a great new national movement. O'Brien tried unsuccessfully to enlist Sinn Féin support for unity meetings organised by D. D. Sheehan throughout Munster. He also addressed meetings at Buncrana and in County Wexford.[122]

Overtures to Sinn Féin were to some extent counter-productive. Harrington wrote that the *Irish People* praising Sinn Féin while its members disrupted meetings of the Irish Party annoyed members who were anxious to see liberty re-established— that is, old Dublin Parnellites like Field and J. J. Clancy, whom O'Brien thought Harrington could influence.[123] The unity campaign did not fulfil O'Brien's hope that by appealing directly to the people he could sweep away opposition; but it won support from several MPs outside O'Brien's little group, notably Tom O'Donnell, Conor O'Kelly, and the Healyite sympathisers Philip O'Doherty (North Donegal) and J. C. R. Lardner (South Monaghan).

Redmond had his own reasons for wanting unity. The party leadership endorsed cattle-driving to retain popularity—especially after the Irish Council Bill—and to acquire some control over it,[124] but this created problems. Some lower clergy supported cattle drives, but the hierarchy predominantly opposed this threat to property. Archbishop Healy was particularly outspoken. The conservative Catholic view is presented in Guinan's *The Curate of Kilcloon,* where the hero's father, a large farmer, faces a vexatious agitation orchestrated by an Irish-American claiming a smallholding vacated during the Famine.[125]

The Liberals might not invoke emergency legislation but could use ordinary law, sometimes with severe penalties, allowing separatists to argue that the Irish Party was either powerless or an accomplice in repression. Several prominent nationalists, including Redmond's close allies J. P. Hayden and John Fitzgibbon—though the latter may have been partly the victim of false accusations—had grazing interests. Redmond needed a counterbalance to agrarian radicals; O'Brien had denounced cattle-driving as obstructing the creation of a conciliatory atmosphere and believed their grievances should be redressed through the conference process.[126] Furthermore, Redmond and many other parliamentarians knew the damage done to the party's reputation by the sight of nationalists engaging in vituperation, and sometimes violence, over apparently mindless personal disputes. If he offered peace and O'Brien refused, it would be clear where blame lay.

Peace talks in December 1907 between O'Brien and Redmond—each accompanied by a clerical witness—broke down over O'Brien's insistence that a national convention should be summoned by machinery other than the UIL organisation to approve the agreement. Nevertheless, Redmond formally summoned all the dissident MPs to the next party meeting, and on 17 January 1908 O'Brien, Healy, Sheehan, John O'Donnell and Esmonde formally rejoined the party.[127]

O'Brien and Healy still despised the other leaders, who regarded the O'Brien-Healy gang with disgust.[128] Dark rumours were current about the extent and origins of O'Brien's financial resources. He was called a dupe of Dunravenism, with limitless Tory funds. Jasper Tully and the cattle-driver J. P. Farrell MP (North Longford) claimed that O'Brien was used by Jewish bankers who wanted high land prices so that landlords could repay their debts.[129] (At the time of O'Brien's resignation, Farrell had written to him pledging loyalty.)[130] John O'Callaghan, secretary of the American UIL, told Redmond that when O'Brien complained about American money he should be asked to account for Jewish money. O'Callaghan suggested disseminating a rumour that O'Brien was related to the Fenian informer Pierce Nagle, and advised that O'Brien's followers be driven from Parliament if they showed insubordination.[131] Meanwhile a letter O'Brien sent trying to persuade C. J. Dolan to rejoin the party shows that O'Brien thought conciliationists and Sinn Féiners had absolute liberty to advance their views while members of the party.[132]

Dolan refused to take this bait and resigned his seat. The local party organisation nominated an AOH man, F. E. Meehan (denounced by Griffith for alleged partiality to music-hall songs), though Redmond would have preferred a nationally known candidate such as John Muldoon.[133] Griffith wrote 'Letters to the electors of North Leitrim', declaring that the decline in Ireland's population in 1879 showed the failure of parliamentarianism.

Violence was used extensively, more by the Irish Party than Sinn Féin, with 'baton-men' brought from Belfast by Devlin and from Sligo by P. A. McHugh, who directed the party campaign. In one notorious incident Parnell's sister, Anna Parnell, who came from retirement to campaign for Dolan, was pelted with rubbish by party supporters.

Dolan was defeated by almost three to one. Sinn Féiners argued that this was a good showing considering the strength of the party machine and the low base from which Sinn Féin started; the Irish Party claimed that half Dolan's vote was personal and the other half came from local unionists voting tactically to exacerbate the split.[134] In local elections soon afterwards Sinn Féin showed a continuing presence around Dolan's Manorhamilton stronghold.[135]

Griffith announced that Dolan was going to America to learn boot manufacture and would return to start a factory, showing how Sinn Féin practicality could benefit his constituency more than a cipher in London.[136] Dolan trained in America and returned, but the factory never materialised and he emigrated again. Leitrim Sinn Féin was reabsorbed by the Irish Party but re-emerged after 1916; and in 1918 Sinn Féin hailed the election of Dolan's brother with the largest Sinn Féin majority in the country.[137]

After the by-election, Sinn Féin showed signs of overstretching. In areas such as Tuam its expansion on local authorities was stalled by shortage of personnel.[138] Divisions between Griffithites and purist republicans re-emerged. Griffith believed a daily paper could make Sinn Féin a serious rival to the Irish Party and announced its imminent appearance; but it had to be postponed on several occasions for lack of capital, and when it appeared in 1909 it survived less than a year.[139]

Even as the Sinn Féin revolt was contained, the O'Brienite rift reopened when the Treasury announced that the guarantee fund under the Irish Land Act (1903) was exhausted and that further land purchases would have to be financed by the Irish ratepayers, unless there was a new Land Act. O'Brien wrote to Wyndham, Dunraven and Plunkett trying to organise a new Land Conference, and at a party meeting on 28 April 1908 he proposed a resolution calling for such a conference, but it was defeated by 42 to 15.[140]

O'Brien stopped attending party meetings and cultivated landlord and nationalist support in the south to demand that the inevitable Land Bill should follow the principles of the 1903 act. At one well-publicised meeting he shared a platform with Lord Barrymore, his old antagonist of the Plan of Campaign. O'Brien saw this as a triumph for the policy of conciliation; the Redmondites denounced it as betrayal, and 'Barrymore' became a Redmondite cry. A Munster delegation of landlords and O'Brienites was organised; Birrell, influenced by the party, refused to receive it.[141] Cork O'Brienites obstructed local party collections.[142]

The party managed to quieten the cattle-drivers by promising that the new bill would make concessions on land purchase. This was not universally welcomed. Ginnell, the most obdurate cattle-driver, who was gravitating away from the party, used a period of imprisonment to produce *Land and Liberty,* a manifesto modelled on Davitt's *The Fall of Feudalism in Ireland,* which presented cattle-driving as the means of doing for the party what the Land League did for Parnell and commented indiscreetly on the notorious grazing interests of prominent activists (including leading cattle-drivers).[143] He also experimented with parliamentary obstruction and—in another reversion to the early eighteen-eighties, in this case *United Ireland's* exposure of a male prostitution ring in the civil service—joined Sinn Féin claims that the theft of the regalia of the Order of St Patrick (popularly called the 'Irish crown jewels') in 1907 was carried out by homosexuals with influential connections in Dublin Castle.[144]

Some unionists also claimed that the cessation of cattle-driving showed that the whole campaign was orchestrated by priests to get a Catholic university. The solution of the university question by the establishment of the National University of Ireland and Queen's University, Belfast, was likewise a mixed blessing for the party. The appearance of a fully recognised Catholic-nationalist rival to Trinity College marked the continuing decay of the old ascendancy. Griffith criticised the new university's orientation towards the professions rather than business and technology and argued that his preferred solution, a reformed Trinity College, would have been less divisive.[145] Moran predicted gleefully that Trinity would collapse as northerners went to Belfast, the new university obscured its prestige, and the southern Protestant community decayed.[146]

The establishment of the National University, with only a small group of unionist diehards denouncing it as a Catholic university in all but name, could be presented as a solid achievement of the Liberal alliance. Irish Party influence over the academic body was considerable, though fresh accusations of corruption were inspired by the appointment of two MPs—Tom Kettle and Swift MacNeill—as professors; the *Freeman's Journal* leader-writer R. T. Donovan also became a professor, and John Muldoon received an administrative position.[147] Another controversy arose over the professor of Spanish and Italian, Marie Degani, whose defeat of Helena Walsh Concannon was attributed to Lady Aberdeen.[148]

A new storm erupted over Irish as a compulsory subject for matriculation. This was opposed by the bishops and leading Catholic notables, who feared it would drive middle-class Catholics to Trinity, while the Gaelic League, seeing a chance to spread Irish in the schools, produced a mass agitation led by MacNeill in support.[149] The league appealed to resentment against the 'Clongowes snob', arguing that the will of the people was being thwarted by unrepresentative notables and that obligatory Irish would be a democratic measure offsetting other advantages that upper and middle-class students enjoyed over the lower-class students of Gaelic League classes.[150] Not all anti-compulsionists were conservatives: Francis Sheehy-Skeffington and Frederick Ryan opposed compulsion because they attributed the demand to clericalist Irish-Irelanders who saw Irish as a shield against modernity.

The Irish Party was caught in the middle. Many of its leaders were unwilling to endorse the campaign, from fear of the bishops, from prejudice against Irish, or from a belief that compulsory Irish would be divisive; many rank-and-file activists and some MPs supported it. Redmond was privately hostile; Dillon spoke against compulsory Irish and was joined by Gwynn. (Griffith commented that this showed the folly of the Gaelic League's appointment of Gwynn to the Coiste Gnótha to conciliate the Irish Party, and demanded his expulsion from the league.)[151] The two other MPs most closely associated with the league, J. P. Boland and Thomas O'Donnell, joined the Gaelic League campaign, as did Field.[152]

O'Brien resumed denunciations of the party leadership, and the factions clashed. Four Redmondite MPs, with a bodyguard of fishermen, held a meeting in Newcastle, County Limerick, on 5 September 1908. They were attacked by an O'Brienite mob; their platform was destroyed, Kettle and Gwynn were injured, and Michael Joyce was knocked unconscious.[153]

The Land Bill introduced by Birrell in November 1908 was denounced by O'Brien, who argued that its terms, apparently favourable to tenants, would kill land purchase by provoking refusal by landlords to sell and would worsen relations between unionists and nationalists.[154] O'Brien decided to appeal to the national convention called to consider the bill, though the convention was evidently loaded against him. Sheehan's Land and Labour Association was refused representation, on the grounds that O'Shee's organisation was the only one recognised by the party.[155]

On 9 February 1909 O'Brien was howled down at the gathering, which he later called the Baton Convention. It was attended by large contingents of Belfast Hibernians and midland cattle-drivers. The Wexford Sinn Féiner Seán Etchingham reported the summary exclusion at the entrances of delegates suspected of pro-Ginnell or O'Brienite leanings.[156] There were shouts of 'Down with the Russian Jewess and her moneybags!' Eugene Crean, the MP for Cork South-East, stood up to advise O'Brien to sit down and was attacked on the platform by Hibernians with batons; this developed into a fight involving Devlin, Gilhooly, and the O'Brienite Father James Clancy, within feet of Redmond's chair. Redmond showed himself unable—and, O'Brien claimed, unwilling—to guarantee free speech. O'Brien convinced himself that the convention would have supported him but for the baton-men, just as he believed the people would follow him if given a lead.[157]

Other targets of abuse from the floor were speakers from the Young Ireland Branch, including Frank Cruise O'Brien and Francis Sheehy-Skeffington, who demanded greater independence from the government, and Laurence Ginnell, who moved that MPs should resign from Liberal clubs in London. Cruise O'Brien and Sheehy-Skeffington, seething at their treatment by the delegates and Devlin's use of demagoguery to evade the issue, privately called the Belfast MP 'this brainless bludgeoner' and declared in print that he represented all that was worst in the party, while the 'statesmanlike' Redmond represented all that was best. Sheehy-Skeffington argued that to guarantee proper debate and greater accountability, conventions should last a week instead of one or two days, so that delegates could meet and concert action rather than being isolated before a well-prepared leadership controlling the agenda.[158]

The floor was not, however, completely controlled by the leadership. A motion proposed by Boland and Thomas O'Donnell supporting compulsory Irish for the NUI was passed by a three-to-one majority, though Dillon opposed it. Boland admired Dillon's decision to make his case in straightforward terms rather than invoking personal sympathy to gain support.[159]

Crean sued Devlin and the secretary of the UIL, Denis Johnston, for abetting in the assault on him. Healy, as Crean's counsel, asked party witnesses embarrassing questions and ridiculed the AOH. Meanwhile Dillon and Muldoon convinced themselves that the baton-wielding stewards were harmless and that the court case was a put-up job by O'Brien, aimed at getting control of the *Freeman's Journal*.[160] Crean's case was dismissed; Healy attributed the decision to Liberal-appointed judges who owed their elevation to the party.

O'Brien set about organising a new All-for-Ireland League in Cork but discovered that many sympathisers opposed a definitive break with the party. The *Cork Examiner,* hitherto neutralised by fear of a rival O'Brienite daily, denounced O'Brien as a factionist. O'Brien planned a new daily with Lord Dunraven.[161] The Cork clergy, never friendly to O'Brien, feared that the new movement would mean contested elections, strife, and actual fighting.[162]

On 20 March, Redmond publicly denounced the All-for-Ireland League. On 23 March a party meeting voted by fifty to nil that membership of the All-for-Ireland League was incompatible with party membership. O'Brien, Healy, Crean, Gilhooly, Sheehan and John O'Donnell stayed away, but Augustine Roche supported the motion. Roche's unexpected defection prostrated O'Brien, emotionally and physically. On his doctor's orders he abruptly resigned his seat, closed the *Irish People,* announced his retirement, and left for Italy, where he wrote *An Olive Branch in Ireland and its History,* an account of his career from 1890, intended as his political testament.[163] Griffith regretted the disappearance of one of the main sources of trouble for the party but declared hopefully that Irish politics had not heard the last of O'Brien.[164]

O'Brien's advice to his followers was to obey party discipline rather than sacrifice themselves needlessly. He promised Sheehan he would return if the party tried to displace them. Sheehan never doubted that O'Brien would return;[165] nor did the party leadership, which moved to eliminate the O'Brienite bridgehead. On 19 April 1909 a meeting in Cork to choose O'Brien's successor as MP broke up in disorder between O'Brienites and Redmondites. Roche and Redmond, with clerical support, nominated George Crosbie; the O'Brienites, supported by trade unionists (who resented Crosbie's attitude during a recent strike) and an opportunist ward politician, Sir Edward Fitzgerald, nominated Maurice Healy, who took the party pledge. On 30 April, Healy defeated Crosbie, despite a personal appearance by Redmond.[166]

The new MP was refused admission to the party, and an attempt to reunite the LLA was blocked by Dillon's ally Thomas Lundon, newly elected MP for Limerick

East, who suspected that Sheehan planned to take over the reunited organisation.[167] Lundon was to score a narrow victory in the by-election following his father's death; the poll took place shortly after Maurice Healy's victory in Cork, and while Lundon's opponent was not an O'Brienite, he won O'Brienite support.

The O'Brienites, now headed by Healy, led Irish opposition to the budget of 1909.[168] The duties on beer and spirits and provision for a land tax introduced by Lloyd George followed traditional Liberal policies but were unpopular in Ireland, while party opposition was muffled by a desire to preserve the Liberal alliance.

Griffith joined the attack, seeing the budget as another attempt to wreck Irish industries. He presented it as proof of the Irish Party's subservience to the Liberals, symbolised by the surrender of Irish seats to 'Englishmen' (i.e. Irishmen living in Britain) such as Thomas Scanlan, Matthew Keating, and Dr John Esmonde,[169] and 'handing back Carlow to the landlords' by the election of Walter MacMurrough Kavanagh, whose conversion from unionism Griffith denounced as coinciding with the Carlow vacancy.[170] Griffith was later to praise Kavanagh for standing down at the general election in protest at the budget.[171]

Griffith, as an old Parnellite, despised Tim Healy, but he praised Healy's attacks on the budget,[172] accused the Irish Party MPs of surrendering Ireland's historical case against overtaxation, predicted that farmers would soon face land taxes more exorbitant than the old rackrents,[173] and even endorsed unionist statements that in this instance Ireland's interests would have been better served by Tory MPs.[174]

As Redmondites reorganised the Cork UIL to challenge the O'Brienite MPs at the general election following rejection of the budget by the House of Lords, violence erupted in County Cork constituencies. Sheehan recalled:

> Hordes of organisers were dispatched to our constituencies to pull the strings against us. I can aver, with a certain malicious satisfaction, that wherever they made their appearance in Cork, we met them and we routed them … Mr. Redmond was to speak at Banteer, on the borders of my constituency. I could not allow that challenge to pass unnoticed without surrendering ground which it would be impossible to recover; and so I took the earliest opportunity of proclaiming that if Mr. Redmond came to Banteer my friends and I would be ready to meet him. He never came.[175]

Messages went to Italy, and O'Brien decided to go to Cork. He notified Healy and Dunraven and arranged for Herlihy to bring out a new paper, the *Cork Accent,* from 1 January.[176] Attempts were made to enlist Sinn Féin support. The O'Brienites attracted some Cork Sinn Féiners, notably the erratic Edward Sheehan, chief lecturer in the Cork branch, who helped draft the constitution of the All-for-Ireland League in 1909.[177] The Independent Sinn Féin councillor James Brady of Dublin[178] proposed that O'Brien should finance Sinn Féin candidates in Dublin in return for compromise on abstention and for Sinn Féin votes elsewhere—including South Dublin, held by unionists, where the O'Brienites thought of running Lindsay

Crawford. Crawford had been in contact with O'Brien for some time and encouraged his optimism by taking for granted the prospective conversion of the unionists and concentrating on the rosy prospects of winning over members of the AOH.[179]

O'Brien told his allies that he would not stand for Parliament.

> This ... would put an end to any possible imputation as to ambitions for leadership and would strengthen my hands enormously for other and better work outside as things progress. At the same time, it would secure in the next Parliament, which is sure to be a very short one, the nucleus of a Party believing in the principles of National reconciliation, which, without any unnecessary aggression would be able to do a thousand things to overthrow the present tyranny and gradually attract the bulk of the Irish people to its side. If Cork can be held for the Policy of Conciliation, sooner or later it will be the nucleus for a great National Movement. If any able man turned up who could go into the House of Commons, there are already ample materials for a great reaction in dozens of constituencies; but I am more clear than ever that I am not that man. That would not, of course, preclude me from giving whatever help I could to any such movement.[180]

O'Brien hoped to create a new United Irish League. He still characteristically desired to address public meetings in Ireland rather than lead at Westminster, and he deceived himself by claiming that he could persuade his followers to nominate someone else. On 4 January 1910 he accepted the Cork City nomination.[181]

4

BALANCE OF POWER
1910

The general election of January 1910 was notable for the consolidation of the unionist bloc and the unexpectedly strong showing of O'Brienite candidates and various local dissidents. This latter phenomenon, however, represented localism rather than a serious nationwide challenge. In the following months, as Redmond took advantage of the balance of power, he grew in stature, while O'Brien (and Griffith, who tried to present Redmond as a tool of the Liberals and called for an Irish-Tory alliance) appeared as a wrecker, weakening Redmond's hand in negotiations with the British government.

O'Brien's negotiations with federalist elements within the Tory party failed to produce any significant result, and at the 1910 election his attempts to extend his base were decisively crushed and his All-for-Ireland League reduced to a Cork splinter group. As the passing of the Parliament Act nullified Griffith's and O'Brien's predictions that Tories and Liberals would unite at the expense of the Irish, and the House of Lords would retain its powers, Redmond seemed for the first time to have inherited Parnell's stature as a national leader.

The election of 1910 amazed commentators, who assumed that O'Brien's antics had destroyed his political base. In Cork city O'Brien headed the poll, though Augustine Roche held the second seat for the party. Sir Edward Fitzgerald, defeated in his attempt to become O'Brien's running-mate, stood as an independent and got some supporters to vote for the Irish Party after realising he would lose.

O'Brien was strongest in the poorer parts of the city, particularly the North Parish and Blackpool and the 'Liberties' (outside the city boundary but in the city constituency).[1] Many working-class voters supported Redmond, and political division produced violence. The trades council divided, with skilled unions supporting the party while the unskilled went O'Brienite. The Quay Lane and Barrack Street Bands were Redmondite; Butter Exchange and Quarry Lane Bands backed O'Brien. Redmondites rallied at the Victoria Hotel in the city centre, while O'Brienites met at Turner's Hotel in a staunch O'Brienite area.[2]

The unionist tactical vote (about a thousand votes) went O'Brienite; he was also supported by some wealthy 'whigs' who had not been politically active since Parnell's triumph.[3] Redmondites pointed out that what Roche called 'Orange dogs creeping from their holes'[4] made the difference between defeat and victory for O'Brien, 'senior Unionist member for Cork City'; but even with a reorganised machine the Irish Party had not defeated O'Brien in the largest constituency in Ireland. In the county O'Brien also received some Protestant support: notable Protestant O'Brienites included J. W. Wood-Wolfe, chairman of Skibbereen Urban District Council,[5] and Langley Brazier-Creagh, a Charleville landlord who sat on the county council from 1911 to 1914. Further research may determine how far this reflected opportunism, adaptation to the prospect of home rule, or genuine O'Brienism. O'Brien also contested his native North-East Cork, overwhelming the sitting MP, William Abraham. He responded to charges that unseating a Protestant was inconsistent with conciliation by denouncing Abraham as a stooge of the AOH.[6]

O'Brien resigned Cork North-East in favour of Maurice Healy, returned un-opposed. The party also lost North Cork. J. C. Flynn MP, challenged by the Land and Labour Association at the nominating convention of 1906,[7] did not stand (though he was still active locally in 1914), and the party candidate was defeated by Patrick Guiney of Kanturk, whose political experience in America and family connections in the constituency built up a personal political base as an LLA activist skilled in deploying land agitation to make landlords agree sale terms.[8] Guiney's activities represented the difference between O'Brien's conciliationist attitude to land agitation and the need to deploy it at local level. This caused problems where a Protestant farmer claimed that O'Brienites boycotted him on sectarian grounds. They argued that they boycotted him as a grabber, not as a Protestant; but the case was used by some unionists to argue that there was no difference between O'Brienites and Redmondites.[9]

In Cork South-East and Cork South-West, Eugene Crean and James Gilhooly fought off local opponents to secure re-election. Kinsale and Bandon were Crean strongholds. In Mid-Cork, D. D. Sheehan was challenged by a prominent member of the Young Ireland Branch and party organiser, W. G. Fallon. Sheehan's followers broke up the party convention in Macroom; local feeling and LLA sticks and stones were employed against Fallon,[10] who returned defeated to Dublin and tried to counter O'Brienite attacks on the AOH by starting an LLA scare. He claimed the LLA was a danger to religion, because it caused the voters of Mid-Cork to defy their priests; that it wanted schools run by committees of labourers; and that if farmers did not support the party they would find the LLA ruling the country and their farms divided into labourers' plots.[11] (One wonders what O'Shee thought of this.) A Mid-Cork O'Brienite replied that the labourers were as devout as ever, that the LLA merely suggested that parents should have some say in education, that labourers were a minority in Mid-Cork, and that many farmers supported Sheehan because of O'Brienite commitment to land purchase and a feeling that O'Brienism deterred the party from subservience to the British government.[12]

Despite a massive campaign spearheaded by Richard Hazleton as the party candidate, Healy held North Louth by ninety-nine votes. Cardinal Michael Logue was persuaded not to publicly endorse Healy but gave Bernard Hamill, a Dundalk Healyite, a 'private' letter endorsing him.[13] Healy drew on his record as a constituency MP and the personal loyalty of his followers in Carlingford and Cooley. He allegedly received four to five hundred unionist votes, and one journalist claimed that some nominally nationalist large farmers and old-age pensioners voted for Healy to prevent home rule, fearing that a government without the resources of the British Treasury would tax land and cut pensions.[14]

In South Mayo, John O'Donnell defeated Conor O'Kelly. O'Kelly's supporters, furious at the role of the local clergy, staged a concerted walk-out from Sunday Mass and overturned collection tables. A church hall and some statues were destroyed during a riot in Claremorris.[15]

In East Kerry, Eugene O'Sullivan defeated John Murphy, and this defeat in a local dispute of the official candidate—however disloyal—was a blow to the party. O'Sullivan had co-operated with the Sheehanite LLA and O'Brien's 1907 unity campaign; the O'Brienites claimed his victory as theirs.[16]

Elsewhere it is difficult to determine the inclinations of candidates, often local opportunists, who opposed sitting MPs. In North Kerry the O'Brienite T. N. Stack, a London stockbroker from a Tralee family, was crushed by M. J. Flavin.[17] In Limerick city J. H. Rice stood as an O'Brienite. Rice, a Clongowes-educated Dublin solicitor and essayist, was inspired by intellectual attraction to the policy of conciliation. Even the *Leader* described him as an honourable man who argued his case rather than engaging in personal abuse. Rice made a respectable showing, but Joyce was comfortably re-elected.[18]

In West Belfast, P. J. Magee, secretary of the diehard rump of the Catholic Association, stood against Devlin. He declared himself a follower of 'the policy of William O'Brien and Timothy Healy' and called on voters to avenge the memory of Bishop Henry; but his candidacy was so clearly a unionist-backed attempt to split the nationalist vote that it attracted only seventy-five votes.[19]

In West Waterford, O'Shee had been challenged for the nomination in 1906.[20] In January 1910 he was opposed by J. Arthur Ryan of Dungarvan, who disclaimed connection with O'Brien but campaigned on O'Brienite themes, such as land purchase and the budget. He made a strong showing but did not take the seat.[21]

T. W. Bennett, who came within two hundred votes of taking Limerick East, was not an O'Brienite, though he probably received O'Brienite support.[22] His candidacy reflected the grievances of the powerful Kilmallock Branch, excluded from the constituency convention on a technicality. The *Leader* praised Bennett as an 'excellent candidate, and no factionist,' who would make a better MP than the 'more or less nondescript' Lundon.[23] This reflects Bennett's Irish-Ireland sympathies: in 1913 he supported compulsory Irish for county council scholarships and denounced infiltration of the Gaelic League by the UIL.[24]

In North Mayo, Daniel Boyle defeated Bernard Egan by a very slim margin. Egan later established links with O'Brien, but he does not appear to have been an O'Brienite at this time.[25]

In North Westmeath, Laurence Ginnell's agrarianism and his origins in Delvin enabled him to rally rural support to defeat a party challenger, Patrick MacKenna, whose main base was in Mullingar. MacKenna was also a well-known agrarian agitator and industrial revivalist, despite being handicapped politically by the fact that his wealthy family had grazing interests.[26] O'Brien unscrupulously claimed the survival of Ginnell and of Patrick White in North Meath as evidence of popular support for him, though both men strongly opposed him.[27] Ginnell's ambivalent relationship to the party is summed up by the fact that he called his local organisation the 'Independent UIL'.

For some commentators the most startling proof of party weakness came in South Monaghan. O'Brien and Healy were well known; but what was to be made of the victory over the party candidate, after a split in the local UIL and a bitterly fought campaign, by the 'political tomtit' John McKean?[28] McKean was a crypto-Healyite, notable for clericalism and for denouncing reports of Belgian atrocities in the Congo as fabrications; the party nicknamed him 'Congo Jack'.[29] His victory probably reflected local divisions between Devlin's AOH and the Irish National Foresters, a rival friendly society headed by J. C. R. Lardner, whose election for North Monaghan in 1907 had been opposed by the AOH.[30]

The party also lost Mid-Tyrone to the Unionists on a split vote after the de-selected Healyite MP George Murnaghan stood against the party candidate, John Valentine, and the Unionist Bryan Cooper held on to South Dublin, vacated by Walter Long, who moved to an English seat. His party opponent, Alderman W. F. Cotton, was an associate of William Martin Murphy who used his ownership of the Dublin gas-works to give himself a political base on Dublin Corporation. As Cotton was a leading loyal-addresser, regarded as unionist in all but name, his selection aroused criticism.[31] Cooper tried to offset this appeal to the 'whig' and business vote by courting labour voters distrustful of Cotton's record as an employer.[32] The O'Brienite plan to run Lindsay Crawford in South Dublin collapsed through Sinn Féin's failure to co-operate and what Crawford saw as insensitive treatment by James Brady and Healy; he spoke on behalf of Cotton, and left Ireland to become a journalist in Toronto.[33]

The election also saw the defeat of T. W. Russell and T. H. Sloan by official Unionists. Sloan's career was over, though he continued to lead a small Independent Orange rump, denounced by official Unionists as factionists and denouncing them as insufficiently committed to opposing home rule for Ireland as a whole. The recapture of South Tyrone and North Antrim marked the end of Russellism as an independent force, though Russell survived as a discredited office-holder. R. G. Glendinning had retired in North Antrim, and his successor as Liberal candidate declared himself so strongly against home rule that some nationalists welcomed his defeat.

J. J. O'Toole compared the election results to the shock experienced by Dublin Parnellites in 1890 when the Kilkenny North by-election shattered their illusion that the whole country was Parnellite.[34] This reflects the 'decentred' nature of politics in the period. County Mayo was remote from Dublin; the *Leader* was not sure whether John O'Donnell or O'Kelly was the party candidate in Mayo South,[35] and in the immediate aftermath of the election O'Brien listed among signs of national rebellion against the party the survival of Robert Ambrose, who had in fact been displaced in Mayo West after the collapse of a dubious scheme to develop Blacksod Bay as a transatlantic port.[36]

O'Brien pointed to the election results and the failure of the purge as proof that the country was on his side. Bad weather and physical weakness confined him to three speeches in the city and four in North-East Cork, yet he had shaken the party. The *Cork Accent* became a daily evening paper, the *Cork Free Press*. The inaugural meeting of the AFIL was held in April, attended by the O'Brienite MPs (except for Healy, still trying to preserve a semblance of independence), the principal members of the Dunraven group, and the aged T. D. Sullivan.

O'Brien boasted that the AFIL had made greater progress than the UIL at the equivalent stage of its career.[37] This was illusory. The AFIL had existed in embryo since 1904. It was almost entirely confined to County Cork (a few hundred votes would have unseated Healy and O'Donnell). It had only eight MPs, whereas the Irish Party had 73, of whom 53 were unopposed in January. Its base was Sheehan's LLA, and 1910 saw a rapid disintegration of the Sheehanite organisation outside County Cork and its borderlands as members drew back from open revolt.[38]

Sheehan's erratic leadership was a long-standing source of tension.[39] In March a section of the Cork LLA under P. J. Bradley seceded and established itself as an independent organisation allied to the party.[40] The AFIL faced a united party in an unprecedentedly favourable parliamentary situation, not the exhausted factions of the eighteen-nineties. The O'Brien strategy of an alliance of notables lost its attraction as home rule returned to the agenda.

O'Brien assumed that the AFIL could act as a catalyst to purify the party, as the UIL had done. It was not meant to fight every constituency, nor to present itself as an alternative party; the AFIL MPs never appointed whips or elected a chairman. They accepted that there should be a united party but claimed they had been illegally excluded from it. (Redmond warned potential rebels that the newly elected independents would never be re-admitted to the party under any circumstances.) The party was violating its own rules: they were the true upholders of party discipline, and the majority were 'factionists'. O'Brien argued that as the party and the UIL Directory had not disciplined Dillon for rebelling against conciliationist resolutions in 1903, they could not discipline him unless they first disciplined Dillon. It can be seen that the attitude of the AFIL to party membership makes it unsafe to judge candidates' allegiance by willingness to take the party pledge or declarations of support for the party.[41]

To repeat the success of the UIL, the AFIL needed to attract defectors among the twenty or so MPs known to be discontented with the party leadership. There were in fact no defections—though immediately after the election the party had misgivings about P. J. O'Shaughnessy and Tom O'Donnell, and O'Brien claimed that the party's acceptance of O'Shaughnessy and Eugene O'Sullivan as members showed its weakness.[42] Even McKean refused to openly join the AFIL; Healy complained that Lardner, McKean, the Bishop of Clogher and his clergy were sympathetic but too cowardly to support them openly.[43] A Clogher priest had backed an abortive scheme to run Dr E. C. Thompson as an O'Brienite against T. W. Russell in South Tyrone.

Two attempts to assert strength outside County Cork also came to nothing. When the MP for West Wicklow died, O'Brien urged a local businessman and party activist, E. P. O'Kelly, to run as a conciliationist, on the grounds that his victory would bring 'peace'—that is, O'Brien's triumph. O'Kelly wrote a confused, half-distraught reply but was returned unopposed as the party candidate.[44]

O'Brien and Healy intended to contest the Dublin Harbour by-election caused by Harrington's death but were caught unprepared when the party used a little-known regulation to move the writ earlier than expected.[45] The party nominated William Abraham, who praised the AOH for showing tolerance by giving the seat to a Protestant.[46] A feud between Alderman Lorcan Sherlock and C. P. O'Neill, who was supported by the AOH, allowed Redmond to impose a compromise candidate.[47]

The failure to run an O'Brienite merely saved the AFIL from humiliation. Griffith attacked Redmond's claims to the Parnellite legacy by recalling that Abraham moved the deposition of Parnell in committee room 15 and claiming that Redmond habitually gave old Parnellite seats to 'the meaner sort of Anti-Parnellite.'[48] In the annual Dublin Corporation elections the party reversed its long-standing decline: Sinn Féin lost four seats, and James Brady was defeated in the Inns Quay ward.[49]

In East Kerry, Eugene O'Sullivan was unseated on petition, on the grounds that demonstrations outside the polling station in his Firies stronghold had deterred opponents from voting. The Cork Free Press quickly distanced itself from him.[50] The writ had not been moved when Parliament was dissolved.

The AFIL was handicapped by lack of clerical support. When Bishop O'Donnell arranged for most bishops to double their subscriptions to the National Fund, O'Brien responded that three of the four archbishops supported him. Archbishop Healy may have sympathised but kept silent. Cardinal Logue and

Archbishop Walsh were Healyites rather than O'Brienites; Dillon suspected they only tolerated O'Brien as a tool against the party.[51] Logue disliked O'Brien, disapproved of 'conciliationism', and was deterred (though also annoyed) by divisions among North Louth clergy and Redmondite resentment at his support for Healy. The AOH held a protest demonstration in Armagh and burnt Healy in effigy.[52] Walsh had largely withdrawn from politics and as early as 1904 toyed with abstentionism.[53]

All three County Cork bishops opposed O'Brien, Kelly of Ross and O'Callaghan of Cork being particularly active.[54] O'Brien's most prominent clerical supporter was Father James Clancy of Kilkee, County Clare. In Ross, three Kinsale curates organised Crean's support.[55] In his native Cloyne, O'Brien was supported by Canon Sheehan of Doneraile, Canon Wigmore of Mallow, and his curate, Father Madden.[56] In North Louth, politically active clergy divided equally between Healy and his opponents; but the formal accession of Healy to the AFIL in September 1910 brought little clerical support; a few isolated priests who combined Healyism with Sinn Féin tendencies, such as Father Matt Ryan of Knockavilla and Father John Kelly of Ballyfin, aligned with the AFIL. Healy's alliance with O'Brien made Logue less enthusiastic about Healy.[57] Crypto-Healyites failed to follow his lead; the *Irish Independent* continued covertly slanting news coverage against the party but giving it lukewarm editorial support.[58]

The AFIL also failed to attract unionist support on any large scale outside the original Dunraven group. Lord Dunraven regularly appeared on AFIL platforms. He also contributed to the *Cork Free Press,* as did Colonel William Hutcheson-Poe: between them they spent £5,000 on it in 1910–14, the wealthy Dunraven presumably giving more than Hutcheson-Poe. Lady Fitzgerald Arnott, owner of the *Irish Times,* also took a large shareholding; while she had associated with devolutionists in the past, her main motive was a desire to hurt the Irish Party.[59] The AFIL also received political and financial support from Lord Castletown, Lord Rossmore, T. A. Brassey (a Liberal imperialist Ulster landowner and advocate of a federal United Kingdom), and the Waterford landowners and county councillors Captain Villiers Stuart and Sir John Keane,[60] as well as the Healyite former MPs C. J. Engledew,[61] P. G. H. Carvill, and E. C. Thompson,[62] the Parnellite veteran J. G. Fitzgerald,[63] and the former labour-nationalist MP Michael Austin.[64]

Keane symbolises the tensions inherent in O'Brien's attempt to build a coalition whose extremes—Sinn Féin and moderate unionists—were even further apart than those of the unwieldy Irish Party; for while he accepted the Free State and played an active role in its public life as banker, businessman, long-serving senator, and outspoken (usually arrogant and often solitary) defender of minority rights, he also became widely hated in County Waterford for breaking the labourers' strike of 1922–3, those same labourers whose support O'Brien cultivated.[65]

The adherence of unionist landowners to the AFIL allowed its opponents to portray O'Brien as a rich man defending selfish interests. O'Brien added to this impression by living in former gentry homes and adopting such upper-class habits as Continental holidays and visits to hydros, while his wife played Lady Bountiful. Addresses presented to him when he took up residence in Mallow in 1912 resemble those presented to landlords on similar occasions. Such tensions passed almost unacknowledged by O'Brien, who believed that patriotism and the force of his personality would solve all problems and overcome all social differences. He overlooked the difference between his allies' view that power and influence were theirs by right and his own view that he and they earned a high place in the nation by identifying with its cause. Declaring that only commitment to the principle of self-government was required for membership of the AFIL, he allowed them to advocate tariff reform, bimetallism, the House of Lords veto, and various federalist and devolutionist schemes, contrasting their freedom to differ on points of detail with the 'slavishness' allegedly displayed by the Protestant members of the party;[66] but the voluble exercise of this freedom—by Moreton Frewen in particular—provided propaganda for Redmondites, while the devolutionists were exasperated by O'Brien's inability to identify completely with their Tory agenda.[67]

They were united, however, in exasperation at the unwillingness of most unionists to support the AFIL. O'Brien saw any unionist who showed the slightest willingness to compromise, or resignation at the inevitability of home rule, as a secret AFIL sympathiser, restrained only by fear of social ostracism.[68] He claimed he had made Lord Barrymore a home-ruler, extrapolating from their co-operation against the Irish Land Act (1909); when Barrymore declared that he was always a unionist, O'Brien blamed the party for frightening away this potential convert.[69]

Throughout the summer O'Brien and his lieutenants carried out frenetic organisational work in Counties Waterford, Limerick, and Kerry; in early autumn they moved into County Mayo to strengthen John O'Donnell.[70] Meanwhile the party prepared to counter-attack in County Cork.

Redmond and the party leaders announced a huge rally in Cork. O'Brien planned an AFIL rally for the city on the same day, and many observers predicted large-scale violence. The rallies passed off peacefully, despite a provocative march led by O'Brien past the party leaders' hotel, but were followed by fighting in Blackpool between Redmondites and O'Brienites reinforced by agricultural labourers in the city for the AFIL rally; there were many injuries.[71] At Newmarket the RIC opened fire on a party fight involving about forty people, and one man was killed and many others wounded.[72] In Bantry a riot involving 'hundreds of injuries' led to short terms of imprisonment for six Redmondites and sixteen O'Brienites.[73]

These events embarrassed the party and rejoiced unionist propagandists. They reinforced the mainstream nationalist view of O'Brien as a destructive madman enabled to play the fool by his wife's money and as an egoist driven by envy of Redmond. The UIL emphasised the incongruities of the O'Brien-Healy alliance by publishing a selection of the invective exchanged by Healy and O'Brien between 1891 and 1903.[74] Most of O'Brien's supporters saw themselves as engaged in a simple personal contest between O'Brien and Redmond. Only influence in the

House of Commons could make his policy credible; but at Westminster O'Brien had nothing to offer comparable with the balance of power.

Redmond's insistence, in and out of the House of Commons, that the British government must commit itself to the abolition of the House of Lords veto or else the Irish Party would refuse to support the budget won admiration from most of his followers and from the radical wing of the Liberals. He used T. P. O'Connor as intermediary to present himself to discontented government backbenchers as their spokesman against a Cabinet seemingly inclined to compromise with the Tories.[75] Redmond failed to win concessions on the budget, but, despite some grumblings within the party, O'Brien could not make much political capital on the issue. As Lloyd George pointed out in the Cabinet, Redmond could hardly forfeit home rule for minor budget changes.[76] The party countered denunciations of the 'socialist threat' by pointing to increased government spending on Ireland, particularly the Old Age Pensions Act (1908).[77]

O'Brien predicted that, sooner than enter the large-scale constitutional conflict required to abolish the House of Lords veto, Liberals and Conservatives would bypass Redmond through a compromise including limited Irish self-government on devolutionist lines. He declared that Redmond could no more make the British revolutionise their constitution than he could turn the stars pink or pluck up the Galty Mountains and throw them into the sea.

Griffith took the same line, hoping the breakdown of the Liberal agenda might further discredit the party and provide new political opportunities. Editorials in Sinn Féin declared that the 'British democracy' were snobs who loved a lord too much to diminish their powers.[78] Since neither of the British parties would give home rule, and the Irish Party had virtually abandoned the claim to independence (as defined by Sinn Féin), they should have voted in the Tories for an improved version of the Irish Council Bill.[79] Griffith presented Redmond as an incompetent who would pass the budget for Asquith and then see Tory and Liberal join to preserve the House of Lords and leave home rule on the sidelines. Free trade was heading for disaster, and the Tories would return to power for at least two terms.[80] He predicted a nationwide split between Redmond and O'Brien on the scale of the eighteen-nineties.[81] At the same time Griffith announced that he had changed his opinion on one point: he now believed that Ireland could never progress from home rule to independence without becoming completely Irish-speaking.[82]

Expectations of a compromise may have been enhanced by the virtual parliamentary consensus on abolishing the coronation declaration against transubstantiation after King Edward VII's death made it an issue of immediate concern. Only Ulster and Liverpool Orange Tories and a few Liberal 'political Protestants', such as Neil Primrose and T. C. Agar-Robartes, opposed the repeal. Griffith promptly declared the royal declaration issue a red herring and complained about displays of mourning in Dublin, including a requiem Mass in the Pro-Cathedral.[83]

There were indeed attempts by members of both British parties to arrive at a compromise. Elements from both parties contacted O'Brien. As a sideline to his negotiations with Redmond, the Liberal chief whip held conversations with O'Brien and Healy and considered financing the AFIL in order to weaken Redmond. Lloyd George met O'Brien and Healy and offered a budgetary compromise if the party would agree to support it; this was calculated to spread rancour among nationalists, without giving anything in return.[84] In a bizarre exchange in the House of Commons, O'Brien and Lloyd George accused each other of lying; Austen Chamberlain privately said that neither was trustworthy.[85] While some Liberals, including the Master of Elibank and Birrell, briefly considered a federalist settlement, AFIL contacts with the Liberals reinforced the party view of O'Brienism as spiteful factionalism.

O'Brien's contacts with elements of the Tory party seemed more promising. They held out the hope of justifying O'Brien's claim to win unionist support for a limited measure of autonomy.[86] This was based on the contacts of Frewen and Dunraven and the willingness of some tariff reformers and imperial federationists to consider devolution in return for Irish support on tariffs and opposition to Liberal social legislation.

Frewen spent much of 1910 in America, trying to dissuade wealthy Irish-Americans from supporting Redmond and 'socialism'. With the help of Lord Grey, Governor-General of Canada (a former Liberal unionist MP and a business associate of Frewen), he set up the League of Federals as an American-Canadian rival to the UIL of America—in fact a conduit for contributions to the UIL from a few wealthy federalists. £4,000 was eventually sent; £1,000 was publicly acknowledged by the All-for-Ireland Fund, a counterpart of the party's National Fund.[87] This compared poorly with Redmond's triumphant fund-raising visit to America in the autumn of 1910 with Devlin and T. P. O'Connor, when he told enthusiastic crowds that this might be the last time he would ask them for aid. (Some incautious federalist remarks by O'Connor and Redmond were retracted after denunciations by party activists, including Michael Meagher MP.)[88] Redmond raised £48,000.[89]

In the summer of 1910 some unionist newspapers campaigned for a federalist settlement by consent. F. S. Oliver, propagandist of imperial federation and founder of the Round Table group, argued the case in a series of letters in the *Times* signed 'Pacificus'. J. L. Garvin, editor of the *Observer* and a supporter of tariff reform, put in touch with O'Brien by Frewen, campaigned for a conference to work out a federalist compromise. He canvassed the Tory leadership, suggesting that a federal settlement might save the House of Lords, preserve Britain from 'socialism', and safeguard the empire.[90]

There was some debate within the Tory party. Lord Milner, former Governor-General of South Africa, talked privately of accepting federalism to avoid worse evils.[91] Lord Balcarres, Conservative chief whip, wrote in his diary that the Ulster unionists' fears were greatly exaggerated, that they must make sacrifices if necessary, and that the Irish situation had improved so much—as evidenced by the emergence of O'Brienism—that devolution might be considered.[92] During the inter-party Constitutional Conference of June to November 1910, aimed at reaching compromise over the House of Lords, Lloyd George produced an unofficial scheme for a national government, independent of the Irish Party, whose programme would include a federal solution. The former Cabinet minister Alfred Lyttelton wrote to Balfour expressing fear that the Conservatives could not credibly oppose federalism if the Liberals took it up, because Grey, Milner and many bright young Tory intellectuals now advocated it.[93]

Balfour faced the more concrete prospect of rebellion by Irish unionists and traditional Tories; he often declared he would never split the Tory party, as Peel did. Walter Long and Edward Carson declared publicly and privately that they would never accept federalism, and organised an anti-federalist manifesto.[94] Even Conservatives who discussed federalism as a possibility said it was acceptable only as a permanent settlement,[95] whereas O'Brien advocated it as a first step to wider self-government.

The Constitutional Conference broke down over Conservative demands that home rule be regarded as 'organic legislation', requiring a referendum. A snap general election was called for December 1910. Garvin raised funds for the AFIL from Tory devolutionists. Lord Carnarvon, son of the Conservative home rule Lord Lieutenant of 1886, gave £5,000; Lord Desborough, a business associate of Frewen's and a 'Soul' (one of an upper-class social and intellectual coterie of which Balfour and Wyndham were leading members), gave £2,500. O'Brien had qualms but quietened his conscience by recalling Parnell's shady acceptance of money from Cecil Rhodes and refusing some Tory contributors not prepared, even in private, to gesture towards some form of Irish self-government.[96]

An odd feature of this episode was O'Brien's acceptance of £2,500 from Walter Long. After 1916, when Long realised that home rule was inevitable, he advocated federalism as an alternative to partition to safeguard southern unionists; but in 1910 he fiercely opposed compromise in public—though he also made private federalist noises to Redmond.[97] O'Brien, an extreme optimist whose first impressions became fixed opinions, formed a favourable opinion of Long from his attitude towards O'Brien's Munster delegation on the Irish Land Act (1909).[98] *The Irish Revolution* (written after the War of Independence) praises Long as a conciliationist 'maligned by the party as an anti-Irish Conservative … as romantic a lover of Ireland as his mother's Irish blood could make him.' O'Brien claims that Long said 'from the start' that 'I shall have to oppose Home Rule as it stands, but I will only oppose it from the lips out.'[99] This sounds like a fabrication—whether by Long, O'Brien, or an intermediary such as Frewen. Long's spoiling tactics derived from the same desire to maintain nationalist divisions that led the ultra-diehard *Morning Post* to publish euphoric reports of O'Brien's progress. Long channelled a potential subscriber to O'Brien as late as 1912.

On 21 November, Garvin reported to Lord Northcliffe on his fund-raising and O'Brien's scruples. He said that 'the splendid old O'Quixote' would 'have the fight of his life even to hold his own but goes back to Ireland tomorrow night … trumpeting indomitably. He thinks he will gain from three to six seats.'[100]

The party avoided embarrassments at conventions by declaring that they could not be held, because of the abruptness of the election. In the Birr Division of King's County (Offaly) the discontented Ferbane Branch backed an ambitious member of the YIB, Frederick W. Ryan, against Michael Reddy, the sitting MP, claiming that a letter from Redmond describing Ryan as a suitable candidate was a specific mandate to oppose Reddy and that the absence of a convention entitled them to support the candidate of their choice.[101] In general, however, sitting MPs were renominated automatically; even Ginnell and McKean were left undisturbed as the party concentrated on O'Brien and the unionists.

W. F. Cotton unseated Captain B. R. Cooper in South Dublin; with George Murnaghan out of the running, Richard McGhee as party candidate retook Mid-Tyrone. There were ominous signs, discounted at the time. Unionist leaders threatened armed resistance and opened subscription lists.[102] W. J. Harbinson, the most prominent nationalist in Cookstown, had his shop windows broken,[103] and Jeremiah MacVeagh's election agent in South Down was beaten to death by loyalists.[104]

As the party concentrated, O'Brien overreached himself. He was keen to strengthen his claim as an alternative national leader and wanted to show his backers that their money was being put to good use. Despite continued failure to recruit defectors, with a last approach made to Tom O'Donnell just before the election,[105] he was confident 'the people' were on his side. Believing that if the January election produced so many setbacks for the party, greater efforts would produce proportionate results, he ran AFIL candidates not only in constituencies where local independents had done well in January but in several that had not been contested. He tried to capitalise on his personal prestige by contesting East Cork and West Mayo as well as Cork City; Sheehan stood for Limerick West as well as Mid-Cork, while Patrick Guiney contested North Cork and East Kerry (which suggests that there was a shortage of candidates). The *Cork Free Press* predicted the election of twenty AFIL members.[106]

The election began promisingly when O'Brien and Maurice Healy were returned for Cork City. Augustine Roche wanted Sir Edward Fitzgerald as running-mate, but 'Fitzy' was too treacherous and unpredictable to be handled safely. Willie Redmond MP was chosen. Fitzgerald retaliated by not campaigning for party candidates (though he sent his nephew) and letting his displeasure be known; the defection of many of his supporters and the superior organisation of the well-financed city AFIL unseated Roche. After Healy's election, O'Brien nominated Frewen for North-East Cork. The Redmondites did not contest the seat.

The AFIL also narrowly took South Cork, not contested in January. The MP, Edward Barry, had formerly shown O'Brienite sympathies. A Redmondite thought

Barry's defeat predictable, as parts of the constituency were almost 100 per cent O'Brienite. Barry had also been the target of a cattle-drive.[107] The new MP, John Walsh, a director of the Beamish and Crawford brewery, was a former Parnellite who supported O'Brien since the early days of the UIL. His involvement also reflected opposition to the budget's taxes on drink.[108]

Bad news began with the decisive defeat of Healy by Hazleton in North Louth. Logue remained silent, and the election was marked by violence; Healy could not appear in Dundalk without an escort. On polling day Healy was besieged at one polling station; at another a Healyite agent fled a hostile crowd. The party replied to Healy's accusations of corruption by listing government jobs held by his associates; Healy obtained an injunction against the repetition of these allegations.[109]

O'Brien asked Patrick Guiney to step down in favour of Healy in North Cork, where the poll took place a few days after North Louth. Guiney angrily refused. According to hostile rumour, it was then planned to nominate Healy so as to pressure Guiney into standing down, but this was abandoned, as the party, though it could not win against Guiney, would force a three-cornered contest if Healy were nominated.[110] Thus the AFIL, like the party, acquired its own malcontent MP, dependent more on local and family support than on the good will of the leadership.

After the general election, Guiney threatened to turn Redmondite or declare himself independent of both parties.[111] He soon reappeared on AFIL platforms, claiming the party offered him £10,000 to give up the seat,[112] but North Cork's position as a semi-independent Guiney fiefdom was confirmed after Patrick Guiney's death in 1913, when his brother John took the seat unopposed.[113] As the AFIL disintegrated in 1915 and 1916, John Guiney distanced himself from it, and rumours of a deal between the Guineys and Redmond resurfaced.[114]

In Mid-Cork, Sheehan fought off a local candidate. In South-East Cork, Crean also held his ground, and in South-West Cork, Gilhooly survived, though his majority was reduced.

Outside County Cork, most new candidates polled significant minority votes, the exception being T. B. Cronin, a journalist with the *Cork Free Press* and Poor Law guardian in Tralee with some Sinn Féin sympathies,[115] sent to fight J. P. Boland in South Kerry. In East Kerry the O'Sullivans were bought off by giving the party nomination to Timothy O'Sullivan, a relative of Eugene; Guiney was defeated. Killarney jarveys refused to hire their vehicles to him, and transport sent from North Cork was intimidated into turning back.[117] A few years later Eugene O'Sullivan was addressing party meetings in County Kerry.[118]

January discontents did not become O'Brienite votes, as shown by increased party majorities in West Waterford (contested by M. F. Healy, Maurice's son, after T. D. Sullivan turned down the nomination because of age and ill-health) and East Limerick (where the O'Brienite candidate was Hubert O'Connor, a young past pupil of Clongowes Wood later killed in the First World War).[119] In Limerick city Rice's vote dropped slightly. Martin O'Dwyer, a member of Tipperary County Council associated with O'Brien and Sheehan's LLA,[120] tried for the labourers' vote in Mid-Tipperary, held until January by the chairman of the O'Shee LLA. O'Dwyer polled well but did not seriously threaten the sitting MP, John Hackett, whom he accused of having grazing interests. The election was followed by a local purge of O'Dwyer supporters. Despite his obvious O'Brienism, O'Dwyer protested that since there had been no convention in December to test his claim that the January convention that selected Hackett was unrepresentative, he was entitled to appeal to the electorate.[121]

In West Limerick, Sheehan was routed by P. J. O'Shaughnessy. The decision to oppose an MP who was seen as a potential defector shows the isolation of the AFIL.

Three minor O'Brienites appeared outside Munster. Healy and O'Brien ran Healy's solicitor, S. H. Moynagh, in South Armagh, hoping to profit from Logue's annoyance that he had not been consulted when the sitting MP was selected in 1909. Frewen characteristically suggested the ex-Catholic Garvin as joint Unionist-AFIL candidate![122] Moynagh was defeated by three to one, with Redmondites claiming that local unionists voted for him;[123] after the election Healy and O'Brien discovered that he had solicited money for the election from each of them without telling the other and had misappropriated cash given by Healy to pay North Louth election debts.[124] In South Wexford, John Cummins opposed the sitting MP, Peter Ffrench, but lost by three to one.[125]

In Dublin, James Brady tried again to ally the AFIL and Sinn Féin, undertaking to stand as an abstentionist. His proposal was supported by Griffith and the trade unionist and IRB man P. T. Daly, who had opposed the 1909 proposal. The *Leader* claimed that Daly intended to run against J. P. Nannetti in College Green—receptive to a labour candidate—while Brady fought Abraham, and Frewen opposed Field in St Patrick's.[126] This last item sounds fabricated: Moran mocked the AFIL as 'Frewenites'. Griffith's approval reflected his belief that the Dublin candidates would stand as abstentionists; when this was discovered to be mistaken the Sinn Féin executive dissociated itself from Brady and O'Brienite candidates. Brady failed to lodge Daly's nomination papers in time and was routed in the Harbour ward.[127]

The final blows to O'Brien's claim to national leadership came in East Cork and Mayo. O'Brien and Sheehan campaigned in County Mayo for months—coming under revolver fire at Crossmolina—leaving the Healys to campaign in East Cork, where Gwynn and Hazleton directed the campaign of the Irish Party's whip, Captain A. J. C. Donelan. Donelan won healthily. The *Cork Free Press* claimed the constituency was equally divided outside Cóbh, whose Redmondism it attributed to government dockyard patronage; O'Brien claimed he would have won if he got one foot in the constituency.[128] No such excuse could be offered in County Mayo.

In South Mayo clergy and the party reached agreement. Conor O'Kelly was replaced as candidate by the Castlerea shopkeeper and veteran agitator John Fitzgibbon, who had just been appointed to the Congested Districts Board, where he was expected to exercise extensive patronage. P. D. Kenny's hope that O'Kelly and his supporters might join O'Brien was not fulfilled.[129] Facing certain defeat, and with his *Connaught Champion* collapsing before the new *Connaught Tribune,* supported by the party, John O'Donnell yielded without a contest.

In West Mayo, O'Brien was opposed by William Doris, former assistant secretary of the Land League. County Mayo remained a centre of land agitation; the policy of conciliation was less attractive here than in Munster. O'Brien was crushed. Sophie recorded her bewilderment that his votes came from the towns, where they did little in the past, while country people, for whom they did so much, defeated them.[130] Westport and Ballina were traditionally at odds with the countryside. Both had residual AFIL presences after 1910, as had Castlebar. This may reflect local factionalism and possibly separatism.[131] During the First World War, Westport was separatist and supplied few recruits, even before 1916.[132]

The O'Briens sold their home in Westport and moved to Cork. The *Connaught Champion* closed in January 1911, though a few malcontents and O'Brien loyalists travelled to Cork for AFIL conferences. A year later O'Brien announced the suspension of AFIL activities outside County Cork 'as a peace gesture,' though scattered branches remained.

O'Brien's nuisance value was shown by election petitions in North Louth and East Cork. The Louth petition publicised violence and bribery by party supporters; Hazleton was unseated because of a leaflet containing admittedly false insinuations about Healy securing jobs for relatives. In East Cork it was revealed that party expenditure exceeded the legal limits, records were destroyed, and a false statement of expenses was submitted. The party pleaded that O'Brien also spent freely; the petition was brought by 'men of straw' to avoid awkward questions.[133]

Treating and intimidation were also revealed. The results were publicised by O'Brien—and unionists. The *Leader* complained that 'the miserable old man with foreign money' washed dirty linen for the benefit of unionists and lawyers.[134]

Healy thought it hopeless to contest North Louth; the party gave Roche the seat. Neither Donelan nor Hazleton was disqualified from Parliament. Hazleton continued to sit for North Galway, though enmeshed in complex legal endeavours by Healy to make him (or the UIL) pay the costs of the North Louth petition.

Donelan exchanged seats with Muldoon, moving to East Wicklow. Muldoon's unopposed election was 'traded' against Healy's return for North-East Cork. Frewen was persuaded to resign in favour of Healy, thus forced into uneasy dependence on O'Brien.[135] Neither side sought hopeless contests; Redmond lamented that excessive optimism cost a thousand pounds for every unsuccessful contest against sitting AFIL MPs.[136] The All-for-Ireland Fund petered out early in 1911, having produced slightly more than £2,500. O'Brien sold £13,000 of Sophie's investments to meet election costs and to support the *Cork Free Press*.[137] The paper was full of lengthy reports of speeches (and of misprints). It became notorious for excessive optimism about AFIL prospects, underestimating party strength, slanting news reports, and a financial liability maintained by cutbacks and by advertising from sympathetic local authorities.

O'Brien's Cork base was secured for the time being by local elections in January and June 1911, which gave the AFIL a majority on Cork County Council[138] and allowed the O'Brienites to elect a mayor of Cork with unionist and independent support.[139] Redmondites were purged from council committees and employment, with the *Cork Free Press* inveighing against idealistic notions of fairness that might allow Redmondites to retain their places and use them against the AFIL.[140] The prospect of maintaining the lawyers and organisers needed for annual revisions of the electoral register in opposition to an increasingly well-organised party machine meant more long-term expenditure.

Frewen's stated reason for resignation was the AFIL decision to vote for abolition of the House of Lords veto. The *Cork Free Press* continued to predict into early 1911 that the Tories would resist the Parliament Bill to the last and that Redmond would be left discredited and powerless by a Tory-Liberal compromise.[141] As the Parliament Act (1911) was passed, Frewen told Lord Dunraven that O'Brien was beaten; they must find other means to defend their cause.[142] Griffith grumbled that the Liberals moved only for their own ends, and home rule was a long way off; Moran quoted O'Brien's declaration that the stars would turn pink before the House of Lords veto was abolished.[143]

O'Brien was taunted in the House of Commons. As he got up to speak party MPs audibly whispered, 'He married a Jewess.'[144] He had to be restrained when Thomas Lundon suggested that his mother was related to the informer Pierce Nagle.[145] Canon Sheehan's novel *The Graves at Kilmorna* is often seen as prefiguring the Easter Rising; but his picture of a corrupt and Anglicised country ruled by a tyrannical party machine, where political dissent is punished by commercial boycott and a young idealist who rises above his ascendancy background and stands for election as an independent nationalist is met with mob violence, may also mourn O'Brienism.[146]

O'Brien's denunciations of the AOH actually helped to spread the order by publicising its existence and associating it with loyalty to the party leadership. In 1909–10 the AOH established a strong presence in Munster, including Cork, which O'Brien had boasted was 'free of the Molly pest'. The AOH were often called the 'Mollies', usually by their opponents. because of their descent from the 'Molly Maguires', the agrarian secret society active from the eighteen-thirties.

For the first time, Redmond attained national stature resembling that of Parnell. He is a more enigmatic figure than Dillon (who followed a consistent agenda), the florid O'Brien (whose incessant self-representations reveal recurring themes, even if their many distortions await detailed decoding), or the perverse Healy. Redmond was a reserved figure. The attitudes of his class (which exercised less influence on his ebullient brother) were heightened by childhood experience as go-between for his estranged parents, the sudden death of his first wife, and the experience of the Parnell split. His formal classical oratory imposed a distance between the private and the public man. His conversation was designedly noncommittal. His private life remained private; even his second wife's Protestantism escaped public mention in controversies on Catholic intolerance and mixed marriages. Long seclusions at Aghavannagh insulated him from Dublin politics, in contrast to Dillon in North Great George's Street. In a fissile and factionalised party he relied on a small core of confidants—his brother, Pat O'Brien, and J. J. Clancy—who have left little trace in the historical record. Even admirers within the wider party, such as Stephen Gwynn, complained of difficulty in gaining access to him; the Gwynns' lives are written from that remoter perspective with the hindsight of defeat.

Redmond was vulnerable to charges of incompetence and double-dealing because he was a conciliator, slow to commit himself. His negotiations with Dillon and O'Brien before Parnell's death can be seen in this light. He was probably always conservative, despite transatlantic appeals to separatism; if Dillon and Davitt thought of progressive alliance, his project was wider national reconciliation— between Ireland and Britain, rather than between nationalism and Liberalism (and also the unionist upper classes, which Davitt and Dillon saw as permanent enemies). The Redmondite project reconstructed by Paul Bew is conservative with regard to national and social questions, though it can be praised as reconciling creeds.

Redmond's position as leader of a volatile party encouraged reserve; he knew that unnecessary assertions of authority might renew the split. There was certainly indecision here; but he was not simply weak. His insistence on voicing his opposition to Healy's expulsion at the 1900 convention, after chairing the debate when Harrington was shouted down, suggests a desire to assert his own integrity. He committed himself sparingly but completely. Such were his decisions to support Parnell in 1880 and 1890, to support the war, and to step up his recruiting campaign as support fell away, declaring he would continue even if alone. The code of honour behind this commitment can be seen as self-indulgent or as heroic.

By 1911 what Griffith and O'Brien called weakness and cowardice seemed vindicated as prudence and foresight; Redmond had navigated the storms of faction and seemed about to complete Parnell's work. The unveiling of the Parnell statue early in 1911, while the Wolfe Tone project lay in chaos, symbolised the resurgence of constitutionalism. 'Where are Parnell's enemies now?' Redmond asked. Griffith remarked sourly that he need only have looked on the platform (at Dillon and Abraham) and was reduced to denouncing the statue as 'a pigeon-chested American' resembling Davitt more than Parnell.[147]

5

RESPONSIBILITIES
1911–14

O'Brien and Sinn Féin continued to act as gadflies, attacking the specific terms of the Home Rule Bill and the failure of the Irish Party to use the balance of power to secure concessions for Ireland on such matters as tax and a cattle embargo caused by foot-and-mouth disease; but most nationalists continued to accept the party's argument that the enactment of the principle of home rule must take precedence over 'sectional' grievances—including women's suffrage. The extension of state welfare also helped to strengthen the party's position, despite accusations of corruption, resistance to insurance contributions, and fears that a land tax supported by British radicals as an attack on British landlords might be extended to Irish tenant farmers.

Many of these attacks can be seen as attempts by Sinn Féin to strengthen its position in the new home rule parliament by emphasising its shortcomings. The main obstacle to home rule lay in threats of resistance by Ulster unionists, at first dismissed as opportunist bluff inspired by a Tory party anxious to paper over its divisions on tariff reform by a strong stance on the Union. It was pointed out that much unionist rhetoric echoed the arguments used against Catholic emancipation, and it was argued that defeat for the Home Rule Bill would amount to a declaration that the votes of Irish Catholics could be discounted by a unionist minority. Redmond offered safeguards for minority interests—though the effect of this was offset by militant Catholic campaigns against 'tolerance-proving', which in turn were fuelled by sectarian riots in Belfast.

The British government, however, was reluctant to overrule unionist resistance and from 1913 moved steadily towards a compromise based on partition. This provoked the appearance of the Irish Volunteers, whose leaders pledged allegiance to Redmond while in fact wishing to displace him, and attempts by O'Brien and Sinn Féin to use the partition issue to gain support. The majority of nationalists, however, were not prepared to sacrifice home rule by rejecting partition; Redmond was able to force the Volunteers to accept his leadership, and local elections in 1914 saw

Redmondite gains against the dissident factions. The situation was destabilised, however, by the Curragh Mutiny and the Larne and Howth gun-runnings, while the issue of the exact area of Ulster to be excluded continued to prevent an agreement.

⊷⟫⟨⊷

G riffith and the republican monthly *Irish Freedom,* founded in November 1910, claimed that the offer of home rule derived from British fear of Germany and a desire for alliance with the United States.[1] O'Brien and Sinn Féin claimed that they stood aside to give the Irish Party its chance, while denouncing members of the party as incompetents and seizing every opportunity to embarrass them, claiming that the balance of power should make the Liberal government do whatever they wanted.[2]

One such issue was the restriction on Irish cattle exports during an outbreak of foot-and-mouth disease in 1913–14. Most nationalists and some unionists claimed that Irish cattle were treated more harshly than British cattle. Some alleged that the minister, Walter Runciman, imposed the embargo to help the dead-meat trade of his family shipping business.[3] Griffith said it showed the need to develop trade with the Continent, especially Germany.[4] Only Patrick White and William Field among party MPs campaigned strongly on the issue;[5] David Sheehy praised the embargo as a 'blessing in disguise', because it damaged graziers.[6]

Separatists attacked the Irish Party's ambivalence towards the coronation of King George V in 1910, when the party issued a statement regretting that it could not participate, as Ireland had not yet received its freedom (though Redmond privately wished to go further), and towards a royal visit in July 1911, when some members of Dublin Corporation, led by the lord mayor, J. J. Farrell, proposed an address. The party leadership disowned Farrell, and his motion was defeated, but the Corporation allowed a citizens' committee, including William Martin Murphy and George Noble Plunkett (Count Plunkett), to decorate the streets.[7] Cork Corporation voted an address with the support of the AFIL, disquieting some O'Brienites.[8]

Griffithites and purists maintained relations with each other; Tom Clarke chaired a Sinn Féin branch.[9] With the Irish Party reviving, Sinn Féin organisation withering, and representation on Dublin Corporation eroded as Larkinite labour became a rival voice of working-class protest and municipal reform, every paper and activist was needed to counter the Anglicisation and empire loyalty that might follow home rule—or to prepare for a great war offering 'the best chance of freeing Ireland since Napoleonic times.'[10] Griffith predicted that in a long war, Britain would strip Ireland of food, producing a worse famine than the eighteen-forties, though he thought a war would in fact be short, decided by a naval battle.[11]

Sinn Féin called on the Irish Party to demand complete autonomy, including tariffs, and denounced parliamentarians as dupes of jingoism.[12] Griffith prepared ideologically for debate in an Irish parliament. (He never intended abstention to apply to a devolved parliament, which he saw as a local government body.) He edited Young Ireland texts, emphasising critiques of O'Connell's whig alliance.[13] Just as he addressed *The Resurrection of Hungary* to 'patriotic' constitutionalists, he told 'patriotic' unionists how they should 'logically' demand an equal share in the empire.[14] Later historians mistook this for his ideal.[15] (Griffith distinguished between 'Irish unionists', who thought the Union served Irish interests, and 'West British unionists', who gloried in Ireland's subjugation.)[16]

Redmond's triumph came in April 1912 when he returned to Dublin from the House of Commons, where the Home Rule Bill had been introduced, to a national convention. One speaker told critics, 'Put your amendments in your pockets.'[17] A long parliamentary struggle lay ahead; unionists would exploit uncertainty. The prime objective must be the enactment of home rule. Once a home rule parliament existed it would be almost impossible to abolish, strengthening future home rule governments as they bargained for extended powers, though unionists pointed out that minority safeguards could be circumvented if a home rule government with majority support threatened resignation—as the Natal government did in 1907, and as Stormont did in 1925.[18] Dillon's statement, much quoted against him, that they must not use the bill to extract concessions, because they had pledged their honour to the British government to accept it as final,[19] merely excluded amendments to the current bill.

C. J. Dolan attended, though supporting Sinn Féin.[20] James Brady endorsed Redmond and denounced Sinn Féin's incompetence.[21] Some members of Cork Corporation, led by the AFIL lord mayor, James Simcox, defied O'Brien, attended, and praised Redmond's leadership. Simcox resigned, and a Redmondite, Henry O'Shea, became mayor.[22]

The largest Dublin crowd since Parnell's funeral filled O'Connell Street, addressed from five separate platforms; Redmond's was beneath the Parnell statue. Pearse declared that they all knew he was a separatist (he had joined Sinn Féin in 1905 or 1906[23] and published an Irish-language separatist magazine) but he accepted the Home Rule Bill as a stepping-stone, though he warned: 'If we are cheated again there will be red war in Ireland.'[24]

Tom Kettle had promised a women's suffrage amendment but lost his nerve. The Sheehy-Skeffingtons resigned from the Young Ireland Branch.[25] Their position had already become precarious: Francis had joined two other YIBs, Frank Cruise O'Brien and W. E. G. Lloyd, in denouncing the Ancient Order of Hibernians as 'green Orangeism' and hoping that home rule would undermine clerical influence.[26]

Suffrage protesters were manhandled. The AOH broke up a suffrage meeting in the Phoenix Park.[27] Suffragist annoyance increased in February and May 1913 when United Kingdom suffrage bills were killed by Irish Party votes, and some party MPs voted for the forcible feeding of imprisoned women suffragists. Despite hypocritical talk of a 'free vote', an unofficial whip was applied. This reflected social and religious conservatism, exacerbated by suffragist militancy, a fear that since Asquith was anti-suffrage his defeat would weaken the government,[28] and concern that a Suffrage Bill might delay the Home Rule Bill. This was decisive for some Irish Party members who normally supported the demand. Even Griffith—who consistently supported suffrage, praised women suffragists for demanding it as a right rather than a concession,[29] and normally seized opportunities to embarrass the Irish Party—declared that 'sectional demands' must yield to the national interest.[30]

Seven Irish Party MPs voted for the May bill—Willie Redmond (more radical than his brother), Gwynn, Boland, Hazleton, and the mavericks Lynch, O'Shee, and White—for which they were criticised by allies.[31] Any political credit was reaped by the separatists, who denounced the manhandling of suffragists, and O'Brienites, whose support for the bill apparently reflected conviction. O'Brien (whose wife was anti-suffrage) and Healy had suffragist records, and the AFIL's one identifiable anti-suffrage MP, Eugene Crean, abstained.[32] Laurence Ginnell also supported the bill.[33]

O'Brienites and separatists recalled how the AOH 'employed ruffians to insult and beat women,'[34] but its political impact should not be overestimated. Indifference and hostility to suffragism were widespread. Moran combined vague support for limited suffrage with violent hostility to women suffragists, described in terms of long-established stereotypes of female 'soupers'[35] as ugly, patronising harridans. The Phoenix Park incident was commemorated with a rhyme, 'Skeffy in the Zoo', and a cartoon of Sheehy-Skeffington in the chimpanzee cage.[36] (The rhyme became popular, and Sheehy-Skeffington took pride in it.) Calls by suffragists for Derry city voters to oppose the 'Cat and Mouse Act'—as the Prisoners (Temporary Discharge for Health) Act (1913) was generally called—by rejecting the Liberals at the January 1913 by-election were badly received.[37]

Joe Devlin dismissed criticism of the financial provisions with the slogan 'Freedom before finance.' Ever since the eighteen-fifties, when Gladstone compensated for tariff reductions by raising indirect taxes (which hit Ireland, like other poor rural areas, particularly hard) and extended income tax to Ireland to offset famine loans, Ireland had paid more in tax than it received in services; and a popular explanation for industrial backwardness was that investment capital was drained by tax.[39] There had been campaigns by Irish MPs of all parties to lighten the tax load.[38] Such grievances received official backing from the Childers Report in 1896.

The financial situation changed with the Irish Land Act (1903) and the introduction of old age pensions in 1908. Ireland benefited disproportionately from pensions, because it had an unusually large elderly population—survivors of the densely populated Ireland of the eighteen-thirties and forties—and because the absence of official birth registration before 1864 facilitated false claims. There was ill-feeling over the administration of pensions, with allegations that eligible candidates were disqualified so as to save money, but they made a dramatic impression.[40]

When advocating federalism in 1910, J. L. Garvin argued that since Gladstone's time remedial legislation had given the nationalist population a financial interest in the British connection.[41] Kettle noted that the disappearance of the Irish financial surplus affected the case for home rule—though he argued that compensation for past plunder imposed no moral obligation.[42] Unionists seized on Kettle's statement, while Griffith, Moran and the O'Brienites—including Lord Dunraven—denounced him as incompetent.[43] The Irish Party praised benefits conferred by the Liberals when arguing against O'Brien in Ireland, then described economic woes to convince British audiences of the need for home rule.[44] *Irish Freedom* said that no country from which an annual revenue of £8 million was extorted could be poor,[45] while others, including J. J. Horgan, claimed that the deficit was caused by the exhaustion of Ireland's capacity to pay and that Treasury figures were not entirely reliable;[46] but after the National Insurance Act (1911) even Horgan admitted that Ireland was in deficit.[47]

The deficit was the principal reason for the rejection of the recommendation of the Primrose Committee for complete fiscal autonomy. The Home Secretary, Herbert Samuel—helped by the Irish Party's financial expert, J. J. Clancy[48]—instead proposed the annual transfer to Ireland of a fixed sum and allowing Ireland to increase (but not decrease) some indirect taxes. The scheme was to be renegotiated when Irish revenue and expenditure balanced.[49] The complexity of the scheme brought criticism from opportunist opponents and from those like Erskine Childers who advocated clear-cut fiscal autonomy, on the grounds that home rule could not be a final solution if it was unnecessarily cramped.[50]

Devlin considered the advantages of permanent British subsidy for Irish social welfare, and the deficit fanned conservative fears that home rule would bring land tax; but such fears did not cause significant political realignment. Long-established loyalties and hopes were reinforced by expectations that large sums could be saved through rationalising administration. Kettle and Horgan complained that the Union forced Ireland to copy British expenditure; subjection bred financial irresponsibility, but home rule would encourage self-reliance.[51] Bishop Kelly of Ross, Redmond's staunchest episcopal supporter, told an English journalist that the Irish were not materialistic, that in a frugal land of small farmers and rural industries, where life was simpler and prices lower, a five-shilling pension was too much.[52]

Calls for economies implied that the state apparatus was inflated by official patronage; but would this disappear under home rule, or continue with different recipients? O'Brien and Griffith attacked corruption in the Irish Party, linking it to Tory accusations of Liberal corruption over the Marconi affair, when J. J. Mooney sat on the committee that whitewashed ministerial share dealings, and O'Brienites abstained on votes of confidence.[53] Griffith wrote for the *Cork Free Press* on 'Placehunting in Irish politics', claiming that O'Connell's place-hunting caused the Famine and alleging that since Parnell died, the party had been corrupted by servility in London.[54] O'Brien denounced the growth of AOH patronage through the National Insurance Act.

The National Insurance Act was opposed by the Irish Catholic bishops and by the General Council of County Councils, and some Irish Party MPs wished to exclude

Ireland from it—as did Francis Sheehy-Skeffington.[55] But Devlin and John Dillon Nugent persuaded the party to accept it, with some of its provisions watered down.[56]

The National Insurance Act operated through 'approved societies' extending existing friendly societies; the AOH set up an Insurance Section, which became one of the largest societies in Ireland, reflected in increased membership for the parent body. The Insurance Section received government funds to build premises, which could double as AOH halls, important for social activities in rural areas.[57] Other societies linked with the party, notably the Irish National Foresters, also benefited. Many party supporters became administrators under the act.

Irish Freedom jeered at the applicants for administrative jobs—including former Sinn Féiners—adding that Irish contributions would go to Britain and that Lloyd George's slogan 'Ninepence for fourpence' should be 'A penny for twopence'.[58] Griffith saw the extension of state welfare by a British government as bribery, financed by taxes and the takeover of existing societies (though he said a free Ireland should have national insurance).[59] He complained that by subsidising 'maternity rather than matrimony' the Nonconformist conscience, which rejected Parnell, taxed the virtuous Irish for the British workingman's mistress. A correspondent protested that unmarried mothers should not be left in poverty and disgrace; Griffith called him a 'sentimental philanthropist'.[60] He predicted that new taxes would finance a conscript army to uphold the Anglo-French alliance.[61] Tensions between the AOH and trade unions—also registered as approved societies—increased as they competed for members.

O'Brien co-operated with the Tories in trying to prevent the AOH registering as an approved society.[62] He claimed that the AOH had prevented the party from forcing home rule immediately after abolition of the House of Lords veto. In fact the National Insurance Act had been put first in order to placate Liberals annoyed at sacrificing parliamentary time to home rule.[63]

O'Brien campaigned vehemently against the act.[64] He refused to register the AFIL or Sheehan's LLA as approved societies, forfeiting possible finance—and boosting P. J. Bradley's breakaway Cork LLA.[65] Separatists organised an Irish Ireland Benefit Society under the act;[66] but the Irish-American Alliance advertised itself as unconnected with the British Treasury.

More tangible corruption was exemplified by A. M. Sullivan (son of A. M. Sullivan of the *Nation*, first cousin of Healy's wife). In 1900 he was injured by UIL rioters while campaigning for Maurice Healy. By 1908 he had joined the UIL and argued that there was no harm in nationalists taking office if it did not affect their political views; he simultaneously attacked Matthias McDonnell Bodkin—an ex-MP and former *Freeman's Journal* contributor who was appointed a County Court judge in 1908—as a place-hunter.[67] In 1910 Sullivan conspicuously failed to support Healy and campaigned in North Tyrone, held by Redmond Barry, the Attorney-General for Ireland, as a Liberal.[68]

In mid-1911 Barry became Lord Chancellor. Sullivan hoped to secure the Solicitor-Generalship by taking the seat. He won the support of Hugh Gallagher, the

Strabane party boss; Muldoon believed that Sullivan had promised Gallagher's son a job and that Bishop Charles McHugh of Derry tacitly supported Sullivan.[69] The *Leader* endorsed Sullivan.[70] Party leaders were less enthusiastic: Sullivan had recently prosecuted some Hibernians. J. B. Armour, who sympathised with Sullivan, attributed party enmity to Sullivan's kinship with Healy.[71] Sullivan was not a crypto-Healyite: he was merely a careerist. Moreover, Healy and O'Brien were actively hostile to his candidacy.[72] Devlin destroyed Sullivan's hopes by threatening to order AOH members to boycott the poll.[73] Sullivan tried to get the Solicitor-Generalship as the price of withdrawal.[74]

The administration asked Redmond to support T. W. Russell in North Tyrone. Redmond agreed. Russell was seen by both unionists and nationalists as a shameless turncoat.[75] Devlin and J. D. Nugent protested but deferred to Redmond.[76] Some South Tyrone nationalists travelled to North Tyrone to oppose Russell, and his advocacy of temperance led nationalist publicans to vote against him. The Unionist candidate, E. C. Herdman, was a prominent local employer with numerous Catholic workers. Sullivan was persuaded to campaign for Russell,[77] reinforced by priests prophesying damnation for Catholics who supported Herdman, something gleefully quoted by unionist propagandists.[78]

Russell secured a majority of eighteen. (Barry's majority had been 132.) At least forty-five nationalists voted Unionist—probably more, for forty or fifty Protestant Liberals supported Russell.[79] Although Sullivan was made a serjeant-at-law (equivalent to senior counsel), the Benchers of King's Inns—mostly unionist, but including Tim Healy—refused to admit him to membership, traditionally conferred on serjeants.[80]

Suzanne Day connected defections of AFIL activists in 1911–12 with party offers of 'basketfuls of Jay-Payships [justiceships of the peace].'[81] Unionists spoke of graft and jobbery in local government as proof that a home rule government would appoint incompetent time-servers, bleed taxpayers white, then disintegrate through mismanagement. The behaviour of some local authorities supported aspects of this prediction, but the image of self-destructive kleptocracy sprang from prejudice about Catholic and Irish incapacity for self-discipline: Unionist local authorities were hardly immune from corruption. Farmers and tradesmen who supported the Irish Party were no more enthusiastic for increased rates than unionists, and party publicists showed that rates had not increased significantly since the establishment of nationalist-controlled county councils.[82] Indeed home rule was sometimes presented as an escape from a London regime of increasing taxation, exemplified by Lloyd George's 'People's Budget' and the rise of the Labour Party.[83]

Nevertheless many nationalists as well as unionists were dissatisfied. Bribes were often paid to secure appointments as dispensary doctors. Non-monetary influence was widespread. When the cousin of John O'Dowd MP applied for the matronship of Sligo Workhouse, O'Dowd canvassed for her; a rival's qualifications were brushed aside, because 'nurses would not like to be supervised by someone who might interfere in their work."[84] Republicans attributed influence-peddling to servility bred by foreign rule, leading people to seek favours they should claim as rights.[85]

Even the party leadership recognised the need for reform. In 1913 Jeremiah MacVeagh told Redmond that an amendment establishing competitive examinations for local government appointments to safeguard unionists was a blessing in disguise: vested local interests, otherwise too strong for a home rule government to tackle, could not resist it as the price of home rule. MacVeagh wanted this extended to railway companies that discriminated against Catholics.[86]

In official discussions in 1915 about the implementation of home rule, it was decided that a home rule government would assert central authority over local government (as done by post-independence Irish governments, though vested interests were not altogether eliminated). A government that had not gained power by revolution might have tackled vested interests less strongly.[87]

Suzanne Day's description of her experience as a Cork Poor Law guardian was recognised as accurate, though arch and patronising. It shows guardians as ignorant, irresponsible, more concerned with party politics than the hideous workhouse conditions, employing useless hangers-on, mobilising religious, political and personal slander against improvements, and encouraging farmers' belief that they would be beggared if a rate were struck to build a children's ward.[88] Despite atrocious slum conditions, Cork Corporation had built no housing since 1906, partly because the AFIL had problems with the Redmondite-inclined Town Tenants' Association, which helped to secure housing schemes elsewhere.[89] The AFIL had tried to combine D. D. Sheehan's record of housing agricultural labourers and O'Brien's hatred of the National Insurance Act in a campaign for subsidised housing for town labourers, demanding a housing grant paid as compensation for excluding Ireland from certain services—or from the whole of the National Insurance Act.[90]

Dublin Corporation's record was somewhat better, but its schemes catered for respectable workers while doing nothing for displaced slum-dwellers and awarded compensation to slum landlords (including several members of the Corporation) and to building contractors connected with the Corporation.[91] Publicans on the Corporation allegedly supported expensive inner-city schemes rather than cheaper developments on the outskirts, in order to keep customers.

Unionists liked to contrast housing conditions in Dublin with those in Belfast, though there were notorious slums and jerrybuilding in Belfast, and most of its housing stock dated from the city's extraordinary expansion in the nineteenth century, whereas Dublin's buildings were older. Apologists for Dublin Corporation also pointed out that while Belfast secured legislation to preserve its financial base by extending its boundaries, unionist-dominated middle-class suburbs used Dublin's services without paying city rates.[92]

Local government appointments also provoked accusations of religious discrimination. Unionist councils in Ulster gave few positions to Catholics, while nationalist councils employed many Protestants. Many of these, however, were hold-overs from the old grand juries, and southern Protestants, with their business interests and administrative and professional traditions, could less easily be ignored than northern Catholics, while at the same time a voluble body of Catholic opinion disapproved of Protestant appointments. Unionists publicised instances where Protestants and (before 1908) Queen's College graduates were rejected as such.[93]

During the first session of the Home Rule Bill, Protestants received positions from Leitrim Poor Law Guardians and Cavan County Council. These may have been intended to counter unionist arguments; and in County Leitrim local rivalries were also involved. Moran denounced them as slavishness and 'tolerance-proving'. Particular vitriol was reserved for the AOH representatives involved, including the Cavan County President, J. F. O'Hanlon, and West Cavan MP, Vincent Paul Kennedy (Redmond's cousin).[94] When the Listowel Guardians pointed to several Protestant appointments, Moran called this discrimination against Catholics, saying that if the Listowel Guardians were in the Balkans (where war had just broken out), 'the way they would fight is give jobs to the Turk.'[95]

Defensible actions drew suspicion. The MP for Sligo, Thomas Scanlan, was denounced for accepting a government brief in the inquiry into the sinking of the *Titanic*. Like another party activist, J. F. Harbinson, he was briefed by the National Seamen's and Firemen's Union before he knew that the government would pay the legal costs, and he tried unsuccessfully to bring out the role of human error.[96]

The Irish Party supported salaries for MPs (at £400 a year) but asked to be excluded. Party members knew they would be accused of corruption, and salaried MPs were less amenable to discipline. The ultra-reactionary P. A. Meehan opposed parliamentary salaries in principle.[97] A minority pointed out that salaries would help party finances and that Parliament would not let them single themselves out.[98] Parliament refused to exempt them; and O'Brien and Sinn Féin denounced them as hypocrites.

Frank Healy, O'Brienite president of the Irish-American Alliance, recalled the party linking O'Brien to the informer Pierce Nagle, who at least had not pledged himself against taking government money.[99] Party MPs countered accusations by giving fifty pounds each to the party fund; the wealthy Augustine Roche gave a hundred pounds.[100] P. A. Meehan gave his salary to the St Vincent de Paul Society. 'Four hundred pounds a year' became a powerful Sinn Féin propaganda weapon. J. P. Hayden later remarked that Free State TDs, who did not have to travel to London or live at London prices, received salaries of £350 a year in 1922,[101] an argument used against them by republicans.

The widely publicised Derry City by-election in January 1913 was won by the Presbyterian Liberal shirt-manufacturer David Lindsay Hogg, giving home-rulers seventeen Ulster seats against sixteen Unionists. (As parliamentary seats had not been redistributed since 1885, rural west Ulster—predominantly nationalist—was overrepresented compared with the industrial east.)[102] Ulster Liberals, despite their high profile, were few in number, as were Protestant home-rulers in general. James Hannay, William Hutcheson-Poe and the former MP Walter Kavanagh opposed the Church of Ireland Representative Body's resolution against home rule in 1912, but only five votes were cast against it, and only a small minority supported J. B. Armour in the Presbyterian General Assembly. The church assemblies were recognised as the principal deliberative bodies of the Protestant community.[103]

The two Ulster Liberal MPs, receiving less than a hundred Protestant votes apiece, were utterly dependent on Catholic nationalists. The few signs of a Liberal minority—notably in North Antrim, where Captain Jack White got ten local JPs and a county councillor to attend a 'Protestant Home Rule' meeting in Ballymoney—reflected resentment at the slowness of land purchase rather than incipient nationalism.[104]

Both nationalists and unionists thought many Presbyterian Liberals office-hunters. T. W. Russell was despised by both sides. Lord Pirrie's conversion was attributed to social ambition and resentment at his failure to become a Unionist MP.[105] Alice Milligan mourned J. B. Dougherty, the Presbyterian home-ruler who became Under-Secretary in 1907 and an MP in 1914, as a lost leader who abandoned principle for office. J. B. Armour, through his connection with Dougherty, was prominent in the Liberal patronage network. He praised Lord Aberdeen as an exemplary Presbyterian who appointed Presbyterian officials; Moran noted this 'honesty', adding that Presbyterians considered themselves persecuted unless given everything.[106] John Muldoon, an Ulster Catholic, telling Dillon how Aberdeen and Dougherty asked Redmond's son-in-law to yield his position as head of the Prison Service to a Presbyterian, suggested that 'the Protestants on our side are as bigoted as the others.'[107] Maurice Healy junior, an O'Brienite legal humorist, claimed that a Presbyterian unionist lawyer congratulated on his co-religionists' advancement replied, ''Tis not a religion any more—'tis a trade union.'[108]

Unionist leaders announced subscriptions to buy arms,[109] drilling began, and the anti-home rule campaign was launched at a rally on the outskirts of Belfast within days of the home rule rally in Dublin. Moran called for the arrest of Carson and said that if home rule were defeated, nationalists should retaliate with a boycott.[110]

Most nationalist spokesmen declared unionist threats of resistance to be bluff. Bluster about armed resistance to church disestablishment in 1868 was recalled, and the Ulster Volunteers were portrayed as a sham army of greybeards and adolescents, armed with wooden guns.[111] The nationalist strategy of presenting unionism as a continuation of the Orange Toryism that resisted Catholic emancipation and playing down its 'liberal unionist' component rested on actual, though selective, observation. (The Irish were not the only out-group attacked: some Tory propagandists pointed to Jewish Cabinet ministers as proof of the government's unnational character and claimed that Scottish and Welsh 'provincials' were less qualified to understand the situation than the English majority who voted Tory.)

Much unionist propaganda claimed, using arguments advanced against emancipation, that Catholic governments inevitably persecuted and that Catholic voters should be discounted, since they could not call their souls their own. Fringe groups recalled the massacres of 1641.[112] The ballad 'The Old Orange Flute' was composed by a separatist to parody images of Protestant martyrdom but soon became a genuine Orange song.[113]

Eoin MacNeill equated the loss of home rule with reversing emancipation,[114] while some Catholics retorted by denouncing Protestant proselytism and anti-Catholic discrimination and complaining that many Protestants privately read Connellan and Michael MacCarthy and saw Catholics as superstitious fools.[115] Even some Protestant nationalists reduced the relationship between Catholic clergy and laity to straightforward priestly tyranny—just as clericalist apologists idealised priestly paternalism: Griffith complained that a fictionalised account of the Parnell split by Hannay assumed that Catholics would submerge the country beneath the ocean if priests ordered them to do so.[116] Legitimate unionist concerns could thus be dismissed as lies used to justify past oppression, while wild claims, such as assertions that poverty in Belfast was confined to Catholic districts,[117] allowed nationalists to avoid Carson's subtler point that he did not expect formal persecution and feared not legislation but administration.

A Catholic-majority state would be unpalatable to Protestants; and many Catholics did look forward to engaging in discrimination. A foretaste of future events came in 1911–12 with a nationwide 'Literature Crusade' by Catholic groups. Vigilance Associations were formed in most large towns, with strong participation by the Catholic clergy and their associated network of confraternities, though the campaign was modelled on British purity crusades and was endorsed by some Protestants, including Lord Aberdeen.[118] Music-halls and newsagents were picketed, and 'immoral' English papers were seized and destroyed.[119] The crusade was not directly linked to political nationalism. A major target, Reynolds's News, published articles by T. P. O'Connor and Redmond;[120] Griffith at first supported the campaign but pulled out when he saw it as the vehicle of another potential 'Brass Band'.[121] Some secularist nationalists, such as Ryan and the Sheehy-Skeffingtons (whose stance contributed to their departure from the Young Ireland Branch), opposed the campaign because it included the suppression of ideas incompatible with Catholic orthodoxy.[122] Nevertheless, nationalist organisations such as the AOH and individuals like Lorcan Sherlock, Lord Mayor of Dublin—secretly part-owner of a music-hall[123]—were extensively involved.

The epicentre of the crusade was Limerick, notorious for the intimidation of Jews and Protestant evangelists. Much of its rhetoric was couched in nationalist terms, advocating the cleansing of Ireland from English pollution. One of its most distinctive products was the monthly *Catholic Bulletin,* which for the next quarter of a century argued that the mere existence of a separate Protestant or Anglo-Irish identity constituted an unacceptable claim to supremacy and a defiance of majority rule.[124]

R edmond's contacts with unionists made him reluctant to believe unionist threats anything more than irrational prejudice and bluff. If they were faced down, and if fighting was not sparked off by some hasty action, home rule would come into operation, and a few years would prove unionist fears baseless. Accordingly, he advised the government to take no action against Carson and his associates—though the *Freeman's Journal* publicly demanded prosecutions, and Kettle declared that the police should stand aside and let nationalists deal with the Ulster Volunteers and that unionist leaders should be hanged, shot, or imprisoned.[125] Nationalists pointed out that the Tories flirted with devolution in 1885, 1904, and 1910; how could threats of civil war be anything more than a political manoeuvre to exploit the Union as the only issue that united a party demoralised by defeat and divided on tariff reform? Griffith at first called the Ulster unionists catspaws who would find that success meant only home rule passed by Tories rather than Liberals, and after a few riots they would bow to necessity.[126] As matters developed, he decided that the Ulster Covenant was an application of Sinn Féin principles, called on nationalists to resist any attempt by British forces to suppress the Ulster Volunteers, and hoped the rank and file would sweep aside their humbugging leaders and participate in a nationwide Volunteer movement. Griffith liked to claim that only separatism, by removing the possibility of an appeal to higher authority, could reconcile the two Irish factions, and he called appeals by the Irish Party to British Liberalism as great a betrayal as unionist appeals to the Tories.[127]

Social ties between British politicians remained friendlier—though deteriorating—than rhetoric suggested. Carson privately complained that threats of resistance would not be taken seriously while colleagues maintained social relations with alleged revolutionaries and traitors;[128] but, with F. E. Smith, he took a libel brief for accused ministers during the Marconi scandal of 1913, passing up a chance to damage the government and renewing accusations of bluff.[129]

Seeing unionists as grabbers frightened for their loot, nationalists refused to believe they would wage civil war: they had too much to lose. Martyrdom, in their eyes, was a nationalist monopoly; unionists were incapable of self-sacrifice. Griffith recalled that Belfast supplied fewer Boer War recruits than Dublin.[130] To some extent this reflected ignorance of the populist unionism of the north; but even Ulster nationalist MPs refused to believe that people with whom they coexisted (though uneasily) would really plunge into civil war. Sam Young insisted that he had done business with these people all his life and their threats were nothing but bluff.[131] This argument was to resurface in 1914 when J. J. Clancy sent Asquith a memorandum detailing the disastrous consequences of armed resistance on Ulster commerce.[132] As the north moved towards conflict in mid-1914, business confidence declined, and credit tightened, some unionist businessmen had second thoughts but were not in control.[133]

A few Ulster nationalist MPs, notably Hugh Law and J. C. R. Lardner, privately suggested that unionists seemed determined but were told that Devlin, the best judge of the situation, said they were bluffing.[134]

In many respects the unionist campaign was indeed a triumph of well-organised publicity.[135] Despite talk of 'grim determination', even some unionists admitted that they could not defeat the British army. They calculated that no British government could shoot loyal subjects prepared to fight rather than lose the protection of the British constitution.[136] Carson was prepared to fight if it became inevitable, but memories of Asquith at the bar convinced him that the Prime Minister's nerve would break.[137]

Not all Tories and unionists were equally determined. Revolutionary socialists and militant suffragists, citing the Ulster Volunteers as precedent, caused disquiet,[138] and at one point the Fermanagh MP, Godfrey Fetherstonhaugh—a southern unionist—raised nationalist hopes by temporarily breaking ranks and calling for a settlement, to avoid bloodshed.[139]

The Ulster unionists failed to detach significant numbers of British Nonconformists from Liberalism, which the Nonconformists hoped would deliver further victories against Anglicanism once the Irish question was out of the way.[140] Joseph Hocking spoke of the evil effects of Catholicism but argued that by distinguishing religious from national allegiance, home rule offered Irish Protestants opportunities for evangelisation.[141] Harold Begbie declared Irish Catholicism a genuinely popular religion, free of the corruptions of Catholicism elsewhere.[142] An Irish ultra-Protestant declared that he would never believe anything these people said in future. He compared Begbie to commentators who opposed sending missionaries to China, adding that China was less idolatrous than Ireland.[143]

Lloyd George wanted to hold on to office as long as possible after the passing of home rule and to fight the next election on the British land question rather than the Union. He began a publicity campaign on the land, which caused the Tories sufficient concern to produce proposals for smallholdings (with Plunkett as an adviser).[144] It also allowed critics of the Irish Party to whip up fear that long-standing Liberal support for land taxes aimed at large landowners in Britain might hit peasant proprietors in Ireland.[145] The participation in Lloyd George's campaign of Irish Party MPs resident in Britain—notably Thomas Scanlan, Matthew Keating, and Richard McGhee—encouraged accusations of Liberal betrayal and Irish Party subservience,[146] while Dillon's speeches against Liberal foreign policy on Morocco and Persia were mocked as showing a lack of interest in his constituents.[147] These were not personal idiosyncrasies but attempts by the Irish Party to present itself to the British Liberal grass roots as part of a pan-British progressive alliance, portraying home rule as part of the wider struggle against privilege rather than a sectional measure advanced at the expense of social reform.

Devlin publicised sweated labour in the Ulster textile industry as proof that unionist agitation was a bosses' device to distract workers. Labour unionists like Mary Galwey, veteran organiser of mill-girls, accepted help even from the *Leader* in exposing exploitation.[148] The AOH was disingenuously presented as trying to do for urban workers what the Land League did in the countryside. Devlin pointed out that Protestant clergy and unionist politicians concerned about persecuted southern Protestants were conspicuously silent on sweating. (Connolly commented that unionists lacked the sense to point out that the AOH also persecuted Catholics who did not share their political views, and that Belfast Catholic clergy were as inactive in anti-sweating campaigns as their Protestant counterparts.)[149]

Attacks on sweating sometimes became attacks on Belfast's claim to industrial greatness, with sectarian and anti-industrial overtones. In 1886 the *Freeman's Journal* called the linen industry a curse to Ulster, as it encouraged exploitation by landlords.[150] At the time of the second Home Rule Bill the statistician T. Galloway Rigg argued that Belfast was no more prosperous than Dublin according to such measures as the number of professionals (inflated in Dublin by the administration and central law courts) and tax paid (many firms with head offices in Dublin paid tax there on operations throughout the country).[151] In 1911 Rigg used similar arguments in the *Leader* to prove Ulster prosperity illusory. He pointed out that every class in Belfast, except the working class, was equally numerous in Dublin, and explained away the fact that the Belfast working class was twice as numerous as its Dublin counterpart by pointing out that many Belfast workers were mercilessly sweated.[152] (The Dublin working class contained a larger proportion of casual labourers without regular employment—a major reason for differences in army recruiting rates.) Rigg also pointed to the large nationalist minority in Ulster and suggested that, far from 'marching to Cork,' as Craig boasted, the Ulster Volunteers would be hard put to secure Ulster—especially since Catholics were mostly fine, sturdy countrymen, while Protestants were predominantly stunted mill-hands and weedy urban wage-slaves.[153] Rigg produced a county-by-county analysis of the 1911 census 'proving' that, taking discrimination into account, Catholics were as active in business as Protestants and that in many counties Protestants had declined so drastically in the last fifty years that they could hardly do worse under home rule.[154]

Higher rates of 'illegitimate' births in Protestant Ulster and fraudulent insurance claims in Belfast were emphasised to dispute the unionist image of Protestant Ulster as a haven of industry, religion, and respect for law.[155] A Falls Road political activist and member of the Gaelic League, Father Richard Fullerton, compared Belfast to Babylon and the South Sea Bubble.[156] One contributor to the *Leader* called it a sham built on Protestant bankers lending money lodged by unenterprising southern Catholics on easy terms to northern co-religionists, while refusing credit to Catholic entrepreneurs.[157] The idea of Belfast as parasite recurred in response to the Belfast riots of July 1912, showing how minor incidents could trigger an avalanche of violence, embittering both sides and diminishing the chance of compromise.

The chain reaction began when the leadership of the Irish Party responded to the Agar-Robartes amendment. During the second reading of the Home Rule Bill, Agar-Robartes proposed that the four mainly unionist counties of Derry, Down, Antrim and Armagh be given the option of excluding themselves from the provisions of the bill. This was in effect the first serious proposal for the partition of Ireland. The Irish Party organised a rally in Maghera, County Derry, in July to demonstrate the depth of anti-partition feeling in the affected counties. J. B. Armour was invited to take the chair. When the amendment was defeated in Parliament it was decided to abandon the meeting, not least on the grounds that such a rally in a mixed area so close to 12 July could cause trouble. However, the publicans had stocked up in anticipation, and they prevailed on the local party leadership to go ahead.[158] Drunken Hibernians returning from the rally duly attacked a Protestant Sunday school excursion carrying Union Jacks at Castledawson.[159]

Castledawson sparked riots in Belfast. Thousands of Catholics were driven from their places of work, many being attacked and injured. Refugees fled Belfast on the Great Northern Railway, and a shipload also arrived in Dublin.[160] Pirrie ended expulsions at Harland and Wolff by threatening to close the yard until Catholic workers were reinstated; but most unionist employers connived at expulsions, from bigotry or from fear of the reaction of Protestant employees. Nationalists went beyond pointing out the influence of unionist rhetoric, suggesting that unionist leaders organised the riots.[161] Devlin claimed that the Sunday school excursion was deliberately provocative (in the eighteen-eighties, Sunday school excursions passed provocatively through nationalist areas as an assertion of supremacy),[162] though this hardly excused the Hibernians' violence or Devlin's claim that the incident was an unprovoked attack on peaceful Hibernians. Unionists called Devlin a liar; Carson and his lieutenants never publicly condemned the rioters.

Some nationalists realised that unionist leaders were trying to restrain their followers and that uncontrolled riots might alienate British opinion and allow military intervention; but they drew questionable conclusions. A Belfast nationalist argued that the best way to avert riots was to press on with home rule: if the bill were passed, unionist leaders would restrain their men so as to prepare for resistance, while if it collapsed, Orangemen would celebrate with a pogrom, as in 1886 and 1893. He did not explain what would happen afterwards.[163]

A. P. Wilson told Asquith that many respectable unionists joined the Ulster Volunteers to restrain the rougher element, and prevented an attack on the Ballymoney Protestant home rule meeting; but Wilson took this to mean that the Ulster Volunteers would not fight.[164]

Redmond and Devlin ordered nationalist parades in Ulster suspended until further notice.[165] Nonetheless, sporadic small-scale riots continued in Belfast, often sparked by soccer matches between the rival teams of Linfield and Celtic (Linfield being the Protestant and Celtic the Catholic club in Belfast).[166] Expelled Belfast Catholic workers appeared on Liberal platforms in Britain to counteract boycotted southern Protestants sent by the Irish Unionist Alliance.[167] Several nationalist areas organised boycotts of northern firms. In East Limerick the United Irish League sent Protestants a petition condemning the riots, hinting that they would be well advised to sign and contribute to the fund for distressed Belfast Catholics.[168] A meeting of the Irish Unionist Alliance in Limerick had been attacked some time previously; a *Times* reporter was told that large-scale violence in the north would start in Portadown, and any southern equivalent in Limerick.[169]

The *Leader* constantly published accounts of Orange violence and intimidation, past and present. To stereotypes of the braggadocio Carson, the sham army with wooden guns and the fat sweating Belfast industrialist was added the 'Bolt-Thrower', a gorilla-like figure attacking innocent Catholics or ridden by an exploiter while Carson led him by the nose,[170] a portrayal mirroring long-established British stereotypes of the Irish. Why should such creatures enjoy the benefits of home rule, retarding Gaelicisation, Catholicisation, and nationalist industrial development? Moran toyed with the idea that partition might remove the last obstacle to home rule, allowing nationalist Ireland to develop on 'native lines' and ultimately absorb an enfeebled north on its own terms.[171] He never developed this idea systematically; it coexisted in his writings with suggestions that the AOH should influence British opinion by parading Union Jacks and daring unionists to attack them,[172] and calls for the arrest of Carson and suppression of the Ulster Volunteers.

Arthur Clery also revived his partitionist proposals. The better-known views expressed in 1916–18 by Father Michael O'Flanagan (an occasional contributor to the *Leader*) were probably influenced by him. O'Flanagan urged that Ulster unionists not be subjugated by force but hoped they would come in freely when democracy revived in Ulster.[173] Clery saw them as a separate nationality, which might never come in.

Clery disliked both Ulster communities, once remarking that he never understood Ulster Protestants until he met an Ulster Catholic.[174] The main drawback of his plan was the fate of west Belfast. Clery distrusted Belfast Catholics—especially Devlin—as urban creatures suspiciously resembling the British working class. He predicted that as the only significant Catholic minority in the excluded area, too few to threaten its existence, they would be assimilated like the Irish in Glasgow, Liverpool, and Newcastle. In the same way the small southern Protestant minority would be absorbed.[175] He pointed out that while economic constraints encouraged landlords to come to terms, and a significant minority showed some sympathy for nationalism, neither condition applied to northern unionists. Clery claimed that northern unionists had a genuine national identity, while southern unionism was primarily a class phenomenon.[176]

Meanwhile, despite the continuing decline of the AFIL, the presence of O'Brienites in the House of Commons and the prominence of O'Brien and Healy attracted more attention—especially from British observers vaguely acquainted with the Irish situation—than its strength warranted.[177] O'Brien continued to call for a conference between unionists and nationalists. During the debate on the Home Rule Bill the AFIL proposed amendments to meet unionist fears. They advocated changes in the composition of the senate, a provision specifying that land purchase—a reserved service—should be completed within three years, to prevent the home rule government delaying it to force landlords to accept lower prices, and provision for an appeal to the British Parliament by Unionist MPs against legislation damaging to their interests. (Dillon called this 'a veto for ten Orangemen'; O'Brien complained that this was no way to describe the representatives of a million Irishmen.)[178]

AFIL MPs supported an unsuccessful attempt to get proportional representation for all seats in the lower house of the home rule parliament.[179] The government accepted this for the senate and for urban seats in the lower house. The AFIL also called for fiscal autonomy, claiming that once agreement by consent was reached, unionists would join in reforming the financial provisions. When their financial amendments were guillotined, AFIL MPs left the House of Commons and held a protest rally in Cork.[180]

O'Brien knew that some Ulster unionists would oppose any settlement, but selective recollections of divisions in the Ulster bloc, and the optimism of his Ulster contacts, led him to believe it possible to convert or neutralise moderate unionists by reasonable concessions; the hard core of fanatics would then be isolated and could be suppressed—by force if necessary. Alternatively, if unionists refused reasonable terms they would lose British support; the Liberals could go to the country, and their victory would deprive unionists of any pretext for further resistance.[181]

O'Brien used his allies' contacts among British politicians. Lord Dunraven and Moreton Frewen lobbied Bonar Law in the hope of winning him to a federalist compromise. Frewen supplied party propagandists with useful ammunition by signing the Ulster Covenant and talking of his intention of bringing over a force of English unionists when the fight began. His real concern was for the empire and his fellow-aristocrats: he thought Ulster 'not worth the bones of a Pomeranian puppy.'[182]

Frewen also approached Carson—helped by Carson's friendship with his niece, Ruby Frewen, who became Carson's second wife in 1914. Carson was exasperated by Frewen's habit of taking any mildly sympathetic remark as proof that Carson had turned federalist.[183]

The O'Brienites also lobbied right-wing federalist Liberals.[184] Healy had most impact through friendship with Lord Loreburn,[185] the Liberal Lord Chancellor, who had opposed a partition proposal in the Cabinet. Loreburn, who retired as Lord Chancellor in 1912 because of a heart condition, shared O'Brien's view that the offer of a reasonable compromise would make Ulster resistance impossible and bring settlement by consent. In March 1913 he told Healy:

A little incident, like the electric spark which can produce a chemical combination, may any day bring about the collapse of the Unionist anti-Home Rule
bubble, and if the atmosphere were national, a good many improvements
might by consent of all, be made in the Home Rule Bill.[186]

In July, Loreburn joined Dunraven and Grey in calling for a federal settlement.
O'Brien invited him, with other British federalists, to a demonstration in Cork.
Loreburn refused to join any Irish political demonstration, but on 11 September
1913 he published a letter urging settlement by consent. This was seen as evidence
that the Cabinet was weakening and encouraged the King in feeling he should act to
stave off bloodshed. O'Brien urged Redmond to meet Carson without preconditions.
Redmond ruled out any conference unless Carson accepted home rule.[187]

The party leaders, who knew he was involved with Loreburn,[188] were furious
at O'Brien's activities, which they saw as heartening unionists and weakening
Liberal will. O'Brien seemed genuinely oblivious. For years he claimed the Irish
Party was dominated by a sinister secret society of sectarian place-hunters—which
was regularly quoted by unionist propagandists; but he was puzzled that Carson
seemed to believe that Protestants would be persecuted under home rule.[189] Healy
had fewer illusions: during the Loreburn controversy he told his brother Maurice
that the conference O'Brien wanted could only end in partition.[190] Healy had more
contact with Ulster unionists than O'Brien, secluded in Mallow; this convinced him
that partition in some form was inevitable. Healy even grasped that an autonomous
parliament in the excluded area would make unification more difficult and that
nationalists should concentrate on having the excluded area run directly from
London;[191] but Healy, as O'Brien's political dependant, concealed these views.

Healy was not the only politician who thought partition inevitable. On
8 October 1913 at Dundee, Churchill hinted at compromise and suggested that an
election might be held between the enactment and the implementation of home
rule. A few days later Asquith had the first of three meetings with Bonar Law (the
others were on 6 November and 10 December). Law believed that Asquith had
committed himself to a four-county or six-county exclusion scheme.[192] Asquith did
not believe he was committed to anything so definite (which severely affected his
relations with Law) but approached Redmond and Dillon. Both reluctantly agreed
to an offer of partition but insisted that it be made at the last possible moment, lest
the Tories use it as a lever for further concessions. Sporadic contacts between
Liberals and Unionists continued into early 1914.

In a memorandum to the King in September 1913, Asquith hinted that while
the electorate had decided on home rule in 1910, partition had not been placed
before them and it was therefore arguable that a dissolution could be sought on the
issue. He told Bonar Law that, even if no dissolution took place on the issue, there
would probably be an election before home rule came into effect. Bonar Law replied
that by then a new Tory government would be in an impossible position. Asquith

thought this already the case: the defeat of home rule by threats of violence would trigger uncontrollable agitation in Ireland, while nationalists and radicals in Parliament made the new government's position unbearable.[193]

Asquith told colleagues that the summer or autumn of 1914 would be best for the next general election—annoying Lloyd George, who wanted more time to build up his land campaign and who knew that his position as second in the party would be endangered if the Liberals lost office. Many Liberals expected defeat.[194]

The Irish Party had another motive for refusing to take the Ulster problem seriously. If the Unionists won by threatening force, the logic of parliamentary nationalism would be undermined. In June 1913 O'Brien advanced compromise proposals, arguing that even a weak measure with unity was better than a stronger measure imposed by force on Ulster. Dillon responded that this meant a surrender to minority demands to remain top dog.[195] Eoin MacNeill compared the implicit threat of anti-Catholic pogroms to the behaviour of the Ottoman empire[196] and argued that abandoning home rule practically meant disfranchising Ireland (a proposal occasionally made by unionists). Tom Kettle's witticisms at the expense of the Ulster Volunteers—his polished, knowing tone insinuated confidence based on intimacy with high politics[197]—were fatally vulnerable to Pearse's retort that an Ulsterman with a gun was less ridiculous than a nationalist with only a pun.

The British government was indeed fearful of the consequences of resistance by the Ulster Volunteers, especially when unionist demands shifted from all-out opposition to the more defensible request that Ulster, with its unionist majority, should remain under London. During the drafting of the bill, Lloyd George and Churchill proposed partition to the Cabinet. Several ministers, including Asquith, looked on the proposal favourably, the main opposition coming from the Gladstonian veterans Loreburn and Morley and from Birrell, who did not want to complicate his relations with the party; and it was decided that Redmond should be informed that the government reserved the right to adopt it if necessary. Amendments at committee stage by the dissident Liberal Agar-Robartes[198] and at the third reading by Carson, proposing the exclusion of all nine counties of Ulster, were voted down. This seems to have been due in part to the large-scale amendments that would have been required (Samuel's financial scheme would have to be completely recast, further delaying the bill and helping the unionists to kill it by obstruction), and partly also because unionists had been slow to propose partition. The principal obstacle, however, was nationalist unwillingness.[199] Lloyd George, knowing he would be reported to Bonar Law, complained that they wanted compromise on partition but the Irish Party wouldn't allow it.[200]

Sinn Féin hinted that the government was moving towards partition, ostentatiously reassuring readers that the Irish Party was not degraded enough to accept it.[201] The *Cork Free Press* drew readers' attention to Churchill's sympathy for partition and predicted that Redmond would cave in, as on the budget and the cattle embargo.[202] Redmond urged the government to stand firm and made speeches intended to calm Protestant fears. Moran grumbled that the Land War ended with landlords bought out at fat prices, and now home rule might leave Protestants running the country.[203] At Limerick, Redmond declared: 'As an Irishman I am as proud of [the siege of] Derry as of [the siege of] Limerick,' while claiming that O'Brien's call for a conference would throw the principle of home rule back in the melting-pot, and declaring (prompted by Devlin) that 'the two-nation theory is to us an abomination and a blasphemy.'[204]

P. S. O'Hegarty claimed that Ulster unionists were unconverted because nationalists after Mitchel concentrated on winning English opinion.[205] *Irish Freedom* declared that money spent by the Irish Party on putting the case for home rule to British audiences would have been better spent evangelising Ulster.[206] The illusion was fostered by individual separatists from Ulster Protestant backgrounds. Purists often claimed that compromise and safeguards only helped Britain to play off Irishmen against one another. Given the obvious truth of separatism, watering down the full national demand confused the issue, and unionists were more likely to be converted by 'honest' separatists than by servile, treacherous constitutionalists.[207] This was encouraged by opportunist unionist praise of 'honest' separatists. *Irish Freedom* predicted that the Ulster Volunteers would soon fire on their erstwhile leaders;[208] and O'Hegarty, criticising the view that Belfast was un-Irish because materialist, said that ordinary unionists believed their political ideals as sincerely as nationalists, but argued that this made it easy to convert them.[209]

The purists' welcome for the Ulster Volunteers was not entirely based on such intangible hopes. They argued that the central sign of British domination was the denial to Irishmen of the citizen's right to bear arms. They spoke of martial virtues as antidotes to the beggarly whine of constitutionalism.[210] These ideas went back through Davis and Kickham, when the right to carry arms was a visible distinction between rulers and ruled in rural Ireland,[211] to the eighteenth-century Patriot tradition, and were kept alive by the distrust shown by the reluctance of the War Office to extend the Territorial Army to Ireland[212] and by nineteenth-century proclamations against the importing of arms. This prohibition was dropped by the Liberal government at the request of Redmond, who boasted that he had restored to Irishmen their rights as citizens; the result was the extensive use of firearms during elections in 1910–14.[213] These ideas also echoed contemporary European glorification of the warrior. Symbiosis between Irish and British versions of this cult is reflected in the use by some separatists of rifle clubs affiliated to the right-wing pro-conscription British National Service League.[214]

The Ulster Volunteers inspired thoughts of a nationalist counterpart—often centred on the AOH, whose activities, like those of their Orange counterparts, had military overtones; and AOH members often spoke of themselves as an embryonic national army.[215] Moran suggested that the drilling of the Hibernian Boys' Brigade might come in useful.[216] In mid-1913 a 'Midland Volunteer Force' in Athlone—in fact a stunt by a local journalist—attracted widespread attention.[217] The Irish Citizen Army had been established in Dublin as a workers' self-defence force in answer to police brutality during the 1913 strike, accompanied by comment about the contrast between the treatment of Carson and of Larkin.[218]

The immediate inspiration for the Irish Volunteers was an article by Eoin MacNeill, chosen as front man by a group associated with the IRB and Sinn Féin.[219] MacNeill's interpretation of the northern problem reflected memories of the Glens of Antrim, where even some Protestants shared the local Scottish and Gaelic culture.[220] MacNeill, like other Ulster nationalist commentators, was deceived by outwardly friendly relations between Catholics and Protestants in rural Ulster into ignoring concealed hatreds.[221] In 1905 he claimed that Ulster Protestants were no different from Catholic or nationalist neighbours but believed themselves different through English policy, aided by the folly of Ulster Catholics in responding violently to provocation. He suggested that nationalists should help to convert unionists by controlling Ulster nationalists.[222]

MacNeill declared that the Presbyterian and Episcopalian democracy were home-rulers, since they wished to hold Ulster against Britain. The decaying feudal elite, the only true 'unionists', had unleashed a democratic movement they could not control. Since the Tories admitted that the British army could not suppress the Volunteers of four counties, the rest of the country should organise Volunteers— ostensibly, as in 1782, to hold Ireland 'for the Empire'—to regain self-government and prosperity won by the Volunteers of 1782 and lost through their disbanding. He called Carson a secret home-ruler (thinking of his role in the 1896 anti-tax campaign) and predicted that Ulster Volunteers would march to Cork—cheered by Irish National Volunteers.[223]

A Provisional Committee was established; Griffith and Moran were invited to join, but preferred journalism. On 25 November the Irish Volunteers were launched in Dublin.[224] MacNeill declared himself a follower of Redmond, wishing to strengthen his hands, but his interpretation of the aims of the Irish Party was more radical than that held by the party, and around him stood separatists and IRB men. MacNeill treated Redmond as he suggested Carson was treating his British allies.[225]

The Home Rule Bill denied the right to raise an army. Unionists predicted that this was worthless and that an Irish parliament would form paramilitary forces;[226] Edward Martyn complained that Volunteers should have been established after home rule.[227] Now the prediction was coming true, and British Liberal opinion was affected.[228] MacNeill saw this as irrelevant, because he believed the Liberals would abandon home rule anyway.

The presence of two private armies raised the prospect of civil war. The Arms Proclamation was revived; the Irish Volunteers claimed that this showed a bias towards the Ulster Volunteers. Redmond and Devlin reacted with alarm and inde-cision; Dillon, always opposed to movements independent of the party, was more hostile.[229] Richard Hazleton—inspired by Redmond—attacked the Volunteers.[230] Lundon denounced the new movement.[231] Cork Hibernians attended an inaugural meeting, waited for MacNeill to call for three cheers for Carson (as usual), then rioted.[232]

Many Irish Party activists favoured the Volunteers. At the inaugural meeting in Dublin, Michael Davitt junior of the Young Ireland Branch pleaded for loyalty to Redmond (received with hostility by sections of the audience).[233] Dissidents—AFIL in Cork, McKeanites in Monaghan,[234] Sinn Féiners, and republican purists—flocked to the new movement. O'Brien at first tried to restrain his followers. P. J. O'Shaughnessy declared support,[235] and Willie Redmond endorsed the Volunteers.[236] Unable to stifle the new organisation, the party leadership ordered AOH and UIL members to join, swamp it by weight of numbers, and elect their own officers. The Volunteer leaders took counter-measures, declaring their movement 'above politics' and planning a national convention to elect a representative committee, whose mandate would rival the party's.[237]

Redmond did not see himself as an ordinary political leader. He was the national leader of the national organisation, which needed national unity to attain the national demand for home rule. As he often said when criticising the Gaelic League's 'non-political' refusal to declare itself nationalist, 'Nationality is above pol-itics.' Redmond's prestige had risen almost as high as Parnell's. The 1913 national collection was so successful (while state salaries for MPs diminished expenses) that there would be no collection in 1914, 'Home Rule Year'. While discontent was voiced over the foot-and-mouth epidemic, at the decision of the Cunard company to stop its liners calling at Cóbh (presented as British sabotage of Irish trade),[238] and anti-ranch agitation in parts of Connacht,[239] only the most embittered wanted the Irish Party to threaten the British government if this risked home rule.

The party was certainly damaged among the Dublin working class by the 1913 strike. The traditional practice of incorporating craft unions as a subordinate element in the nationalist coalition and of authority figures brokering disputes on the grounds that employers and workers shared common interests—the policy in whose name Griffith also attacked Larkin[240]—could not cope with a mass industrial union organising unskilled workers and an employers' organisation responding with a full-scale lock-out. Attempts at mediation by the eccentric William Field (the other Dublin 'Labour nationalist', J. P. Nannetti, being paralysed by illness)[241] and by middle-class intellectuals such as Stephen Gwynn[242] and Tom Kettle could not offset the pro-employer stance of conservatives such as W. F. Cotton (a director of Murphy's tram company) and the St Stephen's Green MP, P. J. Brady,[243] or the AOH counter-attack in the name of Catholicism and traditional labour relations (which produced widespread resignations in Dublin), or Redmond's perceived indifference and perceptions that the party did not use its influence to intervene. Some rural

MPs, including David Sheehy, denounced the strike leaders as godless syndicalists and dismissed any comparison with the Land War, with the *Cork Free Press* heading one such intervention 'The creature [Thomas] Lundon talks of religion and morality.' The *Cork Free Press* gloated over newspaper photographs of Redmond golfing during Dublin disturbances and claimed he could no longer speak publicly in Ireland's three largest cities,[244] though conservatism and relations with Murphy kept the AFIL leaders from taking up suggestions that they should opportunistically endorse the strikers.[245] (The *Cork Free Press* regularly attacked the Irish Party for allying with 'socialists, secularists, and land nationalisers.')[246] But the party's agrarian core supporters were relatively indifferent to urban problems and hostile to socialism.

The property-based local government franchise and Stephen 'the Stuffer' Hand, who oversaw party interests at annual register revisions, underpinned the Irish Party in the Dublin Corporation elections of January 1914, despite an increased Labour vote.[247] Enniskillen passed from unionist control after a gerrymander aimed at a 14-7 unionist majority produced a 14-7 result in favour of the Irish Party.[248]

In Cork, O'Brien's housing campaign failed to reverse the decline of the AFIL. The Irish Party won an absolute majority in the Corporation and purged opponents.[249] After self-pitying denunciations of 'dirty municipal politics',[250] O'Brien resigned his seat to secure a fresh mandate. Some Cork Redmondites believed he could be defeated, but Redmond held that the risk of violence was too great.[251] O'Brien appeared on nomination day with a retinue of MPs, councillors, and supporters; and 156 nomination papers, containing thousands of names, were submitted.[252] O'Brien's extravagant claims soon devalued whatever political capital he had gained.

Redmond was thus in a strong political position when claiming command of the Volunteers. He also had tactical justifications. Local Volunteers might trigger conflict. Bishop MacHugh, disregarding the prohibition on Ulster demonstrations, planned a huge anti-partition Volunteer review at Derry; the party leaders managed to stop him.[253] The *Irish Times* opportunistically praised the Volunteers as idealists resisting a corrupt political machine.[254] When Redmond threatened a rival force unless allowed to add 25 nominees to the 25-member Provisional Committee, which already contained several Redmondites, a majority accepted to prevent disruption. The minority, though embittered, stayed on the committee. Tom Clarke accused Bulmer Hobson of being paid by the Castle; they never spoke again.[255] In the event, many of Redmond's nominees rarely attended, and while the Provisional Committee saw angry quarrels between Redmondites and separatists, its administration remained under members of the old committee.[256]

The *Cork Free Press* lamented that 'naïve idealists' were no match for hardened intriguers and predicted that the Volunteers would be corrupted and destroyed by party politics.[257] In County Cork the Volunteers split, with Bantry and Charleville O'Brienites forming their own Volunteers, alleging that local groups were dominated by Redmondites,[258] while the Fermoy Volunteers fought for Redmondites in an election riot.[259]

In the House of Commons the party leadership was forced towards partition as the price of peace. Having suggested to unionists that they should accept 'home rule within home rule' and an Ulster veto, Asquith told Redmond he would repeat these proposals publicly so that unionists would be placed in the wrong by refusing. He clearly intended to go further and was 'softening up' Redmond. On 10 February he announced that the government would soon make proposals, producing wide-spread expectations of the exclusion of Ulster.[260] On 27 February and 2 March, Asquith and Lloyd George privately proposed to the leaders of the Irish Party that four counties with unionist majorities should opt out for three years. Redmond accepted this as the last word, with the bill unchanged if it were rejected; within a few days he had to agree an extension to six years, thus annoying Devlin, who had difficulty persuading Ulster nationalists to accept three.[261]

Negotiations hitherto were conducted by Redmond, Dillon, and T. P. O'Connor, with Devlin brought in when compromise could not be avoided, rank-and-file MPs being kept in the dark. Now Redmond hinted that partition might be unavoidable. Arthur Lynch told MPs to 'reject the abomination,' but they were soothed by exhortations from the chief whip, Pat O'Brien, to trust the leadership.[262] Lynch, whose belief in a united nation of Catholics and Protestants was encouraged by fear that a homogeneous state would have no room for heterodox people like himself,[263] lacked the political weight necessary to challenge the new policy; privately he decided that the weakness of Redmond and Asquith would defeat home rule.[264]

Since Conservatives were certain to win one of the two elections in the six-year exclusion period, and if the act were amended to make exclusion permanent the Liberals would be unlikely to plunge back into controversy, the new concession amounted to permanent partition.[265] It is not clear how far the leaders of the Irish Party realised the full implications of their agreement; they may have hoped—as Redmond did—that the north would come in once it saw home rule in operation, or that unionists would refuse. In fact, by admitting that compromise was necessary, the government precluded a return to the previous position.

When Asquith announced his proposal on 9 March, Carson rejected 'a sentence of death with a stay of execution for six years,' and Bonar Law offered to abide by a British referendum. Protests by local Irish Party activists were squashed; as Gorey Poor Law Guardians rescinded a hastily passed anti-partition resolution, a Sinn Féin member, Seán Etchingham, protested that not only Redmond but the whole nation lacked backbone.[266]

As the government moved towards temporary exclusion for six counties, ill-considered moves to send soldiers north produced the Curragh Mutiny. The War Office ordered troops based in the Curragh to prepare to move north. The purpose was the protection of arms depots from loyalists. Fifty-six officers, under the leadership of Major-General Sir Hubert Gough, offered to resign rather than move against Ulster. The government fudged the issue, and the Great War a few months later finally removed it from view. In the meantime, however, attempts to settle the crisis led some ministers, without notifying their colleagues, to guarantee that the army would not enforce home rule. The government distanced itself from the guarantee, but separatist commentators spoke of collusion. Moran claimed the mutiny would strengthen British determination to pass the bill.[267] It had this effect on some Labour and radical activists—even Neil Primrose toured Britain demanding action against the mutineers; but in effect it deprived the government of the ability to threaten a military response. The Curragh Mutiny strengthened the argument that Ireland must rely on its own armed strength; Dillon told Blunt that it convinced him of the need for the Volunteers.[268]

Dissident nationalist groups protested against partition. Attempts were made to organise a Dublin anti-partition rally uniting Labour, AFIL, Sinn Féin, and the Irish-American Alliance. These broke down[269] because Sinn Féin and Labour did not want to associate with O'Brien. Though some supporters, notably Tadhg Barry and Frank Healy, held pro-labour views, O'Brien hated and feared socialists even more than Healy did,[270] and his opposition to the 1913 strike probably increased Labour disinclination. Sinn Féin and Labour protested in Dublin, while O'Brien rallied the AFIL in Cork.[271]

Griffith put forward proposals including extra urban representation for Ulster, competitive examinations for civil service positions, and an Ulster veto over certain types of taxes and measures affecting the linen industry. In return, Sinn Féin wanted unionists to accept complete financial autonomy for Ireland.[272] At some level this 'compromise' was sincere. Griffith insisted on proposing that the Irish parliament meet alternately in Dublin and Belfast, despite opposition from William Cosgrave.[273] But it is hard to think that acceptance was seriously expected. It would have broken down when unionists opposed the tariffs that Griffith's demand for financial autonomy was intended to allow; Sinn Féin had no mandate; and the proposal was drawn up without reference to the unionists, who were expected to accept it without criticism. Its effect was to prepare for Sinn Féin to attribute partition to the Irish Party's incompetence and to claim they could have prevented it. Griffith declared that if any part of Ulster were allowed to secede—even with the consent of the nationalist minority in the excluded area—or offered the right of secession and chose not to exercise it, Ireland would deny its historical identity and forfeit any claim to self-government.[274]

AFIL MPs abstained on the second and third readings of the last circuit of the Home Rule Bill in protest against partition and joined a revolt of conservative Liberals on Lloyd George's 1914 budget to cut the government majority on one division to twenty-three.[275] The budget had been incompetently drafted, and Lloyd George had to revise it and make concessions to critics, severely affecting his preparations for the next election.[276]

O'Brien's position that no home rule at all was better than partition[277] contributed to the loss of the last major AFIL local government bastion, Cork County Council, in the local elections of 4 June 1914, ten days after the third reading.[278] At the lower level of rural and urban district councils, the AFIL held its ground and even gained slightly.[279] The dissident group was held together by local factional allegiances, rather than O'Brien's charisma as alternative Leader of the Irish Race.

Illustrating the separatist view of the Ulster Volunteers as potential allies, Dr Pat McCartan lent his car for the transporting of arms smuggled into Larne on the night of 24/25 April.[280] The Cabinet dithered and then, influenced by Irish Party leaders, by fear that arrests might spark general conflict, and by the doubtful loyalty of the armed forces, took no action. There were rumours that the government colluded with the gun-runners. Moran asserted for several weeks that the gun-running was a sham and that no guns were landed.[281] Meanwhile the hard core of the Provisional Committee of the Irish Volunteers prepared their own gun-running.

On 23 June the government introduced an amending bill in the House of Lords excluding six counties for six years; the House of Lords amended it to exclude nine counties permanently. On 21–24 July, with the amending bill about to be debated in the House of Commons, Redmond, Dillon, Carson, Craig, Asquith, Lloyd George, Bonar Law and Lord Lansdowne met at Buckingham Palace. (O'Brien protested furiously at his exclusion.) Asquith told Bonar Law that the conference, by admitting the need to compromise, ruled out a return to the status quo—whatever Redmond might think—and that if it broke down the King would be entitled to demand a general election on partition as soon as the bill became law, though he rejected Bonar Law's response that the King should refuse to sign unless an election were first held on home rule.

By now the Irish Party leaders tacitly accepted partition, but the conference became deadlocked over the area to be excluded. Both sides felt (or claimed) that their supporters would not stand many more concessions. In informal contacts before the conference, the government offered Carson the four counties except for south Armagh, most of County Tyrone and parts of Counties Donegal and Monaghan if he would give up a quarter of County Tyrone—presumably mid-Tyrone, with its nationalist majority. Carson replied that his followers would reject such an arrangement.[282] He declared that if nationalists acted as statesmen and offered the 'clean cut' of nine counties, Irish interdependence and the large nationalist minority in the excluded area might bring eventual reunification, whereas any attempt to coerce Ulster would make unity impossible for a lifetime. Redmond and Dillon agreed but said if they made such an offer their supporters would repudiate them.[283] Asquith lamented that both Carson and Redmond incomprehensibly refused to divide County Tyrone while declaring that they understood each other perfectly.[284]

As the conference developed, Liberal backbenchers denounced talk of further concessions, though some observers thought they would be restrained by the growing Balkan crisis.[285]

Redmond and Dillon were summoned to Downing Street on 25 July and persuaded to agree to permanent exclusion for four counties as positively the last offer to the unionists. The proposal was immediately approved by the Cabinet; but before it could be put to the unionists, events in Ireland intervened.[286] On the morning of 26 July the *Asgard* landed guns and ammunition at Howth. Irish Volunteers who mobilised to receive them were met on the way back by police and soldiers under Assistant Commissioner David Harrel. After several injuries from police clubs and bayonets and the firing of revolver shots by individual volunteers, it became clear that Volunteers would resist and that the police were not entirely reliable. While government forces hesitated and Volunteer officers argued with Harrel, most of the Volunteers slipped away. As the soldiers marched empty-handed through Dublin they were followed by a taunting, stone-throwing crowd. At Bachelor's Walk they fired into the crowd. Four were killed, and many more injured.[287]

There was outrage in nationalist Ireland. No attempt had been made to disarm Ulster Volunteers parading with smuggled guns.[288] In Parliament, Redmond denounced the shootings; Dillon told C. P. Scott, the influential editor of the *Manchester Guardian,* that party MPs could not now support compromise.[289] But the party soon began to back down; Unionists, O'Brienites and Sinn Féiners protested that it was preserving relations with the government by scapegoating Harrel, when Dougherty, Birrell and Aberdeen were equally responsible.[290]

'Long John' O'Connor and Tom Kettle were in Belgium arranging gun-running on behalf of the Redmondite section of the Provisional Committee, with the guns to be landed on the County Cork coast.[291] A row broke out in the committee because J. D. Nugent sent sixty Howth guns to his native south Armagh.[292] Pearse complained privately that Redmondites wanted to arm the Ulster AOH; Pearse and his associates thought the guns should be kept for the real enemy—Britain.[293] Ireland seemed on the verge of civil war.

Then the First World War broke out.

6

UNLIMITED LIABILITY
1914–16

Redmond's support for the war, after consulting only a few intimates such as J. P. Hayden (Dillon and Devlin being in Ireland),[1] was later condemned as sentimental folly. Margot Asquith's claim to have been responsible is often quoted.[2] Separatists argued that he should have returned to Ireland, demanded immediate home rule, then stayed out of the war. Maurice Moore, who sided with Redmond in the Volunteer split, urged him to tell reservists not to report for duty until instructed.[3] Redmond's declaration that staying out would have forfeited Ireland's soul—reminiscent of separatist attitudes to their own beliefs—could be seen as confirming this view.[4]

Redmond supported Britain and its allies and believed that Ireland owed a moral debt to Britain for home rule; but his decision did not merely reflect personal prejudice. Just as it was never clear whether nationalists saw home rule as a final settlement or a lever for separation, there had always been ambiguity about whether home rule Ireland would support Britain in a war. Needing to decide immediately, Redmond took responsibility as leader.

His critics, especially those writing after nationalists definitively abandoned home rule, assume that with its army diverted to the Continent, Britain must have conceded whatever Redmond demanded. This forgets the Ulster Volunteers; and since the war was expected to be short, might civil war not end with victorious Britain intervening in favour of those whose prophecies had been vindicated? This might not have mattered had Redmond hoped to secure independence by assisting in a German victory, as Griffith and Casement desired;[5] but even a victorious Germany might not be able to dictate terms on a position so strategically important to Britain. With such disparity in military strength, which was acknowledged—even exaggerated—by most nationalists, might not a rebellious Ireland obtain worse rather than better treatment?

These, though not Redmond's primary considerations, help to explain why so many nationalists accepted his policy as the only one possible under the circumstances. Even Redmond's personal belief that, apart from home rule, the Allied cause was just and that Germany represented aggressive militarism can be seen as a reasonable stance rather than craven acceptance of British propaganda. Retrospective knowledge of how the war developed and revulsion at the Hun-hatred and romanticising of war that pervade many of Redmond's speeches obscure what was to be said for this view.[6]

Although the German invasion of Belgium was the pretext for intervention by a British government already committed to France, aggression had been committed. 'Little Catholic Belgium', though remote from Ireland, was a favourite with Irish Catholic opinion-formers, who idealised its governing Catholic Party as evidence that Catholicism was compatible with good government. This, and links with Belgium through his order, may explain why in 1914 the Jesuit Timothy Corcoran—later the mainstay of the *Catholic Bulletin*—published sonnets on the rape of Belgium and told J. J. Horgan that an Irish expeditionary force should be sent, provided an upper limit was set on its numbers.[7]

The Redmonds had personal links with Belgium; John's niece continued a tra-dition of Redmond women joining the Irish convent at Ypres, which moved to Ireland because of the war.[8] Tom Kettle, gun-running in Belgium on his mission, was deeply affected by the destruction he saw.[9] The arms acquired by Kettle and O'Connor were detained in Belgium; the Irish Party handed them over to the Belgian government. The Ulster Volunteers refused suggestions that its rifles also should go to Belgium.[10]

Devlin and Dillon were at first reluctant to commit themselves, and for a while after Redmond's speech the *Irish News* of Belfast warned against hasty commitment to war.[11] But neither could propose any alternative. Dillon, in line with Radical views on foreign policy, held the British government partly responsible, because past contacts encouraged Russia and France to act recklessly, expecting British support; but he believed the government could not now abandon its allies and that, having committed themselves to the empire, Irish nationalists had to support it.[12]

Not all lovers of freedom saw Germany as the greatest danger to free insti-tutions. Some Radicals who distrusted Britain's alignment with the reactionary Russian monarchy attributed German actions to fear of Russia. Russian strength was overestimated; and the fate of the Russian army and monarchy later brought forgetfulness of how in 1914 many anti-war radicals, such as Sheehy-Skeffington[13] and to some extent Connolly, believed that Britain and France had become agents of Russian aggression and that Allied victory would strengthen Tsarist despotism at the expense of the relatively advanced Germans.[14] Some predicted that Britain and France, after beating Germany, would fight Russia.[15] Some separatists founded a short-lived Irish Neutrality League, but the identity of those advocating neutrality, and the absence of any means of enforcing it, left even sympathetic observers convinced that 'neutrality' simply meant hostility to Britain.[16]

Redmond's initial statement merely offered the Volunteers for home defence in Ireland—jointly with the Ulster Volunteers—to free British troops, and while relations between Redmondites and separatists on the Provisional Committee of the Volunteers deteriorated further, there was no immediate split. MacNeill, still hopeful, pointed out that Redmond's speech in the House of Commons was compatible with the Volunteers' commitment to defend Ireland. He dismissed Carson as a place-hunter because he had not taken advantage of the war to demand independence.[17]

Redmond, while appealing for the Irish Volunteers and the Ulster Volunteers to work together, pressed the government to formally enact home rule.[18] German-owned shops were attacked in Dublin,[19] the *Freeman's Journal* took a pro-recruiting stance, and individual MPs called for recruits. Arthur Lynch made a speech to this effect in his constituency. Lynch was a Francophile who had developed a distrust of Germany while studying there. A few months previously, during the last circuit of the Home Rule Bill, he had declared that if home rule were granted he would fight for the empire if war came. He actively called for war in August, and tried to enlist but was turned down because of his Boer War record.[20]

The *Cork Free Press* declared during the Agadir Crisis of 1913 that if war broke out Ireland must support Britain—though it also taunted 'Billy the Bould Militia Boy' (Willie Redmond) for declaring that the Home Rule Bill reconciled him to the empire, and recalled his youthful declaration that he hoped to see Cossacks stabling their horses in the Palace of Westminster.[21]

Within days of Lynch's speech, O'Brien and Healy called for recruits at a joint meeting with Cork unionists. Local Redmondites stayed away.[22] Some separatists urged O'Brien to lead resistance to the war, but the logic of conciliation, and links with France through his wife's family, led O'Brien to his decision.[23] He called for home rule to be left unratified during the war (which was expected to be short) and for the Volunteers to be placed under the War Office. This would humiliate Redmond and remove the Volunteers from his control. O'Brien and Healy met the Secretary for War, Field-Marshal Kitchener, to express their views; this may account for some suspicion when Redmond proved less unconditionally co-operative.[24]

Redmond would have found it difficult not to call for recruits had he wished to draw back. On 18 September the Home Rule Bill, accompanied by the Suspensory Bill, suspending its operation for one year or the duration of the war, received the royal assent at a special session of Parliament, despite complaints by Unionists that this violated all-party agreement to suspend controversial measures. They were not consoled by Asquith's announcement that under no circumstances would Ulster be coerced. Party leaders had already tacitly accepted this, but its explicit statement was later used to support claims that they had been outwitted and betrayed.[25]

Irish Party MPs returned to Ireland amid euphoria at the long-awaited enactment of home rule. It is often suggested that Redmond's speech at Woodenbridge, County Wicklow, was arbitrary and unexpected; this reflects separatist shock when Redmond actually did the unthinkable. He had already obtained the party's approval for recruitment, and issued a declaration the day the bill became law. He meant to inaugurate the new policy at a major rally, but while travelling to Aghavannagh on Sunday 20 September he was asked to inspect local Volunteers at Woodenbridge. There he declared that it would shame Ireland and its martial traditions if Irishmen refused to fight in defence of 'right, of freedom and religion.'[26] On 23 September, Asquith spoke in Dublin with Redmond, Dillon, and Devlin. He called Irish recruits 'the free gift of a free people' and was understood to promise that the government would arm and train the Volunteers and organise the three divisions containing Irishmen (the 10th, the newly formed 16th, and the 36th, recruited from the Ulster Volunteers) into an Irish corps.[27]

The day before the Asquith meeting, MacNeill, Pearse and their associates on the Provisional Committee declared that Redmond had violated Volunteer principles, his nominees were no longer members of the committee, and Volunteers would defend Ireland against any assault on its liberties.[28] MacNeill kept the weekly *Irish Volunteer* and about 10,000 members, including a disproportionate number of activists—large enough to be significant, small enough to be manipulated by IRB infiltrators. About 150,000 followed Redmond as the National Volunteers, but they lacked experienced officers. Reservists and old soldiers had gone to the front, and many committed Redmondites had enlisted. A Volunteer Executive was established and a weekly, the *National Volunteer,* published from the *Freeman's Journal* office.

Irish-American activists, traditionally more hostile to Britain and used to co-operating with German-Americans, went overwhelmingly against Redmond. Only a few activists, led by the former Land Leaguer Patrick Egan, remained loyal to Redmond, and messengers sent to reorganise the American UIL met little success.[29] Middle-class Irish America remained sympathetic to Redmond but saw no particular need to contribute to his support. The Irish Party thus lost an important source of funds, while Clan na Gael, around John Devoy's *Gaelic American,* continued to assist separatists in Ireland. Devoy's co-operation with German agents laid the basis for claims by the Irish Party that the separatist movement was run on German gold.

Pro-British and Redmondite sentiment swept Ireland, influenced by the granting of home rule, by the Irish newspapers' propagation of British war hysteria, and perhaps by relief at the postponement of civil war. It surprised many observers who remembered the Boer War—or the enthusiasm surrounding the Volunteers and the atmosphere after Bachelor's Walk. As the great majority of County Kerry Volunteers sided with Redmond, Desmond Fitzgerald and his friends realised that Redmond and not the separatist Volunteer organisers represented Irish opinion. They contemplated the possible disappearance of Irish nationality as they saw it.[30]

Some months later, Arthur Clery (who supported MacNeill) wrote that for centuries Ireland had retreated from one defence line to another. Independent statehood had been crushed, language given up; now instinctive hostility to Britain had evaporated. Catholicism was the last citadel. Clery asked: 'Could our religion be crushed?' Some nationalist newspapers echoed British criticisms of Pope Benedict XV as pro-German, unthinkable a few years earlier. Clery feared that Ireland might fall into schism while—like England under King Henry VIII—remaining superficially Catholic. Ireland might see anti-clerical laws like those of France; he depicted Father Finlay deported as a Jesuit with only John McKean protesting, and Devlin reading letters from English Nonconformists to a joint Orange and Green meeting in Belfast and declaring he would no longer allow an Italian priest to separate Irishmen of different faiths.[31]

Clery was notoriously pessimistic (shortly before the Easter Rising he predicted a decade of Anglicisation before a last desperate attempt to revive Irish identity in 1925).[32] But his fears were shared by observers more sympathetic to the Irish Party. A commentator—possibly Patrick Hogan, future Cumann na nGaedheal Minister for Agriculture—wrote in a new magazine associated with the Young Ireland Branch that Ireland must accept partition, because it could not have home rule without it and had abandoned so much traditional Anglophobia that without home rule it would be irretrievably Anglicised.[33] Even after the Rising, when Dillon realised that separatists might destroy the party, he thought they could never replace it; T. P. O'Connor spoke of a return to the politics of the eighteen-seventies.[34] If such reflections occurred even among Redmondites it is not surprising that Seán Mac Diarmada told Tralee Irish Volunteers that Irish nationality was dying and that only blood sacrifice could revive it.[35]

In rural areas, rising prices heightened war euphoria. There was a rush to profit, reflecting the expectation of a short war; even in-calf heifers were exported for slaughter.[36] Yet war euphoria had limits. It reflected long-accumulated expectations; now the Irish Party faced anti-climax and the burdens of war without the resources of a home rule government. P. S. O'Hegarty later remarked that most nationalists' support for Britain extended only to selling cattle and cheering from a safe distance.[37] Rising prices fostered urban discontent—especially since war prices were not offset by increased employment and high wages in expanding war industries, as in Belfast and in British industrial cities.

Moran alleged that Carson's threats of civil war had led Germany to expect British non-intervention,[38] and that Ireland owed no moral debt and must follow self-interest.[39] He endorsed Redmond's initial support, arguing that nationalists accepted the empire as inevitable and must take the consequences, but opposed overseas service, arguing that Ireland had been depopulated by British policy. It could best contribute by increased food production; perhaps, as an absolute maximum, it might spare 20,000 men.[40] Moran denounced the Woodenbridge speech, though remaining a critical Redmondite for lack of alternatives.[41] As war enthusiasm spread, he complained that those who denounced his 'Collar the King' policy now adopted it, without his nuances.[42]

The *Leader* depicted farmers exporting crops and farm animals, discovering too late that they could not eat paper money.[43] A satirical rhymester suggested that the Volunteers should force 'Mickey Rustyspade' and 'Patsy Pennywise' to till their land.[44] Home truths were told about farmers' treatment of their children and their labourers. Contributors, more enthusiastic than experienced, attributed a long-continuing decline in wheat acreage to stupidity. Moran predicted that food prices would remain high after the war, so farmers should adopt tillage immediately (thus employing more labour).[45] This reflected a consciousness among Moran's white-collar contributors that the Dublin poor were going hungry and that a long war might place them in the same situation. As winter came and the Western Front stagnated, Moran recalled food exports during the Famine.[46]

Redmond predicted that after sharing 'the bloody sacrament of the battlefield,' unionists and nationalists would avert partition by consent. Many prominent south-ern unionists joined the National Volunteers, or shared recruiting platforms with nationalists. In mid-1915 J. H. Bernard, Anglican Bishop of Ossory, declared that after fighting side by side it would be intolerable for Irishmen to turn against one another. Bernard's elevation to the archdiocese of Dublin was taken as showing that he represented a significant body of Church of Ireland opinion.[47] When Redmond proposed a joint recruiting meeting with Carson in Newry, Archbishop Crozier of Armagh, active in the Ulster agitation, agreed to appear; Carson did not.[48]

The willingness of some southern unionist leaders to seek compromise (rank-and-file activists were less moderate) reflected an awareness that home rule for the south was inevitable. No such constraint affected northern unionists. Individuals may have been influenced to prefer home rule to war in Ulster;[49] but most were unchanged. Carson said he refused to appear with Redmond lest his followers think he had betrayed them. Recruiting for the Ulster Division was encouraged by predictions that Ulster's contribution would underpin partition—while Devlin told Belfast working-class Catholics they would return as trained soldiers to fight the Ulster Volunteers.[50]

Redmond's capacity for attracting unionists was limited by nationalist opinion. Soon after the Asquith meeting, Redmond toned down his suggestion that every eligible Irishman should enlist.[51] Pearse claimed that Redmond was plotting to hand over the Volunteers to the War Office,[52] but Redmond refused to hand over the National Volunteers unless he kept the final say on their disposition. The War Office refused to train and arm forces not under its control. Southern unionists resigned, while nationalists resented the non-fulfilment of Asquith's pledge.[53] Nationalist Ireland did not identify with the conflict to the same extent as Britain and was not willing to make the same sacrifices. Redmond and his followers saw him as equal to dominion prime ministers, a national leader with a national army,[54] but to the British official mind he was a politician with no official position and with no authority to limit British state demands on Ireland.

Seven nationalist MPs served in the British army during the war: William Redmond (Redmond's brother) and William Archer Redmond (Redmond's son), Dr John Esmonde, and his son John Lymbrick Esmonde, Stephen Gwynn, Arthur Lynch (under special circumstances), and the O'Brienite D. D. Sheehan. Admittedly a disproportionate number of nationalist MPs were too old to serve, and Gwynn and

Willie Redmond were too old to be much use.[55] Several MPs had sons in the forces. The only surviving son of the enthusiastic recruiter William O'Malley (and nephew of T. P. O'Connor) joined up against his father's wishes (he was deaf in one ear and could have claimed exemption) and died in action.[56] The three eldest sons of D. D. Sheehan went with their father; two died. Gwynn's son Denis joined up. Two sons of John Fitzgibbon were killed, one at Gallipoli, the other as a chaplain in France.[57] Dr Esmonde's son Geoffrey died in the Tyneside Irish Division, aged nineteen.[58] Sir Thomas Esmonde's second son, a midshipman, died at Jutland.[59] Redmond's eccentric nephew Louis Redmond-Howard served with the naval reserve.[60] A son of Michael Joyce was wounded in 1918 in the American army.[61] Sheehy's son Eugene and son-in-law Kettle joined up.[62] Tim and Maurice Healy each sent a son; Tim Healy's eldest son was severely injured.[63] A brother of V. P. Kennedy was wounded.[64] Others were held back by political or family commitments. Stephen Gwynn claims that Devlin wanted a commission but was asked by Redmond to stay, as the party needed him.[65] Tom O'Donnell, the most enthusiastic recruiter after Redmond, had ten young children and was in financial difficulties (though no doubt some of his recruits were similarly circumstanced).[66] Richard Hazleton had personal difficulties.

Nevertheless, several MPs of military age conspicuously abstained from enlistment and were pointed out as evidence of the Irish Party's hypocrisy and degradation. This was correct in some cases. Others had doubts about the war, or resented the lack of attention to nationalist sentiment. Such doubts soon led Dillon to withdraw from recruiting; opponents noted that none of his sons joined up.[67] Dillon's doubts may also explain the non-enlistment of his ally Thomas Lundon, a young bachelor. The largest Irish Party contribution to the war effort was made by two Catholic gentry families with military traditions.

The limits of Irish commitment were also reflected in the decline of the National Volunteers, encouraged by the split and its bitter polemics, the enlistment of committed activists, and fear that military training might bring conscription. Moran claimed the National Volunteers were in an impossible position: if they followed Redmond's advice they should enlist.[68] Colonel Maurice Moore, inspector-general of the National Volunteers, urged Redmond to maintain the National Volunteers and criticised hysterical denunciations of the Irish Volunteers by Kettle and the *National Volunteer*.[69] Thomas Sexton left to run Boland's Mills in 1912; the *Freeman's Journal* was now run by the veteran editor W. H. Brayden and the ultra-conservative Redmondite MP for South Westmeath, Sir Walter Nugent, a baronet from an old Catholic family, who had extensive business experience. Kettle accused Moore of attempting a *pronunciamento*.[70]

A few rallies were organised, culminating in a national review in the Phoenix Park at Easter 1915, but the National Volunteers dwindled into sporadic local parades and meetings. They succumbed to Irish Party 'vampirism'—co-opting new organisations, absorbing their activists, and leaving a shell.[71] Redmond and Dillon were no more willing to nourish a potential rival than they had been to let the original Volunteers operate outside their control. Separatists had suggested that the National Volunteers would depose Redmond.[72]

In December 1914 Cork National Volunteers guarded railway bridges. Irish Party and National Volunteer leaders hoped that this heralded similar schemes elsewhere, but the War Office—prompted by O'Brien, who claimed that an undisciplined 'Molly militia' would terrorise political opponents—forbade the Cork military to delegate to unrecognised organisations. Party supporters complained of stupidity— or sabotage.[73] Volunteers who equipped themselves at their own expense and spent unpaid hours wearing out boots on marches and in guarding places in the middle of nowhere were less dismayed.[74]

Redmond focused on Irishmen in the army, particularly the embryonic 16th Division. He saw them as the Irish national army but had to deal with military authorities for whom he was not the Irish prime minister directing an Irish army but a politician meddling in military affairs. He could not get the nationwide recruiting campaign adapted to Irish circumstances until vital months were lost. He could not make General Parsons, commander of the 16th Division, ask for recruits from the Irish in Britain (Parsons saw them as 'slum-birds' and preferred to wait for Irish country lads) or give prominent nationalists commissions to encourage recruiting and so offset Protestant and unionist predominance among professional officers. Gwynn enlisted as a private. Redmond's son, refused an immediate commission, obtained a commission in the Irish Guards, where he served with distinction. Willie Redmond, who escaped cadetship because he once held a militia commission, was the only nationalist in the divisional officers' mess until Gwynn joined him.[75]

Redmond fretted at the time required to prepare the division. He thought glorious deeds by Irish soldiers the best stimulus to recruiting. There were complaints that Irish regiments in France and Belgium received insufficient recognition. Nationalists spoke of professional soldiers in these regiments as entirely nationalist, overlooking many English recruits and some Ulster Protestants. Some neglect reflects the confusion of the retreat to the Marne, and some nationalist soldiers achieved recognition: Sergeant Mike O'Leary of Inchigeela, the first Irish VC of the war, was given a commission and spoke at recruiting meetings around Ireland.[76] But complaints multiplied after the 10th Division suffered heavy losses at Gallipoli. Particular outrage was caused by a despatch that gave details of all the other forces involved but passed over the Irish sector with 'Here the troops performed prodigies of valour,' without mentioning their nationality. Gwynn accepted claims that bureaucratic error was responsible,[77] but recent research suggests it reflected hostility between General Ian Hamilton, the overall commander, and General Bryan Mahon, commanding the 10th Division. When the division withdrew to Salonika, 90 per cent had been killed or injured or suffered illness, though many recovered and engaged in subsequent fighting against Bulgaria.[78]

New Ireland published articles by Mrs Victor Rickard, widow of a professional officer killed in France, on Irish regiments in France, followed with a series on Gallipoli by Michael MacDonagh;[79] both series appeared as pamphlets. *New Ireland* claimed that several soldiers received medals as a result.[80] The London-Irish journalist Michael MacDonagh published *The Irish at the Front,* lavishly prefaced by Redmond, to accompany the recruiting campaign of late 1915. A companion volume, *The Irish at the Somme,* appeared in late 1916. These and similar books addressed British opinion as well as potential Irish recruits.[81]

As Irish regiments suffered, questions were asked about the Ulster Division. If they were so formidable, why were they not ready?[82] Unionists claimed the south was shirking and that all Ulster recruits were unionists, while Griffith predicted that unionists would shirk military service, as in the Boer War,[83] and the Irish Party complained that the War Office gave the Ulster Division privileges denied to the 16th and kept the Ulstermen back from the front.[84] MacNeill told Tyrone Hibernians that the government intended to use the Ulster Division to expel nationalists from Ulster.[85]

There was some foundation for these suspicions. Early in 1915 Kitchener wanted the Ulster Division kept in Ireland as long as possible in case of rebellion by Irish or National Volunteers. Kitchener fancied himself an expert on Ireland, and while he accepted Redmond's bona fides he suspected Dillon and Devlin.[86] His willingness to allow the Ulster Division distinctive badges while refusing them to the Irish Division showed political bias, though he had at first refused them to Carson, and both Parsons and Ulster Volunteer officers resisted such badges as obscuring traditional regimental identities. The Welsh Division met similar resistance, overcome by Lloyd George, whose government position gave him authority not available to Redmond. Both divisions were given badges, but too late to erase nationalist grievance.[87] Kitchener moderated his attitude by mid-1915.[88]

Continuing suspicion of the Irish Party's motives fuelled the perception of the War Office's anti-nationalist bias.[89] Redmond's talk of an Irish national army aroused Tory suspicions; and the Home Rule Act precluded an independent army. Redmond may have been hoping that Ireland's war record might bring dominion status.

The War Office was not the only government department to attract criticism. 'Treasury tactics' were often blamed for Irish underdevelopment, while the Treasury thought the Irish Office a particularly wasteful spending department.[90] In September 1914 Sir Matthew Nathan was appointed Under-Secretary to cut Irish expenditure and prepare the administrative groundwork for home rule. The *Freeman's Journal* defended the appointment,[91] but there were complaints about the appointment of a non-Irishman (the *Leader* described Nathan as Asquith's free gift to a free people),[92] Nathan's past as a colonial governor,[93] his Jewishness,[94] and his links with the Treasury.[95] One economy was a freeze on the purchase, reclamation and division of land by the Congested Districts Board, seen as overelaborate and costly. There were complaints that this was ridiculous when officials were appealing for increased food production.[96]

Nathan struck the separatist press on 28 November 1914. Griffith's claims that the war was a piratical attempt to cripple German economic strength and that home rule was as dead as the Treaty of Limerick, and his comparison of 'German atrocity' stories with unionist 'Irish atrocity' propaganda, had already excluded his paper from postal distribution and had brought official pressure on distributors.[97] Now the *Irish Review* (a literary monthly turned Volunteer mouthpiece, run by Joseph Plunkett and Thomas MacDonagh), *Sinn Féin, Irish Freedom,* Larkin's *Irish Worker* and Terence MacSwiney's *Fianna Fáil* perished; two Griffith vehicles, *Éire-Ireland* and *Scissors and Paste,* soon followed. The *Irish Volunteer* survived, but its printing was transferred to a Belfast firm.[98] Patrick Mahon, the Dublin printer of separatist journals, was threatened with prosecution, and the *Leader's* printer was warned that his plant might be confiscated. Traditional commitment to freedom of the press was slow to disappear, especially with Irish Party influence against a wholesale crackdown. New separatist journals sprang up,[99] but Birrell responded to ultra-Tory complaints by dismissing them as a 'mosquito press', small but noisy.

The Treasury was also blamed for the absence of major new war industries in Ireland outside Ulster, where, after initial shock to the linen industry caused by a shortage of imported flax, shipyards and linen mills were taken up with war contracts. Some complaints were legitimate: for years Dublin MPs had campaigned for an army receiving depot in Dublin, making it easier for Irish manufacturers to submit samples and to tender for contracts; none was established. Others exaggerated Irish industrial capacity and claimed that Ireland should share war contracts irrespective of cost or quality. Some ammunition factories were established in southern towns, and manufacturers and food exporters received some contracts, but not enough to employ labour on the scale needed to affect urban poverty. Separatists claimed this showed that Britain would risk destruction rather than develop Irish industrial resources, an argument to which some industrial spokesmen were receptive.[100]

War taxes erased the deficit. By late 1915 Ireland once again paid more than it received, and it was clear that the financial provisions of the Home Rule Act needed revision. Soon the tax issue would be used against the Irish Party. In April 1915 Lloyd George increased duties on alcoholic drinks to raise revenue, boost war production, and please Nonconformist opinion. The Irish Party negotiated behind the scenes to ameliorate them, but Healy declared publicly that they would destroy Irish brewing and distilling. O'Brienites forced a division—the first since the outbreak of war.[101] The Irish Party, reluctant to attack war measures, abstained. The Irish drink lobby—including unionists—stirred up public opinion. Even the *Leader,* no friend of O'Brien or of the drink trade, responded.[102]

The members of the parliamentary party could not resist such pressure, and at a meeting in the Houses of Parliament they passed a resolution denouncing the duties.[103] When Redmond and Dillon asked Lloyd George to exempt Ireland, he refused, sneering that one county in Wales did more for the war effort than all

Ireland.[104] Irish Party MPs returned to Ireland. A national protest meeting was held in the Phoenix Park, at which Field was interrupted by hecklers demanding to know why he had not voted against the duties in Parliament.[105]

The Liberal government, faced with pressure from the Irish Party and restless Tories (allied to the drink trade), exempted Ireland. The British drink trade demanded concessions, and Lloyd George's scheme was crippled. Nonconformists were annoyed.[106] Lloyd George said privately he would never subject sober Ulster Protestants to degraded drunkards.[107] Unveiling a portrait of the Nonconformist Hugh Price Hughes, he made easily deciphered remarks about Hughes's opposition to drink and dealings with spineless politicians.[108] Attempts by the Irish Party to sort matters out behind the scenes had irritated both the government and Irish opinion. Redmondites retained some credit;[109] but if the government tried again, how long could the party resist?

When the war brought a coalition government in June 1915, Redmond's vulnerability became clearer. The reduced role of Parliament and Redmond's commitment to the war effort cost the Irish Party most of its ability to use the House of Commons as a forum for grievances. Only the mavericks Lynch and Ginnell used it regularly.[110] Lynch campaigned for the effective prosecution of the war, denouncing military incompetence and championing scientific and technological innovations.[111] Ginnell kept up questions about the non-development of Irish resources and about the arrest and harassment of separatists under the wide-ranging Defence of the Realm Act (1914), the non-recognition of Irish, and the conduct of the war, with particular reference to the seamier side of Allied diplomacy and the horrors of army life. Perhaps his most notorious question, having claimed that Allied troops on the Western Front were ordered to take no prisoners, asked whether Irish recruits had been told that the Germans might retaliate. This was a reaction to incitements to kill prisoners by elements of the British press.[112] An English member asked the government to notify Germany that the allegation came from an MP of unsound mind.[113]

Swift MacNeill campaigned for the removal of British titles from German relatives of the royal family. This was done after the sinking of the *Lusitania*.[114] The MP for East Waterford, Mike Murphy, who owned Tramore racecourse, lobbied for the exemption of Ireland from the wartime ban on horse-racing.[115] The *Leader* and the separatist press ridiculed such efforts as trivial while Ireland hung in the balance.

Redmond's support for the war effort prevented systematic criticism of the government's activities. How far should he take that responsibility? When the coalition government was formed, Asquith asked Redmond to become Postmaster-General. It could be argued that the party pledge against taking office did not apply since home rule had become law. Moran argued that as Redmond took responsibility for committing Ireland to war, he should claim a share in its direction.[116] T. P. O'Connor took care not to communicate with Redmond until the decision was taken, since he knew his ignorance of Irish public opinion; he believed the party would disintegrate if its leader entered the Cabinet, but a party representative should do so—perhaps Devlin as counterweight to Carson and a reminder of Ulster nationalists.[117]

Redmond refused the offer. He might have considered the Irish Office, with control over the Irish administration; this would have been a formal admission by the Tories that home rule was inevitable. Taking any other office would make the Irish Party responsible for decisions they could not veto and would help opponents accusing them of selling their souls for £400 a year. One separatist paper claimed that Redmond refused because he was not made Colonial Secretary.[118] Acceptance might plunge Ireland into political chaos; but Redmond had given up his chance of official influence through Cabinet membership, while unionist opponents gained office.[119]

Redmond asked that his absence be counterbalanced by a refusal of office to Carson; but British national unity was the rationale of coalition government, and Carson was too prominent (in British terms) to exclude if the Conservatives wanted him—especially since the Liberals retained most major positions. In any case Bonar Law, Balfour and F. E. Smith were equally obnoxious in nationalist eyes. Carson became Attorney-General.

Carson's appointment aroused in Ulster unionists some of the suspicion Redmond would have received if he had taken office. Lord Northcliffe, visiting Derry, was asked, 'Is Carson going to betray us?'[120] Ulster recruiting declined; it was said that its best men were getting killed while nationalists remained at home, and they would be left defenceless.[121] Fears and suspicions stimulated by the coalition government similarly affected recruitment in nationalist Ireland.[122]

O'Brien thought Carson had sold his followers and that Redmond was politically bankrupt. He thought a few more Ulster unionist jobs would solve everything if the Cabinet could be persuaded to adopt the conciliationist policy and make Walter Long Lord Lieutenant, with Cabinet rank, to impose a compromise settlement. O'Brien urged Healy to lobby for this fantastic proposal.[123] Healy hinted that Ulster unionists were less tractable than O'Brien thought but agreed that Carson had sold his followers and could never recover. Healy went to Westminster for his own purposes.

The Lord Chancellor of Ireland, Ignatius O'Brien, former counsel for the *Freeman's Journal,* featured prominently in the standard lists of Irish Party jobbery. Healy's court case against Hazleton over the costs of the North Louth election petition had reached the Irish Supreme Court of Judicature, presided over by O'Brien. Hazleton divested himself of all assets except his parliamentary salary; Healy wanted the salary attached to pay the debt. O'Brien's court overruled the lower courts and declared parliamentary salaries immune from seizure. The decision was reversed by the House of Lords; Healy believed O'Brien acted from political prejudice.[124]

Unionists pressed to extend the coalition to the Irish administration by appointing J. H. Campbell as Lord Chancellor of Ireland. Campbell, one of the most distinguished Irish barristers, was heavily involved in the Ulster agitation. His appointment would increase fears that home rule was in danger and deprive the

Irish Party of useful patronage, as it was the Lord Chancellor who appointed magistrates. Healy may also have supported Campbell as an old bar crony. He soon boasted to O'Brien that Campbell would become Lord Chancellor through his intervention.[125]

The Irish Party managed to block Campbell, though it had to accept an Ulster Unionist MP, John Gordon, as Attorney-General for Ireland. The *Leader* complained that Gordon was as bad as Campbell.[126] The *Cork Free Press* jeered that with their country at stake, the Irish Party fought for Ignatius O'Brien.

Despite Gordon's appointment, the party guided the Irish administration through Birrell and Nathan, and Birrell dissuaded the Cabinet from meddling by claiming all was going smoothly; but how long could this be maintained?[127] The decline in Irish recruiting was not entirely due to political reasons. In Britain the limits of voluntary recruitment had been reached, and political opinion moved towards conscription. In July, Parliament voted to register the population in case conscription became necessary. Birrell announced that Ireland was excluded because the RIC would provide lists if required.[128]

Irish harvesters in Britain for seasonal work were called shirkers and told to join up.[129] In the west of Ireland, rumours of conscription—which separatists claimed the RIC was spreading to encourage enlistment—increased emigration. Some emigrants were attacked by a mob at Liverpool; the ship refused to carry them, and they returned to Ireland.[130] Subsequent restrictions on emigration were to trap potential conscripts—and resisters—in Ireland. The incident provoked an open letter from Bishop Edward O'Dwyer of Limerick. 'Why should they die for England?' he asked. 'What has England ever done for them or their country?' He suggested that the British would never grant home rule.[131] The situation was not helped by a pompous reply from Serjeant Sullivan[132] and a furious British press reaction, with one paper regretting that O'Dwyer could not be tried for treason. Separatists started an anti-conscription campaign; a rally in the Phoenix Park was addressed by Alderman Alfie Byrne as well as by Connolly, Markievicz, and the veteran separatist Henry Dixon.[133]

After the formation of the coalition government, papers that had avoided explicit editorial opposition while publishing articles hostile to Redmond and the war, such as the *Meath Chronicle* and *Catholic Bulletin,* became more openly hostile.[134] *New Ireland,* the weekly close to the Young Ireland Branch, founded on the assumption that since home rule was achieved it was time to discuss its operation,[135] campaigned for home rule to be implemented when the initial period of suspension expired in September 1915.[136] Sinn Féin joined the 'Septembrist' campaign. Redmond rejected it, and an attempt to have it endorsed by Dublin Corporation was defeated by Irish Party pressure.[137] The party acquiesced in the renewal of the Suspensory Act (1914), suspending the implementation of the Home Rule Act.

New Ireland continued to profess loyalty to the party but grew increasingly critical, especially after Denis Gwynn, its original editor, joined up in February

1916, being succeeded by P. J. Little, and it was added to the RIC list of publications under surveillance.[138] Lynch planned an anti-partition campaign.[139] T. J. Condon went to County Clare to disrupt Lynch's meetings; Lynch got word and returned to London.[140] Lynch promptly destroyed his political base by publishing a book on the Irish situation containing unorthodox religious sentiments.[141]

Dillon and many other MPs muted their support for the war and recruiting,[142] though only one openly opposed them. Michael Meagher, MP for Kilkenny North (an old Fenian and a friend of the maverick editor of the Kilkenny People, E. T. Keane),[143] told constituents he had never stood on a recruiting platform and never would and that Ireland would be taxed heavily to pay for the war. He predicted a land tax of four shillings an acre (a lesson to farmers who had been overhasty in buying their land) and called for the abolition of the National Insurance Act, whose payments had become increasingly burdensome as prices rose.[144] Meagher had opposed the act from the start.[145]

Dillon began a nationwide reorganisation of the United Irish League, on the grounds that a delay in implementing home rule and the continuance of the war made it necessary to prepare for all eventualities. MPs visited each constituency to hold meetings; but the campaign was not very successful.[146] Critics claimed that most meetings were held behind closed doors and that their main business was passing votes of confidence.[147]

While Dillon and his allies pulled back, Redmond and some associates committed themselves even further to a partial equivalent of the Derby Scheme, undertaken in Britain as the last effort to meet requirements through voluntary enlistment. Redmond became the first Irish Party leader to enter the Viceregal Lodge, to attend a recruiting conference presided over by the Lord Lieutenant and including prominent unionists. He then launched the campaign with a speech in the Mansion House.[148] The new campaign aimed at farmers' sons, the most obvious untapped source of manpower. Redmond appealed to national honour. D. D. Sheehan declared Ireland eternally dishonoured if Munster farmers' sons did not fight Prussian militarism.[149] Sheehan's campaign may be connected to RIC observations that many Cork farmers' sons turned separatist from fear of conscription;[150] nor was the party helped when applicants for land redistribution were told to join up and to reapply after the war.[151]

Kettle published a manifesto, To the Man on the Land in Ireland, and declared that if farmers' sons did not join up he would support conscription.[152] Redmond said the land problem had been solved; farmers had their land and had accumulated large sums in savings accounts. He claimed that Germany would confiscate farmers' savings (a separatist replied that Britain had already confiscated them by suspending sterling convertibility into gold) and their land would go to German settlers.[153] This bizarre suggestion was advanced at recruiting meetings since 1914,[154] accompanied by lurid atrocity stories. Redmond described Germans chasing Belgian nuns naked through the streets. It was not his finest hour; one separatist suggested that vigilance committees should examine recruiting literature.[155]

The Irish Party's core support rested on passive agrarian conservatism expressed in non-recruitment. Redmond might make farmers and their sons receptive to separatist propaganda:

> Ye farmers of Ireland, John Redmond commands:
> 'In the trenches in France take your place right away,
> 'Tis a double-damned shame to be minding your business,
> When the Empire in ruins ye may find any day …
> To Hell with your land and your crops and your cattle,
> To Hell with your future, John Redmond obey.
> You may die, but from John you'll get passports to Heaven,
> Along with Home Rule, boys, upon the Last Day.[156]

The Irish Party called its opponents dreamers, cranks, soreheads, red revolutionaries (tarring the whole movement with the socialism of the Citizen Army), pro-German, and in receipt of German gold. This led to accusations of felon-setting when separatists were arrested, imprisoned, deported, or saw their newspapers suppressed.[157] Nationalist opinion might not be separatist but it did not like such measures against nationalists by an alien government. On several occasions nationalist juries or justices of the peace acquitted or imposed nominal sentences on separatists accused of political offences, even if manifestly guilty. Justices of the peace in Macroom who stayed away from the bench rather than antagonise the resident magistrate by acquitting a Gaelic Leaguer arrested for answering police questions in Irish were ridiculed by a widely circulated satirical rhyme from the *Leader*.[158] The acquittal of the County Sligo IRB activist Alex McCabe, who was caught with explosives, by an intensively canvassed jury surprised McCabe himself. John O'Dowd MP made representations on his behalf, a significant fact whether it was from sympathy or from expediency.[159]

Prohibitions were not confined to separatists. A Town Tenants' Association meeting in Sligo organised by Field and attended by three MPs was suppressed; when this was raised in Parliament, Birrell took full responsibility.[160]

In an early twentieth-century liberal state adjusting to total war, it was extraordinary by later standards—or by comparison with nineteenth-century Ireland—that a government should tolerate journals praising its enemies and allow armed paramilitaries to march openly, to police the capital city, and to rehearse the capture of buildings. This forbearance reflected the delicate political situation and the influence of the Irish Party; but when the party restrained the government from taking action against separatists it did so in secret and received little credit, while encouraging official suspicions of its motives.[161] The only consolation was that separatists would be widely seen as ridiculous: who would attempt armed rebellion under such hopeless conditions?

Separatists were generally described as 'Sinn Féiners'. Griffith's new paper, *Nationality,* which appeared early in 1915, had Mac Diarmada as manager and was financed by the IRB.[162] MacNeill adopted the Sinn Féin policy of abstention, self-help, and passive resistance. His editorials denounced Redmond's 'sharp curve' and accused him of sacrificing the national cause to personal vanity and perversity.[163] Articles recalled coercion and provocations by Liberal and Conservative governments in the eighteen-eighties;[164] contemporary harassment and surveillance of separatists were cited to prove that nothing had changed and that only the Irish Volunteers prevented wholesale repression.[165] MacNeill repeated the details of Irish taxation, confident this would convert nationalists and unionists to his own standpoint,[166] now essentially that of Griffith.[167] He wrote two pamphlets, in a series edited by Herbert Moore Pim, calling the Sinn Féin policy the policy of O'Connell.[168] Griffith himself contributed a pamphlet that used official statistics to support claims of Irish misgovernment and demanding to know whether 'the Government publishes sedition.'[169]

Pim, a member of a prominent Quaker business family and minor man of letters living in Belfast, was a convert to Catholicism and to nationalism. He had been a Belfast UIL lecturer until the outbreak of war but thereafter became an Irish Volunteer organiser, brought to public notice by a brief imprisonment in 1915.[170] He wrote extensively for both *Nationality* and the *Irish Volunteer.* One of his 'Tracts for the Times' praised Emmet's rising as a spiritual triumph—a blood sacrifice keeping the spirit of nationality alive.[171]

Griffith retained editorial control of *Nationality.* More intransigent separatists wrote for the *Spark,* a four-page weekly brought out from December 1914 by Seán Doyle (under the pseudonym Edward Dalton).[172] Pearse published (anonymously) in the *Spark* some of his best-known articles: 'Peace and the Gael' with its notorious praise of war,[173] and his vision of the future Ireland as a peaceful, prosperous land without ugly industrial conurbations, sustained by agriculture and rural industries, rejoicing in recovered Gaelic culture and creating a new literature ranking with the sagas of the heroic age.[174]

Other contributors included the County Wexford Sinn Féin journalist Seán Etchingham[175] and Father Michael O'Flanagan, who lamented that while a single year taught Belgians to hate Germans, the Irish had not learnt their lesson after seven hundred years.[176] O'Flanagan claimed that Redmond failed because the Irish expected him to be ambassador and leader simultaneously: an ambassador had to be polite and ingratiating, suppress his personality, and if necessary accept insults and humiliation; a leader must be aloof, strong, and decisive. O'Flanagan argued that Ireland needed true leadership, based at home—in other words, abstention. O'Flanagan had been on the Sinn Féin executive committee since 1911.[177]

The *Spark* was also a virulent scandal-sheet. It led the 'mosquito press' in attributing moral corruption to the Irish Party, AOH, Dublin Corporation, British army, government, and British people generally. One article describing the horrors of the trenches and soldiers made drunk before battle 'like raging gorillas' was raised in the House of Commons.[178] Another suggested that John Dillon Nugent was in league with the Freemasons; during the College Green by-election Nugent's opponent repudiated it, though Nugent circulated equally vicious slanders.[179] One contributor attributed drunkenness in Ireland to parliamentarianism, claiming that political servility diminished self-respect;[180] another alleged official concealment of murders and sexual crimes committed in Dublin by soldiers.[181]

Separatists drew on the oppositional idiom dating back to the Young Irelanders, further developed by Parnellites during the split and deployed by the Irish Party against 'whigs' and by Griffith against the party. Redmondite exaltation of recruits as heirs to the eighteenth-century Irish Brigade and traditional sympathy with France[182] was met with reassertions of the image of the soldier as debauched corner-boy. *Honesty,* an imitator of the *Spark,* lampooned Mike O'Leary as 'Pat McGinty V.C.', a drunken criminal and fraudulent hero who joined the army to escape arrest and who secretly hates the British.[183] This alternated with denunciations of union-ist and Redmondite employers forcing workers into the army and suggestions that arrests, deportations and dismissals of separatists were preparations for full-scale military repression, aimed at the final destruction of the Irish nation.[184]

Anti-British statements by MPs during the Boer War and a pre-war article by Redmond praising Germany for granting home rule to Alsace-Lorraine were cited as proof that the Irish Party knew the British cause to be unjust.[185] The AOH were described as pseudo-Catholic drunken louts and place-hunters, solely responsible for the failure to convert Ulster unionists.[186] One writer declared that the AOH showed their true colours by supporting Masonic employers against Catholic workmen.[187]

Kettle's alcoholism and his abuse of separatists made him a particular target. When he addressed a joint unionist-nationalist meeting in County Tyrone, one writer asked when he intended to join the Royal Black Preceptory.[188] There were repeated insinuations that neither he nor any other Irish Party recruiter would ever see action.[189] Redmond was depicted reassuring his son:

> William Archer, my boy, now don't be afraid;
> You're not for the front, and neither is Quaid.
> You're only got up as a swank and decoy
> To show that the choice is—enlist or Mountjoy.[190]

> (Alderman Denis Quaid, who had joined up, was a former Sinn Féiner who campaigned for the removal of the German Celticist Kuno Meyer from the list of honorary freemen of Dublin.)

Party accusations about 'German gold' were met with claims that the *Freeman's Journal* and *National Volunteer* survived through recruiting advertisements and secret service money.[191] Griffith recounted the history of the *Freeman's Journal,* emphasising its founding by the informer Francis Higgins, its initial opposition to the Land League, and its betrayal of Parnell in 1891. He described the career of James Birch, a journalist paid by Dublin Castle to slander the Young Irelanders, remarking that as far as British policy in Ireland was concerned there was nothing new under the sun.[192] The traditional litany of past British atrocities in Ireland was recited as a guide to the future.[193]

The image of Redmondism as utter moral corruption—the unprecedented betrayal of a hitherto unbroken national tradition—is familiar to readers of *Ghosts,* one of Pearse's contributions to the 'Tracts for the Times'.[194] Separatists claimed to represent a pure, honest Irish tradition, voiced in Pearse's funeral oration for O'Donovan Rossa. Attempts by the Irish Party to claim O'Donovan Rossa were rebuffed. (He accepted a sinecure from Cork County Council in 1906 and attended UIL rallies in New York, but claims that he endorsed Redmond on his deathbed were invented by a British journalist.)[195] The Irish Volunteers dominated the arrangements for the funeral of O'Donovan Rossa and policed Dublin for the day.[196] Ginnell and Field were the only MPs to take a prominent role, though Patrick Crumley, William Doris and John Fitzgibbon also attended.[197] Writers to the ultra-Tory *Outlook* seized on Pearse's speech as proof that the Irish situation was getting out of control.[198] A Liberal retorted that the Volunteers were harmless and Pearse was 'an Ulster Protestant like myself.'[199]

Separatist propaganda fed on moral anxieties over British cultural influence in Ireland, echoing jingoist denunciations of the British populace as decadent 'shirkers'. Griffith jeered at British failure to implement conscription as sending others to fight their battles.[200] Declarations that the war provided golden opportunities to capture German trade, and similar exhortations addressed to Irish manufacturers by John Pius Boland and the *Freeman's Journal,*[201] were seen as proving the source of the conflict.[202]

British militarist denunciations of trade union demands were drawn on to depict British workers as living in luxury on fat wartime wages, buying fur coats and diamonds for their wives.[203]

> Rinse your throats, my boys, and cheer,
> Every day we're wiser O;
> By drinking floods of British Beer
> We'll surely swamp the Kaiser O ...
> Let fools go out to fight in France
> Or in the land of Heligo,
> We'll stay at home and sing and dance
> And drink a health to Jellicoe.[204]

Increases in the rates of divorce and sexually transmitted diseases in Britain, the expression of 'advanced' views on marriage, the behaviour of soldiers on leave and the decision to extend separation allowances to cohabitants and the 'illegitimate' children of soldiers were taken as proof that Britain was irredeemably debauched and that Ireland could save its soul only by total separation.[205] Some writers detected a plot to drag Ireland down to British standards: 'One might as soon hope to turn lions into baboons.'[206] W. J. Brennan-Whitmore claimed that Jews and Freemasons plotted the country's destruction, because Ireland was destined to defeat their centuries-old plots by re-Catholicising Europe and restoring the Middle Ages.[207] (A Protestant separatist pointed out the shortcomings of the Middle Ages and the shameful national record of the Irish hierarchy.)[208]

It was claimed that French Freemasons engineered the war to secularise Germany, dismember Catholic Austria, and de-Christianise the schools of Europe.[209] Irish Party claims that suffering had led France to religious revival were derided, though the *Spark* hoped that defeat would make repentance sincere and lasting.[210] The refusal of the French authorities to let priests see wounded soldiers unless this was requested in writing, or to bring up orphaned children of Catholic soldiers in their parents' faith, was publicised,[211] as were shortages of Catholic chaplains in the British forces.[212]

Early in 1915, T. P. O'Connor organised an Irish Party delegation (including Devlin, J. D. Nugent, Stephen Gwynn, W. A. Redmond, and the Lord Mayor of Dublin) to visit President Viviani in Paris as a sign of international support for the party. During the abrogation of the Concordat and the passing of anti-clerical laws ten years earlier Viviani had boasted, 'We have put out the lights of Heaven.' Dillon worried about repercussions; O'Connor responded that the Catholic political leader Augustin Cochin was also involved and that Viviani was a moderate anti-clerical.[213] The separatist press seized on the visit; one paper asked whether the ceremonies included a Black Mass.[214] The AOH demonstration of 1907 was recalled; a photograph of the delegation with Viviani was circulated, and separatists replied to accusations of 'atheism and anarchism' by referring to 'Jean Viviani Nugent' and 'M. Clemenceau Devlin'.[215]

Despite suggestions that the Belgians had provoked Germany, Belgium was usually presented as a hapless pawn. Its population and economic statistics were regularly cited as proof that German oppression in Belgium paled into insignificance beside Britain's continuing crimes against Ireland.[216]

Early in the war, separatists emphasised the Russian threat, both with regard to religion and to politics. Francis Sheehy-Skeffington voiced radical fears that Tsarist power would strengthen reaction everywhere. Clery worried that the war might extend 'the Eastern Schism' over Catholics in eastern Europe.[217] The *Catholic Bulletin* discussed the subject, and Ginnell publicised the persecution of Uniates in Russian-occupied Galicia and the arrest of Archbishop Sheptitsky of Kiev to counter Allied complaints about German treatment of the Belgian Cardinal Mercier.[218]

The 'Russian threat' receded with Russian defeats but was replaced by the well-founded suspicion that Italy's accession to the Allies included a promise to exclude the Papacy from the peace conference—and territorial annexations that cast doubt on Allied rhetoric about the 'principle of nationality'.[219] The *Catholic Bulletin* declared it hypocrisy to talk of Belgium without restoring another 'small nationality'—the Papal States.[220] Separatists also capitalised on the appeals of Pope Benedict XV for a negotiated peace; several separatists justified their views on the war by the Pope's position.[221] Acceptance of the British position on the war placed the Irish Party at odds with the Pope. T. P. O'Connor sent Dillon an article from the ultra-Tory *Morning Post* as 'proof' of Papal pro-German intrigues; Dillon replied that the article seemed completely unsubstantiated.[222] Bishop O'Dwyer publicly asked Redmond to influence the government in favour of the Pope's appeal and received (as he probably expected) an embarrassed, noncommittal reply.[223] When Joseph MacRory, who was seen as hostile to Devlin, was appointed Bishop of Down and Connor, Griffith enquired whether Devlin wanted to be Pope of an Irish Catholic Church.[224]

Bishop O'Dwyer privately feared that Allied victory would destroy the last Catholic great power, Austria-Hungary.[225] This view was openly expressed by separatist writers, who emphasised the strength and fervour of German Catholicism and the advanced nature of German civilisation.[226] Griffith said that under the Allied economic blockade Germany was stronger than ever before, proving the superiority of national over cosmopolitan economics.[227] He cited the growth of Prussian Poland as proof that at worst, Ireland would be better off under German rule.[228] The *Hibernian*, established by the Irish-American Alliance, reprinted American praise of Germany and the Kaiser.[229] Even the Turks were praised during the Gallipoli campaign.[230]

The *Spark* claimed that wounded Irish soldiers who were burned to death at Gallipoli when scrubland caught fire, and soldiers' wives getting drunk on separation money, showed the curse of God on those who fought for the Allies.[231] *Honesty* implied that those who died on the Allied side would go to Hell for fighting in an unjust cause.[232] The Allied invasion of Greece in 1915—loudly supported by Lynch—was compared to the German invasion of Belgium.[233]

Such hatred of opponents and making sacred one's own cause were not confined to separatists, or to nationalists. It was natural in a community where political unanimity had been treated as the highest virtue and where widespread formal devotions and religious literature made such language familiar. Neither should this brand of separatism be seen as the direct political expression of Catholic devotionalism:[234] Catholic devotees were often apolitical or deferential.[235]

It is clear that the Anglophobia of some separatists was fuelled less by the relatively secular tradition of separatist political action than by Catholic anti-modernism, similar to that of pre-war vigilance committees, and that after the collapse of the Irish Party's political strategy following the Rising it helped to mobilise support for Sinn Féin. At the same time many separatists, from the 'mosquito press' to more sophisticated intellectuals such as Griffith, were not primarily religious in inspiration but used the emotional power of this familiar language to convey their own political message. Even Pearse's devotional language can be seen, like earlier attempts to develop Celtic revival themes in religious art, as appeals to the simple faith of the people against clerics and lay conservatives who saw Heaven in the form of the social hierarchy of the time. Some can be explained as a response to attempts by the Irish Party to use religion for similar purposes. Home rule propaganda was not confined to such respectable statements as Hugh Law's riposte to Griffithian conspiracy theories—that nobody who witnessed the difficulty of getting the British Cabinet to maintain a consistent policy during the home rule crisis could believe them capable of executing such deeply laid plans.[236] One recruiting poster depicted an Irish saint showing a Belgian church in flames to a ploughman. (A separatist remarked that if Irishmen wanted to fight for ruined churches they had plenty at home.)[237] The *Gael* depicted an elderly reader of the *Freeman's Journal* realising the falsity of its portrayal of the separatist leaders as godless revolutionaries after hearing Pearse speak: '… a most estimable and religious man … I could almost have thought it was a young priest speaking.'[238]

Long-standing distrust of the British revived among the nationalist population as the early euphoria died away, and with it revived older suspicions about the Irish Party's political competence, but this did not necessarily amount to separatism. The Irish Volunteers were growing but still had only a small fraction of the pre-split membership. The 'mosquito press' added new titles and increased circulation but still reached only some tens of thousands of readers.[239] Separatist language might be familiar to the general public but would gain general acceptance only when linked to concrete grievances. We have seen some: urban poverty exacerbated by rising food prices, cessation of land distribution and of emigration, continuing fear and suspicion between unionists and nationalists, rising taxes, and the growing threat of conscription. Separatists—like most nationalists—saw these issues as facets of the national question but engaged in specific campaigns as a means of consciousness-raising.

Father Michael O'Flanagan combined separatist proselytism[240] with denunciations of the Congested Districts Board and participation in smallholder agitations for turbary rights and land division, citing calls by the CDB for food production. He wrote on the food question and land division for the *Leader*,[241] reserving explicit separatism for the *Spark*; but he saw the land question as intrinsically bound up with separatism. He claimed that the Congested Districts Board could solve the land problem within two years and had not done so because it was spinning out the process to keep people quiet while Ireland was depopulated by emigration.[242] He argued that if farmers stopped producing wheat and cattle for export and grew oats for their own sustenance, Ireland could support fifteen million smallholders living in the frugal comfort their ancestors experienced before the Famine. He linked this ideal to the separatist campaign against food exports, telling smallholders, 'Hold on to the oats!'[243]

How far had such linkage progressed before the Easter Rising? How far did Redmond and the Irish Party retain support? Paul Bew has attempted to answer by discussing by-elections contested between the outbreak of war and the Rising.[244] The first, in the Tullamore division in December 1914, saw the narrow defeat of the official Irish Party candidate, P. F. Adams, by William Graham, whom he had defeated at the nomination convention. Bew argues that this defeat was of little importance, because it reflected local rivalries, because Graham protested loyalty to Redmond and claimed he was forced into the contest by a rigged convention, and because the failure of Adams's imprisonment for anti-grazing agitation to secure his election in a cattle-driving area of the midlands shows the electoral appeal of agrarian radical- ism declining even in its heartland.[245] It may be added that Graham's victory was aided by large personal wealth.[246] In late 1916 Graham bought two hundred acres in the constituency for resale to smallholders at fair prices (as defined by local opinion). This practice by wealthy party activists was known elsewhere: it was the explanation offered by John Fitzgibbon when he was accused of land-grabbing. Graham could also appeal to agrarian radicalism, and its decline should not be overestimated; two years of wartime shortages would have strengthened it.[247]

The party treated the contest more seriously than it deserved. Several MPs were sent to campaign for Adams, and voters were told that support for Graham consti- tuted rebellion against the party and Redmond's leadership.[248] Graham also opposed the imprisonment of an anti-recruiting activist at Tullamore.[249] The party refused to admit Graham, and its MPs refused to sponsor his introduction to the House of Commons. They hoped to force him to use O'Brienite sponsors, discrediting him by association.[250] In the event, Graham was sponsored by two English MPs.[251]

The second by-election took place in the College Green division of Dublin in June 1915. John Dillon Nugent had cultivated the seat for at least two years.[252] Many local activists, including several councillors and the representative of the Harbour division on the Directory of the UIL, claimed the selection convention had been packed, with organisations favourable to Coghlan Briscoe (secretary of the Town Tenants' Association) excluded. Briscoe threatened to stand against Nugent.[253] Healy privately offered £100 to Briscoe's campaign. He told O'Brien, disturbed at alliance with this notorious opportunist, 'Any stick will do to hit a dog.'[254]

Briscoe did not stand; but Dublin Trades Council refused to send delegates to the selection convention, and Robert Farren, a prominent ITGWU official who had resigned from the AOH during the 1913 strike, appeared as a Labour candidate. Farren stood on a separatist programme drawn up by Connolly; despite a rushed election that gave only three weeks for campaigning, and AOH smears presenting him as a red revolutionary opposed to Catholic education, Nugent was saved from defeat only by long cultivation of the register.[255] Even New Ireland, which sup- ported the Irish Party, complained that the election severely damaged the party's reputation.[256]

The by-election a fortnight later in Tipperary North marked a complete contrast. No convention could be held, because of the near-total disappearance of the UIL in the constituency: there were only four functioning branches.[257] The seat had been vacant for months, and Pat Hoctor, a miller and former IRB activist with clear separatist sympathies, had spent the time campaigning in the constituency.[258] Hoctor was decisively defeated by John Lymbrick Esmonde (son of the dead MP), a lieutenant in the British army. When the vote of the third candidate, Richard Gill (a strong Redmondite, with a son at the front)[259] is added, it is clear that a solid majority of North Tipperary voters supported the party against an explicit separatist challenge. In the 1918 general election Esmonde found support so weak that he withdrew.[260]

In October 1915 another Dublin seat, in the Harbour division, was contested after the death of William Abraham. No convention could be held, as there was only one active UIL branch in the constituency.[261] This was surprising, given the strength of the AOH in the Harbour division in 1910. Possible explanations include high recruitment and post-strike defections. Harbour was seen as the most promising constituency in the country for Labour. Connolly was urged to stand but refused, saying it was undesirable to direct workers' attention towards Westminster.[262]

Two local aldermen came forward. J. J. Farrell, as Lord Mayor of Dublin during King George V's visit in 1911, had defied the party and tried to get himself knighted by greeting the King. Alfie Byrne, a publican and opponent of Larkin, was a well-known opportunist, then flirting with separatist front organisations (but also supported by the local UIL remnant).[263] *New Ireland's* suggestion that Erskine Childers be nominated was not taken up.

At the last moment Pierce O'Mahony (who called himself 'the O'Mahony'), a prominent member of the National Recruiting Committee and speaker at recruiting meetings, came forward. He was a Protestant landowner with property in Counties Kerry and Wicklow and Parnellite MP for North Meath from 1886 to 1892. He had spent most of the intervening years running an orphanage in Bulgaria; he had thought of establishing one in Ireland but feared that as a Protestant he might be suspected of proselytism.[264] His relations with the Irish Party were strained by his sympathetic attitude to O'Brien in 1907–9[265] and by his campaign on behalf of his half-brother, who was dismissed on suspicion of stealing the regalia of the Order of St Patrick;[266] but these differences were submerged by the war. He also supported the strikers in 1913.[267]

O'Mahony campaigned in British uniform, declaring himself a supporter of Redmond's recruiting policy;[268] Byrne and Farrell avoided mentioning Redmond. O'Mahony claimed that Parnell would have supported the war.[269] He was backed by the Dublin unionist press, which told the four hundred unionist voters in the constituency to support him. He was attacked by Moran as 'the Bulgarian phil-anthropist'[270] and by the separatist press. Seán Etchingham suggested that votes for O'Mahony were votes for conscription.[271]

Byrne won, with over 2,200 votes; O'Mahony got 917. Farrell got a derisory vote, which he attributed to an allegation that Farrell favoured the abolition of Catholic schools, circulated too late for an effective rebuttal.[272] Even some separatists thought Farrell, who had been involved in campaigns against the Defence of the

Realm Act, was badly treated. *New Ireland* thought the proceedings disgraceful and hoped that Byrne would be unseated on petition.[273]

The Harbour election was a setback for Redmond, though O'Mahony was not an official candidate and had only a short campaign (though he received unionist votes, not necessarily available to another nationalist). Byrne was above all an opportunist, who stood for Parliament only because he could no longer make a living from 'my little pub'.[274] He was admitted to the party, unlike Graham, as he had not opposed an official candidate, but he soon established a reputation as a critic of the government. Moran praised Byrne and Ginnell as the only two Irish MPs who addressed the concerns of Irish public opinion.[275] After the Rising, Byrne continued to attend separatist-sponsored events, but when offered Sinn Féin support in return for abstentionism he stayed with the party.[276]

After the House of Lords decision, Hazleton turned down an offer from the party to pay Healy's costs from UIL funds. He decided to resign and emigrate to Canada but wanted the party to provide for his sister's family, whom Hazleton supported.[277]

It was thus that the North Louth convention after the death of Gussy Roche was visited by Hazleton and J. T. Donovan. They announced that the leadership supported Hazleton's eldest nephew, 23-year-old Patrick Joseph Whitty; if the convention nominated anyone else, the party would repudiate him. Whitty also received support from T. F. McGahon of the *Dundalk Democrat*. Two of the three local candidates—a man called O'Hagan, based in Cooley and the borderland with County Armagh, and Sir Edward Bellingham, a member of a prominent Catholic gentry family serving in the British army—accepted the diktat. The third, Patrick Hughes, tried to protest but the chairman refused to allow him to speak. Hughes and many supporters walked out; the remaining delegates unanimously nominated Whitty.[278]

There was widespread outrage at these proceedings.[279] Hughes endorsed a prominent Healyite, Bernard Hamill. Healy provided £200 and advice behind the scenes. He told O'Brien that so many old opponents supported Hamill that victory seemed certain, and even party supporters in the Law Library expected Whitty to lose.[280] William Martin Murphy also heard that Hamill would win and told his editor to use the *Irish Independent* to support him;[281] but Devlin brought in Belfast activists and personally directed the campaign.[282]

Support for Hamill by local separatists and some separatist papers allowed the party to portray him as a quasi-separatist.[283] Four hundred unionists who voted for Healy in 1910 supported Whitty, causing the *Cork Free Press* to complain that they supported Redmond to kill home rule—as if the same was not true of their support for Healy.[284] Hughes's dissident Dundalk Redmondites were counterbalanced by the loss of much of Healy's personal vote in Cooley and Carlingford, perhaps reflecting the influence of O'Hagan and a Redmondite priest in Carlingford.[285] The *Cork Free Press* claimed forlornly that Healyites stayed home because Hamill was not an official candidate of the All-for-Ireland League.[286]

Whitty beat Hamill with almost exactly the same majority that Hazleton enjoyed in December 1910. This showed some loss of nationalist support—concealed by the unionist change of sides; and Louth was untypical as a Redmondite and AOH stronghold up to 1918, and even afterwards. Some separatists disowned Hamill after realising he was chairman of the local recruiting committee and attributed his defeat to hostility to his recruiting activities.[287] Yet victory with a weak candidate against a strong challenge can only be seen as a triumph for the party; and some Hamill voters might not have supported a separatist. The *Leader* made 'Kid Whitty' a regular fixture in portrayals of the party.[288] Hazleton intended to leave a discreet interval between Whitty's election and his resignation, but he had not resigned when the Easter Rising made it unsafe to risk a by-election. Healy's costs were settled in 1919.[289]

A sixth contest, in County Laois, took place during the Easter Rising. This was a simple personal rivalry between the official candidate, J. Lalor Fitzpatrick, a large farmer related to James Fintan Lalor and to Lord Castletown, and J. J. Aird, a prominent local merchant and vice-president of the county AOH. It says much about organisational disarray that such a senior figure opposed the official candidate; but Lalor Fitzpatrick won comfortably.[290]

This analysis gives qualified support to Bew's view that the Irish Party faced discontent in Dublin but retained traditional rural support before the Rising. Bew thinks that Hoctor was less separatist and Hamill more so than is presented here; he also plays down the strength of opposition to Nugent and the setback caused by Byrne's victory. Three by-elections took place close together in the southern midlands (though in an area traditionally subject to agrarian discontent), and separatists may have made inroads into the party's rural base elsewhere. In County Kerry the *Kerryman* was one of the few local papers openly separatist before the Rising, and several recruiting meetings were broken up in the weeks before Easter 1916.[291] The agrarian-populist *Mayo News* regularly published resolutions by 'No. 1 Parent branch of the UIL, Westport' denouncing Redmond as a traitor.[292]

Nevertheless the general interpretation remains valid. Edward MacLysaght, not predisposed towards the Irish Party, wrote shortly before the Rising that unless some opposition came forward more formidable than the motley individuals who contested the by-elections, Redmond would dominate Irish politics for at least two elections after home rule. Political realignment would follow, with a conservative party based on the farming vote coming out strongest.[293] Indeed the unusual number of contested by-elections (when parliamentary salaries meant that dissidents could no longer be starved out by being refused party funds) reinforced Dillon's fear that the party was threatened not by separatism but by disintegration into undisciplined place-hunting.

Two caveats must be entered. The Irish Volunteers, claiming to be 'above politics', did not take part in elections. A proposal that the Volunteers should develop a political wing and contest elections was not taken up. Pim (in an unreliable memoir written after his reversion to unionism) attributed its abandonment to fear by the IRB that political activity would distract it from preparations for the Rising,[294] but the MacNeill wing also feared the disruptive effect of electoral politics.[295] A political split in which both factions had significant support might revive the days of the Parnell split and benefit Dublin Castle administrators, who MacNeillites as well as IRB men believed were conspiring to enslave Ireland. Many critics of the Irish Party's war policy (and some Volunteer supporters) hoped that they might be reconciled and that the Volunteers could function as the military wing of a purged party. Clery regularly recalled how the division between Grattan and the United Irishmen proved disastrous for both and predicted that unless the breach were healed, MacNeill would end as a martyr, while Redmond protested eloquently and in vain against another British betrayal.[296]

Despite occasional successes in embarrassing the Irish Party, the war finally crippled the All-for-Ireland League. O'Brien's support for the war alienated separatist-inclined activists such as the Hales family of Ballindee.[297] Tadhg Barry, an activist of the Land and Labour Association and member of the staff of the *Cork Free Press,* published a verse, 'To Maurice Healy, All-for-Englander,' hoping the tongue of the former O'Brienite candidate for West Waterford might burn in Hell for scurrilous recruiting speeches.[298] Healy suggested that separatist hecklers lived in brothels on their wives' immoral earnings.[299] Relations between O'Brien and Lord Dunraven grew more distant after Dunraven called for conscription in Ireland.[300]

The war devastated Sophie O'Brien's fortune, which derived from German and Russian securities. Without her financial support the *Cork Free Press* had become a weekly by mid-1915, kept going at a loss. When the coalition government was formed, O'Brien and Healy lamented that they had neither men nor money to seize this opportunity.[301] Sheehan was in the army. Gilhooly was dying. John Guiney had lost interest. O'Brien raged at his MPs in self-pitying letters to Sophie.[302] Some separatists still maintained links with him. Frank Gallagher, editor of the paper, and many of the staff were separatists.[303] Frank Healy, national president of the Irish-American Alliance from 1911 to 1915, delivered an O'Brienite speech to Cork Volunteers predicting that the Ulster Volunteers' march to Cork would be welcomed in the one part of Ireland loyal to conciliation.[304] (Healy was defence counsel when the deputy commander of the Irish Volunteers in Cork, Terence MacSwiney, was tried for sedition; nationalist justices of the peace let him off with a nominal fine.)[305]

Tim Healy defended several cases brought under the Defence of the Realm Act, claiming that Seán Milroy could not be accused of discouraging recruiting because he asked a heckler 'Why aren't you at the front?'[306] It is not clear whether Healy acted from a desire to embarrass the party, a wish to keep on good terms with all sides, or sentiment—probably all three. Batt O'Connor claimed that Healy's generosity to clients in such cases influenced his appointment as Governor-General of the Irish Free State.[307]

So, despite growing discontent, Redmond—or at least the Irish Party— retained majority support in the absence of a national political alternative. Some

Tory leaders, including Austen Chamberlain and Bonar Law, admitted that Redmond had shown that home rule could be safely conceded to nationalist Ireland—though unionist Ulster must be allowed to opt out.[308] Most prominent southern unionists were prepared to acquiesce in the inevitable; many conceded that Redmond was not as bad as he seemed. Details of the transfer of power to a home rule administration were being worked out. Redmond's influence with the government had averted the large-scale repression of separatists and the consequent alienation of Irish public opinion.

In some respects things were improving for Redmond by the end of 1915. Carson resigned from the government over the failure to aid Serbia. (Redmond amused the House of Commons by asking whether Asquith now shared his opinion about the unwisdom of appointing Carson.)[309] A visit to the front in November as part of his recruiting campaign, and a subsequent speech at a recruiting meeting in London, attracted favourable publicity.[310] Kitchener had become more attentive to Redmond's suggestions. Suspicions that the 36th (Ulster) Division had been kept back abated as it arrived in France and began to suffer casualties.[311]

These improvements were outweighed by the voracious demands of the war, which was going badly for the Allies. Russia, once expected to steamroll triumphantly into Berlin, had been driven from occupied Galicia and Russian Poland and was now fighting on home territory. Gallipoli had been evacuated. Bulgaria entered the war on the side of the Central Powers and helped to crush Serbia and Montenegro. (The separatist press remarked that this showed the fate of small nations enticed by British promises.)[312] The French and British were stalemated on the Western Front, as were the Italians in the Alps.

British overseas assets were run down and debts accumulated in order to buy war materials abroad. This was further complicated by the unexpected effectiveness of submarine warfare. In Britain conscription was inevitable to keep up the huge armies recruited and trained in 1914–15, which would suffer heavy losses in the great offensive of 1916 even if it succeeded; yet Cabinet opponents of conscription pointed out that it would damage Britain's industrial capacity outside areas vital to the war effort (thus reducing Britain's ability to pay for purchases abroad), while the cost of a vast conscript army would further strain the economy.[313] In Ireland the separatist press claimed that the Allies had lost and were only fighting for better terms. Some participants in the Easter Rising believed that Britain was about to seek a negotiated peace and that Ireland would lose any chance of raising its claims unless the Volunteers acted immediately.[314] With every corner searched for money and men (however inefficiently), government demands on Ireland would be bound to increase and Irish Party resistance to cause increased tension.

In November 1915 an Irish Retrenchment Committee, similar to one that already existed in Britain, was set up to cut government expenditure. The Irish committee had a government-appointed chairman, a government-nominated expert (Walter MacMurrough Kavanagh, Protestant nationalist and financial expert), one unionist, and one nationalist. Redmond nominated Boland as the Irish Party's representative, but when it became clear that savings would go to the general war effort rather than to other Irish needs, Redmond withdrew him. MacMurrough Kavanagh followed suit, and the committee collapsed.[315] Unionists complained that Redmond demanded the authority of a prime minister of Ireland.[316] Separatists claimed that Britain plotted to bankrupt the home rule government by creaming off the savings intended to make it solvent and that Redmond and the Irish Party acted only to preserve fat jobs for party supporters.[317]

Nathan cut Irish educational grants. An agitation was started by industrial campaigners, who complained that scientific and technical education would be devastated, and by the Gaelic League, because grants for teaching Irish were affected. It was pointed out that in Britain similar grants had been increased. Amid allegations that the government was trying to destroy Irish industries and the Irish language, Nathan restored the grants.[318]

In February 1916 an attempt was made to organise a nationwide campaign against overtaxation. The organisers included Councillor P. W. Kenny of Waterford, a Gaelic Leaguer and long-standing critic of the Irish Party on financial issues, later involved in attempts to establish an alternative constitutionalist party after the Rising;[319] in the nineteen-twenties he was a Cumann na nGaedheal senator.[320] A meeting was held in the Mansion House and a co-ordinating committee established. Sexton, still seen as a financial expert, had not forgiven the party for being deposed from the *Freeman's Journal*; he supported the campaign and criticised the party's indifference.[321] Redmond denounced the campaign as a separatist front and ordered party supporters to avoid it,[322] but Byrne and Ginnell attended the inaugural meeting.[323] Moran attacked the party's attitude.[324] Francis Sheehy-Skeffington, a committee member, hoped it would become a national political movement, an alternative to the 'militaristic' Volunteers and the Irish Party.[325]

In March 1916, J. H. Campbell became Attorney-General, after John Gordon was made a judge. Redmond spoke of breaking with the administration and going into opposition.[326] Dillon refused to go to London for political discussions, because Sinn Féin was very active and a party leader was needed to watch the Dublin situation. He reported that young Davitt had gone over to the separatists (he spoke at the overtaxation meeting).[327]

The probable reason for the increase in separatist activity was conscription. After the failure of the scheme to supply enough voluntary recruits, a Conscription Bill was introduced, with Ireland excluded. O'Brien stated that the fact that Irish conditions ruled out conscription did not cast doubt on Ireland's commitment to the Allied cause. Ireland was a separate nation helping as it thought best; conscription that was applied to Britain only was no concern of Ireland's, and AFIL MPs would abstain rather than meddle in the internal affairs of another nation.[328]

Redmond, thinking of future relations with the British government, believed the party should abstain. Dillon took a different view. Apart from the possibility that a show of independence would improve the party's standing with public opinion, Dillon instinctively identified with radical Liberal and Labour opponents of conscription, whom he saw as Ireland's truest friends.[329]

Dillon initially prevailed, and the party voted against the second reading, but the Liberal revolt collapsed; one Cabinet minister resigned, but fewer than forty British MPs voted against the second reading. The Irish Party then announced that it would abstain on the remainder of the bill, though Dillon privately saw this as a betrayal of British anti-conscriptionists.[330] Ginnell and Byrne continued to oppose the bill.[331] The effect on Irish public opinion is not known, though *New Ireland*— no friend of O'Brien—thought the party's tactics brought the worst of both worlds: as the passing of the bill was inevitable, they should have taken the same position as O'Brien.[332] Dillon and Redmond unintentionally gave the separatists propaganda material during the debates.

Dillon opposed a Conservative amendment exempting clerics from conscription. He felt that priests who incited young men to go to war should not be exempted from going themselves;[333] and for the rest of his career Dillon was accused of wishing to imitate French anti-clericals and to fling young Irish priests into the horrors and vices of military life.[334] Redmond stated that the party opposed Irish conscription not in principle but because it would not help the war effort, and that it would support it if it became necessary.[335] This was immediately seized on by the separatist press.[336] It was the logical implication of his commitment to the war: Stephen Gwynn thought Redmond privately believed Ireland should accept conscription but that it could not be imposed unless the people were persuaded to accept it.[337] (Dillon stated that he opposed conscription under any circumstances.)[338] Parliamentarians argued that Irish exemption was due to the influence of the Irish Party.[339]

Redmond's commitment to the war effort had been increased by his visiting Irish troops at the front. Speaking at a recruiting meeting, he pleaded with the Irish people not to desert them by failing to keep up the supply of recruits. He had no doubts he had done the right thing:

> If I stood alone, I would still raise my voice, even if it were in vain, and I would willingly face any consequences, political or otherwise, that might ensue upon taking a line of action that my heart and conscience told me was best for the freedom and prosperity of my country.[340]

New Ireland commented that this was magnificent but it was not politics.[341] Whether seen as blind pride or heroic commitment to what he believed to be righteousness, it indicates the strain placed on Redmond by the prolongation of war beyond the expectations of August 1914.

Meanwhile Griffith wrote that sending representatives to Westminster implied accepting its right to conscript, and separatists boasted that Ireland's exemption derived from fear of armed resistance by Volunteers.[342] MacNeill declared that the

Volunteers would resist any attempt to impose conscription on Ireland or to disarm them as a prelude to conscription.[343]

The need for unity against the threat of conscription may explain MacNeill's reluctance to confront the IRB group on his staff when he realised they were intriguing behind his back. A memorandum he prepared criticising the romantic-nationalist version of 'duty to Ireland' (restated by Pearse in four 'Tracts for the Times', the last scheduled to come out immediately before the Rising) and calling rebellion without hope of success morally equivalent to murder was put in a drawer.[344]

Fears of crackdown and conscription were increased by a raid on the Gaelic Press, which printed most separatist papers as well as the *Catholic Bulletin*. The mosquito press had grown increasingly bold.[345] The *Spark* fantasised about a German landing in the west of Ireland, an Irish Volunteer rising with MacDonagh among its leaders, the proclamation of a republic by a provisional government, the rout of the British army, the flight of Kettle, Gwynn, and company, and the establishment of an internationally recognised neutral Irish state, defended by German submarine bases. Ulster unionists were not mentioned.[346]

The raid was directed at the *Gael* because of an especially provocative article. Other separatist publications continued to predict military despotism until the Rising ended them. The raid lent credence to the 'Castle document', revealing supposed British plans for a crackdown but in fact partially or completely a forgery by Plunkett, publicised by *New Ireland* and the Sinn Féin alderman Tom Kelly on the eve of the Rising, which temporarily persuaded MacNeill to acquiesce in the plans of his subordinates.

T he motives of the insurgent leaders have been much discussed, though research usually concentrates on a few individuals, without enough attention to less prominent associates and the general milieu in which they moved.

It has been questioned whether before the seizure of the *Aud* the Rising had a serious hope of success through German aid.[347] Given British command of the seas, such a hope was naïve. Success would have required aid far larger than the shipload of rifles sent. When Plunkett visited Germany in 1915 he submitted a plan requiring a large force of German regular troops. This plan resembles the *Spark* fantasy, which also portrays a German landing in County Clare and the capture of Athlone, followed by a push towards Dublin to link with a Volunteer rising and the establishment of German naval bases on the north coast to cut British sea routes. The Germans refused. The slow-moving transports needed would have been intercepted by the blockading British fleet.[348] For this reason it is difficult to believe that Volunteer leaders were convinced Germany could inflict such a crushing defeat on

Britain as to dictate an Irish settlement permanently crippling British naval power, as Casement and the *Spark* prophesied.

Perhaps the leaders in Ireland preserved unrealistic hopes through lack of contact with the Germans;[349] but Charles Townshend points out that the plans outside Dublin were extremely vague, and some MacNeill associates showed more appreciation of the possibilities of guerrilla warfare than the planners of the Rising.[350] The theme of blood sacrifice is found in literary works by Pearse, Plunkett and MacDonagh well before the Rising;[351] it was also advocated by the erratic Pim and even the professional revolutionary Mac Diarmada. At the outbreak of the war—that is, shortly before Mac Diarmada's speech—the Supreme Council of the IRB decided that a rising should at all costs take place during the war, and it established the Military Committee that made the preparations.[352] In 1915 Connolly threatened to call out the Citizen Army by itself unless the Volunteers made serious preparations for a rising; even allowing for Connolly's overestimate of the ability of urban insurrectionists to defeat regular troops, this suggests that he was less concerned that a rising should succeed than that it should take place.[353]

Some insurgents may have been naïve about the prospect of victory, or the extent to which Germany might help them gain recognition as combatants. Others remembered taunts at 'tin-pikers' after the Boer War. Mac Diarmada's 1914 speech suggests that he saw blood sacrifice not so much as a means of converting the nation as of ensuring the continuation of the separatist tradition. This may be taken as the central aim of the professional IRB revolutionaries—Clarke, Mac Diarmada, and Ceannt. They had worked for years to keep alive the organisation that allowed separatists to capture and direct the Irish Volunteers; it was not surprising that in later years some associates argued that the IRB men were the real architects of the Rising, and resented their eclipse by flamboyant intellectuals.[354]

This was not the only way in which the Easter Rising grew out of the long-standing separatist sub-culture. The rhetoric of Pearse drew on a separatist idiom forged by Mitchel and Griffith, given credibility by the petty repressions, snobberies, hypocrisies and corruptions of early twentieth-century Ireland. It appealed to the contrast between the ideals the Irish Party invoked against unionists, 'whigs' and Castle Catholics and its own compromises, whether motivated by responsibilities of power or personal advantage, with forces it claimed to oppose. Pearse sought, in separatism and the cult of Cú Chulainn and Robert Emmet, to validate heroic perceptions of nationalism formed as a child and disappointed by the subsequent discovery of the factionalism and incompetence of his childhood heroes, just as he sought in the language of Catholic devotional asceticism and the simple faith of Connacht to validate his commitment to Catholicism against the social and political shortcomings of many of that faith's earthly representatives. To some extent this was a cry for a miracle—a belief that the world was not transformed only because others had not desired it enough to risk everything. It was also a political strategy— propaganda by the deed. The Mitchel-Griffith belief that the strategy of progressive alliance masked a settled plot by the entire British political elite to exterminate the Irish implied that compromise was worse than useless, because it blinded people to their true situation. The apparent moderation of the Asquith government masked an enmity as determined as that of the most outspoken Tory diehard. A blow that forced the British to show themselves in their true colours might dispel illusions and spark a nationwide resistance no force could subdue. Students of separatist literature were inculcated with Mitchel's belief that this would have happened had O'Connell refused to call off the Clontarf meeting, or the Young Irelanders risen the moment Mitchel's conviction by a packed jury revealed the lawlessness of the 'constitution'.

This underlay the insurgents' attitude to MacNeill's fears that a premature rising might precipitate the repression the Volunteers existed to prevent. Ireland was destined to suffer military tyranny and conscription, and a protest in arms, however hopeless, should be made while possible, rather than waiting for seizure of the leadership and paralysis of the movement. The question whether Redmond had a mandate from the people was, in this way of thinking, simply irrelevant: Redmondites were fools or traitors, outside the moral universe; no attention need be paid to them. Revelation would show them in their true colours.

The insurgents succeeded, to some extent, partly because the British government of Ireland still rested on force rather than the consent that Redmond and Dillon hoped home rule would produce, partly because it was not as single-mindedly repressive as Griffith and his disciples claimed. A government guided by nationalist politicians in touch with Irish feeling might have isolated the insurgents as an extremist minority; a government as ruthless and determined as Griffith alleged it was might have destroyed the insurgents so savagely that effective resistance would have been impossible for another generation.

For good or ill, the Easter Rising brought down the project over which British statesmen and Irish constitutionalists of the stature of O'Connell, Davitt and Redmond had laboured, squabbled, gained and lost throughout the Union: an Ireland recognised and accepted as an equal partner within a remodelled Union. The Easter Rising transformed Ireland, but less completely than Pearse and Griffith hoped. Much of the separatist political and economic ideology that developed in reaction against the British social model proved unequal to the business of post-independence state formation, for intrinsic or extrinsic reasons, and was laid aside. Many social formations of early twentieth-century Ireland survived into the new state, justifying themselves by selective use of the rhetoric of the Rising; and those who saw the divergence between rhetoric and reality but not the extent to which the triumph of Sinn Féin after the rising depended on specific circumstances, which drained away the political legitimacy of the Irish Party, could appeal to the rhetoric of the Rising to justify a militarism revealing darker implications of the insurgents' claims to know the will of the people better than the people themselves.

7

THE PRICE OF WAR
1916–18

After at first provoking a recoil—brought about by the possibility that it might provoke a full-scale military crack-down as much as by hostility towards its organisers—the 1916 Rising and its repression triggered the collapse of the home rule position. The security threat that some British politicians saw in home rule helped to doom the attempt to bring about immediate home rule in return for partition; and the Irish Party was left with the blame for the British government's actions, without having anything to show for it, and found itself having to denounce the government to retain credibility while remaining dependent on it to deliver a deal that might shore up its position.

The second half of 1916 saw the appearance of several splinter parties, but they lacked credible leadership, and the Irish Party even took an O'Brienite seat in a by-election; but the victory of George Noble Plunkett (Count Plunkett) in North Roscommon early in 1917 was followed by massive defections among party activists and marked a decisive point in the alienation of the party's rural core vote under the demands of the warfare state.

As Sinn Féin won successive by-elections and united its disparate factions under a single leadership, a division grew within the party between those, such as Redmond, who sought a deal with the government and with moderate unionists and those, such as Dillon, who demanded a more radical strategy, repudiating past compromises in order to maintain their Irish base.

In all probability neither strategy could have succeeded. Land hunger and food shortages provoked fears of a new famine; the trend towards repression and towards increased taxes visible before the rising grew rapidly afterwards, culminating in the conscription crisis in 1918. Dillon, succeeding as leader after Redmond's death, found himself tarred with past compromises and hindered by the continuing support of sections of the Redmondite right for the war effort, while the ascendancy of the Tories and their Coalition Liberal allies in Britain seemed to vindicate the separatist view that it was futile to seek home rule through a progressive alliance.

The result of the 1918 election confirmed that the home rule party had been reduced to an incoherent network of local factions held together more by personal allegiance and local considerations than by any coherent policy. It was now the constitutionalists who were 'factionalists' and the separatists who offered a coherent national leadership.

T he Easter Rising finally disrupted Redmond's strategy. As southern unionists, including Archbishop J. H. Bernard, demanded severe punishment, Arthur Clery pointed to such outbursts as proof that their previous accommodating noises were a sham.[1] It is not clear how much popular support the insurgents enjoyed. It suited unionists, home-rulers and separatists alike to emphasise hostility by elements of the Dublin population towards the defeated insurgents, since this let them blame British leniency, stupidity or tyranny for subsequent events. There is evidence of sympathy for the insurgents in some areas. James Stephens recorded that the better-off and very poor denounced the insurgents, while the rest kept their views to themselves.[2]

Some initial hostility may have reflected fear that the rising would allow the government to drop home rule, impose martial law, and enforce conscription—as the separatists claimed it intended. Unionists claimed the insurgents' popularity revived when Asquith came to Ireland, visited the prisoners, and showed that the rising brought home rule back to the government's agenda.[3] Separatists claimed credit for forcing the government to address the issue.[4]

The executions took place amid rumours of large-scale summary executions followed by secret burials in unmarked graves. These rumours, publicised by Ginnell in the House of Commons, derived from such atrocities as the Bowen-Colthurst killings and the shooting of civilians in North King Street, the fact that many killed in the fighting were buried in the nearest available ground pending reinterment, the non-recovery of some bodies amid ruins and fires, and the difficulty in getting immediate news about prisoners.[5]

Within a month of the executions, pro-separatist demonstrations reappeared in Dublin, associated with religious services for the dead. The *Catholic Bulletin* fostered a quasi-religious cult of 1916, based on the potent mixture of religion and politics in separatist literature before the rising. Brian Murphy's claim that this was simply an attempt to evade censorship is unconvincing, since this rhetoric was in use before the rising, and censorship was only introduced after it.

Bishop Edward O'Dwyer's quasi-endorsement of the rising proved useful in its sacralisation.[6] The Auxiliary Bishop of Tuam, Michael Higgins, refused to say Masses for the dead leaders, calling them political demonstrations.[7] The Inspector-General of the RIC reported youths in O'Connell Street calling 'Up the Kaiser' and 'Three cheers for the torpedo that sank Kitchener.' He believed separatists had majority support in the towns.[8]

Reactions outside Dublin are more obscure. In Achill, Darrell Figgis recalled initial sympathy turning to hostility when old age pensions were not paid and fears grew that food supplies might be disrupted, then resurgent sympathy after the executions.[9] Joseph Lee's study of provincial newspapers reveals confusion and initial suspicion of the rising as the work of 'socialists'. This may indicate acceptance of slurs by the Irish Party against separatists rather than a literal belief that the rising was confined to the Citizen Army.[10] Hasty and indiscriminate arrests that swept up many Irish Party activists as well as separatists had a radicalising effect. J. G. Douglas, a Quaker home-ruler and future Free State senator, was one of many who felt that the military crack-down validated claims that Ireland was ruled by force.[11] The RIC Inspector-General reported that most farmers supported the Irish Party for fear that a large-scale upheaval might endanger their farms, but added that they supported Dillon (who took the first opportunity to condemn the treatment of the insurgents) rather than Redmond.[12]

When Frank Gallagher went to London to discuss the attitude of the *Cork Free Press* to the rising he found that O'Brien attributed it to Larkinites. Gallagher said the staff would walk out unless the paper took a more favourable attitude. O'Brien capitulated and soon developed admiration for the insurgents' idealism and their desperation at possible consequences.[13]

The influence of the Irish Party over Dublin Castle was destroyed with the resignations of Birrell and Nathan. While Redmond (and, less vocally, Dillon) accepted that an example should be made of the prominent leaders, they grew alarmed and eventually persuaded Asquith to stop the executions. Party apologists later argued that a rising under home rule would have been treated with greater tact, pointing to leniency towards pro-German rebels in South Africa; the party had been severely damaged by its inability to control the crack-down, easily seen as complicity.

In some places National Volunteers helped to suppress the rising. Redmond in the House of Commons denounced the insurgents as tools of Germany attacking the Irish Party as much as the government. Party MPs cheered British victories over the insurgents. Laurence Ginnell (who greeted the announcement by shouting 'Murderers!') later claimed they cheered the first executions, but O'Brien, despite his hatred for the party, said Ginnell was mistaken.[14] As with cases under the Defence of the Realm Act before the rising, many nationalists instinctively disliked seeing rebels shot or imprisoned by a British government.

The party needed immediate home rule, if it was not already too late. Dillon privately believed a home rule settlement based on partition would never be accepted by the country, though he supported it for the sake of party unity.[15] Separatists, already blaming partition on the party, could now attribute home rule to the rising and were strong enough to cause a home rule government considerable difficulty; but the Irish Party was stronger than it would ever be again. Home rule (and patronage accompanying it) might underpin party support; without it, who could tell what demands might be made by a Castle administration appointed by a coalition Cabinet and lacking the contacts built up by Birrell and Nathan?

Could a home rule government implement unpopular security measures to prevent separatists endangering the safety of Britain? Many Conservatives and unionists feared they could not; and such fears were reinforced when party MPs denounced Britain's handling of the rising. MPs soon raised the case of individuals claiming to have been arrested or harassed on insufficient grounds. (Arthur Lynch infuriated Griffith by demanding his release and compensation as a harmless advocate of passive resistance.)[16] Mavericks—Arthur Lynch, Laurence Ginnell, Alfie Byrne, William O'Brien, and Tim Healy—took the lead but were soon joined by party members such as M. J. Flavin. Attention was drawn to prison conditions, and MPs went to Frongoch to hear complaints. Ginnell smuggled out letters; he was later forbidden to visit prisons and was briefly jailed after evading the ban by using an Irish form of his name.[17]

An amnesty movement appeared, as in the eighteen-sixties and eighteen-nineties. The party set up an Irish National Aid Association to compete with the separatist Volunteer Dependants' Fund under Kathleen Clarke, but the organisations eventually merged, under separatist control. The new body provided a national network of contacts for the separatists who staffed it—most famously Michael Collins, secretary from April 1917.[18]

Such party activities—though not fully developed until after the collapse of the negotiations following the rising—lent credence to paranoid beliefs that Dillon, Devlin and other party members were in league with the insurgents. MacNeill's claim (raised in Parliament by Lundon) that Major Ivor Price, Director of Intelligence, tried to browbeat him into implicating Dillon and Devlin has been disputed; but similar wild allegations were made by the Tory journalist Arnold White, citing informants in the Castle administration.[19] Herbert Moore Pim suggested that Price's allegations derived from a malicious letter he had sent to Devlin in 1914, referring to a pact between party leaders and separatists, in the hope that it would be read by British intelligence.[20]

Lloyd George, sent to Dublin by the Cabinet, decided that the only possible solution was immediate home rule for the twenty-six counties, and he offered this to Redmond and Dillon. One Tory minister, Lord Selborne, resigned in protest at Lloyd George's mission on the grounds that it would lead to such an offer; others thought Lloyd George would report back before taking action.

The scheme equivocated on partition. Officially it was a temporary arrangement, to be reviewed after the war; all 103 Irish MPs would remain at Westminster until a final settlement. (The Home Rule Act reduced Irish representation to forty-five.) Redmond and his lieutenants claimed that Ulster would automatically come in. Lloyd George encouraged this impression, while giving Carson a written guarantee that Ulster would not be forced in, conveyed by Carson to his lieutenants. Carson put down opposition led by unionists from the three Ulster counties to be given up; they had got as much as they could expect under the circumstances, and Carson's critics could not offer an alternative leader. The *Irish Times* protested, and southern unionists lobbied their British allies.[21]

Lloyd George's negotiating tactics involved incompatible assurances in the hope that neither side would find out before a compromise was implemented. It was perhaps less treacherous than later claimed. Irish Party leaders themselves accepted that Ulster unionists could not be coerced; they claimed that Ulster would come quietly at the end of the war, through conversion, weariness, or loss of Tory support, deceiving themselves as much as they were deceived by Lloyd George. The real treachery lay in Lloyd George's promise to underwrite the proposal by threatening resignation.[22]

Since the principal separatists were dead or imprisoned (though two thousand republicans demonstrated in Dublin as early as 16 June 1916),[23] nationalist public opposition focused on the *Irish Independent,* seconded by O'Brien and Healy; but the *Independent's* denunciations of the rising made it an incongruous champion.[24] Growing discontent might have posed problems for a home rule government but was too disorganised to effectively oppose the proposals. The *Independent* could encourage discontent but it could not provide leadership; neither could the decomposing All-for-Ireland League. O'Brien organised an anti-partition rally in Cork City Hall, hoping to launch a nationwide campaign, but his speech was drowned by heckling from separatists (orchestrated by Tadhg Barry), who had no intention of allowing him to recoup his political fortunes. The AFIL lacked the activist muscle needed to protect its meetings. O'Brien informed Father James Clancy of the fiasco, declaring he would fight to the last at Westminster and lamenting that 'Sinn Féiners … the one remaining uncorrupted element in the country,' destroyed the last hope of defeating 'the traitors' Bill.' O'Brien consoled himself by thinking that 'Sinn Féiners' feared him as the one person who might revive constitutionalism.[25]

Fifty-eight MPs attended the party meeting that debated the scheme. Two—Philip O'Doherty and P. J. O'Shaughnessy—opposed it. Lynch was absent,[26] but he and other mavericks could not mount serious obstruction. *New Ireland* and the *Leader,* despite their critical attitude to the party, both supported the proposed settlement as the best obtainable. The most serious nationalist opposition came from the north and from the Catholic bishops. Episcopal opposition to partition offset initial condemnation of the rising. Bishop O'Dwyer told northern nationalists they were the authors of their own misfortune, through submission to a leader (Dillon) who had sunk so low as to visit a Nonconformist meeting-house in London to make a political speech.[27]

Bishop Charles MacHugh of Derry organised northern nationalist opposition, strongest in Counties Tyrone and Fermanagh. Devlin, sent north to gather support, reported near-total opposition outside his Belfast base. Hard campaigning won majority support at a convention of six-county party members in Belfast on 4 July, but only after Redmond threatened resignation and Devlin promised that partition would be temporary and that the home rule government would suspend the Defence of the Realm Act and declare an amnesty.[28] The party could claim a mandate, however fragile and dubiously obtained (anti-partitionists claimed that Belfast was overrepresented, that the convention had been prolonged to make some west Ulster delegates leave before the vote, and that the count was rigged);[29] but the assurances that obtained it strengthened unionist opponents. Hard-line ministers asked whether a home rule government could prevent separatist revival and whether it might hinder attempts to put down such a threat. Redmond's loyalty was unquestionable, but he lacked administrative experience, while Dillon's speech after the rising revealed him as an enemy of Britain, and Devlin seemed little better.[30]

The principal Cabinet opponents were Lord Lansdowne and Walter Long, influenced by southern unionist opinion. They were joined by Lord Robert Cecil, who thought home rule unsafe in wartime. Other Conservative ministers, notably Curzon and Austen Chamberlain, were indecisive. Bonar Law, whose main concern was for Ulster unionists, supported the plan; but its strongest Conservative supporter was Balfour. T. P. O'Connor was told that Balfour fought 'as if he had been a Home Ruler all his life.' Lloyd George and Asquith, fearful of more wartime Cabinet resignations, tried to accommodate the dissenters, who finally agreed on the understanding that partition was permanent and that the British government retained control of Irish wartime security matters. These conditions directly contradicted Devlin's Belfast speech. Lansdowne promptly announced them;[31] Redmond accused the government of treachery. The scheme collapsed, and the party announced it would oppose the government, while supporting the war effort.[32]

Lloyd George evaded his promise of resignation by claiming that his continuance in the Cabinet was so vital to the war effort that he could not honourably sacrifice it.[33] From the British point of view it made sense to sacrifice Irish settlement to immediate exigencies; with hindsight, and with the war won, it would be seen as Lloyd George's greatest failure.[34]

The Irish Party accepted partition without receiving its prize; now, accusing the government of treachery, it convicted itself of folly. It was humiliated and damaged; nor could it escape by going into opposition. Several younger MPs, notably Richard Hazleton, William Lundon, and P. J. Meehan, with help from T. P. O'Connor, took up parliamentary skirmishing and kept debates going late into the night; but this had little effect. Critics accused them of play-acting, pointing out that support for the war effort precluded all-out opposition.[35]

These activities aimed as much at limiting the parliamentary exposure of the mavericks as embarrassing the government. Lynch, Ginnell and Byrne were joined by Patrick White, who had advocated recruiting a month before the rising but now rediscovered Sinn Féin sympathies.[36] Ginnell asked if the Turks had shot General Townshend (captured at Kut al-Amara) in line with British treatment of 'Irish prisoners of war'.[37] He appeared in the House of Commons wearing a Tricolour,[38] and prefaced a parliamentary question with 'May I ask my right honourable enemy …?'[39] When the Duchess of Connaught, wife of the King's uncle, died and condolences were offered to duke and king, Ginnell suggested condolences to another relative, Kaiser Wilhelm.[40]

The party had to take responsibility for former decisions; nor could it escape continued connection with government actions. Redmond refused to support clemency for Casement after seeing the Black Diaries.[41] The offence was compounded when J. D. Nugent cited Casement's homosexuality against the separatist movement.[42] J. J. Mooney represented the party on the Sankey Commission, which determined the release of prisoners. Mooney was hostile and encouraged the commission to retain many prisoners;[43] at the same time several colleagues were visiting prisoners and demanding their speedy release.

On 1 July members of the 36th (Ulster) Division died in thousands at Thiepval on the opening day of the Battle of the Somme. Further up the line the Tyneside Irish—whom General Parsons thought 'slum-birds' unfit to serve in the 16th (Irish) Division—also pierced the German lines; like the Ulster Division, their breakthrough was isolated, lacked support, and was crushed with huge loss for infinitesimal gains.[44] In September the Irish Division suffered heavy losses in its turn. Among the dead was Tom Kettle, killed at Ginchy on 9 September. After the rising he had applied to go to the front; despite health problems and offers of staff posts, he insisted on going up the line.[45] Kettle's biographer points out that his motives should not be reduced to a simple death wish. He intended to take up a post behind the lines if he came through his first battle; he made plans for life and work after his return, had planned a book on Anglo-Irish relations as a history of misunderstandings, and spoke of using his knowledge of Ulster Division soldiers to help a settlement.[46] At the same time he went beyond the requirements of military duty: in his own words, he diced with death. His inclination to melancholy and despair played a part, but he also wished to prove his sincerity. Before the rising he was accused of cowardice and hypocrisy by separatists. As Irish dissatisfaction grew, he developed doubts; at one time he talked of deserting. Such attacks and doubts increased after Easter 1916, when Kettle actually helped to suppress the rising (as did J. L. Esmonde).[47] Friends recalled that he was deeply affected by the bravery and deaths of the insurgent leaders and the popular response, and the thought that he himself would be remembered as 'a bloody British officer'.[48] Service at the front would give him moral authority.

Kettle also seems to have been influenced by a hope that his death might help his political cause. He left a political testament, pleading for immediate all-Ireland dominion home rule; 'Ulster will agree.'[49] As with Pearse, there is some self-conscious collusion with the hoped-for cult.

After the rising Dillon took control of efforts to revive the *Freeman's Journal*, whose premises had been destroyed. Sir Walter Nugent was displaced as Dillon urged the paper to follow a stronger nationalist line so as to regain circulation while the *Irish Independent* was recovering from the loss of its own plant. W. H. Brayden was replaced as editor by P. J. Hooper. The finances of the *Freeman's Journal* were still disastrous. In the immediate aftermath of the rising T. P. O'Connor had naïvely relayed an offer of help from Lloyd George; Dillon rejected this immediately. Sinn Féiners duly suggested that the *Freeman's Journal* was maintained by secret service money disguised as compensation payments.[50]

The *Irish Independent* soon recovered, and Dillon lamented that the whiggery of the *Freeman's Journal* destroyed its best chance of recovering its position.[51]

In the autumn Redmond spoke at Waterford and Sligo, declaring his unalterable opposition to conscription, disowning permanent partition (though he reiterated that Ulster could not be coerced), and announcing that they could not under present circumstances negotiate with the government.[52] Dillon believed this had repaired much damage; but his belief that the party should avoid negotiations and concentrate on winning back public opinion[53] also evaded the party's dilemma. Separatists seized on any sign of renewed contact between the party and the government as proof of impending betrayal; but the party was too deeply implicated with the war and the government to escape responsibility—though Dillon soon claimed, equivocally, that he 'never stood on a recruiting platform.' Opponents, less subtle, called this a straightforward lie.[54] The party's only hope of justifying past actions lay in concrete results—and only the government could deliver home rule.

It was necessary to talk to the government if anything was to be achieved, especially since the government might completely alienate nationalist opinion unless the party could restrain it. Some form of home rule was needed to have its advice taken into consideration; but could it ever restrain a British government engaged in total war from following perceived necessity, whatever the consequences in Ireland? Dillon's distrust of negotiations reflected well-founded suspicion that the price the British government required was more than nationalist opinion would pay. And the price demanded on both sides increased the longer settlement was delayed.[55] T. P. O'Connor lamented that Redmond lost Ireland in trying to gain England, while Dillon lost England trying to gain Ireland.[56]

The main advantage possessed by the party was the absence of any organised national alternative to direct and rapidly increasing grass-roots discontent. After the July debacle, attempts were made to produce a rival national political organisation. Michael Judge was first in the field. He was a Board of Erin man, a former member of the Provisional Committee of the Volunteers injured at the Howth gun-running, and briefly editor of the separatist-inclined *Meath Chronicle*. Judge founded the weekly *Irish Nation* as organ of a Repeal League, seeking to replace the home rule demand for a subordinate legislature with repeal of the Union and a return to 'the constitution of 1782', with Britain and Ireland linked only by the Crown. Judge had a histrionic streak. Former colleagues claimed that several other Volunteers were wounded at Howth, but only Judge publicised his injury.[57] He claimed hundreds of Repeal League branches, existing largely in his imagination. Jasper Tully adopted the League as his latest flag of convenience, but this hardly entitled Judge to be taken seriously.[58] He was disregarded, though his paper survived until 1919.

Pim was slightly more substantial. Released a few months after the rising, he revived his weekly Irishman and circulated leaflets summarising Griffith's policy.[59] Pim called himself a 'constitutional Sinn Féiner'. He claimed that Griffith and the other prisoners mandated him to direct the separatist movement. He may have had some mandate from Griffith (though his closest ally was MacNeill); he was helped by Sweetman and a few Sinn Féin veterans. Opponents ridiculed him as a political weathercock. He had not made the blood sacrifice he had advocated before the rising. His vanity was outstanding, and he cultivated a physical resemblance to Parnell. Pim's claims to exclusive leadership and his insistence on abstentionism antagonised Judge and the new Irish Nation League,[60] and Judge published letters written by Pim to the new censor, Lord Decies, in which he told Decies he wished to steer the national movement into constitutional Sinn Féin channels. (Formal censorship was instituted after the rising, as distinct from the informal peacetime variety—by detectives—which was intensified during the war.) Judge called Pim a British agent.[61]

Judge's allegations reflect the personal rivalries besetting attempts to give political form to the dissatisfactions accumulated by the war and stimulated by the rising, and show nationalist bureaucrats leaking official documents to separatists. Pleas for official toleration embarrassed Pim's claims to uncompromising nationalism but do not support the allegation. If Pim were a British agent he would have been managed by intelligence officers able to influence the censor, who was notoriously dimwitted and inefficient.[62] As Pim was running a weekly paper it was natural that he should contact the censor. His talk of constitutional means derived from Sinn Féin, as Griffith originally defined it; Pim attached his megalomaniac fantasies to a ready-made programme. The strongest point against Judge's allegation is the fact that Pim became a Sinn Féin organiser and prospective candidate for West Belfast.[63] Even allowing for favouritism by MacNeill and Griffith, who was notoriously suspicious of possible traitors, Pim would hardly have received such positions if the letters constituted proof of treachery.

The Irishman and Young Ireland (a sister paper aimed at young people) became notorious for egomania and for reprinting the talentless literary productions of Pim and his friend Lord Alfred Douglas, who flirted with Sinn Féin and Scottish nationalism. Early in 1918 the Sinn Féin leadership took control of his weeklies; soon afterwards Pim declared himself an Ulster unionist and published a lurid propaganda pamphlet.[64] If he had been a British agent his handlers would have kept him in Sinn Féin while he could still be useful. Pim justified himself by claiming that Sinn Féin had abandoned Griffith's constitutionalism and become a physical force front. Peeved with Sinn Féin, he fantasised about becoming Carson's *eminence grise*. Ulster unionists shunned him, and he went to London to run an ultra-rightist paper with Douglas.[65]

Judge and Pim were one-man bands. The Irish Nation League was more substantial. It grew from an Anti-Partition League established by Bishop MacHugh with the Healyite Omagh solicitors F. J. O'Connor and George Murnaghan.[66] It attracted some dissentients from the Belfast convention (though others, notably T. J. S. Harbinson of Cookstown, stayed with the party) and some separatists, notably Ginnell, the Gaelic Leaguer J. J. O'Kelly (known by his pseudonym 'Sceilg'), Louis Walsh, and George Gavan Duffy, a long-time Griffith associate and Casement's solicitor. It made limited headway in the Derry area, held a large rally in the Phoenix Park, and established a foothold in Waterford with P. W. Kenny. It was also endorsed by *New Ireland* and the *Mayo News*[67] as the strongest rival to the Irish Party.[68]

These divisions reflected the problem of the Irish Nation League in making a single-issue anti-partition campaign into a political party. Most nationalists opposed partition, but outside Counties Fermanagh, Tyrone and Derry this was not enough by itself. A few nationalists still supported partition, on grounds of political expediency or because they believed Ulster unionists were entitled to self-determination. A controversy developed in the *Leader,* with Father Michael O'Flanagan and J. J. O'Toole arguing for partition against Louis Walsh and a County Fermanagh nationalist.[69] There was a similar dispute in *Irish Opinion* between M. J. MacManus and the Protestant home-ruler R. J. Smith, who argued that it was neither possible nor desirable to plunge Britain and Ireland into civil war over Counties Tyrone and Fermanagh and urged nationalists to concentrate on keeping the excluded areas under direct London control to save the nationalist minority from an Ulster parliament governing by 'seventeenth-century Orange ideas'.[70] Smith, Clery and O'Flanagan did not represent any large body of nationalist opinion, but the fact that Clery and O'Flanagan later held prominent positions in Sinn Féin[71] indicates that partition was subsidiary in the discontent with the Irish Party.

MacHugh and Tyrone Healyites saw the Irish Nation League as an alternative constitutionalist party. Its MPs would not be abstentionist on principle but would attend only when the fifty-member ruling Council ordered it; MPs were to be excluded from membership of the Council, to insulate it from the corrupting Westminster atmosphere.[72] Pim denounced the INL for compromising on abstention and for refusing to allow himself, as representative of the imprisoned leaders, to nominate a majority of the Council.[73]

Separatist members tried to move the Irish Nation League towards outright separatism. The INL lacked prominent leaders. 'The Irish people will not depose John Redmond to make P. W. Kenny Leader of the Irish Race,' wrote Moran.[74] Opponents sneered at 'the league of seven solicitors'.[75] Its Dublin leader, Councillor

J. J. O'Meara, who supported the loyal address in 1900,[76] was terminally ill and died in December 1916, as did the ex-MP George Murnaghan (senior).[77] Thomas Sexton endorsed the INL but was a neurotic recluse who had not been a public representative for twenty years.[78] Negotiations with the AFIL also proved troublesome.

The quasi-separatist attitude of the *Cork Free Press* increased sales, though paper shortages and lack of capital left its financial position hopeless. A Limerick supporter asked when it would become a daily; O'Brien replied he would gladly make it one—if the Irish people repaid the £20,000 he had spent on it.[79]

O'Brien contacted the INL through a Wexford-born supporter, Lawrence Casey,[80] a member of the Council of the INL. George Murnaghan junior visited Cork, and negotiations took place.[81] One anonymous pamphlet giving the INL view of the partition proposals based its critique of the Irish Party on an O'Brienite view of recent history and was later attributed to John Herlihy.[82] O'Brien got Moreton Frewen to contact British political friends seeking help for a new federalist centre party; Frewen secured £500 from Lord Milner.[83] Meanwhile, Healy and William Martin Murphy established friendly relations with the Chief Secretary, H. E. Duke.[84]

O'Brien's hope of a coalition stretching from Tories to separatists clashed with the aims of the INL. He complained that his old enemy Ginnell was INL ambassador at large, with liberty to insult everyone, and the only MP allowed on the Council. He said that no self-respecting MP could be the puppet of a remote Council. (In fact O'Brien had tried to do this when he set up the United Irish League; his real objection was that he was not the leader.) He thought the INL should stop debating minutiae and build a broadly based movement.[85]

While these contacts continued, Gilhooly died. O'Brien moved to fill the vacancy. On the evening of the funeral he met friends in Bantry and nominated Frank Healy, who had been deported to Britain after the rising. O'Brien presented Healy as a prisoners' candidate whose election would bring general amnesty. At the same time he reassured Frewen that Frank Healy 'had no more to do with the Rising than you or I.'[86] Healy was personally loyal to O'Brien and prepared to take his seat but had long-standing separatist connections. He was a friend of MacBride and Connolly[87] and was prominent in the Irish-American Alliance, whose military wing, the Hibernian Rifles, participated in the rising.[88] Healy supported Sinn Féin in the 1918 election, and his home was an IRA 'safe house' during the War of Independence. He supported the republicans in the Civil War and Sinn Féin in the 1926 split with Fianna Fáil. His family attributed his death in 1931 to grief at the political situation.[89]

This speedy nomination of Frank Healy forestalled Serjeant Sullivan, who, having boasted of letting the British army use his Dublin house during the rising, hoped to exploit Bantry family connections and his prestige as Casement's defence counsel to secure unopposed election as an independent; it also prevented a possible attempt to put up the deportee J. J. Walsh.[90] Lack of consultation with local O'Brienites and Healy's origins outside the constituency caused resentment. J. B. M.

Shipsey, son of a prominent O'Brienite from Schull, County Cork, stood as an independent O'Brienite. Daniel O'Leary, the Redmondite defeated in 1910, then entered the race, ostensibly also as an independent.[91]

Crean, Walsh and the Healy brothers campaigned with O'Brien in west Cork. The party ran a low-key campaign, concentrating on O'Leary's local support and family connections. If he won, this would be a party victory; if he lost, the party could dissociate itself. No major party leaders participated.[92] The AFIL candidate acquired the support of many former Redmondites, notably Canon Jeremiah Cohalan, parish priest of Bantry and brother of Daniel Cohalan, Bishop-elect of Cork,[93] but this was offset by the loss of the Protestant and unionist vote cultivated by Gilhooly, numbering about five hundred and now facing a separatist in all but name. Jasper Wolfe, Gilhooly's former election agent and the most prominent Protestant political activist in west Cork, campaigned for O'Leary.[94] Bishop Cohalan was enthroned shortly before the by-election; when he declared his support for Redmond and, by implication, O'Leary, Canon Cohalan walked out.[95]

Many separatsts saw Frank Healy as a decoy. Pim corresponded with O'Brien, demanding that the AFIL adopt abstentionism. O'Brien told Pim he was semi-abstentionist but that growing support for 'Sinn Féin' represented discontent with the party and was insufficient to justify abstention in principle. Pim then dissociated Sinn Féin from Healy, declaring it better for a corrupt Redmondite to go to Westminster than for an Irish political prisoner to be degraded by attending the British Parliament.[96] Some Cork prisoners, led by Tomás MacCurtain, disowned Healy and Shipsey.[97] When questions in Parliament revealed that Healy wrote to the Home Secretary promising good behaviour if allowed back to campaign, the party derided him as a bogus Sinn Féiner.[98] Not all separatists agreed. Griffith allegedly wrote to O'Brien dissociating himself from Pim and MacCurtain.[99]

The vote in west Cork virtually replicated that of December 1910, but Shipsey took enough votes to give O'Leary the seat. After wild recrimination and despair, O'Brien closed down the *Cork Free Press* while there was enough money to pay debts and give employees severance payments.[100] The paper had cost the O'Briens £24,715.[101] This ended the All-for-Ireland League, though O'Brien and Healy engaged in freelance activity until the 1918 election.

There were rumours that the party would get John Guiney to resign his seat.[102] As T. P. O'Connor told British readers that victory over the AFIL and Sinn Féin combined in an AFIL stronghold proved that Ireland supported the party, separatists argued among themselves. Some thought Frank Healy's national record deserved support;[103] others argued that separatists acted wisely in refusing to bolster the decaying fortunes of O'Brien and that the party's victory would soon be reversed.[104]

Hindsight shows the limitations of the victory. Apart from its dependence on Shipsey's intervention, the unionist vote concealed a swing of nationalist opinion away from the Irish Party. O'Leary played down party links but claimed to be a 'Sinn Féiner' (as had Shipsey, who occasionally wrote for Griffith before the war).[105] This reflected a radicalisation of the party, as of nationalist opinion in general; the party was reduced to claiming the slogan 'Sinn Féin', associated with opposition to the party itself. O'Leary proved troublesome: within a year Dillon described him as worse than useless, only tolerated for fear of a by-election.[106] In 1918 West Cork fell uncontested to Sinn Féin, and Tim Healy told O'Brien that O'Leary's relatives refused to finance a hopeless candidacy.[107]

Nevertheless the party won the by-election and secured another success when J. D. Nugent arranged for members of Dublin Metropolitan Police to protest against conditions of employment by joining the AOH. Policemen were forbidden to join secret societies, but the DMP men protested that it was unfair to forbid them to join the AOH while Protestant policemen could become Freemasons. The government agreed to prohibit policemen joining the Masons in future.[108]

By the end of the year Dillon could tell O'Connor that the danger of immediate destruction had been overcome, and public opinion was swinging back. He blamed Redmond's neglect of organisation and excessive identification with the war, and feared the party might still be destroyed.[109] Dillon suspected that the government desired such an outcome; he complained that when Lundon was pulled off a platform in Limerick, beaten up and severely injured, the police made no effort to apprehend the culprits.[110]

The growing crisis on the Western Front led to the removal of Asquith as Prime Minister and his replacement by the more vigorous Lloyd George, who governed with Tory support. Asquith's fall did not cause the Irish Party much regret (it opposed his government since July 1916, even joining Tory hard-liners in one important division),[111] but the installation of a Tory-dominated government under Lloyd George determined to fight the war to the finish, and the consignment of many Liberal home-rulers to opposition, were disquieting. Carson was prominent in the coup and became First Lord of the Admiralty, though he soon proved unsuccessful. He turned down the Lord Chancellorship to remain free to take up the Ulster leadership if necessary.[112]

The new government announced a Christmas amnesty for Irish internees (as distinct from those tried and convicted), which returned hardened separatists and radicalised detainees to Irish politics.[113] These included Griffith, who set about re-organising Sinn Féin; Michael Collins; and George Noble Plunkett (Count Plunkett). At this point J. J. O'Kelly, veteran MP for North Roscommon, died. A few local separatists asked Michael Davitt junior to stand, but he refused. A group in Dublin centred on the *Catholic Bulletin* office and including Father Michael O'Flanagan then put forward Plunkett.[114] Plunkett's credentials seemed more dubious than those of Frank Healy. A former Parnellite, he had written for a Fenian-inclined magazine as a young man and was a long-standing advocate of Irish and a patron of Irish arts and crafts[115] but was known as a lukewarm nationalist. When he wished to stand with Irish Party support in St Stephen's Green in 1904, John Muldoon told Dillon it was not worth bothering to vote for him, even to save the seat from a unionist.[116] Plunkett was secretary of the royal reception committee in 1911,[117] and had applied for the position of Under-Secretary in December 1914.[118] Whether influenced by failure to secure this post or the views of his daughter and sons, prominent in the Volunteers, he carried messages between the separatist leaders and Germany during visits to the Continent, and asked the Pope to bless the rising.[119] He remained a justice of the peace[120] and when exiled to Britain wrote to the government pledging good behaviour.[121]

Plunkett's record was publicised by the party and by Jasper Tully (standing for the Repeal League), who attacked him as 'an old Whig'.[122] It was offset by the execution of his son Joseph, one of the signatories of the 1916 proclamation, and the imprisonment of another son, George. The impression of vindictiveness was reinforced when he was dismissed as Director of the National Museum and expelled from the Royal Dublin Society after unionists brought in backwoodsmen from the Kildare Street Club, despite opposition led by William Field, John Sweetman, Charles Oldham, and Pierce O'Mahony.[123]

O'Flanagan turned up at the selection convention and demanded that it nominate Plunkett, in protest at his treatment. The chairman, J. P. Hayden, refused to accept Plunkett's nomination unless he took the party pledge. Now able to accuse the party of manipulating the convention and of complicity in the treatment of Plunkett, O'Flanagan walked out.[124] The convention nominated Thomas Devine, a Boyle shopkeeper formerly involved in land agitation on the de Freyne estate and Roscommon County President of the AOH.[125]

Dillon was confident of victory.[126] Hazleton led a strong force of MPs; Field and O'Mahony came from defending Plunkett in the RDS to oppose him in Roscommon. When a parliamentary question revealed Plunkett's application for the Under-Secretaryship, supporters claimed that this showed the government trying to prop up the party. Plunkett's supporters, led by O'Flanagan and Ginnell, stretched from out-and-out separatists to Moran and the Irish Nation League. O'Flanagan and Louis Walsh dropped their dispute over partition to campaign. W. G. Fallon, working for the party, encountered his former YIB colleague Rory O'Connor campaigning for Plunkett. There were large-scale defections of party activists. Alderman Henry Monson, President of the AOH in Connacht and representative for North Sligo on the UIL Directory, campaigned for Plunkett, as did many local Hibernians.[127] The Roscommon County Board of the AOH was suspended after the by-election so that it could be reorganised and dissidents excluded.[128] Irish Volunteers reappeared in force; after polls closed they guarded the ballot boxes jointly with the RIC, claiming that the government might stuff them.[129]

Throughout the country the Volunteer network was reconstituted under the leadership of long-standing local separatist activists, who recruited from the youth sub-culture that traditionally formed the basis of political activism.[130]

Plunkett secured a comfortable majority over Devine and Tully. Tully welcomed the blow to the party and thereafter supported the growing movement loosely called 'Sinn Féin', though he had denounced the rising as perpetrated by socialists and suffragist cranks.[131] Moran had feared that farmers were too parochial to vote against the Irish Party.[132] Griffith declared that Roscommon buried the slander 'that the farmer had a farm but not a country.'[133] Redmond talked privately of resignation and the end of the party.[134] Dillon said publicly they might lose thirty seats at the next election.[135]

Why did the British welfare legislation of the previous decade not bring home the advantages of a continuing British connection, as Paul Bew argues might have been the case? The party certainly invoked it in 1917–18. Sinn Féin complained that old age pensioners were told they would lose their pension if Sinn Féin won.[136] The AOH obstructed members of its insurance section who wished to transfer to other approved societies because their views had changed.[137] 'Separation women' receiving welfare payments for male relatives in the army were prominent among party supporters—though this was hardly due entirely to financial motives. Some would have failed to see the full implications of their actions, or took these benefits for granted and assumed that an independent Ireland would provide for all its citizens. During the East Cavan by-election Father O'Flanagan jeered at the Irish Party for saying that Sinn Féin victories would end the old age pension, when it had been increased from five shillings to seven and sixpence.[138]

During the Waterford by-election, Devlin claimed the party was responsible for extending the wartime increase in the old age pension to Ireland. Alice Milligan replied that the need for such efforts showed British selfishness and talked of independence as the solution to all Ireland's economic problems.[139] The fact that much government spending was inefficient and was aimed at the political appeasement of local vested interests reinforced separatist perceptions that it was simply a form of political corruption and that a national government could deliver the same services at lower cost.[140] Many separatists advocated social reforms such as replacement of the Poor Law with a more humane system. Sinn Féin's abstention did not extend to non-recognition of the welfare system, and the subsequent records of the British and Irish states were not available for comparison. The National Insurance Act had little time to make benefits felt, and the payment of contributions was unpopular. Many beneficiaries—the old and the poor—were less likely to be politically active and were worse affected by wartime conditions. The question meant less to the young men who provided political activists and muscle, who feared conscription and were leaving the UIL and AOH for 'Sinn Féin'. Perhaps with hindsight it can be said that they lost out, but this is irrelevant to expectations in 1918.[141]

Why did farmers break with the Irish Party? The collapse of the party's rural base partly reflected the other side of the welfare state: the demands of a 'warfare state'. Farmers and their sons were made the target of recruiting campaigns, while tax increased and conscription in Britain extended to married men. In late 1916 the government overcame resistance from English grazing interests[142] and introduced compulsory tillage. A Food Controller was appointed to oversee food supplies throughout the United Kingdom. If agrarian radicals and urban consumers denounced the government for allowing food prices to rise and not encouraging tillage, farmers were equally annoyed at being told what to grow and at having prices fixed below the market rate.[143] Griffith also claimed that tillage orders were disproportionately enforced against smaller cattle farmers, while big graziers and landlords secured lenient treatment.

There was a bad potato harvest in 1916, affecting pig-rearing small farmers as well as urban consumers.[144] Farmers at Athlone market clubbed together to raise prices; the RIC forced them down. While Moran jeered at the 'Potato Shylocks of Athlone',[145] Griffith denounced this attempt to present the RIC as friends of the people and claimed that farmers and customers could have worked matters out by themselves.[146] Sinn Féin had acquired the traditional Irish Party ability to use nationalism to appeal simultaneously to incompatible interests. The first Food Controller, Lord Devonport—a prominent grocer—concentrated on keeping down prices paid to producers and paid little attention to prices charged by retailers.[147] This was interpreted as a British plot to bankrupt Irish farmers and starve Irish consumers.[148]

Plunkett dismayed some supporters by announcing himself an abstentionist who believed Ireland's hope lay in the peace conference.[149] He circulated invitations for a National Convention in the Mansion House on 19 April. While J. D. Nugent put out black propaganda representing the Convention as socialist and anti-clerical,[150] seventy local authorities sent representatives, as did some AOH divisions, reflecting continuing upheavals within the organisation. County boards were suspended and reorganised in Counties Limerick, Kerry, Wicklow and Clare after the North Roscommon by-election and in County Longford after the South Longford by-election.[151] Throughout 1917 and 1918 numerous AOH and UIL members defected to Sinn Féin, sometimes after disrupting Irish Party activities and voting through anti-Redmond and pro-Sinn Féin motions. Griffith suggested that where separatists were the majority they should transfer assets to Sinn Féin.[152] This took place on a large scale in 1918, when many AOH and UIL halls were taken over—usually voluntarily, sometimes by force—and became Sinn Féin halls.[153] The Irish-American Alliance was also represented at Plunkett's Convention but thereafter was absorbed into the wider movement.[154]

Preparations for the Convention were marked by fierce negotiations between rival separatist groups, including Labour. Plunkett excluded the Irish Nation League because of its non-abstentionism, though individual members argued their case.

The Convention was dominated by disputes between Plunkettites, who wanted a new organisation (the Liberty League) and Griffithites, who wanted Sinn Féin as the national organisation. This reflected the perennial division between compromisers and republican purists. As the Griffithite George Gavan Duffy noted, Plunkett adopted republicanism with the fervour of a convert.[155] Sinn Féin was better known, better organised, and had a weekly paper (*Nationality,* which Griffith had revived), while Plunkett had a closer personal link with the rising and the support of hard-line Dublin separatists.[156]

Early in March, T. P. O'Connor put down a motion in the House of Commons on the state of Ireland. Lloyd George told Dillon through C. P. Scott that unless the debate was postponed he would 'irrevocably' endorse partition. Dillon told Scott the party could not postpone the debate without losing its position in the country, and that to give Ulster the right of secession meant denying Irish nationality[157] (an argument used against the party by Griffith).

The debate was dominated by an appeal from Willie Redmond, making his last appearance in the House of Commons; he called for an Irish settlement in the name of fellow-soldiers about to die. Lloyd George declared that the government was committed to home rule for parts of Ireland that wanted it, but Ulster unionists were as distinct from the Irish nation as inhabitants of Fife or Aberdeen.[158] Redmond led the party out of the chamber in protest; Ginnell jeered that they were trying to fool the Irish people.[159]

South Longford fell vacant soon afterwards. No convention was held; three rival party candidates appeared. This was a throwback to the factionalism of pre-1916 by-elections, with one candidate leaning towards Sinn Féin and another identifiably clericalist.[160] Separatists united behind Joseph McGuinness, a convicted prisoner whose family were prominent in County Longford politics.[161] Some prisoners had doubts about 'politics', seeing it as a distraction from military preparations and a source of factionalism and compromise. Thomas Ashe, later president of the reconstituted Supreme Council of the IRB, decided they could use the British electoral system to show Irish opinion.[162] The rival home-rulers agreed to abide by Redmond's decision. He chose Patrick McKenna, the strongest and most experienced candidate.[163]

County Longford was traditionally a stronghold of agrarian politics, but despite the agrarian radicalism of McKenna and the North Longford MP, J. P. Farrell, whose *Longford Leader* poured abuse on separatists,[164] rural districts went against the party. Redmond said that young men refused to work for their fathers unless they voted for Sinn Féin.[165]

Fifty motor-cars working for McGuinness showed middle-class involvement,[166] car ownership being uncommon and petrol being rationed. Tully's *Roscommon Herald* and the *Westmeath Independent* endorsed McGuinness. Moran recalled how both papers published recruiting advertisements and supported the war. (The editor of the *Westmeath Independent* had two sons at the front.)[167] Moran supported

McKenna, 'an assiduous reader of the *Leader*.' He pointed out that the country supported Redmond's policy up to 1916 (judging by the by-elections) and had to share responsibility.[168] He feared that a split reminiscent of 1890 would divide Ireland for years and kill home rule.[169]

Irish Party support centred on Athlone, a garrison town with a long recruiting tradition. 'Separation women' and AOH strong-arm men fought Volunteers; Redmond told Scott that their 'fierce mob' broke Sinn Féiners' heads with bottles.[170] When J. D. Nugent declared that Sinn Féin showed its 'depravity' by encouraging women to stay out late at political meetings, *New Ireland* pointed to the separation women.[171]

Redmond did not appear in Longford. His health had broken down. He had never fully recovered from the effects of a car accident in 1912, and the strains of leadership and defeat were increased by the death of a daughter in America and the wounding of his son on the Western Front.[172] Dillon and Devlin campaigned in the constituency. Dillon thought that if they could not hold Longford with the Athlone mob, the town merchants, the bishop, and nine-tenths of the priests, the party could not survive.[173]

The issue was turned by events at Westminster. Despite the April debate, the party renewed contact with the government. T. P. O'Connor discovered that Lloyd George was thinking of imposing simultaneous home rule and conscription.[174] He would go no further than the 1916 proposals, whereas even Redmond now talked of dominion home rule, though he told Scott that an Irish dominion would not want an army and would never start a trade war with Britain.[175] In response to rumours of settlement, twenty-three Catholic bishops, three Church of Ireland bishops and several prominent laymen issued a joint anti-partition statement. Archbishop Walsh issued a 'clarifying' letter, claiming that the Irish Party was plotting to accept partition on the eve of the poll, too late to be rebutted; it was widely reproduced by Sinn Féin.

McGuinness won by thirty-seven votes. Walsh's 'information' was never made public. When his secretary (who had Sinn Féin sympathies) published an official life a decade later he merely declared it outrageous to accuse an archbishop of lying.[176]

Dillon snapped at Lloyd George, 'You have destroyed the Parliamentary Party,' and told Scott the Sinn Féiners would 'wipe the country with us' if they found a leader.[177] Redmond talked of getting the party to resign *en masse,* making a last appeal to the country or withdrawing altogether and leaving Sinn Féin and the government to take the consequences. He lamented the failure of his policy of conciliation by active co-operation in the war; he blamed the military authorities but thought he would have succeeded had the war lasted no longer than a year.[178]

A new source of hope appeared for Redmond when the government took up his suggestion, as an alternative to immediate home rule with partition, that an Irish Convention representing all shades of opinion should work out a settlement.[179] Few were as sanguine as Redmond. Dillon thought the Convention a waste of time. He insisted on enlarging it to include more nationalists, making it more unwieldy and prolonging its debates, then refused to serve on it himself.[180] Lundon joined the Convention as a representative of O'Shee's Land and Labour Association, perhaps as Dillon's eyes and ears.

Lynch organised a round-robin demanding that the party should insist that partition be ruled out in advance and advocating dominion home rule. It received six signatures: Lynch, Meagher, O'Shee, O'Shaughnessy, and the by-election victors Lalor Fitzpatrick and O'Leary. It was hastily organised; Philip O'Doherty and Byrne did not sign.[181] News of the round-robin leaked out. The Sinn Féin press, denouncing the Convention as a trick to keep the Americans quiet, cited it as proof that members of the Irish Party secretly agreed with Sinn Féin policy but were silenced by their £400 a year.[182]

Sinn Féin refused to take five seats allocated to it, though George Russell and Edward MacLysaght represented the Sinn Féin viewpoint. O'Brien refused to take up the two AFIL seats, though he had demanded a unionist-nationalist conference for years. He argued that it was too large and unwieldy, and he wanted partition ruled out in advance and any settlement submitted to a referendum. The chairman, Sir Horace Plunkett—who, as a southern unionist, disliked partition—negotiated with O'Brien but could not get the government to agree to his conditions.[183]

Healy had doubts about O'Brien's attitude but submitted, and soon found it useful to be free to capitalise on the party's difficulties.[184] An unnamed Cabinet minister—perhaps Long, who wanted to safeguard southern unionists by a 32-county federal settlement—sent Frewen to say that Ulster unionists knew of O'Brien's sacrifices for reconciliation and that he could persuade them to compromise. O'Brien included this in his memoirs, though he did not respond.[185] Lord Dunraven joined the Convention as an independent working with southern unionists. O'Brien told Healy he had parted company with Dunraven over conscription but that Dunraven's behaviour was perfectly honourable. To disown him would cast doubt on the political sacrifices of the previous fourteen years. Dunraven maintained friendly personal relations with O'Brien.[186]

On 7 June, as preparations for the Convention went ahead, Willie Redmond was killed on the first day of the Battle of Messines. He had insisted on going forward with the rest of the 16th Division; had it not been for age and fatigue he might have survived his wounds.[187] He was resigned to death: descriptions of trench life he wrote for English newspapers contain the language of blood sacrifice.[188] He talked to Stephen Gwynn of political defeat.[189] He seems to have been inspired by a desire to prove his sincerity, both to the British and the Ulster unionists and to Irish nationalists (he had received anonymous letters accusing him of cowardice) and to strengthen his brother. Much was later made of the fact that he had been carried by Ulster Division stretcher-bearers.[190] Redmond had intended to nominate his brother to the Convention as a reminder of party commitment to the war effort. Gwynn was chosen instead.[191] This was followed by the death of the chief whip, Pat

O'Brien.[192] Redmond's health deteriorated further. Doctors prescribed six months' total rest; his wife urged him to retire.[193]

Sinn Féin chose Éamon de Valera, the senior surviving Volunteer officer who had taken part in the Easter Rising, to contest the vacancy in East Clare caused by the death of Willie Redmond. At first the party decided not to run a candidate, though some on its right wing wanted a serving soldier with links to Parnell—probably Henry Harrison or Pierce O'Mahony.[194] Patrick Lynch, a member of a prominent County Clare family with a long record as a successful defence counsel, resigned as Crown Prosecutor for County Kerry to stand as an independent—like O'Leary.[195]

De Valera campaigned in person, as the government tried to help the Convention by general amnesty. Prisoners were greeted in Dublin by enthusiastic crowds. Hoardings for recruiting posters were torn down to make bonfires; 'separation women' were attacked. Once more the police were demoralised by the release of those so recently rounded up; Lord Midleton, the southern unionist leader, complained that the government forfeited all credibility by its leniency.[196] Soon after the opening of the Convention, Redmond was hooted and jostled in the street and narrowly escaped injury.[197]

Bishop McHugh tried to organise another constitutional anti-partition party to replace the defunct Irish Nation League. Its most prominent remaining leader, F. J. O'Connor, who endorsed George Russell's critical support for the Convention, died shortly before it opened.[198] Several prominent Catholic laymen spoke at a rally in the Phoenix Park, including Patrick White MP, who left the Irish Party. The Catholic hierarchy's decision to attend the Convention inhibited McHugh, and the new movement fizzled out.[199]

In East Clare the party backed Lynch with activists, including Devine and McKenna,[200] and a fleet of motor-cars.[201] Appeals to the memory of Willie Redmond[202] and Lynch's local connections were met by contrasts between Crown Prosecutor and Crown prisoner.[203] De Valera declared it useless to send Irish representatives to Parliament, since the British combined to crush them. He spoke of overtaxation and predicted land taxes, and he denounced claims that Sinn Féin planned a new rising. He ridiculed Lynch for not openly campaigning as a British army recruiter and jeered at his local connections; this was not an election for dispensary doctor.[204]

All Irish Party candidates in by-elections after the rising appealed to localism; of Sinn Féin candidates only McGuinness and Dr Vincent White (defeated in Waterford city) had strong local ties. The party spoke of old loyalties and asked voters to trust the leadership to deliver a settlement, as it had when invoking national unity against local factionists. Such tactics were less effective against an alternative national movement.

Some thought Sinn Féin were setting the agenda and that the Irish Party were factionists endangering national unity. Moran gave this reason for supporting Sinn

Féin. He had ridiculed Devine's campaign for parochialism,[205] though one contributor remarked that separatists had forced the Irish Party to heed local opinion rather than imposing P. J. Whittys.[206] Moran's initial reaction to McGuinness's victory in Longford was that Ireland faced a devastating split,[207] but he gradually realised that the rural vote had turned against the party. He detested the idea of talking to Protestant notables and was accordingly hostile to the Convention.[208] That, together with clear signs that Patrick Lynch was being routed by de Valera in East Clare, swung the *Leader* behind Sinn Féin.[209] However, Moran continued to complain that Sinn Féin abstentionism, combined with the Irish Party's sensitivity to accusations of corruption, gave Freemasons the best jobs by default.[210]

A few days before the election the businessman M. L. Hearn held South Dublin unopposed for the Irish Party. Sinn Féin did not put up a candidate, because almost half the electorate were unionists, who might vote for the Irish Party; or a unionist might capture the seat through a split vote. A prominent Catholic solicitor appeared as an independent dominion home-ruler but withdrew when an independent unionist talked of standing.[211]

South Dublin was eclipsed by Clare. De Valera received over five thousand votes, Lynch barely two thousand. Once again the rural vote turned against the Irish Party. Lynch was strongest in Ennis, where party supporters and police clashed with Volunteers.[212] As separatists had long known, dissenting minorities found it easier to survive in towns, where conformity was less easily enforced.[213] An important element in de Valera's victory was Bishop Michael Fogarty of Killaloe, who endorsed Sinn Féin soon after the death of Bishop O'Dwyer. (O'Dwyer was succeeded by another new Sinn Féiner, Monsignor Denis Hallinan, who opposed recruiting from the beginning of the war, though he tempered his endorsement by saying he would denounce Sinn Féin if it involved secret societies or a new rising.[214] The majority of younger priests supported Sinn Féin; Dillon lamented that younger clergy worked with fierce energy for Sinn Féin, while older priests were quiescent.[215]

The Clare by-election was followed by increased repression, already seen in February, when, after the Roscommon by-election, several separatist activists were arrested in what was later called the 'first German Plot'.[216] One Sinn Féiner was killed by police during victory celebrations; another was fatally wounded a year later during a search of the Irish-language training college at Carrigaholt.[217] Ginnell withdrew from the House of Commons and published a collection of his parliamentary interventions (exempted from censorship by parliamentary privilege) to show that free discussion had been stifled in Parliament.[218]

The government, wanting Ireland quiet as long as possible, nervously alternated leniency and repression. While southern unionists grumbled that the government was outrageously lenient and allowed Sinn Féin to police large areas of countryside,[219] *Nationality* protested that County Clare lay under martial law and accused the Irish Party of complicity.[220] The temporary suppression of E. T. Keane's *Kilkenny People,* a long-standing critic of the Irish Party, now pro-Sinn Féin, may have helped

William Cosgrave to victory in the Kilkenny city by-election, showing the party's decline even in urban Ireland. Once again Volunteers virtually policed the constituency.[221]

Irish Party organisation disintegrated throughout wide areas. The remnant of National Volunteers broke with the party and reunited with the Irish Volunteers, an insignificant fragment remaining loyal to Redmond.[222] The government raided National Volunteer halls and seized such arms as could be secured. *Nationality* published a letter from Devlin written during the 1916 negotiations that agreed to the disarmament of National and Irish Volunteers if the Ulster Volunteers were disarmed as proof that the party colluded in rendering Ireland defenceless.[223] *Nationality* regularly published letters leaked by sympathisers in the civil service and party apparatus.

W hile Sinn Féin's growing membership subscribed plentifully, the Irish Party faced bankruptcy. Only a guarantee from party funds, backed by Dillon and Hearn, kept the *Freeman's Journal* alive.[224] O'Connor and Hazleton were sent to America, where they were greeted with abuse that focused on O'Connor's religious beliefs, marriage, and recent appointment as film censor.[225] This appointment was certainly a breach of the party pledge against taking office and a sign of unhealthy closeness to the British establishment; at the same time, O'Connor, a diabetic and short of money, endangered his post by his absence.[226]

It was impossible to hold public meetings in New York, and O'Connor concentrated on wealthy sympathisers.[227] The envoys met more success in Chicago, supported by the Irish Fellowship Club of wealthy Irish-Americans and the *Chicago Citizen,* founded by the 'fire-eating' Congressman John Finerty and now owned by his daughter Nora.[228] O'Connor gave speeches about the war effort in general, to attract American sympathy.[229] He sent back £10,000 for the *Freeman's Journal,*[230] publicised as proof of American support; Sinn Féin (and O'Brien) suggested that the donor was the British Secret Service.[231]

O n 25 September 1917 Thomas Ashe died in Mountjoy Prison, Dublin, from forcible feeding during a hunger strike for political status. He had fought in 1916, had his death sentence commuted to life imprisonment, was released, and then sentenced again for making seditious speeches. He had been one of the most prominent survivors of the rising. Redmond urged the Irish Secretary, H. E. Duke, to concede Ashe's demand for political status, but Duke declined.[232]

Ashe's funeral was a show of strength by the Volunteers, who virtually policed Dublin for the day.[233] Archbishop Walsh, too ill to attend, sent his car; Byrne was the only party MP present.[234] A volley was fired at the graveside. Michael Collins, Ashe's successor as head of the IRB, called this the only fitting speech for a dead Fenian.[235]

In Ashe's native County Kerry, which showed separatist leanings even before the rising, the county council (the only one to refuse to send a representative to the Convention) passed a resolution condemning his death, endorsing the rising, and ordering Kerry MPs to resign. Healy acted as counsel for relatives at the inquest and cross-examined ruthlessly. Prison officials—including Max Green, whose role as head of the Prison Service reflected on his father-in-law, Redmond—acquitted themselves poorly, refusing to answer questions on the grounds of privilege.[236] When the Convention visited Cork harbour they were stoned, and Redmond narrowly escaped being thrown into the river.[237]

Despite such occurrences, the Convention did some technical work—its proposals for a final land settlement formed the basis of the Free State's Land Act (1923)[238]—and progress was made towards agreement between southern unionists and Redmondites, whose positions were now equally precarious. Saying he did not regret his attitude towards the war and would do it all again, Redmond declared that if Ulster unionists accepted a home rule settlement he would make Carson coalition Prime Minister and content himself with some minor office.[239] Stephen Gwynn thought he meant the Speakership.[240]

These were desperate illusions. A Carson-led coalition would hardly have been acceptable to Ulster unionists; and most nationalists would have seen it as a new Protestant ascendancy. Clery attacked the idea of an elite-driven deal as an attack on democracy and partial reversal of Catholic emancipation.[241] Sinn Féin was still gaining strength, and it achieved unity of command in October 1917, when Plunkett and Griffith yielded to de Valera. A National Executive was elected—a shadow cabinet, with portfolios. The divide between compromisers and purists was bridged by stating that Sinn Féin wanted a republic, after which the Irish people could choose their own form of government.[242]

Clearly republicans gained more than dual-monarchists; 'the Republic' became one of Sinn Féin's main slogans. It stood for total separation and complete disentanglement from Westminster intrigues. Many believed that republics encouraged honesty, frugal smallholder egalitarianism, pure morality, and fellow-feeling derived from equal citizenship—in contrast to snobbery, jobbery, and ceremonial display. Such views were encouraged by a short-lived republican upsurge in Britain after the downfall of Tsarism. (Arthur Lynch headed an English Republican League.)[243]

Ulster unionist delegates made it plain that they attended the Convention with no authority to make concessions. Midleton and Bernard complained that unionists had no incentive to compromise if Ulster could not be coerced; if the Convention agreed a settlement, Ulster should not be allowed to block it.[244] In private, Carson, who resigned from the Cabinet in January 1918 to resume the unionist leadership, considered a federalist scheme (that is, less than the existing bill) with separate parliaments as the utmost concession. Carson told Archbishop Crozier that even this risked all their political influence in Ulster.[245] Redmond wanted modified dominion home rule, without an army but with full financial autonomy, including customs and excise. This was further than even southern unionists would go.

In the winter of 1917/18 deaths from starvation were reported in Dublin; talk of a new famine increased.[246] In several places clergy and political activists on both sides organised the purchase and stockpiling of food and fuel, to be sold during shortages to keep prices down.[247] Sinn Féin clubs in Counties Clare and Kerry organised food and fuel supply and land division; *Nationality* and the *Leader* called on others to follow suit.[248] Sinn Féin demanded restrictions on food exports. Volunteers led by Sinn Féin's Food Controller, Diarmuid Lynch, intercepted pigs going to Dublin docks and drove them to an abattoir to be slaughtered for consumption in Ireland. The government restricted bacon exports; Sinn Féin took the credit. British politicians complained that Ireland was treated better than their constituents.[249]

Land hunger and agitation increased. Field founded a Plotholders' League, to campaign for Dublin workers to be given allotments. He was pursuing the party tactic of piggybacking on existing agitation; the Irish Plotholders' Union complained that his league was a political vehicle.[250] Byrne joined in with a Back to the Land Association.[251] Crowds of labourers and small farmers, headed by political activists, turned up at land auctions, offered a 'fair' price, and forbade rival bids, announcing that they would divide the land into smallholdings—'moral economy' in action. David Sheehy and Patrick White did this in County Meath,[252] as did Lundon in County Limerick.[253] In Clifden, William O'Malley and Irish Party supporters campaigned against a Sinn Féin shopkeeper who bought land that was expected to be divided among smallholders; at one point the Redmondite parish priest preached virtual incitement to murder.[254] Commenting on Lundon's auction activities, Moran remarked that it was ridiculous for the Irish Party to say that Ireland could be saved only by constitutional means while disregarding them itself. The failure to punish Carson and arbitrary measures against Sinn Féiners showed that there was no constitution in Ireland.[255] Such developments (involving a member of the Convention) cannot have made unionists more receptive to assurances that alliance with the Irish Party would safeguard their liberty and property.

In the Convention, William Martin Murphy argued for full dominion status, claiming that anything less would breed rebellions. He was encouraged by Healy and O'Brien, who annoyed him by refusing to come in and support him.[256] Hopes that Lord Dunraven might second Murphy's proposal were dashed when Dunraven supported a southern unionist compromise giving excise but not customs.[257] (Murphy had never met Dunraven.)[258]

Redmond accepted the compromise, hoping Ulster unionists could not stand against a united Convention. News leaked out, despite a ban on newspaper reports, and Sinn Féin tried to make it an issue in the South Armagh by-election;[259] but by polling-day, 2 February, the proposal—and Redmond—had been defeated.

Many Irish Party delegates, notably Devlin, Bishop O'Donnell, and Lundon, believed the proposed settlement unacceptable to nationalist opinion. On 14 January, when Redmond was expected to move the motion, he announced he would not do so, as Devlin and the bishops were against it.[260]

Soon afterwards, advised that he needed an immediate operation for gallstones followed by lengthy convalescence, Redmond resigned.[261] Complications set in, and he died on 6 March 1918.[262]

After his death, 'Redmondites', led by J. J. Clancy[263] and Stephen Gwynn, joined southern unionists to produce a report embodying the proposed compromise, supported by a small majority of the Convention; but with Ulster unionists and almost half the nationalist delegates opposing it, consensus was wholly lacking.[264] The authors could not speak for their followers. Lord Midleton was deposed by the rank and file of the Irish Unionist Association; under Dillon, the Irish Party moved away from immediate settlement and tried to reclaim support by forceful opposition.

J. J. Horgan writes of Redmond: 'With him were buried the hopes of a generation.'[265] Yet for a time it seemed that Dillon's policy might bring results. South Armagh returned the party candidate. Redmond's funeral in Wexford produced a display of party support, though no priest from the Dublin archdiocese was present. Bishop Denis Hallinan mimicked Bishop Higgins's attitude to the 1916 leaders and prohibited Masses for Redmond as political demonstrations, and Griffith contrasted tributes paid to Redmond by British politicians with their attitudes to Parnell.[266] Pim accused Redmond of betraying Parnell and wrote demented verse depicting Redmond's soul seized by demons.[267] William Archer Redmond resigned East Tyrone to fight and win his father's Waterford city constituency. T. J. S. Harbinson held East Tyrone for the party.

These victories were less significant than they may appear. The AOH was strongest in Ulster, where it was longest established and kept in trim by the struggle against unionism, while Sinn Féin organisation had not reached east Ulster to any great extent, and the *Irish News* exercised a dominance the *Freeman's Journal* had long lost. West Ulster, aggrieved over partition and with the *Ulster Herald* group backing Sinn Féin,[268] was less promising; yet the party countered the memory of the 1916 controversy to some extent by taking a strong anti-partition line and pointing to Father Michael O'Flanagan's advocacy of partition and the fact that Dr Patrick McCartan, the Sinn Féin candidate in South Armagh, had lent his car for the Larne gun-running. McCartan was a particular target of Irish Party attack, perhaps because he was in America and could not defend himself. Dillon and McGhee, linking Sinn Féin with the IRB, spoke of the vulnerability of secret societies to informers and alleged that McCartan was a British agent.[269]

Clery, spurred by fear of Masonic compromise from the Convention,[270] said he would have fought to include south Armagh in the home rule area. 'They have taken

Carson to their bosom. Let him take them to his bosom.'[271] He reiterated that unionists were entitled to self-determination and asked how a peace conference would treat an Irish delegation claiming self-determination for Ireland while denying it to Ulster unionists.[272] Louis Walsh retorted that the Irish Party majority in south Armagh coincided with the unionist vote; south Armagh was at the same stage as south Longford a year earlier.[273]

Sinn Féin and the Irish Party argued about unionist by-election votes. The party claimed that unionists supported Sinn Féin to destroy home rule; Sinn Féin claimed that unionists voted for the party to uphold British rule.[274] A County Kerry Sinn Féin activist in County Armagh saw graffiti declaring, 'Vote Donnelly and to Hell with the Pope.'[275] *Nationality* revealed that the leading unionist in south Armagh, Alex Fisher, persuaded an independent unionist to withdraw and worked to bring out unionists for the Irish Party. It alleged that only in Crossmaglen had the party outvoted Sinn Féin among nationalists. It added that had unionists abstained, instead of voting tactically for Donnelly, there would have been a Sinn Féin majority of forty in the constituency.[276] Darrell Figgis later said that the Irish Party would have won without unionist support, but he does not give his reasoning.[277] In any case nationalist opinion in the constituency was more finely balanced than it seemed, and *Nationality* claimed that some party supporters elsewhere resigned in protest.[278]

The same factors applied in East Tyrone, despite its long tradition of Sinn Féin activity. Half the electorate were unionists, and the Irish Party candidate had opposed the 1916 compromise. Sinn Féin allegedly considered leaving the seat uncontested but decided to fight as a preparation for the general election, and considered its vote good under the circumstances.[279]

The Redmonds' long connection with Waterford, and loyalties going back to the Parnell split and the pig-buyers' strike of the eighteen-nineties, played a part. Ballybricken pig-buyers provided muscle to take on the Volunteers.[280] (*Nationality* complained that constitutionalism was upheld by 'constitutional' stones and bludgeons.) Waterford had drawn some benefit from the war. A cartridge factory was built, and Redmond got war contracts for Waterford firms.[281] Sinn Féin stressed the unionist vote; the Church of Ireland Bishop, Dr Henry Stewart O'Hara—an outspoken unionist—supported William Archer Redmond.[282] Moran mocked a man who declared the young men of Waterford loyal to John Redmond's policy: if they were they should enlist.[283] Sinn Féin claimed that a vote for Redmond was a vote for conscription.[284]

It can be argued that the by-election victories, by raising morale, could have achieved the retention of enough seats to let the party survive as an alternative to Sinn Féin. This is doubtful. The party was still committed to the war, for fear of government retaliation: when John McKean called on the government to accept Papal peace proposals, no party MP supported him.[285] The party lost its best chance of avoiding annihilation through the Franchise Act (1918), which doubled the electorate and increased the number of young voters with no established party loyalties. The party objected to it, lest constituency redistribution reduce the number of Irish seats, as attempted in 1905. Griffith claimed their real aim was to exclude Ireland from the bill.[286]

The party let the main bill through in return for a separate Irish Bill, negotiated by two unionist and two party MPs chaired by the Speaker. Irish seats were not to be diminished but would be redistributed to reflect population changes. From the party point of view the committee achieved very little. Details of bargaining were leaked (perhaps by Jeremiah MacVeagh, one of the party representatives, who was in contact with Healy)[287] and were used by *Nationality* to claim that the party sold seats to unionists.[288] The new Ulster arrangements improved the unionist position—predictably, given changes since 1885. O'Brien feared the party would get proportional representation introduced, allowing it to survive as a minority and disfranchising many voters unable to handle its complexities.[289] The party representatives asked for PR; unionists opposed it, as it would weaken them in marginal areas, and the Speaker refused to impose such a major constitutional change by his casting vote.[290]

O'Brien had now practically given up attending the House of Commons except on special occasions to denounce the party. He moved closer to Sinn Féin as the only alternative, though he still regarded Sinn Féiners as naïve.[291] He published several pamphlets attacking the party, some of them reproductions of speeches in Parliament, protected by privilege.[292]

Healy attended Parliament when he felt like it, for example helping his friend Lord Beaverbrook, Minister of Information, to fight off a censure motion.[293] When female suffrage was passed by the House of Commons, Healy told O'Brien he wanted to support it to the end. O'Brien considered this too trivial a reason to go himself but said Healy could do as he liked.[294]

During the spring by-elections, William Graham, elected for County Offaly in November 1914, died. All indications suggest that the party would have lost the by-election. While Sinn Féin quickly nominated McCartan, the Irish Party was turned down by three potential candidates before it put forward E. C. Dooley, chairman of the county council, whose vigorous recruiting record was now a handicap.[295]

On 21 March 1918 the Germans began a great offensive on the Western Front. The collapse of the Fifth Army, which included the 16th (Irish) Division, was attributed by some unionists to Irish discontent; this was unfounded, though there had been discontent among Irish troops during the winter of 1917. As the Allies retreated towards Amiens, Healy told O'Brien that within a year a Labour government would rule a defeated Britain.[296] Lloyd George revived the idea of simultaneous home rule and conscription. A bill tightening conscription in Britain and extending it to Ireland was passed in the first two weeks of April, fiercely opposed by nationalist MPs, with some Labour and Liberal support. At the end of the debate Dillon led his MPs to Ireland to help organise resistance.[297] O'Connor and Hazleton returned from America, their mission rendered hopeless.[298]

Dillon and Devlin joined Griffith and de Valera, Healy and O'Brien and two Labour representatives in a conference at the Mansion House under the Lord Mayor of Dublin, Laurence O'Neill, to co-ordinate opposition to conscription. Approval was received from the bishops. Healy and de Valera drew up a formal national protest addressed to President Woodrow Wilson.[299] Ulster unionists sent a counter-protest, quoting Redmond's 1915 recruiting speech on Irish prosperity.[300] Dillon later told C. P. Scott that the party and the bishops joined the conference to forestall any rash attempt at armed rebellion, and managed to get the pro-Sinn Féin majority to agree that major decisions must be unanimous.[301] This did not prevent accusations of treason and Catholic plots, linked by British no-popery agitators to alleged Papal pro-Germanism and resistance to conscription by Archbishop Daniel Mannix in Australia and French-Canadians.[302] Dillon withdrew Dooley, and McCartan was returned unopposed.[303]

A national anti-conscription pledge, modelled on the Ulster Covenant, was taken after Mass at churches throughout the country. Protestant nationalists who asked church-goers at St Patrick's Cathedral in Dublin to sign were driven away; Moran sneered that this showed Catholics were for Ireland and Protestants against it.[304] A National Defence Fund was opened; subscriptions, organised on a parish basis, soon reached an impressive sum. (Private individuals organised a Spiritual Defence Fund of rosaries.)[305] A one-day stoppage was observed everywhere except for unionist districts of Ulster. *New Ireland* complained that Belfast inaction might impose conscription on the whole country and published cartoons of 'Belfast' as an ugly, disobedient schoolboy ordered to toe a line marked *Ireland a nation*, and of a crowded Belfast street, full of recruiting posters, captioned *Belfast looks the other way.*[306]

Sinn Féin kept up attacks on the party. It claimed that Lloyd George had vindicated all its prophecies—particularly that the election of William Archer Redmond would be taken as a mandate for conscription.[307] The withdrawal of the party from the House of Commons was claimed as vindicating abstentionism; and by associating with Sinn Féin, the party diminished the credibility of subsequent condemnations.[308]

Three MPs from the Redmondite right—Gwynn, Law, and Sir Walter Nugent—issued a statement opposing conscription but distancing themselves from co-operation with Sinn Féin.[309] When the government announced that conscription would not be enforced if Ireland provided fifty thousand recruits voluntarily in six months, the three joined a Recruiting Committee of conservative nationalists (including Serjeant Sullivan)[310] and moderate unionists and embarked on a recruiting campaign.[311]

The campaign was led by Arthur Lynch, who persuaded the government to commission him to raise an Irish Brigade, with distinctive uniform and flags.[312] Gwynn and Lynch held one public meeting in Dublin—the first for over a year. Sinn Féin had been taken by surprise at their recklessness. Their second meeting was broken up, but they continued to speak in work-places. Recruiting increased but came nowhere near the desired level.

Some of the Recruiting Committee activists talked of a centre party allied with Midletonites. In the general election Sir Walter Nugent stood in Westmeath as an independent nationalist, while Gwynn contested Trinity College. Both were heavily defeated.[313] They may have encouraged a belief that if the Irish Party disintegrated, a centre party of notables would arise to implement administrative devolution. Long sent Frewen to Ireland to tell O'Brien that if he accepted conscription, funds were available for a centre party to operate the Lloyd George scheme.[314]

The party remained aloof from the campaign, saying Lloyd George's actions were so contrary to the spirit of the Allied cause that they could not advocate recruiting until conscription was withdrawn; but they never entirely repudiated the Recruiting Committee MPs, since others, such as J. J. Clancy, privately sympathised with them.[315] The recruiting campaign and Redmond's acceptance of a post on the staff of Lord French—sent as Lord Lieutenant to oversee conscription—gave Sinn Féin new sticks with which to beat the Irish Party.[316]

The AOH was still strong in County Cavan,[317] but Sinn Féin organised energetically in east Cavan in anticipation of the death of the nonagenarian Sam Young and could draw on local factions hostile to the AOH.[318] When Young died soon after the assembly of the Mansion House Conference, Dillon suggested that the party retain Cavan as quid pro quo for Offaly.[319] Sinn Féin replied that Griffith should have it, since the election of a member of the Conference would prove its representative character, and Sinn Féin was underrepresented in proportion.[320] The party suggested the lord mayor, O'Neill, as a neutral interim candidate. Griffith denounced this as an attempt to shield the party.[321] He asked O'Brien to have the writ moved. Two AFIL MPs went to Westminster and moved the writ.[322]

The party put forward a strong local candidate, the newspaper proprietor and AOH county president J. F. O'Hanlon. Sinn Féin accused the party of undermining national unity and of resistance to conscription, while Dillon protested at the nomination of 'the bitterest slanderer of the Party.'[323]

The campaign acquired a new edge when Griffith and most Sinn Féin leaders were arrested by the British on the grounds of a 'German plot', based on pre-1916 contacts and the capture in County Clare of a member of Casement's Irish Brigade. The Mansion House Conference claimed he was an *agent provocateur* planted to justify repression.[324] (He was in fact a messenger from Germany, asking for a new rising to divert troops from the Western Front.)[325]

Sinn Féin now claimed that a vote for Griffith was a vote against the plot, while victory for O'Hanlon would bring conscription. Support by local unionists for the party did not help.[326] Dillon claimed that Lloyd George was deliberately destroying the party so he could impose his will on Ireland.

Griffith was elected, with a sizable majority.[327] Father O'Flanagan, whose political activities after Roscommon were circumscribed by his bishop (an Irish Party supporter), went to Cavan to spearhead the Sinn Féin campaign. Patrick White also spoke for Griffith.[328] O'Flanagan's bishop suspended him after the election;[329] one Sinn Féiner argued that O'Flanagan was justified by the need to save the Irish people from extermination.[330]

❧

The Prophecies of St Malachy enjoyed a new vogue. Hysterical children saw ominous visions. A child three hours old was supposed to have prophesied an end to the war.[331] One Sinn Féiner suggested that these stories were disseminated by the British government to cause alarm and despondency.[332] While the Irish Party called Sinn Féiners socialists, anti-clericals, and red revolutionaries undermining sexual morality, Griffith claimed that the Allied cause was supervised by Illuminati and Grand Orient Freemasons, irritating the separatist-labour *Irish Opinion*.[333]

As these stories were sometimes presented as reflecting a distinctively Irish irrationality,[334] it should be pointed out that under the stress of war, spiritualism revived in Britain, accompanied by apocalyptic prophecies[335] and rumours that thousands of Russian soldiers were being secretly transported to the Western Front, that the British Expeditionary Force was protected by angels during its retreat from Mons, and that German agents were propagating homosexuality among the upper classes.[336]

Sinn Féiners indulged in joyful millenarian predictions of the downfall of the British empire.[337] Writers like Darrell Figgis, Aodh de Blácam, Father Patrick Coffey and Father William Ferris of County Kerry (a long-standing Sinn Féin sympathiser and contributor to the *Catholic Bulletin*) fantasised about a 'Gaelic state', seen as a decentralised, egalitarian, frugally moral federation of artisans and smallholders.[338] It was presented as the fulfilment of Catholic social theories and the aim of James Connolly[339] and identified with the Bolshevik regime in Russia, praised for its commitment to national self-determination, its supposedly democratic structure, and its resistance to Allied military intervention.

It is unlikely that much attention was paid to such detailed blueprints, but the idea that Sinn Féin would bring a new social order was widely held. The trade union movement aligned itself with Sinn Féin. A new wave of militancy swept Ireland.[340] Even white-collar trades that prided themselves on professional status experienced unionisation. In a few areas, bodies of agricultural labourers remained loyal to the Irish Party, which had organised them, and were absorbed into the trade union movement only after 1918.[341]

Conservative counter-mobilisation by farmers' unions resisting wage demands provided support for the Irish Party in some areas, but big farmers were numerically too weak to provide an electoral counterbalance. When a farmers' union leader became party candidate for Kilkenny North, Labour threatened to oppose him.[342]

Resentment at the social pretensions of big farmers was also important for young men who flocked into the Volunteers in increased numbers during the conscription crisis (though many withdrew as the threat abated).[343]

Such hopes were accompanied by vivid fears. Fogarty claimed that conscription was intended to send the young men of Ireland to death in Flanders while the rest of the Catholic population were massacred by Ulster Protestants.[344] Lloyd George, always interested in the old Radical idea of replacing feudal land monopolies with smallholders, had long talked of settling ex-servicemen on the land in Britain. Now he tried to encourage Irish recruiting by promising land to the hoped-for fifty thousand recruits on their return.

Individual unionists suggested that Ireland should be secured by colonies of soldiers from Britain in the southern provinces[345]—with British wives to keep them from corruption by intermarriage. Such suggestions produced a widespread belief that Lloyd George planned large-scale land confiscation and plantation.[346] Dillon declared that this could be prevented only by sending Irish MPs to Westminster.[347] The last major Irish debate in the House of Commons before the dissolution was on this topic, with the Irish Party questioning government assurances that only Irish ex-servicemen would receive land in Ireland.

Ex-servicemen also served as a focus for fears of British moral corruption. Hallinan denounced proposals to build hospitals for syphilitic soldiers in Ireland, and Griffith commented: 'Syphilis is not an Irish disease. It comes to Ireland from the country which is fighting for Christianity and civilisation.'[348] Two Sinn Féin activists, Dr Kathleen Lynn and Dr Richard Hayes, called for returning servicemen to be interned and tested for sexually transmitted disease.[349] James Stephens equated syphilis with Redmondite support for the war,[350] subliminally echoed in Fogarty's description of the Irish Party returning empty-handed 'with the leprosy of Anglicisation visibly developed on their persons.'[351]

So ended Redmond's crusade, with the sexual hysteria and fears of land confiscation he directed against the Germans turned on those who fought 'for freedom, for religion and right.' Sinn Féin literature called dead soldiers traitors and 'damned souls',[352] a line that Devlin turned against Sinn Féin in west Belfast.[353]

Griffithian conspiracy theories were eagerly received; wartime constraints gave plenty of material. The new Food Controller, the Welsh coal magnate Lord Rhondda, whose duties made him unpopular throughout Britain, was a favourite target.[354] Drink duties fought off in 1915 had long since been imposed and extended. *Nationality* denounced duties on heavy beers as being directed against Irish brewers. When restrictions were placed on Irish distilleries to conserve grain, *Nationality* called this a plot to keep Irish distillers from taking the markets of Scottish distilleries commandeered to make industrial alcohol. (Irish distilleries used pot stills, which cannot make industrial alcohol.)[355]

A wave of takeovers occurred in preparation for post-war competition. *Nationality* denounced the 'Clutching Hand' of Britain reaching out to seize Irish industries, a sardonic allusion to British conspiracy theories of a pro-German 'Hidden Hand' sabotaging the war effort.[356] When Belfast banks were taken over by British competitors, *Nationality* called for them to be boycotted as no longer Irish.[357] The 1918 spring budget increased income taxes further, bringing more Irish farmers into the tax net. Some commentators claimed the government intended to reintroduce rackrents disguised as taxes until farmers went bankrupt and were replaced by military planters.[358]

These conspiracy theories were not mere outbursts of irrationality but reflected the long-standing nationalist experience of misrule under the Union. Plans for the colonisation of Ireland by British farmers had been seriously advanced in the nine-teenth century; the Famine was a relatively recent memory. Constitutionalists from O'Connell to Redmond gained concessions and moderated discontent by combining British politics with Irish agitation within an alliance with progressive British forces. Now the demands of the war called many gains into question, while the dis-integration of the British progressive alliance on which the Irish Party pinned its hopes seemed to confirm separatist claims that the British parties secretly shared an understanding that excluded Ireland and in the last resort would combine against it. The Lloyd George coalition seemed to be this combination made manifest. Erstwhile progressives and supporters of home rule placed the war effort before Irish rights and supported conscription. Even Dillon voiced this conspiratorial view of British politics when advocating a strong representation at Westminster to defeat these intrigues; but what could they do against ruthless hypocrites, united in over-whelming strength?

The Asquithian Liberals opposed conscription, as had the dominant wing of the Labour Party, but this could be accommodated by conspiracy theorists. MacNeill attributed a pro-Irish statement by Asquith to conspiracy among British politicians to distract the Irish from the peace conference.[359] Dillon talked of co-operation with Labour, and the United Irish League of Great Britain endorsed Labour in the general election.[360] But Asquithians and Labour were clearly heading for defeat, and 'patriotic' Labour groups allied with the coalition under prominent Labour defectors seemed to confirm Griffith's claim that the British democracy were as jingoistic as the upper classes. Coalition advocates in Britain and Sinn Féiners in Ireland predicted a British 'patriotic' cross-class alliance transcending party divisions and ruling for a generation.[361]

In the last months of the war, as arrests, censorship, arms raids by police and Volunteers and prohibitions of Sinn Féin meetings were stepped up, constitutional politics seemed increasingly irrelevant. When Dillon decided that the Irish Party should return to the House of Commons, *New Ireland* and the *Catholic Bulletin* com-pared it to the Biblical dog returning to its vomit.[362] *Nationality* claimed the party knew abstentionism worked but were too fond of their pay to adopt it.[363] The defeat of a motion of no confidence put by Dillon was presented as proof of the party's futility (Lloyd George gloated that the German offensive in France and the Irish offensive at Westminster failed simultaneously);[364] and the fact that the police did not break up party meetings allegedly showed that the party were Lloyd George's tools.[365] *Nationality* declared opposition to Sinn Féin treasonable—'Sinn Féin is Ireland'—just as the Irish Party had claimed to transcend faction and represent Ireland as a whole.[366]

Healy was persuaded to resign his seat so that a prisoner could be nominated. This was done inexpertly, and Healy resented it, and the writ was not moved before the end of the war and dissolution of Parliament.[367] Healy urged O'Brien to stand again, refusing O'Brien's urgings to stand himself—though at one point Healy hoped he might become a compromise candidate in a marginal Ulster seat.[368] O'Brien replied that even if elected he could achieve nothing in isolation. The House of Commons, Healy's natural element, was a place of torture to him.[369]

Despite misgivings about abstention and Sinn Féin inexperience, the O'Brienites endorsed Sinn Féin and stepped down.[370] Healy appeared on a Sinn Féin platform and declared that he was still a constitutionalist but that Sinn Féin deserved 'a chance. Moran marvelled at a former recruiter with a son in the army proclaiming his constitutionalism on a Sinn Féin platform, amid cheers.[371]

Despite the arrest of leaders and the suppression of meetings, Sinn Féin was well supplied with money, workers, and hope. With the defeat of Germany it transferred its hopes for a peace conference to Woodrow Wilson, now seen throughout Europe as a messiah. Earlier denunciations of Wilson as Britain's catspaw were glossed over.[372] The Irish Party was short of money and men; its organisation was a ramshackle remnant.[373] Even in Dillon's constituency of East Mayo his supporters were surprised at the dissolution; the party organiser, Michael Conway, reported to Dillon on his attempts to mobilise such local remnants as he could find. Affairs were even worse in neighbouring constituencies. Party supporters in South Mayo did not want John Fitzgibbon—old and associated with the war—but had no other candidate. North Mayo did not know whether or not it had a candidate: until the last minute Boyle was in Manchester threatening to stand against the Labour leader J. R. Clynes if Labour did not leave the coalition.[374] South Mayo fell without a contest, despite talk of nominating a party organiser;[375] Boyle was crushed in North Mayo.[376]

Dillon blamed Redmond, claiming he had allowed the party organisation to run down; in fact activists defected to Sinn Féin because the party seemed to have nothing to offer. 'As to the future he saw nothing for it but to mark time and wait for their opportunity,' Dillon told Scott.[377] Even some party loyalists wished to preserve 'national unity' by stepping down, to return after Sinn Féin failed, or accepting abstention as the price of an election pact that might preserve some residual influence. J. J. Horgan advocated the latter course; Dillon turned it down as entailing responsibility for Sinn Féin actions.[378]

Sinn Féin remarked that the Irish Party admitted it had been deceived for years and now avoided mention of Redmond or recruiting.[379] Just as members of the Irish Party could not defend their recruiting record (though Dillon pointed out that Sinn

Féin's pro-Germanism made it unlikely that the victors would welcome them to their conference),[380] they could not point to the Home Rule Act, for they admitted it was unsatisfactory. The party called for dominion home rule; Sinn Féin pointed to the difference between home rule and dominion status and accused them of hypocrisy, then pointed out the shortcomings of dominion status compared with a republic, with a vigour that haunted some a few years later.[381] Calls for dominion status made it harder to cite welfare legislation against Sinn Féin, since dominion status meant financial autonomy. Moran ridiculed P. J. Brady, MP for St Stephen's Green, who simultaneously advocated dominion home rule and argued that abstention would deprive Ireland of post-war British reconstruction finance.[382] Irish Party talk of going to the peace conference was dismissed as echoing Sinn Féin.

The party spoke of Parnell and Davitt; Sinn Féin replied that Parnell was a Sinn Féiner in all but name and that Davitt's children campaigned for Sinn Féin.[383] Dillon warned of violence and bloodshed; Sinn Féin denied that it intended any such thing, and Father O'Flanagan declared that lives lost in the Easter Rising were outweighed by those saved by stopping recruiting.[384] Dillon spoke of the need for Irish MPs at Westminster to safeguard Catholic education; this won some episcopal and clerical support, lukewarm beside those who worked for Sinn Féin and believed (according to the erstwhile Irish Party supporter and *Catholic Bulletin* writer Bishop Cohalan) that it would re-create a pure, manly, religious Gaelic civilisation safeguarded from corrupting foreign influences.[385] Party MPs ran localised campaigns, arguing that local problems could be solved through the British Parliament; *Nationality* replied that local interests must give way to a national demand for independence,[386] and Moran ridiculed the idea of Field going to the peace conference to discuss Dublin roads.[387]

Twenty-six seats fell uncontested to Sinn Féin, including seventeen of the twenty-four Munster seats; O'Brien called this his triumph.[388] Only fifty-seven party candidates stood. Dillon admitted the party could not get a majority;[389] Muldoon said it would take two elections to win back the country.[390] T. P. O'Connor calculated that the party needed fifteen to twenty seats to survive;[391] Dillon hoped for ten; his chief whip thought they would get six.[392] They won only two in direct contests with Sinn Féin: Waterford city and the Falls division of Belfast, where William Archer Redmond and Joe Devlin were preserved by personal machines.[393] They got four more from a pact with Sinn Féin to avoid splitting the nationalist vote in Ulster, and T. P. O'Connor held his Liverpool seat.

In a last echo of Liberal alliance and old habits in marginal Ulster seats, Dillon tried to secure Derry city for W. H. Davey, editor of the Ulster Liberal paper *Ulster Guardian*; he may have calculated that a Protestant Ulster Liberal might be valuable in opposing partition in the House of Commons. MacNeill, negotiating for Sinn Féin and already selected as a candidate for Derry, thought this an academic gesture and an insult to Derry nationalists.[394]

In East Down, party activists rebelled against the pact and outpolled Sinn Féin, despite being disowned by party leaders and even by the candidate; the Unionists took the seat on a minority vote.[395] Only three other seats can be identified as marginal: South Wexford, where Redmondite loyalties brought the sitting MP, Peter Ffrench, within six hundred votes of victory; Louth, battle-hardened from past struggles, where Hazleton surprised party colleagues by coming less than three hundred votes behind J. J. O'Kelly (Sceilg); and South Donegal, with its strong Hibernian presence and belated support from Bishop O'Donnell, where Devlin thought J. T. Donovan would have been elected had the party machine been sufficiently well organised.[396] Donovan pushed out Swift MacNeill, who recalled that Protestant friends always told him the party would let him down.[397] Pierce O'Mahony was left to fight West Wicklow, which Donovan abandoned as hopeless.[398]

Some claimed that Sinn Féin stole the election through intimidation and personation. Dillon claimed that the authorities ignored violence against the Irish Party. Certainly widespread violence and personation took place. The South Sligo MP and former Fenian John O'Dowd was beaten up when he remonstrated with Sinn Féin activists.[399] There was fighting between party supporters and Sinn Féiners in County Donegal, and a Hibernian was fatally wounded near Glenties.[400] In some cases crowd intimidation allowed under-age voting to go unchallenged.[401] In old age, County Meath Sinn Féin activists boasted that they voted dozens of times in 1918.[402]

The impact of such behaviour should not be overestimated. It was a function of organisational strength, which in turn reflected wider support. Rural Ireland always showed intolerance for dissent and exerted strong pressures for unanimity; the Land League and United Irish League forced reluctant members to join by threats and boycotts. Where loyalty to the party remained strong, violence was used on its behalf. On Armistice Day soldiers and 'separation women' attacked the *Nationality* office, and the acting editor, Séamus O'Kelly, died of a heart attack.[403] Sinn Féiners, including Davitt's daughter Eileen, were attacked by Devlin's Falls supporters.[404] Ballybricken pig-buyers fought for William Archer Redmond in Waterford and broke up a Sinn Féin meeting in Wexford.[405]

There was a clear nationwide voting pattern, with Irish Party support strongest in the east, in Ulster, and in the towns, particularly middle-class nationalist Dublin—though Alfie Byrne held a considerable working-class vote and was to bounce back to a colourful career as Lord Mayor of Dublin and TD. Despite its tribulations, the party held about a third of the votes cast.[406] In 1950 Ernest Blythe, arguing for the abolition of proportional representation, stated that the display of national unity achieved in 1918 would not have been possible under PR.

All Irish Party factions were involved in a common ruin. Philip O'Doherty's anti-partitionism did not save him in North Donegal, and he did worse than other Donegal party candidates because his seat was in the Derry diocese, where partition exacerbated hostility to the party.

Michael Joyce withdrew in Limerick, talking of a hung Parliament and another election within a year.[407] Of the six signatories to Lynch's round-robin, only O'Shee faced the Irish electorate; he was defeated by Cathal Brugha in the new County

Waterford constituency. The Dillonite radical Tom Lundon and the Redmondite conservative J. J. Clancy were both defeated. William O'Malley, the former recruiter, was routed in Connemara.[408] Field's 'labour nationalism' was displaced by the Connollyite Constance Markievicz in St Patrick's.

Dillon's defeat in East Mayo shows the mixture of material and ideological appeals behind the Sinn Féin triumph. Lily MacManus, a Protestant Sinn Féiner, recalled: 'The farmers spoke of taxation; their sons spoke of Easter Week.'[409] Dillon claimed he was defeated by the cry 'De Valera and no taxation!'[410]

Epilogue

REFLECTIONS ON A REVOLUTION

E lements of support for the Irish Party survived its defeat. Some right-wing Redmondites joined with moderate southern unionists in trying to broker a settlement based on dominion status, while the remnants of the Dillonite leadership and their associates at local level clung to the belief that after Sinn Féin had failed, the country would return to its old leaders. Although this never happened, the limits of its strength forced Sinn Féin to accept a settlement whose constraints were condemned by hard-liners in the same terms that Sinn Féin had used against the Irish Party.

The resurgence of conservatism within the Cumann nGaedheal governments of the nineteen-twenties, the appearance of neo-Redmondite groups that were allowed parliamentary seats by proportional representation and the self-justifications of Redmondite memoirists led to the formulation of retrospective justifications for the party, arguing that a home rule settlement could have averted a civil war. Such retrospections tend to overlook the contemporary context that shaped the party's actions, to present the heterogeneous pre-war party in the image of its more right-wing and middle-class remnants, and to ignore the strength of the political, religious and economic factors that were to defeat Cumann na nGaedheal—now with a strong neo-Redmondite presence—and bring about the ascendancy of a Fianna Fáil whose cultural and economic agenda was in many respects that laid down by Griffith. The limitations of that agenda in their turn inspired later intellectuals to look back to the home rule party as a possible alternative.

Such counter-factual speculations are ultimately undecidable but draw their force from the continuing debate about what it is to be Irish and what course the country should follow.

G riffith once depicted a confused elderly man, living in the glorious future Ireland that had been attained by Sinn Féin, claiming that the long-forgotten Irish Party would have done better if given the chance but unable to remember any achievements except talk. Some commentators may suggest that the party's reputation has undergone similar retrospective rehabilitation at the expense of its separatist critics. Why is the reputation of the party so much higher among historians than among contemporaries in 1918?

Certainly the Irish Party never 'came back' after a Sinn Féin collapse, as some expected. Some home-rulers feared, and some unionists hoped, that the withdrawal of Irish MPs from Westminster would see Dublin Castle governing Ireland through notables without reference to wider Irish opinion. This did not anticipate the level of support (through commitment or fear) that Sinn Féin could command or the extent (however exaggerated by propaganda) to which it succeeded in constructing its shadow administration. It is important to realise, however, that one reason for its success was that the British government was not as monolithic or as utterly committed to retaining control of Ireland as separatists had claimed in order to discredit parliamentarianism. Griffith's *Nationality* claimed that Britain's failure to develop Irish resources showed that it would rather lose the war than do anything to strengthen Ireland. If this had been so, nothing short of utter British defeat could have prevented the crushing of the IRA; it succeeded not only because it fought off attempts to crush it but also because most of the British political elite had come to accept some degree of Irish self-government as inevitable, and the political will to commit the forces needed to subdue Ireland at a time of severe imperial overstretch did not exist. In later life some Sinn Féin veterans acknowledged that long campaigns at Westminster by constitutional politicians helped to create this mood.

This did not mean that the British government was immediately prepared to accept that only Sinn Féin could operate Irish self-government. For some time it cherished the illusion that a moderate alternative might emerge if the IRA threat were removed. After the 1918 election most Irish Party activists, including the few surviving MPs, pursued a reactive policy, distancing themselves from the British government and Sinn Féin while refusing to advance concrete proposals, as they had no mandate. Some on the right joined moderate unionists and 'whig' notables in advocating dominion home rule. This agitation centred on Sir Horace Plunkett's Irish Dominion League, with its weekly *Irish Statesman,* Stephen Gwynn's short-lived Irish Centre Party (absorbed into the IDL), and Captain Henry Harrison, former Parnellite MP and future biographer of Parnell. The *Irish Independent* also continued to advocate the dominion proposals that William Martin Murphy had made at the Irish Convention.

In this context, the first apologias for Redmond were produced by Stephen Gwynn[1] and a journalist associated with Sir Horace Plunkett.[2] Sinn Féin leaders were worried enough to devote some attention to counter-propaganda, just as the unexpectedly strong showing of the remnants of the Irish Party in urban elections in January 1920 produced a new wave of electioneering-cum-intimidation; but government repression made it hard to advocate anything less than the full republican agenda without being presented as accomplices of the Black and Tans. The prominence of 'the Republic' as a slogan helps to explain some impulses that led to the Civil War. A few months after the 1918 election the *Catholic Bulletin* suggested that the advocacy of dominion home rule constituted treason.[3] Like the Irish Party, the new Sinn Féin saw itself as no mere political party but as the incarnation of the Irish nation. Its members disliked being called 'politicians', a term they applied exclusively to the Irish Party.

The British government's eventual willingness to negotiate with Sinn Féin came only after it sidelined the Ulster issue by partition through the Government of Ireland Act (1920). The great losers from the settlement were northern nationalists. Divided, alienated from the Dublin leadership, with their remaining representatives in the House of Commons unable to influence the act, they suffered the fate that some had feared abstentionism would inflict on Ireland. Even the veteran partitionist Arthur Clery—now a Sinn Féin Supreme Court judge—protested at the inclusion of nationalist-majority areas in the new statelet. Griffith denounced Redmond as a traitor for accepting partition, declaring that the mere acknowledgment of a right to secede betrayed Ireland's claim to be a nation. He accepted such a settlement himself, giving less protection to the northern minority than might have been obtained with an Irish presence at Westminster.

Like the Irish Party, the Sinn Féin movement that fought the War of Independence had a central leadership apparatus directing a network of semi-autonomous local groups; as with its precursor, the centre was less securely in control than it wished. Some veterans of early twentieth-century separatism were disquieted by the level and nature of violence in the War of Independence: they had expected non-violent passive resistance, or a 'soldierly' fight in the open field. This disquiet was heightened by the Civil War and the obvious comparison (freely employed by republicans) between justifications for rebelling against elected leaders in 1916 and in 1922. For years Griffith declared that the Irish people could liberate themselves if only they had the will, and denounced those who thought otherwise as degenerate traitors; but in the last months of his life the idiom he forged against the parliamentarians was turned against him. In vain Moran recalled how Irish life had been poisoned by Irish Party faction fights;[4] Dillon soon remarked that at least the party's splits were not fought with bullets and high explosive.[5] Reviewing Dan Breen's memoirs, J. J. O'Toole pointed out the ominous consequences of Breen's belief in the right of a minority to wage war without consulting the majority and thanked God he had voted for the Irish Party and was free of responsibility for the consequences of Sinn Féin's victory.

The high point of this intellectual rehabilitation of Redmondism came with Denis Gwynn's authorised life of Redmond—though Gwynn's Westminster-centred perspective, combined with Dillon's refusal to write memoirs and the death of P. J. Hooper before completing the authorised life of Dillon, led to overestimates of the conservatism of the party as a whole. Not all party veterans agreed with the Redmond cult: Arthur Lynch told William O'Brien, 'He was the worst leader Ireland ever had.'[6]

T his partial rehabilitation of Redmondism was not confined to literature. Some elements of the Treaty agreement were carried over from the Home Rule Acts. The Free State senate was intended to fill the role of the second house under home rule, giving representation to the minority and reassuring the business class by providing a platform for notables—though its influence was less than might have been expected and its historian complains of the Free State government's decision to play down its role as much as possible.[7] A few former Redmondites and devolutionists, such as Lord Dunraven and Sir John Keane, joined southern unionists as members.

The old Sinn Féiners in the Cosgrave government were partially supplanted by a conservative element that differed from Griffithian attitudes on several important issues, notably protectionism, and whose increasing ascendancy led some Griffith associates, such as Tom Kelly, Seán Milroy, and Jenny Wyse Power, to defect.[8] It would be a mistake to see this element as purely Redmondite, as it included veteran separatists such as Ernest Blythe, but some prominent members had gone through the Young Ireland Branch of the United Irish League—whether they passed on to Sinn Féin after 1916, as did Kevin O'Higgins, or remained loyal to the party, as did the Attorney-General and Chief Justice, Hugh Kennedy.

This did not translate into neo-Redmondite political revival, though attempts were made in the nineteen-twenties and early thirties to use residual Irish Party support—associated with Counties Waterford, Louth, and Donegal, as well as the AOH, ex-servicemen's groups, and sections of the drink trade—as a focus for elements opposing Cumann na nGaedheal from the right. These included the short-lived National League under William Archer Redmond, whose candidates in June 1927 included twelve former MPs as well as former activists such as Coghlan Briscoe and J. J. Farrell, and the Centre Party, led by James Dillon and the former Irish Party candidate Frank MacDermott. There was also a strong Redmondite presence in the Farmers' Party, whose TDs included the former Irish Party by-election candidates J. F. O'Hanlon and Patrick McKenna; McKenna advocated a merger with the National League.

Most of this support was absorbed into Cumann na nGaedheal when the appearance of Fianna Fáil as an alternative government after 1927 consolidated the right behind its strongest faction. William Archer Redmond ended as a Cumann na nGaedheal TD, and some self-conscious Redmondism survives among Fine Gael supporters in County Waterford, as also in Counties Louth and Donegal, where former National League TDs held Fine Gael seats into the nineteen-fifties. There were Esmondes as Fine Gael TDs for County Wexford until 1977; and two Fine Gael leaders, James Dillon and John Bruton, had Redmondite family backgrounds.

To some extent this neo-Redmondite tradition distorts historical understanding of the pre-1914 Irish Party, which also contained radical elements later absorbed into Fianna Fáil, or into the British Labour and Liberal Parties, which inherited much of the Irish Party network in Britain. Charles Diamond, D. D. Sheehan and Arthur Lynch stood as Labour candidates for British seats; Richard Hazleton and Dan Boyle were Liberal candidates. An element of Irish Catholic machine politics, discernible in certain British urban areas into the nineteen-seventies, is as much part of the Irish Party's historical legacy as its Irish remnants.

On a more personal level, while many Irish Party MPs and activists retired from politics into the comfortable classes, some less firmly rooted in local bases were reduced to penury; one spent his last years under Battersea Bridge in London. For years a minority of sympathetic TDs lobbied for their services to be given financial recognition by the new state.[9] If the Irish Party was remembered in some quarters, in others it was forgotten, as the generation that remembered it passed from the scene, and the political situation that formed it changed beyond recognition. By the thirties even Parnell seemed a remote figure, eclipsed by more recent heroes, though William Field organised dwindling anniversary processions to Glasnevin Cemetery until his own death in 1935.

Some Catholic upper-middle-class elements retrospectively seen as 'Redmondite' would have been 'whigs', beyond the right wing of the Irish Party, before 1906—or before 1914. Many institutions, especially among middle-class sections of the clergy, that had seen their task as producing an Irish governing class and suspected the Irish Party as demagogues and potential anti-clericals came to terms with the new state of affairs, in some cases developing an alternative version of Irish history, reminiscent of D. P. Moran, playing down political nationalism in favour of amorphous Catholic populism. This project, which fulfilled Griffith's fears that the Irish revival might underpin a deferential world view erasing Anglo-Irish and nineteenth-century nationalist traditions, was helped by the fact that the disappearance of the British state from Ireland reduced (without altogether eliminating) the tendency for church institutions to accommodate British attitudes and loyalties and thus relaxed the anti-clerical resentments this had encouraged among some separatists and nationalists.

Conversely, some of the Fianna Fáil elite also had Irish Party connections, though they were less likely to emphasise them than their pro-Treaty rivals. Éamon de Valera's first two Attorneys-General, Patrick Lynch and Tom O'Donnell, came from Irish Party backgrounds. One minister, Patrick Little, was a former member of the Young Ireland Branch. In County Cork, Fianna Fáil inherited the remnants of

O'Brienism, though more as a form of protest politics than as intellectual affinity. O'Brien refused a Senate seat, opposed the Treaty over partition, continued—though less measuredly than Tim Healy, with whom he retained suspicious and uneasy contact—to pour out correspondence and commentaries asserting his own historical importance, and endorsed Fianna Fáil in 1927. One Fianna Fáil Taoiseach, Jack Lynch, came from a family that supported O'Brien, though this heritage lacked any conscious ideological element.

In some respects the Fianna Fáil governments of the thirties and forties were closer to Griffith's vision of Ireland than his ostensible heirs in the twenties. De Valera's formula of 'external association' aimed at the same objective as Griffith's 'dual monarchy': combining Irish sovereignty with a temporary residual link to the Crown to placate those who had not yet fully accepted the nationalist version of Irishness. Under de Valera the economic project Griffith inherited from earlier patriots—industrial development with protectionism, and state-sponsored attempts to replace grazing with tillage as Ireland's agricultural mainstay—was tested and proved unequal to its promises. Whether more might have been done by the sort of political elite Griffith advocated is debatable. Some of his projects, such as surveys of mineral resources, were not pursued for decades; but business associations such as the protectionist National Agricultural and Industrial Development Association, in direct descent from his Industrial Development Association allies, vindicated his opponents' claims that tariffs would bring complacency rather than the vigorous developmentalism Griffith predicted.

Republicans of the twenties attacked Cumann na nGaedheal on the same grounds on which Griffith attacked the Irish Party: that its free trade policy failed to prevent emigration and depopulation and showed an intrinsic relationship between political subjugation and economic decline. De Valera faced the same criticism from his own republicans; when protectionism was abandoned in the sixties, some republicans called this neo-Redmondism.

The new state inherited the version of Irish history popularised by Young Ireland and taken up by Griffith and the 1916 leaders, seen as a struggle by uncompromising patriots against foreign usurpation and weak-kneed temporisers, whose attitudes needed no detailed examination but could be assumed to derive from the basest motives. With its project of a historic compromise destroyed by events, the Irish Party took the place assigned to it by Griffith as the latest exhibit in this rogues' gallery. This view dominated popular perceptions of Irish history until the founding generation of the new state passed away. With them passed much of the canon of literary and political history that formed them, outmoded by the passage of time and the fall of the Union against which it defined itself. Davis and Mitchel faded from view; Yeats and Synge were no longer mistaken for Lord Ashtown. Reassessment was encouraged by the disappearance of the memory of British rule, the failure of independence to herald the end of history, and the awkward presence of those like the aged Brian O'Higgins who equated the rulers of the Irish state with the Irish Party and saw those who resisted them in arms as true inheritors of the apostolic succession.

At the same time some intellectuals from Irish Party or southern unionist traditions found an outlet for discontent with the shortcomings of the new state in historical rehabilitation of the Irish Party. While the new state guarded most of its records from public scrutiny, and the conflicts of its early years were too painful to probe deeply, sources for the Irish Party were plentiful, both from the papers of home rule leaders that were becoming available and the publications of the great home rule debates in Britain, their memory kept alive by Liberal historians such as J. L. Hammond, who looked back on home rule as the great lost opportunity for Anglo-Irish relations and the bloody consequences of its denial as a retrospective vindication of the Gladstonian tradition. It became acceptable to argue that home rule might have led to independence without bloodshed, perhaps without partition.

How far is this view justified? It glosses over not only the strength of unionist resistance—easy to underestimate in a state where unionism was virtually dead and Protestants a dwindling minority—but also the sectarian divisions of the time, north as well as south, the degree of anti-British fear and resentment among nationalists, and the contempt and ignorance of Irish affairs among much of the British political establishment. Redmond certainly won some respect among that establishment by 1914, but how much would this have been worth against the demands of war? The 1916 Rising can be defended as a pre-emptive strike, bringing to a head tensions already gathering because of the different degree of commitment to the war felt by the people of Britain and the nationalist population of Ireland; perhaps if there had been no rising in 1916 there would have been one in 1918, or whenever the British government placed the need to enforce conscription or to repress separatists above the desire to conciliate the Irish Party.

That differential commitment reflected Irish experience during the Union, particularly the decades of home rule agitation. Home rule presented by Gladstone as a historic free-will gesture of national reconciliation might have been widely acceptable; home rule conceded by Asquith after years of delay through a parliamentary bargain might have proved less durable. Even a lasting home rule settlement would have been subject to tensions; in the nineteen-twenties and thirties Republicans regularly accused Free State governments of selling out to Protestant and British commercial elements whose interests lay in grazing, retailing and importing rather than production and the development of Irish resources, sacrificing Irish interests to the dictates of British policy, and disguising as safeguards for the Protestant minority measures safeguarding a corpulent and parasitic bourgeoisie. If a dominion government was vulnerable to such attacks, what might have been said of a home rule government more clearly subordinate to London, more solicitous to Protestant and unionist influence, and under more obligations to local vested interests like the Jinkses of Sligo? Other Morans and *Catholic Bulletins* might have arisen; a delayed civil war might have been more bitter and sectarian.

Another problem in assessing home rule lies in the difficulty of assessing its impact on British politics. The third Home Rule Bill encouraged Scottish and Welsh demands for equivalent legislation; when the secession of Ireland removed the driving force behind proposals to federalise the United Kingdom, the issue faded from the political agenda for almost fifty years. How might a home rule Ireland operating within the United Kingdom have reshaped the British constitution? Irish home rule made more political sense in the context of a Liberal-led Progressive Alliance than the class politics of Labour versus Conservative that displaced it. Might the need to accommodate a home rule Ireland have helped to keep the idea of a progressive alliance alive in inter-war Britain, or was that alliance doomed anyway by the impact of war and economic decline on Liberal attitudes and on the strength and confidence of the British periphery vis-à-vis the centre? Might a home rule Ireland have become a political slum like Stormont or the Québec of Maurice Duplessis—corrupt, authoritarian, bargaining cynically with the national parties in return for toleration to mismanage its own affairs?

Ultimately the answer offered depends on contemporary attitudes. Those who think that Ireland's central identity should be Gaelic or European rather than British or Anglo-Irish, who look upon the subsequent decline of the British empire and the disintegration of the United Kingdom, when traditional elites lost the ability to manage the union state, as vindicating the Irish revolution, who value republicanism as having diminished the deferentialism and self-conscious class system derived from Britain, who attribute the shortcomings of the early decades of the Irish state to the residual effects of colonialism rather than flaws in the original nationalist project, who blame the Northern Ireland conflict primarily or entirely on the unionists and the British rather than the shortcomings of nationalism and the republican tradition, who share with Griffith the belief that the Continental tradition of state intervention associated with the German-American economist Friedrich List offers a surer basis for economic and social development than Anglo-American liberalism, will see the advances of the Republic within the European Union as vindicating the decision of separatists to insist on complete sovereignty so that their successors might freely dispose of it. Those who look more favourably on the Anglo-American model and residual British elements in Irish culture, north and south, who believe that nationalism must accept some degree of responsibility for the historical failures and cruelties of the state and the consequences of the tradition of republican militarism looking back to Easter Week, will be more inclined to assess the home rule project sympathetically as a means of criticising contemporary shortcomings. Some issues that divided early twentieth-century Ireland are dead; others resonate today.

WHO'S WHO

ABRAHAM, WILLIAM Protestant nationalist, former member of the IRB. MP for Limerick 1886–92, Cork North-East 1892–1910, and Dublin Harbour 1910–15 (nominated as a gesture against William O'Brien and a compromise between rival local factions). His age and lack of local contacts made him ineffective as a Dublin MP. He is best remembered for proposing the vote of no confidence in Parnell in committee room 15 of the House of Commons in 1890.

ASHTOWN, LORD (FREDERICK TRENCH, THIRD BARON ASHTOWN) Unionist and ultra-Protestant publicist who thought even the hard-line Chief Secretary Walter Long too compromising and denounced land purchase as 'paying the loyalists to leave the country.' His monthly *Grievances from Ireland* (1905–10) was seen as the epitome of anti-Catholic and anti-nationalist bigotry, and he was even accused of faking bomb plots against himself. Unexpectedly elected to Galway County Council in 1911. His family owned large estates in Co. Galway (where he experienced severe land agitation) and Co. Waterford; he was often reminded that his peerage derived from a deal struck publicly between an ancestor and Lord Castlereagh during the Irish Parliament's debates on the Act of Union.

BOLAND, JOHN PIUS MP for South Kerry 1900–18. A member of the family that founded Boland's Mills; active in the Gaelic League and industrial movements. After political defeat and financial losses in war he emigrated to England, where he worked for the Catholic Truth Society. Father of the novelist and playwright Bridget Boland.

BOYLE, DANIEL Irish Party leader and councillor in Manchester, known for his running of the tramway system. MP for North Mayo 1910–18.

BRADY, JAMES Prominent Dublin solicitor and city councillor. Supported address to Queen Victoria in 1900 but later recanted and joined Sinn Féin. Tried to forge electoral alliance between Sinn Féin and All-for-Ireland League in 1909–10 and stood unsuccessfully for the College Green division in December 1910. Rejoined the Irish Party in disgust at the ineffectiveness of Sinn Féin, but broke with them again in 1914 over partition.

BYRNE, ALFRED Dublin publican, city councillor, and MP for Dublin Harbour 1915–18; he declared openly that he stood for the House of Commons because he could no longer make a decent living from 'my little pub'. His attendance at anti-conscription and anti-taxation meetings from the early stages of the war indicates how opinion was shaping in Dublin. From his election Byrne established himself as one of the small group of nationalist MPs who were outspokenly critical of government policy. He was the only Irish Party MP to attend Thomas Ashe's funeral, and was even offered a Sinn Féin nomination but chose to remain with the Irish Party. Despite defeat in 1918 he enjoyed a long career as an independent TD for Dublin constituencies and became one of Dublin's most celebrated and long-serving Lord Mayors.

CASTLETOWN, LORD (BARNABY FITZPATRICK, SECOND VISCOUNT CASTLETOWN OF UPPER OSSORY)
Landowner of native Irish descent with estates in Queen's County (Co. Laois) and Co.
Cork. Active opponent of the Land League in the eighteen-eighties, subsequently
prominent in the Masonic Order, the Gaelic League, and the Irish industrial movement
(with particular reference to reafforestation). Lived mostly at Doneraile, Co. Cork (his
wife was the heiress of Lord Doneraile), where he maintained friendly relations with the
parish priest, the novelist Canon Sheehan. A leading activist in the 1896 campaign
against overtaxation, which produced short-lived hopes of a political realignment
involving 'patriotic' Unionists. (Carson's participation in this campaign explains Eoin
MacNeill's subsequent delusion that Carson was a crypto-nationalist.) Involved in the
negotiations that produced the Irish Land Act (1903); one of the more prominent
Unionist supporters of William O'Brien's All-for-Ireland League. An ineffectual eccentric,
never able to capitalise on his political opportunities, he suffered severe financial losses
on the stock exchange and spent his later years as a recluse.

CLANCY, J. J. MP for Dublin North County 1885–1918. Headed the Irish Press Agency
1886–90. Seen as the Irish Party's financial expert after the retirement of Sexton. One
of John Redmond's closest confidants and allies; after Redmond's death he was seen as
the leader of the remnants of the Redmondite right within the party. Uncle of Piaras
Béaslaí, the Gaelic Leaguer, Sinn Féiner, and biographer of Michael Collins.

CLERY, ARTHUR (1897–1932) Contemporary of James Joyce and Tom Kettle at University
College; one of the principal contributors to D. P. Moran's *Leader*, in which he wrote
extensively on such topics as the employment problems of Catholic graduates. From
1905 advocated the right of Protestant majority areas in Ulster to exclude themselves
from home rule. A barrister; professor of the law of property at University College,
Dublin, from 1910. Member of the Sinn Féin Supreme Court during the War of
Independence; supported the Republicans in the Civil War and subsequently.

COLE, WALTER Dublin fruit merchant and city councillor. A shareholder in the Healyite
National Press during the Parnell split; later a Sinn Féiner and one of Griffith's main
allies on Dublin Corporation. Lost his seat in 1907 after criticising a demonstration
against the French government's treatment of the Catholic Church (it was being used
as a political vehicle by the Ancient Order of Hibernians and other Catholic groups),
though he later returned to the city council and served in the Dáil.

CONNELLAN, THOMAS Catholic priest of the diocese of Elphin, whose decision to escape the
priesthood by faking his own drowning became the basis for George Moore's novel *The
Lake*. He converted to Protestantism in London and returned to Ireland as a Protestant
missionary, for twenty years publishing a monthly journal, the *Catholic*, notorious for
its retelling of Catholic scandals in Ireland and abroad and its attacks on Catholic
influence over the Dublin Castle administration. A hero to many Protestants and a hate-
figure for many Catholics, his activities helped to increase sectarian tensions in early
twentieth-century Ireland.

COTTON, W. F. Dublin brewer and chairman of the Dublin Gas Company (whose employees
in Ringsend provided him with a secure political base). A highly conservative figure,
regarded as crypto-unionist for much of his career; he headed the section of Dublin
Corporation that favoured presenting loyal addresses to visiting monarchs after the
retirement of Thomas Pile. His business links to Timothy Harrington caused the latter

to fall under suspicion by extreme nationalists. Chosen as Irish Party candidate for Dublin South in 1909; defeated by Bryan Cooper in January 1910 but won the seat in December 1910 and held it until his death in 1916.

CRAWFORD, LINDSAY Dublin journalist, originally prominent as a critic of ritualist tendencies within the Church of Ireland. In 1902 joined with T. H. Sloan MP to found the Independent Orange Order, with Crawford as first Grand Master. Influenced by the writings of M. J. F. McCarthy to believe a more democratic unionism could win the support of anti-clerical nationalists, he moved increasingly towards support for devolution, expressed in the 'Magheramorne Manifesto' of July 1905 rapidly disowned by the Independent Order. He briefly edited the Ulster Liberal paper the *Ulster Guardian* but was sacked because of his pro-labour views; after abortive contacts with William O'Brien he emigrated to Canada in 1910 and later served as a Free State diplomatic representative.

CREAN, EUGENE President of Cork Trades Council in the eighteen-eighties until deposed in 1890 for his opposition to Parnell in the split. Elected 'Labour Nationalist' MP for Queen's County (Ossory Division) 1892–1900 at the suggestion of Michael Davitt. MP for South-East Cork 1900–18; one of William O'Brien's closest allies, he followed him out of the party and into the All-for-Ireland League.

DAVITT, MICHAEL (1846–1906) Former IRB leader and founder-member of the Land League, marginalised in the eighteen-eighties by his opposition to Parnell and support for land nationalisation. A vehement opponent of Parnell in the split; MP for Meath North 1892 (unseated on petition), for Cork North-East 1892–3, and Mayo South 1896–1900 (when he resigned in protest against the Boer War). Helped to organise the United Irish League in 1899–1900. Strongly opposed to the Irish Land Act (1903), which he saw as biased towards the landlords. A fervent supporter of the belief that Ireland's best hope lay in alliance with British Liberals and Radicals (representatives of the 'British democracy') against their common enemy, the Tory aristocracy. His outspoken support for the British Liberal policy of state control rather than denominational control of schooling was developing into a major dispute with the Catholic Church when Davitt died in 1906. While Davitt was alive Griffith denounced him as a traitor because of his treatment of Parnell and alliance with British Liberals; by 1918 Davitt was invoked by Sinn Féiners as the symbol of older ideals supposedly betrayed by the Irish Party.

DEVLIN, JOSEPH (1871–1934) A former barman, active in Belfast nationalist politics from the eighteen-eighties. Founded the United Irish League in Belfast and led it in a struggle with Bishop Henry's Catholic Association. Grand Master of the Ancient Order of Hibernians (Board of Erin) from 1904. MP for Kilkenny North 1904–6 and for Belfast West 1906–22. The only member of the younger generation to belong to the inner circle of the party leadership, he was widely seen as heir-presumptive but tended to defer to Redmond and Dillon at crucial moments. His advocacy of social reform sat uneasily with his alliance with nationalist business interests, and his use of the Ancient Order of Hibernians as a base led to accusations of sectarianism and machine politics. His popularity in Belfast and east Ulster survived the downfall of the Irish Party, but his acceptance of temporary partition as the price of a home rule settlement in 1916 was resented by west Ulster nationalists, undermining his attempts to achieve a united nationalist front after partition. His last years were spent as the powerless leader of the Nationalist opposition in Northern Ireland.

DILLON, JOHN Son of the Young Ireland leader John Blake Dillon. MP for Mayo East 1885–1918. Achieved popularity as one of the pre-eminent leaders of the Plan of Campaign in the late eighteen-eighties; led the anti-Parnellites after the retirement of Justin McCarthy. Associated with the maintenance of an alliance with the Liberals and of a centralised and Westminster-centred organisation; intensely suspicious of those who believed in alliance with Irish landlords and Tories on matters of common concern, on the grounds that this merely propped up Ascendancy power and distracted attention from the need for home rule; he therefore played a decisive role in opposing the Irish Land Act (1903) and William O'Brien's Policy of Conciliation. His gloomy and rather self-righteous temperament led to the hostile nickname 'the melancholy humbug'. He inherited a prosperous shop in Ballaghderreen from a cousin in 1906; this may have influenced his hostility to Horace Plunkett's co-operative movement (which also had political sources). His alliance with Redmond lay at the core of the Irish Party after 1903, but his alignment with anti-war Radicals led him to distance himself from Redmond's fervid identification with the war effort. He succeeded to the leadership of the Irish Party after Redmond's death but lost his seat at the 1918 general election. In retirement, regretting that an Irish Mussolini had not arisen to vanquish Sinn Féin, he oddly resembled those Unionists who indulged in nostalgia for the resolute rule of Arthur Balfour. A son, James Dillon, was TD for Donegal and Monaghan (Centre Party, Fine Gael, and independent), Minister for Agriculture, and leader of Fine Gael 1957–66.

DONOVAN, J. T. One of Joseph Devlin's group of Belfast-born lieutenants; later based in Glasgow. MP for West Wicklow 1914–18; unsuccessful candidate for Donegal South in 1918.

DORIS, P. J. Joint founder and editor of the *Mayo News* (Westport), established in 1899 as a cheaper and more radical alternative to the *Connaught Telegraph* and a supporter of the UIL agitation for land division. Doris always remained an agrarian radical. After 1910 his support for local feeling that the Irish Party had neglected the issue of land division and his hostility to Redmond's war policy alienated him from his Redmondite brother, William Doris MP, whom he held personally responsible for his arrest and internment after the 1916 Rising. At first supported the Treaty but became a strong advocate of Fianna Fáil and its agrarian policies.

DORIS, WILLIAM A solicitor in Dublin, active in nationalist politics since the Land League period. Joint founder of the *Mayo News,* he severed his connection with the paper when elected MP for Mayo West (1910–1918). His defeat of William O'Brien's candidacy in Mayo West in December 1910 was a decisive defeat for the All-for-Ireland League. His support for Redmond's war policy exposed him to increasingly vitriolic attacks from his brother, P. J. Doris.

DOYLE, CANON THOMAS As a curate in New Ross in 1852 he supported Charles Gavan Duffy's parliamentary candidacy against the wishes of his bishop, who responded by sending him to the small parish of Ramsgrange. Doyle proved a successful community leader and did much to develop the area; he was one of the earliest priests to support Parnell and defended the Land League against criticism from other clerics. He turned on Parnell as a result of the O'Shea divorce and denounced him and his followers in the most unbridled terms both before and after Parnell's death. An outspoken Healyite, he lived to denounce the reunification of the Irish Party in 1900. (He also held that it was an act of immorality for a woman to ride a bicycle.) His nephew and political ally Councillor John Cummins of Ballyhack later allied himself with William O'Brien and contested South Wexford as an AFIL candidate in December 1910. Doyle's combination of community leadership and vituperative tyranny illustrates some of the ambiguities in the political role of the nineteenth-century Irish priest.

DUNRAVEN, LORD (WINDHAM THOMAS WYNDHAM-QUIN, FOURTH EARL OF DUNRAVEN AND MOUNT EARL) Co. Limerick landlord, former Tory junior minister and political associate of Lord Randolph Churchill (he resigned with Churchill in 1886). Prominent opponent of the Land League in the eighteen-eighties, later a pivotal figure in the negotiations that produced the Irish Land Act (1903). His subsequent calls for devolution as a basis for compromise between Home Rule and Unionism led to an alliance with William O'Brien but helped to precipitate the Ulster Unionist revolt which brought down George Wyndham. The wealthy Dunraven (he owned coal mines in Wales) was O'Brien's main Unionist ally and a significant financial backer of the All-for-Ireland League. He wrote extensively on the need for Irish administrative reform. Dunraven broke with William O'Brien over his support for conscription from 1915 and his participation in the Irish Convention, where he worked with the Midleton group of southern unionists in seeking a Unionist-Redmondite compromise. Nominated to the first Free State Senate but never took his seat.

ENGLEDEW, C. J. From a landed family; MP for Kildare North 1895–1900. Later associated with William O'Brien's All-for-Ireland League. Extremely conservative.

ESMONDE, DR JOHN From a junior branch of a Co. Wexford Catholic landed family; worked as a doctor in Yorkshire. MP for Tipperary North 1910–15, when he died of an illness contracted at a recruiting meeting.

ESMONDE, JOHN LYMBRICK Son of Dr John Esmonde; after his father's death elected MP for Tipperary North while serving in the British army. Served in the forces that put down the Easter Rising. Withdrew without defending his seat in 1918. Subsequently Fine Gael TD for Wexford; inherited the baronetcy when the senior male line died out. Attorney-General in the government of John A. Costello 1948–50; in 1948 he had been suggested as a possible Taoiseach by Seán MacBride, on the grounds that he had no link to either side in the Civil War.

ESMONDE, SIR THOMAS GRATTAN MP for Kerry South 1886–1900, for Wexford North 1900–18. Senior representative of an old Co. Wexford Catholic family, descended in the female line from the eighteenth-century Protestant patriot Henry Grattan. Spoken of by some as a potential leader of the Irish Party even before the Parnell split. Affiliated with the Healyite faction in the eighteen-nineties, he managed to make his peace with the victors in 1900 but was seen as unreliable. His General Council of County Councils—devised to bring together all local representatives on matters of common interest—was brought under increasing Irish Party control, leading to the withdrawal of Unionist-controlled Ulster councils. Resigned from the party in 1907 to join Sinn Féin in protest at the Irish Councils Bill, but returned to the party in 1908; maintained business connections with the pro-Sinn Féin *Enniscorthy Echo*. Defeated by a Sinn Féin candidate in 1918. His house was burned by Republicans during the Civil War. He served briefly as a Free State senator in the nineteen-twenties. One son, John, joined the Royal Navy and was killed at the Battle of Jutland; another, Sir Osmonde, was active in Sinn Féin during the War of Independence and became Fine Gael TD for Wexford.

ETCHINGHAM, SEÁN Journalist on the *Enniscorthy Echo* and local councillor in Gorey; wrote pro-Sinn Féin political satires attributed to 'Patsy Patrick'. Strongly pro-labour. TD for Wexford 1918–22; opposed the Treaty shortly before his death from tuberculosis.

FARRELL, J. J. Dublin city councillor, a leader of opposition to the address to Queen Victoria in 1900. He suffered financially for his opposition. In 1911, as Lord Mayor, he unexpectedly tried to get an address to King George V passed on his visit and was suspected of angling for a knighthood. He stood in the Dublin Harbour by-election of 1915 but was defeated by Alfred Byrne. During the War of Independence, Michael Collins took delight in planting false information that led to a raid on Farrell's house by British forces. In the mid-twenties Farrell was active in the neo-Redmondite National League.

FARRELL, J. P. Proprietor of the *Longford Leader* and a local historian, active in land agitation from the eighteen-eighties. MP for Cavan 1892–5 and North Longford 1900–18. Allied with William O'Brien and the United Irish League, but became one of O'Brien's fiercest enemies after 1903. A leader of anti-grazier agitation during the Ranch War.

FIELD, WILLIAM Nationalist activist from Blackrock, Co. Dublin, and MP for St Patrick's Division 1892–1918. His father was a Young Irelander, and his political activism went back to the amnesty movement of the eighteen-seventies. Presented himself as both a spokesman of business (he ran one of the biggest butchers' businesses in Dublin and took a leading role in organising the British Meat Trades Federation) and a friend of labour (he attended the first two conferences of the Irish Trades Council as representative of the Knights of the Plough, a labourers' union). He was active in the GAA, the Gaelic League, and many other Irish-Ireland bodies. He seems to have had tenuous IRB links as late as 1900. His effectiveness was limited by extreme personal eccentricity, but as one of the few MPs with extensive contacts among the Dublin working class he was a significant obstacle to the challenge of Sinn Féin and independent labour groups. He was proud of his memories of Parnell and until his own death played a leading role in organising Parnell commemorations.

FITZGIBBON, JOHN A leading shopkeeper, land agitator and former IRB man in Castlerea, Co. Roscommon; Parnellite candidate for East Mayo and MP for South Mayo 1910–18. A strong supporter of Redmond and in later years a significant power-broker through membership of the Congested Districts Board. He was a leading agitator against ranchers but was accused of having ranch interests himself (the truth of these allegations remained unclear; he claimed he was holding the land involved in unofficial trust before its acquisition for division among smallholders). Two of his sons were killed in the First World War. John MacBride worked as an apprentice in his shop.

FREWEN, MORETON A financial adventurer from an English landed family, known for reckless financial and political schemes; he became involved in Irish affairs through inheriting a small estate and through friendship with Lord Dunraven and T. M. Healy. O'Brienite MP for North-East Cork 1910–11. (He resigned because the seat was needed for Healy and because his reactionary public statements were proving a political liability.) Later signed the British Covenant in support of Ulster, while continuing to engage in political intrigues. He was a brother-in-law of Lord Randolph Churchill and Sir John Leslie of Glaslough. His niece Ruby (with whom he was not on good terms) was the second wife of Sir Edward Carson.

GALLAGHER, FRANK London correspondent of the *Cork Free Press,* subsequently its final editor; though himself a separatist, he personally admired William O'Brien. Subsequently de Valera's director of publicity and editor of the *Irish Press.*

GARVIN, J. L. Journalist born in Birkenhead of Irish descent; first came to prominence by his report of Parnell's funeral. During the eighteen-nineties drifted away from nationalism and became an advocate of imperial federation; hero-worshipped Joseph Chamberlain (and became his first official biographer). Editor of the *Observer* 1908–42; during the crises of 1910 tried to persuade the Tory leadership to accept a form of Irish devolution on a federal basis. Said to have discoursed to the surrounding Tories on the greatness of Parnell while queuing to sign the British Covenant in support of Ulster.

GILHOOLY, JAMES An old Fenian and Bantry storekeeper. MP for West Cork 1886–1916, imprisoned during the Plan of Campaign in the late eighteen-eighties. One of William O'Brien's closest political supporters; joined his secessions from the Irish Party after 1903.

GINNELL, LAWRENCE Lawyer and nationalist activist from a small-farming family; organiser in the Irish National League in the eighteen-eighties and nineties and the United Irish League 1900–4. Author of books on early Irish history; research assistant to John Morley during composition of the *Life of Gladstone.* MP for Westmeath North 1906–18 (independent nationalist from January 1910, Sinn Féin from 1917), TD for Westmeath 1918–23. An agrarian radical fiercely hostile to O'Brien's conciliationist policy and showing traces of Sinn Féin sympathies as early as 1906, Ginnell's criticisms of the Irish Party leadership's closeness to the Liberals, his choleric and unstable personality and his uncontrollable pursuit of the Ranch War after 1907 (though, unlike many other anti-ranch leaders, he had no hidden interests at stake) led to his break with the party. After the outbreak of war in 1914, and particularly after the Easter Rising, he became celebrated among separatists as 'the member for Ireland' because of his denunciations of official repression and his frequent pro-German and pro-Sinn Féin speeches. He became an abstentionist in 1917; he was briefly Minister for Publicity in the first Dáil and was then sent to Latin America as an official envoy. He opposed the Treaty and died when acting as a Republican representative in New York.

GRIFFITH, ARTHUR (1871–1922) A Dublin printer active in separatist politics from adolescence, Griffith came to prominence from 1899 as editor of the weekly *United Irishman* (later replaced by *Sinn Féin*) and as founder of Sinn Féin (though he did not become party leader until 1910). A disciple of John Mitchel, he can be seen as the last Young Irelander as much as the founder of a new era; the anti-liberal aspects of his thought (which he emphasised after 1906 in order to attack the alliance between the Irish Party and the Liberals) have contributed to the eclipse of his reputation.

GWYNN, DENIS A pupil of Patrick Pearse at St Enda's, later active in the Young Ireland Branch of the United Irish League; founded the weekly *New Ireland* in 1915 to urge the Irish Party to take a more assertive role in preparation for Home Rule. Joined the British army early in 1916. Subsequently a journalist and academic; his official life of Redmond was decisive in shaping Redmond's posthumous image.

GWYNN, STEPHEN Grandson of William Smith O'Brien, the Young Ireland leader, and one of a numerous Church of Ireland clerical and professional dynasty. MP for Galway city 1906–18. A prolific journalist and author of books, he was one of the few Irish Party

MPs to have close links with the literary revival; he was active in the Gaelic League and a founder of the Dublin publishing house of Maunsel and Company. He was in charge of much of the party's official publicity and its replies to criticism from Sinn Féin. He joined the British army on the outbreak of war and served in the Irish Division until recalled to take part in the Irish Convention, where he sided with the Redmondite faction of the party in supporting compromise with the southern unionists. During the conscription crisis he broke with the majority of the party by supporting a renewed voluntary recruiting campaign. In 1918 he contested Trinity College as an independent nationalist; he then founded the Irish Centre Party (subsequently merged with Horace Plunkett's Irish Dominion League) to press for a settlement by consent on the basis of dominion status, but he broke with the IDL over his willingness to accept partition as a temporary compromise. His later career was spent as a historian and journalist (he was the *Observer's* Irish correspondent in the nineteen-twenties); he and his son Denis did much to shape the retrospective image and self-justifications of Redmondism. Another son, Aubrey, became a well-known Jesuit and historian. (Gwynn's wife converted to Catholicism and the children were brought up in her religion.)

HARRINGTON, TIMOTHY Born in Co. Kerry, a journalist who became the chief organiser of Parnell's Irish National League in the eighteen-eighties; one of the few leading Irish Party MPs to remain loyal to Parnell in the split, and the second most prominent Parnellite after Redmond. MP for Dublin Harbour 1885–1910. Sided with the United Irish League from its early days and briefly considered as a possible alternative to Redmond as leader in 1900. Strongly identified with the negotiation of the Irish Land Act (1903). As Lord Mayor of Dublin accused of equivocation on the subject of royal addresses. (A celebrated challenge on the subject by Maud Gonne at a meeting in 1903 sparked a riot, but it was revealed after his death that Harrington had turned down tempting offers from Wyndham to support an address.) Excluded from Redmond's tight circle of confidants, retaining sympathy with William O'Brien, and seeing his Dublin local base eroded by the rise of Sinn Féin, Harrington was a marginalised figure well before his death in 1910.

HAVILAND-BURKE, EDMUND A former member of the Irish Protestant Rule Association, his activities as a political organiser in England in the 1880s led opponents to dismiss him as a British Liberal. He stood as a Parnellite candidate in the eighteen-nineties, worked with William O'Brien as a UIL organiser in 1899–1900, and served as MP for the Tullamore Division of King's County (Offaly) 1900–14.

HAYDEN, J. P. Brother of Luke Hayden, Parnellite MP for Roscommon South 1885–98, whom he succeeded as MP 1898–1918. Proprietor of the *Westmeath Examiner,* and subjected to extreme hostility by Bishop Nulty of Meath and his clergy during the Parnell split. A close associate of Redmond. Target for anti-grazing agitation headed by Larry Ginnell, who saw him as symbolising the Irish Party's hypocritical tolerance of graziers.

HAZLETON, RICHARD A young professional from Blackrock, Co. Dublin, seen as one of the Irish Party's most promising younger members; active in the Young Ireland Branch of the United Irish League. MP for North Galway 1906–18. His career was disrupted after his defeat of T. M. Healy in North Louth led to a petition followed by protracted court cases, in which Healy tried to recoup his costs by having Hazleton's parliamentary salary seized. In 1918 came within a few hundred votes of retaining the Louth seat for the Irish Party. He later emigrated to England, where he worked as an engineer and stood as a Liberal candidate. Was briefly engaged to the singer Margaret Sheridan.

HEALY, FRANCIS J. A solicitor from Cóbh, cousin of T. M. Healy. Active in the separatist Irish-American Alliance faction of the Ancient Order of Hibernians, in which he served as Grand Master c. 1909–15, and in William O'Brien's All-for-Ireland League; defended separatist prisoners charged under the Defence of the Realm Act. Deported after the Easter Rising, put forward by the AFIL in the West Cork by-election of November 1916. Subsequently supported Sinn Féin and, in the Civil War, the Republicans.

HEALY, MAURICE A solicitor in Cork, younger brother and closest confidant of T. M. Healy. MP for Cork city 1885–1900 (when he was defeated by William O'Brien in a violent campaign), 1909 to January 1910 and December 1910 to 1918, as well as for Cork North-East January–December 1910.

HEALY, MAURICE (JUNIOR) Son of Maurice Healy MP; educated at Clongowes Wood College. Stood unsuccessfully as AFIL candidate for West Waterford in December 1910; regular contributor (including much satirical verse) to the O'Brienite *Cork Free Press*. He moved to England after the establishment of the Irish Free State, built up a successful legal practice, and wrote the well-known legal memoir *The Old Munster Circuit*.

HEALY, TIMOTHY MICHAEL Journalist and barrister; Parnell's former secretary, whose intrigues during the eighteen-eighties and savage attacks on his former Chief in 1890–1 won enduring distrust from moderate anti-Parnellites as well as Parnellites. MP for Wexford (1880–3), Monaghan (1883–5), South Derry (1885–6), North Longford (1886–92), North Louth (1892–December 1910), and Cork North-East (1911–18). In the eighteen-nineties advocated the abandonment of the centralised party structure created by Parnell and supported by Dillon in favour of what would have been a virtual return to the Buttite or pre-Butt situation of nominally nationalist MPs returned by a mixture of local Catholic notables and the clergy, more interested in lobbying for local interests than in their nominal goal of self-government; himself increasingly a part-time politician financed by his growing legal practice and proud of his intimacy (whose value he overrated) with unionist barristers and politicians. In the late nineties entered an opportunist alliance with Redmond and the Parnellite rump but saw his followers purged from Parliament by William O'Brien and John Dillon at the general election of 1900. He survived by dint of his assiduous constituency work and the influence of Cardinal Logue and recruited new malcontent MPs to harass the party. His power for mischief was greatly increased by his opportunist and somewhat uneasy alliance with William O'Brien from 1905. Shifted to support for Sinn Féin from 1915 and especially after 1916 (though a son served in the British army during the First World War). Resigned his seat at Sinn Féin's request in 1918 but returned to public life as Governor-General of the Irish Free State 1922–8.

HENRY, HENRY Catholic Bishop of Down and Connor, who believed Belfast Catholics should avoid involvement in nationalist politics in favour of a representation of communal interests led by notables through a Catholic Association; he was challenged and defeated by the populist nationalism of Joseph Devlin. Henry's ineptitude was a warning to the Catholic bishops of the limits of their influence but left Devlin open to accusations of anti-clericalism from conservative Catholics. A bitter remnant of the Catholic Association tried unsuccessfully to split Devlin's Westminster vote in January 1910 and deliver his seat to the Unionists.

HERLIHY, JOHN London-Irish journalist, editor of the O'Brienite *Irish People* (1904–9), *Cork Accent* (1909–10), and *Cork Free Press* (1910–11, when he quarrelled with O'Brien). Later editor of the *Irish Press*.

HOBSON, BULMER Lisburn Quaker from a Liberal family, converted to separatism as an adolescent through contact with Alice Milligan. A leading figure in the post-1906 IRB revival, founder of the *Republic* (later succeeded by the *Peasant and Nation* and *Irish Freedom*) as a platform for the republican wing of Sinn Féin. Hobson was seem by some friends as a potential second Mitchel but was permanently marginalised by his decision to support acceptance of Redmond's nominees to the executive of the Irish Volunteers in 1914 and his opposition to the Easter Rising.

HYDE, DR DOUGLAS Son of a Church of Ireland rector from Co. Roscommon, picked up Irish as a boy from the local people and became a folklorist and scholar. (His subsequent clashes with Irish scholars in Trinity College reflected scholarly as well as political differences, the dons wishing to have Irish studied as a dead language based on ancient texts and seeing the spoken language as worthless.) He played down his nationalist views in order to unite the Gaelic League and keep as wide a range of support as possible, and was criticised for this by Griffith (who nonetheless supported him and his associates on the grounds that their Munster rivals would fragment and provincialise the movement). Resigned from the Gaelic League in 1915 after it became explicitly nationalist under the influence of separatist infiltrators.

JOYCE, MICHAEL A Limerick pilot whose political career began in a Temperance Debating Society. MP for Limerick city 1900–18. President of the United Kingdom Pilots' Association 1910–23; he proved helpful in steering legislation concerning piloting through the House of Commons.

KEATING, MATTHEW Irish Party activist born in Wales, MP for South Kilkenny 1909–18. One of the party's main advocates of industrial development (he had been a coal-miner for a time in his youth). Subsequently a director of Irish Shell Ltd. His brother Joseph wrote several popular novels about the mining communities of the Welsh valleys.

KELLY, TOM Dublin alderman and shopkeeper, first elected to Dublin Corporation as an Irish Party candidate in 1899 but defected to Sinn Féin on its foundation. Became Sinn Féin leader in the corporation after Walter Cole's defeat in 1907; a strong advocate of housing reform. Publicised the 'Castle Document' by reading it at a meeting just before the Easter Rising. TD for St Stephen's Green 1918–21 and Lord Mayor of Dublin during the War of Independence. A temporary mental breakdown while imprisoned by British forces may account for his failure to attain greater prominence thereafter, though he was a Dublin TD in the twenties and thirties, at first for Cumann na nGaedheal but moving to Fianna Fáil in the late twenties in protest at the Free State government's abandonment of Griffithian policies.

KENNY, P. D. (PAT) Journalist and controversialist; self-educated son of a small farmer in Co. Mayo, long-time resident in England until he returned to Ireland on inheriting the family farm. He became notorious for combining anti-clericalism, criticism of Irish social mores, and advocacy of land reclamation. First editor of the *Irish Peasant,* he defected to Unionism on its demise.

KENNY, P. W. Nationalist from Co. Waterford who had spent much of his career in Australia, active in local politics and the Gaelic League. Although a nominal follower of the Irish

Party, his relations with its leaders were awkward, and he took a leading role in wartime campaigns against overtaxation. After 1916 he took a prominent role in the Irish Nation League and subsequently in Sinn Féin. Briefly a Free State senator in the nineteen-twenties.

KETTLE, THOMAS M. Son of the Land League veteran Thomas Kettle and son-in-law of David Sheehy. One of the leading members of the group of young professionals who founded the Young Ireland Branch of the United Irish League in the hope of giving new intellectual life to the Irish Party. MP for East Tyrone 1906–1910. A brilliant wit and orator who failed to advance because of a drink problem, possible distrust by elements of the leadership, and a certain dilettantism. (He gave up his seat to concentrate on his duties as professor of national economics at UCD but continued to speak widely at political rallies and was accused by some students of neglecting his duties in favour of his political activities.) One of the most fervent advocates of recruitment in the early days of the war, and one of the most prominent targets of abuse from separatists. By the time of his death at the Somme in July 1916 he had lost much of his earlier enthusiasm for the war, a process hastened by the Easter Rising. His personal charm and an intelligence not fully captured in his surviving writings won him the admiration of most of his friends and students and a lasting reputation as a martyr to frustrated ideals.

LARDNER, J. C. R. Educated at Clongowes Wood, a Co. Monaghan solicitor with Healyite sympathies; MP for North Monaghan 1907–18 (after an unsuccessful attempt by the Board of Erin faction of the AOH to pack the convention in favour of John T. Donovan). His position as Chief Ranger of the Irish National Foresters also brought conflict with the AOH, as the two friendly societies were competing for similar customers.

LAW, HUGH Son of Hugh Law, Liberal Lord Chancellor of Ireland in the eighteen-eighties. MP for Donegal West 1906–18. Active in the Gaelic League and the industrial revival movement; one of the few Irish Party MPs to take an interest in the literary revival (he was a close friend of George Russell, who regularly holidayed on his Co. Donegal property). Strong supporter of Redmond's pro-war policy; one of his sons joined the British army and became a professional officer. He broke with the party in 1918 over its co-operation with Sinn Féin in the anti-conscription campaign. Cumann na nGaedheal TD for Donegal 1927–32, fiercely attacked for his criticism of censorship legislation. A convert from Protestantism to Catholicism.

LUNDON, THOMAS Son of William Lundon; MP for Limerick East 1909–18. Closely associated with John Dillon; particularly hated by O'Brienites for his role in splitting the Land and Labour Association and his personal insults to O'Brien. A labourers' representative at the Irish Convention of 1917–18. After his defeat worked in the horse-racing industry and married a daughter of the prominent Cork Redmondite (later Farmer and Fine Gael) county councillor D. L. O'Gorman.

LUNDON, WILLIAM A veteran of the 1867 Fenian rising (though accused by separatists of exaggerating his involvement) and MP for East Limerick 1900–9. At first associated with William O'Brien but turned against him after his resignation in 1903.

LYNCH, COLONEL ARTHUR Australian-born adventurer; his father, John Lynch, was second in command of the miners' revolt at the Eureka Stockade. Educated in German and French universities. Parnellite candidate for Galway city 1892. As a journalist in London in the eighteen-nineties he moved in London poetic circles and worked with

Maud Gonne in France in support of Irish republicans. In 1899 he went to South Africa and commanded the second Irish Brigade in the Boer army. After the occupation of the Boer Republics in 1900 he returned to France. In 1901 he was elected in absentia as Nationalist MP for Galway city, having declared his conversion to constitutionalism. He returned to Britain to take his seat, was arrested and tried for high treason; his death sentence was commuted to a short term of imprisonment, after which he established himself as a doctor in London. In 1909 he became MP for West Clare but made little impression in the House of Commons and was involved in controversy by his religious agnosticism, criticisms of the political role of the clergy, and calls for a greater emphasis on science in education. He saw Redmond as excessively conservative and was fiercely opposed to partition. His Francophilia made him a strong supporter of the First World War. He was always a republican on principle and in 1917–18 led a short-lived English republican movement. In 1918 he took a leading role in a last-minute recruiting drive in Ireland, despite opposition from Sinn Féin and the leadership of the Irish Party. In 1918 he stood as a Labour candidate in a London constituency. His last years were spent in criticising Einstein's theory of relativity.

MacBride, Major John From a Westport shopkeeping family; emigrated to the Transvaal, where he worked with Arthur Griffith in lobbying the Irish community to support the Boer Republics against pro-British intrigues. Second in command of one of the Irish Brigades fighting for the Boers, his exploits made him a hero to separatists in Ireland. In 1900 separatists joined with local Healyites and ranchers to put him forward in the South Mayo by-election after the resignation of Michael Davitt, in the hope of damaging the growing United Irish League and discrediting the Irish Party by forcing it to oppose MacBride. MacBride remained abroad for some years but returned to Ireland after the squalid breakdown of his marriage with Maud Gonne; he was given an official job by Dublin Corporation and remained active in separatist politics. Shot by firing squad in 1916 for his participation in the Easter Rising.

McCann, James Dublin stockbroker, a former Unionist who became Independent Nationalist MP for the St Stephen's Green division of Dublin 1900–4. He advocated schemes for economic revival, including the development of the canal system to compete with the railways and the encouragement of tillage through division of land. His schemes centred on Navan, where he opened a sawmill and bacon factory and the *Irish Peasant,* whose increasing anti-clericalism after McCann's death led to its suppression by Cardinal Logue.

MacCarthy, Justin Born in Co. Cork, a journalist in London and popular novelist and historian; Parnell's deputy leader in the eighteen-eighties. Elevated to titular leadership of the anti-Parnellites at the split, among Parnellite jeers and sniping from the rival claimants to the succession. Retired in 1896 and succeeded by John Dillon.

MacCarthy, Michael Barrister and religious controversialist. Son of a Co. Cork farmer and Land Leaguer, he graduated from Trinity College and in the early eighteen-eighties worked as a barrister and parliamentary lobbyist for the drink trade. A nationalist at first, by 1890 he had become a unionist and from 1900 attracted notoriety as author of a series of books declaring that all Ireland's ills derived from the extortions of the Catholic priesthood. (He later formally converted to Protestantism.) His books were widely read by unionists and exerted significant influence on Lindsay Crawford's brand of 'democratic unionism', while Catholics and nationalists denounced him as a turn-coat and hypocrite. He emigrated to England in 1904 after an abortive attempt to stand as a parliamentary candidate in protest against the Unionist government's alleged temporising with nationalism and the Catholic hierarchy, and remained an active pamphleteer until the early twenties.

McCARTHY, TIM Born in Co. Cork; editor of William O'Brien's weekly *Irish People* 1900–3, subsequently editor of the *Irish News* (Belfast) and one of Joseph Devlin's closest allies.

McKEAN, JOHN MP for South Monaghan 1906–18 (Independent Nationalist from January 1910), chiefly notable for his outspoken clericalism. Attacked Roger Casement's exposé of Belgian atrocities in the Congo as a British fabrication aimed at annexing the Congo. Had Healyite sympathies but never joined the All-for-Ireland League. In 1918 called on the British government to respond to Pope Benedict XV's peace initiative. His local supporters transferred to Sinn Féin on his retirement.

MacMANUS, SEUMAS Separatist activist and prolific author of dialect stories about Co. Donegal. Married the separatist poet 'Ethna Carbery' (Anna Johnston). Grand Master of the Irish-American Alliance faction of the AOH and a prominent Sinn Féin activist until he emigrated to America (where he vigorously opposed performances of *The Playboy of the Western World*).

MacNEILL, EOIN (SOMETIMES CALLED JOHN) Irish scholar and civil servant. His upbringing in the Glens of Antrim and contact with the Co. Antrim Presbyterian Liberal tradition led him to underestimate the depth of Ulster unionist opposition to home rule. Benefited from the extension of competitive examinations for admission to the civil service, which helped to loosen the grip of Ascendancy patronage networks. One of the founders of the Gaelic League with Douglas Hyde, and played a major role in its early years of organisation. One of the great Irish scholars of all time; his nationalist sympathies stimulated him in overturning schematic 'evolutionary' accounts of pre-conquest Ireland, which implicitly took the British state model as the norm. Despite his nominal support for the Irish Party he was (like some members of the Young Ireland Branch of the United Irish League) far more separatist-inclined than the party leadership; his protestations of loyalty to Redmond during the early months of the Irish Volunteers should not be taken at face value, since they were accompanied by a refusal to obey Redmond's instructions. He consistently believed in the existence of a British plot to enslave or even exterminate the Irish, and this brought him near to the Griffithian perspective, especially after the outbreak of war. His strategy, based on waiting for the course of events to reunite Irish opinion behind the Volunteers, required Volunteer unity above all else and expected that at some stage the British would mount a pre-emptive strike against them as a prelude to military dictatorship; this (as well as a certain personal passivity and misplaced trust in his long friendship with Pearse) lies behind his failure to confront the IRB advocates of a pre-emptive strike by the Volunteers and his willingness to accept the 'Castle Document' as genuine. Rejoined Sinn Féin after his release in 1917, despite controversy about his attempt to block the Rising. TD for Derry city and National University of Ireland 1918–21, for Clare 1921–7.

MacNEILL, (J. G.) SWIFT MP for South Donegal 1887–1918; from a Church of Ireland Tory background claiming collateral descent from Jonathan Swift. Eccentric but with a formidable mastery of parliamentary procedure and a habit of campaigning against official corruption. Professor of law at University College, Dublin, from 1911. Highly aggrieved by his deselection in 1918 in favour of John T. Donovan.

MacVEAGH, JEREMIAH Active in the Belfast Gaelic League in the eighteen-nineties; later ran a hotel in London. MP for South Down 1902–22; one of the more prominent Ulster nationalist MPs, known as a parliamentary wit, with some residual Healyite sympathies. An unsuccessful Dáil candidate for Monaghan in the nineteen-twenties.

MacWALTER, DR J. C. An apothecary and leading light of the Dublin Catholic Association, much derided by Griffith and closely associated with Moran. The only Dublin Corporation nationalist to oppose compulsory Irish, he boasted when the bishops spoke on the issue that his opponents would come to heel like whipped dogs. A very prominent exponent of local machine politics combined with an emphasis on Catholic interests rather than nationalism. Attempts to recruit him to a new anti-Sinn Féin centre party after 1918 were frustrated by his death in 1920.

MARTYN, EDWARD A Catholic landlord in Co. Galway, originally a unionist but converted to separatism by reading Lecky in the eighteen-nineties. An early Abbey Theatre play-wright and patron of the arts. One of Griffith's financial backers; first President of Sinn Féin 1905–8. Severely limited by his eccentricities; a recluse in his later years.

MEAGHER, MICHAEL A veteran of the 1867 Fenian rising and MP for North Kilkenny 1906–18. One of the more separatist-inclined members of the Irish Party, highly critical of British taxation and of Redmond's support for the war; an associate of E. T. Keane, editor of the *Kilkenny People,* who—unlike Meagher—supported Sinn Féin after 1916.

MILLIGAN, ALICE Protestant nationalist poet. At first active in support of evicted tenants in Co. Donegal during the Plan of Campaign in the late eighteen-eighties, she became a sepa-ratist after the Parnell split, believing the Liberals had cynically exploited the Irish for electoral advantage. In 1896–9 she ran the pioneering separatist monthly *Shan Van Vocht* in Belfast with 'Ethna Carbery' (Anna Johnston); it later merged with Griffith's *United Irishman.* A frequent contributor to the nationalist and Irish-Ireland press; campaigned for Sinn Féin after 1916.

MOONEY, J. J. Member of a prominent Dublin business and pub-owning family; MP for Dublin South 1900–6 and Newry 1909–18. One of the younger members of Redmond's inner circle; seen as right-wing in nationalist terms. After 1918 pursued a career at the English bar.

MORAN, DAVID PATRICK (1869–1936) Irish-Ireland journalist who founded the weekly *Leader* in 1900. His combination of cultural nationalism with an emphasis on Catholicism as the core of Irish identity and vigorous denunciations of anti-Catholic job discrimination proved attractive to many young Catholic professionals; it also encouraged sectarian divisions and led Griffith to denounce 'D. P. Hooligan' as the inventor of a new ratio-nale for Catholic whig job-hunters. Moran's view of parliamentary orators and separatist 'tin-pikers' as irrelevant fantasists reflected conditions under the long Tory ascendancy of the eighteen-nineties and carried less charge after 1906, but his importance as cultural chauvinist, encourager of political debate and spokesman for economic national-ism should not be underestimated.

MULDOON, JOHN Born in Co. Tyrone, a solicitor and close political confidant of John Dillon. MP for Donegal North 1905–6, but deselected by the local clergy; his difficulties in securing another seat reflect the limits to the power of the central leadership of the Irish Party over local organisations. MP for West Wicklow 1909–11 and Cork East 1911–18.

MURPHY, WILLIAM MARTIN Business tycoon closely associated with T. M. Healy; MP for St Patrick's division, Dublin, 1885–92 and unsuccessful candidate in 1895 and 1900. Disliked by separatists because of his cosmopolitan business interests and promotion of an International Exhibition seen as dominated by snobs and importers; principal target of Larkinite hostility as employers' leader during the 1913 lock-out. Murphy's development of the *Irish Independent* to displace the *Freeman's Journal*, with its orientation towards the Irish Party, as principal paper of the Irish middle class, while keeping its criticisms of the party sufficiently veiled to avoid a political boycott, played a significant role in weakening the party. He saw the third Home Rule Bill as granting insufficient fiscal autonomy, fiercely opposed partition after 1916, and played a leading role in organising opposition within the Irish Convention to Redmond's attempts to work out a compromise with southern unionists.

NANNETTI, J. P. Dublin printer and nationalist activist, MP for College Green, Dublin, 1900–15; he represented an older school of trade unionism, based on skilled workmen and emphasising shared interests between workman and employer, which was challenged by the rise of Larkinite mass unionism. By 1913 he had been incapacitated by a series of strokes; his death in 1915 and the appearance of an independent Labour candidate in the subsequent by-election are seen as significant in the drift of labour voters away from the Irish Party. He appears in the 'Aeolus' episode of *Ulysses*.

NUGENT, JOHN DILLON National secretary of the Board of Erin faction of the AOH from 1904; MP for College Green, Dublin, 1915–18 and member of the Northern Ireland Parliament 1921–5. Devlin's right-hand man, he was widely denounced for orchestrating intimidation against opponents (including suffragists and Larkinites). Engaged in vociferous quarrels with Pearse at meetings of the Volunteer Executive in 1914.

NUGENT, SIR WALTER MP for South Westmeath 1907–18; a baronet from an old Catholic gentry family and a financial expert brought in to help run the *Freeman's Journal* before 1916. Very much on the right of the Irish Party; in 1918 he supported the last-ditch recruiting campaign devised as an alternative to conscription and denounced the party leadership for allying itself with Sinn Féin in the anti-conscription campaign. Associated with Hugh Law and Stephen Gwynn. Crushingly defeated as an independent nationalist candidate for Westmeath in 1918; subsequently a Free State senator and a governor of the Bank of Ireland.

O'BRIEN, PAT MP for Limerick 1886–92, Kilkenny city 1895–1917. A former Fenian, one of John Redmond's small circle of political intimates; Chief Whip 1907–17. His death from a stroke soon after the death of W. H. K. Redmond in the First World War was a devastating political and personal blow to the party leader.

O'BRIEN, WILLIAM (1852–1928) From a professional family in Mallow that had come down in the world, O'Brien became a journalist and made Parnell's acquaintance while covering his political activities. First editor of the Parnellite weekly *United Ireland*; MP for Mallow (1882–5), South Tyrone (1885–6), North-East Cork (1887–92), Cork city (1892–6, 1900–3, 1904–9, 1910–18). Achieved his highest fame as campaigner for the Plan of Campaign in the eighteen-eighties, when he was repeatedly arrested and refused to wear prison clothing. A powerful orator, capable of inspiring immense admiration, but also autocratic, egoistic, and deeply unstable. He retired from Parliament after the defeat of the second Home Rule Bill but returned to prominence with his founding of the United Irish League as a vehicle for western calls for land reform and a means of reuniting the Irish Party. His involvement in the Land Conference that negotiated the terms of the Irish Land Act (1903) convinced him that similar conferences on matters of common concern could convert moderate unionists to a form of home rule; this aroused opposition from sections of the party who saw it as watering down home rule, and O'Brien's decision to resign rather than argue his case within the party was fatal to his influence. Thereafter he operated as leader of an increasingly Cork-centred faction in alliance with Lord Dunraven's devolutionists and his old enemy T. M. Healy; in 1910 this was formalised by the creation of the All-for-Ireland League. He was vehemently opposed to partition and after the final collapse of the AFIL supported Sinn Féin; in 1922 he opposed the Treaty because of partition, and in 1927 he endorsed Fianna Fáil.

O'CONNOR, JOHN ('LONG JOHN') A former Fenian, Parnellite MP for Tipperary South (1885–92) and North Kildare (1902–18). A close friend of Lord Loreburn, Liberal Lord Chancellor 1905–12. Although he nearly involved the Irish Party in scandal by his messy private life (which he had omitted to inform Redmond about when soliciting a candidacy) and on one occasion refused to fight a crucial by-election after he had explicitly applied for the seat, Redmond remained close to O'Connor.

O'CONNOR, THOMAS POWER Born in Athlone, became a journalist in London; MP for Galway 1880–5 and Liverpool (Scotland Division) 1885–1928. His role in the 'new journalism' (widely denounced as immoral), his lax adherence to Catholicism and his marital problems were often used against the Irish Party by its opponents. His close personal contacts with British Liberal and Labour activists made him a useful go-between (and at times allowed him to rouse pro-Irish Radical backbenchers against their leaders) but also encouraged charges of subservience by the Irish Party to British politicians. As head of the party organisation in Britain he also channelled the concerns of the Irish community in Britain. He was criticised in Liverpool as an absentee MP. His Irish accent is said to have fluctuated in inverse proportion to his proximity to Ireland.

O'DONNELL, JOHN A protégé of William O'Brien, who recruited him as UIL organiser in Mayo in 1898–9; MP for South Mayo 1900–10. He became national secretary of the United Irish League but resigned in 1904 because of his continuing support for William O'Brien and was identified as one of the little knot of O'Brien's diehard supporters. More electorally vulnerable than the Cork O'Brienites, he survived in 1906 through a party truce (and a jail sentence for land agitation) and in January 1910 through clerical support against the anti-clerical Conor O'Kelly. He was forced to retire through lack of support in December 1910 while an Irish Party boycott drove his newspaper, the *Connaught Champion,* out of business. He retained links with O'Brien but never made a political comeback. Persistently rumoured to have unsuccessfully sought admission to the RIC before embarking on his political career.

O'DONNELL, THOMAS MP for West Kerry 1900–18, active in the Gaelic League. Despite some flirtations with separatism and with William O'Brien, by 1914 he was seen as one of the Irish Party's rising stars and possible member of a home rule government. One of the party's strongest supporters of recruitment in 1914–16, criticised for failing to join up himself (he had ten children). Returned to politics in the nineteen-twenties as a leading member of the National League; later joined Fianna Fáil, served as de Valera's second Attorney-General, and became a judge.

O'DOWD, JOHN Veteran of the Fenian rising and Land League, active in the United Irish League; MP for North Sligo (1900) and South Sligo (1900–18); author of popular verse. Accused of corruption and of organising violence against Sinn Féin supporters during the North Leitrim by-election of 1908; beaten up and severely injured by Sinn Féiners on polling day in 1918.

O'GRADY, STANDISH JAMES Tory journalist who lamented the decline of the gentry, complaining (in a style of thought derived from earlier Irish Tories like Charles Lever) that they had opened the way for the Land League by abandoning heroic for commercial values. His invocation of the heroic Irish past as exemplar of these virtues (in a style derived as much from Carlyle and Whitman as from Irish literature) influenced the Irish revival and the Gaelic League, though the results were often mutually embarrassing. MacNeill blamed O'Grady's version of the Cú Chulainn story for Pearse's cult of blood sacrifice.

O'KELLY, CONOR MP for North Mayo 1900–1910. His career was marked by conflict with the local clergy, dating back to his youthful activities during the Parnell split. He maintained an ambiguous position between O'Brien and Redmond, though on the whole favouring the Redmondite side. His parliamentary career ended in January 1910 when the leadership of the Irish Party responded to clerical attempts to deselect him by imposing a compromise candidate in North Mayo and sending O'Kelly to South Mayo, where the local clergy opportunistically supported John O'Donnell to keep O'Kelly out.

O'MAHONY, PIERCE Member of a landed family with estates in Co. Wicklow and Co. Kerry (his grandfather was a prominent associate of Daniel O'Connell). Parnellite MP for North Meath 1886–92, when he was deposed in a bitter contest, after which the victor was unseated on petition. O'Mahony spent most of the succeeding decades in Bulgaria, where he founded an orphanage, and campaigning to clear the name of his half-brother, Sir Arthur Vicars, accused of stealing the regalia of the Order of St Patrick. He supported the First World War but tried unsuccessfully to persuade the Allies to make concessions to Bulgaria in order to prevent it joining the Central Powers. Unsuccessful Redmondite candidate in the Dublin Harbour by-election of 1915 and the 1918 general election, when he contested West Wicklow. His son was a Fine Gael TD for Wicklow in the nineteen-thirties.

O'MALLEY, WILLIAM Born in Co. Galway, a brother-in-law of T. P. O'Connor; a journalist in London and MP for the Connemara division of Co. Galway 1895–1918. His involvement with dubious speculative companies was widely criticised. At the beginning of the First World War he took a prominent part in recruiting. His only surviving son joined up and was killed in action.

O'SHAUGHNESSY, P. J. MP for West Limerick 1900–18; seen as having some sympathy with William O'Brien but remained within the mainstream Irish Party. One of two party MPs to formally oppose the partition-based compromise proposals of 1916.

O'SHEE, J. J. A solicitor in Clonmel, MP for West Waterford 1895–1918. Founded the Land and Labour Association with D. D. Sheehan but remained loyal to the Irish Party when the Sheehan faction broke from the LLA to support William O'Brien. One of the more socially radical members of the party, he called on it to adopt a more aggressively nationalist position after 1916.

PEARSE, PATRICK H. Schoolmaster and Gaelic Leaguer. Criticised at first by some separatists, who distrusted his tendency to place cultural above political activism, he was in fact showing separatist sympathies by 1906, though he did not become prominent as a separatist until about 1912. His late pamphlets may be seen as the culmination of the Mitchel tradition as developed by Griffith.

PILE, SIR THOMAS A home-ruler from a predominantly unionist family, Pile became Lord Mayor of Dublin in 1899 as a nationalist and advocate of municipal reform but caused controversy by supporting the presentation of a municipal address of welcome to Queen Victoria. He was rewarded with a baronetcy and moved to England (where he remained an active Liberal home-ruler) in pursuit of business interests.

PIM, HERBERT MOORE A member of the northern branch of a prominent Quaker business dynasty who worked as an insurance clerk in Belfast and a minor man of letters. Pim progressed from conservatism to liberalism to home rule (and membership of the Ancient Order of Hibernians, having converted to Catholicism); for some time he was the leading member of the Belfast equivalent of the Young Ireland Branch. On the out-break of the First World War he defected to the Irish Volunteers, became one of their main northern organisers, and suffered a short term of imprisonment in 1915 under the Defence of the Realm Act. After the failed attempt to mobilise the Belfast Volunteers in 1916 he was arrested and deported to England. On his release in late 1916 he used his weekly, the *Irishman,* to proclaim himself the heir to Griffithian Sinn Féin and to denounce all those who failed to comply with its abstention policy. With the release of the leaders and the consolidation of Sinn Féin he was increasingly marginalised, despite selection as parliamentary candidate for West Belfast, and in 1918 reverted to union-ism and declared his support for conscription. He subsequently went to London and jointly edited a virulently anti-Sinn Féin weekly with his friend Lord Alfred Douglas.

PLUNKETT, GEORGE NOBLE (COUNT) Parnellite candidate for mid-Tyrone 1892 and St Stephen's Green, Dublin, 1895. Director of the National Museum, widely seen as a place-hunting whig nationalist (he was active in the Dublin branch of Joseph Chamberlain's Tariff Reform League and served on a royal reception committee in 1911). Radicalised by the involvement of his sons with the Volunteers and by the rejection of his application to become Under-Secretary in 1914, he served as a Continental envoy for the planners of the 1916 Rising. His imprisonment after the rising, dismissal as Director of the National Museum and expulsion from the Royal Dublin Society were widely seen as unfair and vindictive, and this helped to secure his election as MP for North Roscommon in 1917. A brief attempt to establish himself as national leader of a new republican organisation, the Liberty League, ended with its absorption into a revitalised Sinn Féin under de Valera. He served briefly in the first Dáil Cabinet, opposed the Treaty, retained his Roscommon Dáil seat as an abstentionist Sinn Féiner until 1927, and remained active in Republican politics until the nineteen-forties. His son Joseph, originally a member of the Young Ireland Branch of the United Irish League, was one of the signatories of the 1916 Proclamation; another son, George, served on the IRA Army Council in the nineteen-thirties and forties; and a daughter, Geraldine Plunkett-Dillon, was also an active republican.

PLUNKETT, SIR HORACE Younger son of Lord Dunsany, founding leader of the Irish co-operative movement, Unionist MP for South Dublin 1892–1900, founder and head of the

Department of Agriculture and Technical Instruction (Ireland) 1896–1907. His calls to shelve the national question in favour of economic development were widely admired by intellectuals but won him suspicion from Dillon and from mainstream nationalists (though dissident nationalists often used him as a stick with which to beat the Irish Party). At the same time he was attacked as too conciliatory by hard-line unionists, who lost him his seat in 1900 by putting up a candidate to split the vote, and his book *Ireland in the New Century* (1906) caused controversy for its comments on the power of the Catholic priesthood. Advised the Conservative Party on agricultural reform after 1906. From about 1910 accepted home rule as inevitable, opposed partition, and advocated compromise; chaired the Irish Convention of 1917–18; subsequently active in lobbying for a compromise based on dominion status, for which he was denounced as a traitor by republicans. Appointed to the Free State Senate, but left Ireland after his house was burned during the Civil War.

RAFFALOVICH O'BRIEN, SOPHIE Member of a French family of Russian origin with extensive business interests in Odessa. She made contact with William O'Brien when organising French publicity in support of the Plan of Campaign and became a Catholic on their marriage just before the Parnell split. She provided him with emotional and financial support throughout his later career, acting as his secretary while herself engaging in journalism and extensive charitable activities. Her finances were devastated by the cost of running the All-for-Ireland League and the loss of investments in Germany and Tsarist Russia. After O'Brien's death she engaged in various attempts to perpetuate his memory. She returned to France in the nineteen-thirties, narrowly escaped the Holocaust, and spent her last years in poverty.

REDMOND, JOHN Son of W. H. Redmond, junior member of a prominent Co. Wexford merchant and landed family and Buttite Home Rule MP for Wexford. (Redmond inherited the family estate when the senior line died out, but it was heavily encumbered, and the terms of sale proved a political liability.) MP for New Ross (1883–5), North Wexford (1885–90), and Waterford city (1891–1918). He came to prominence as the most outspoken defender of Parnell—a close friend—during the split and was elected Parnellite leader after the Chief's death. His criticisms of the second Home Rule Bill (1893) as insufficient were to be quoted against him by nationalist rivals during the struggles over the third Home Rule Bill. In the later eighteen-nineties he tried to offset majority support for the Dillonites and the rise of the United Irish League by forging tactical alliances with Healyites and moderate Unionists. Installed as compromise leader in 1900 but subjected to humiliating restrictions, especially by William O'Brien. Joined with O'Brien in negotiating the Irish Land Act (1903) but refused O'Brien's demands to purge Dillon for his criticisms of the act, leading to O'Brien's own resignation. His low-key and conciliatory style of leadership, allied to a certain remoteness, gave the impression of weakness but reflected the problem of keeping together a factionalised party. Grew in stature after 1906 and especially after 1910 with the attainment of the balance of power, but the rebuttal of his attempts at compromise with Unionists and his forced acceptance of partition revived accusations of weakness. His decision to support the British war effort and to continue his recruiting activities even when he knew they were costing him support should be seen as a deliberate political gamble rather than an expression of naïve trust in Britain. After 1916 increasingly eclipsed by ill-health, the rise of Sinn Féin, and the growing dominance of Dillon within the Irish Party. It says much about his attitudes that his second wife was a Protestant and that this fact was never raised in the numerous debates about whether Protestants could expect fair treatment under home rule.

REDMOND, WILLIAM ARCHER Son of John Redmond; MP for East Tyrone 1910–18 and Waterford city 1918–22, TD for Waterford 1923–32. Served in the British army during the First World War, where he was severely wounded and decorated for bravery. Some saw him as over-conscious of his father's influence, and his acceptance of a minor official position at the time of the 1918 conscription crisis embarrassed the party leadership. He led the short-lived neo-Redmondite National League Party in 1926–7 and joined Cumann na nGaedheal in 1930. His widow carried on the Redmond family tradition of representing Waterford until 1954.

REDMOND, WILLIAM HOEY KEARNEY Younger brother of John Redmond; as a young man was a militia officer and had intended to follow the family's military tradition before his conversion to nationalism. MP for South Fermanagh 1885–92, for West Clare 1892–1917. In some ways more radical than his brother (he supported women's suffrage and made several quasi-separatist statements at intervals throughout his career), his reputation is dominated by his decision to join the British army in 1914 as part of what he saw as the home rule bargain and his death in the war in 1917 and subsequent memorialisation as a Redmondite martyr.

ROONEY, WILLIAM Son of a Land League 'suspect' imprisoned in the eighteen-eighties, educated by the Christian Brothers and employed as a clerk; he became active in nationalist literary societies as a teenager in the late eighteen-eighties with his friend and contemporary Arthur Griffith. By the late nineties he was a well-known speaker at separatist meetings, and he was responsible for the choice of Griffith as editor of the separatist weekly *United Irishman* in 1899. Rooney contributed extensively to the *United Irishman* until his death at the age of twenty-nine in 1901 from overwork; Griffith mourned him as a second Davis and published selections of his prose and verse. Griffith's republican critics looked to Rooney as an alternative founder of Sinn Féin. He is best remembered for his ballad 'The Men of the West'.

RUSSELL, THOMAS WILLIAM Scottish-born proprietor of a Temperance Hotel in Dublin, came to prominence as an anti-alcohol campaigner. As Liberal Unionist MP for South Tyrone from 1886 he played a prominent role in campaigning against home rule and was a junior minister 1895–1900. Russell became increasingly critical of the aristocratic Unionist leadership and from 1900 put himself at the head of a tenant-farmer protest movement demanding land purchase, which contested several by-elections against official Unionist candidates (winning East Down and North Fermanagh). This was widely seen as heralding a political realignment in Ulster; in fact it was partly dependent on nationalist tactical voting and went into decline after the Irish Land Act (1903)—which Russell helped to negotiate—and the appearance of a newer and more effective generation of official Unionist leaders. The two Russellite by-election victories were reversed in 1906, though Russell held South Tyrone and a Liberal candidate took North Antrim. Both decided to sit on the government benches and became indistinguishable from official Liberals. In 1907 Russell displaced Horace Plunkett as head of the Department of Agricultural and Technical Instruction. He lost South Tyrone in

January 1910 but was re-elected as Liberal MP for North Tyrone in a by-election in 1911 with nationalist support, though by now despised by nationalists and unionists as an opportunist. He retired from politics in 1918.

RYAN, FREDERICK Journalist, socialist and outspoken agnostic, associated at different times with Arthur Griffith, the Abbey Theatre, and the Sheehy-Skeffingtons. Founded *Dana,* a short-lived journal of free thought, with the literary critic 'John Eglinton' (W. K. Magee) in 1906; died while editing an English-language Egyptian nationalist journal with Wilfred Scawen Blunt. Should not be confused with Frederick W. Ryan, member of the Young Ireland Branch of the United Irish League and unsuccessful parliamentary candidate for the Birr Division of King's County (Offaly) in December 1910.

RYAN, WILLIAM P. Journalist and Gaelic Leaguer; editor of the *Irish Peasant.* His son, Desmond Ryan, was a pupil at St Enda's, fought in the Easter Rising, and became a prominent amateur historian and biographer.

SEXTON, THOMAS Journalist and financial expert; MP for Sligo (1880–6), West Belfast (1886–92), and North Kerry (1892–6). Regarded as one of the Irish Party's finest orators but hampered by a neurotic and reclusive temperament. Anti-Parnellite; he retired from parliamentary politics in disgust at the bitter factionalism following the demise of the second Home Rule Bill. Remained a leading ally of Dillon as chairman of the board of the *Freeman's Journal* 1893–1911; his policy of cutting investment to maintain dividends contributed to the eventual supersession of the paper by William Martin Murphy's *Irish Independent.* Hostile to the Irish Land Act (1903) on financial grounds; seen by William O'Brien as one of the principal agents of his marginalisation. Chairman of Boland's Mills after retiring from the *Freeman's Journal*; denounced wartime taxation and endorsed Sinn Féin in 1918. At the end of his career supported Fianna Fáil because it promised tariff protection for flour-milling.

SHEEHAN, DANIEL DAVID A journalist, first politically active in the labourers' movement in Cork in the eighteen-eighties. (His family experienced eviction during the Land War.) After a brief period in London he returned to Ireland, where he briefly edited the *Southern Star* in west Cork, founded the Land and Labour Association in alliance with J. J. O'Shee, and was elected MP for Mid-Cork (1901–18), despite the opposition of the Irish Party hierarchy. From 1904 he allied himself with William O'Brien, and branches of the LLA became the base for the O'Brienite organisation in rural Co. Cork. He was an able organiser, though at times slightly unstable; despite his work for the labourers' cause he increasingly tended to subordinate it to his political leadership. In 1914 he joined the British army, as did three of his sons (two were killed in action). In 1918 he stood as a Labour candidate in the East End of London, and he worked for a time as a stockbroker before returning to Ireland, where he spent his later years as an organiser for the Irish branch of the British Legion.

SHEEHY, DAVID Former IRB man and miller turned professional politician; closely associated with William O'Brien as UIL organiser but turned against him after his resignation from the Irish Party. MP for South Meath 1903–18, increasingly beset by financial problems.

SHEEHY-SKEFFINGTON, FRANCIS Friend of Tom Kettle, from a similar Catholic professional milieu, but moved from standard Catholic nationalism to agnosticism, radicalism, and feminism. Married Hanna Sheehy-Skeffington. Supported Davitt's campaign on secular education, and with Frederick Ryan founded the short-lived *National Democrat* to continue the struggle after Davitt's death. Though a socialist, he was in many ways an old-style radical, believing that social problems could be resolved by reason and that democracy led to the triumph of reason. (He opposed calls for minority safeguards in the Home Rule Bill as undemocratic.) His pacifism led to a paradoxical alliance with anti-war separatists after 1914, though he continued to condemn their militarism; in 1915 he was imprisoned for making anti-recruiting speeches. He was shot by a British officer who arrested him while he was trying to organise resistance to looting during the Easter Rising; the subsequent official cover-up was deeply resented in Ireland. D. P. Moran, who for years had ridiculed 'Skeffy', thereafter spoke of 'the late Mr. Sheehy-Skeffington, God rest him.'

SHEEHY-SKEFFINGTON, HANNA Daughter of David Sheehy; married Francis Sheehy-Skeffington. A member of the Young Ireland Branch (the only UIL branch to admit women), she faced the same obstacles as her generation of Catholic professionals as well as those imposed by her sex. She was a leading representative of the first generation of Catholic professional women active in the suffrage movement (hitherto dominated by Protestant women). Resigned from the United Irish League over its failure to include women's suffrage in the Home Rule Bill; thereafter increasingly critical of its attitude towards suffrage (and fond of drawing embarrassing comparisons between the former prison treatment of certain nationalists and that which they endorsed for jailed suffragists). After 1916 became a prominent Sinn Féin and republican activist while remaining an active feminist.

SULLIVAN, ALEXANDER M. Son of A. M. Sullivan, the celebrated nineteenth-century nationalist journalist and politician (and therefore a nephew of T. D. Sullivan and a relative of the Healy family). Began his legal career in the eighteen-nineties and became one of the most prominent advocates of his day. Distanced himself politically from his relations after 1900; his behaviour was marked by eccentricity and job-hunting tendencies, attributed by some to head injuries received in an election riot in 1900. In 1911 his candidacy for the marginal North Tyrone seat (seen as a stepping-stone to legal office) was blocked by the party leadership; his subsequent appointment as one of the three Serjeants-at-Law was widely seen as a quid pro quo for persuading his supporters to endorse the successful Liberal candidate, T. W. Russell. An outspoken supporter of the First World War, his actions as Roger Casement's defence counsel during his treason trial in 1916 remain controversial. He supported the 1918 recruiting campaign and was accused of flirting with conscription. After two attempts on his life by the IRA during the War of Independence he moved to England, where he enjoyed legal success and wrote two memoirs, *Old Ireland* and *The Last Serjeant*.

SWEETMAN, JOHN Member of an old Catholic landed family with links to Co. Meath and Co. Wicklow, Sweetman was a founder-member of the Land League's national committee but soon thereafter went to Minnesota to organise an unsuccessful scheme of assisted emigration and agricultural colonisation. He returned to prominence in Irish politics at the time of the Parnell split, when he contributed a large sum of money to the establishment of the Healyite daily paper, the *National Press*. Anti-Parnellite MP for East Wicklow 1892–4; he resigned in protest against the party's continued support for the Liberal government after the retirement of Gladstone, and stood as a Parnellite candidate in Meath in 1895. As a Meath county councillor he was active with Sir Thomas

Esmonde in establishing the General Council of County Councils. He was one of Griffith's main financial backers, and some critics attributed Griffith's rightward shift to his influence. He was the first vice-president (1905–9) and second president (1909–10) of Sinn Féin. Arrested after the 1916 rising, on his release he worked with Herbert Pim to rebuild the Sinn Féin organisation; he was offered a Sinn Féin parliamentary candidacy in 1918 but turned it down because of age. Thereafter he continued to engage in public controversy; he supported the Treaty but later endorsed Fianna Fáil because of its support for protective tariffs. One son was TD for North Wexford 1918–21, resigning in protest at the IRA's use of violence; another became editor of the *Irish Press*.

WHITE, PATRICK Dublin city councillor and MP for North Meath 1900–18. An agrarian radical whose relations with the leadership of the Irish Party were extremely poor (attempts were made to deselect him in 1906 and 1910), he regularly flirted with Sinn Féin in its first decade but never actually defected. He supported the First World War but turned strongly against the government after the Easter Rising. In 1917 he formally left the Irish Party and campaigned for Sinn Féin candidates in 1918, but (unlike Larry Ginnell) was unable to win a Sinn Féin candidacy or to revive his political career after the War of Independence.

YOUNG, SAMUEL The wealthiest member of the Irish Party, a Presbyterian distiller from Belfast. MP for Cavan East 1892–1918. Despite advancing age and right-wing views (including outspoken hostility to the Gaelic League and defiance of the Irish Party's ban on attending royal functions) he was able to defeat repeated attempts at deselection and to retain the seat until his death.

NOTES

ABBREVIATIONS

BL   British Library, London
HLRO   House of Lords Record Office, London
MDA   Meath [Catholic] Diocesan Archive
NA   National Archives
NLI   National Library of Ireland
NUIC   Library, National University of Ireland [formerly University College], Cork
NUID   Archives Department, National University of Ireland [formerly University College], Dublin
TCD   Trinity College Library, Dublin

INTRODUCTION (P. 1–13)

1. O'Hegarty, *History of Ireland Under the Union*; Ryan, *The Phoenix Flame*.
2. Farrell, *The Irish Parliamentary Tradition*; Lyons, *The Irish Parliamentary Party*; O'Halpin, *The Decline of the Union*.
3. Cruise O'Brien, *States of Ireland*; Bew, *Ideology and the Irish Question*.
4. McDowell, *The Irish Administration*; O'Brien, *Dublin Castle and the Irish People*; McBride, *The Greening of Dublin Castle*.
5. MacIntyre, *The Liberator*.
6. Kerr, *A Nation of Beggars?*
7. Bull, *Land, Politics and Nationalism*.
8. Murphy, *Catholic Fiction and Social Reality in Ireland*.
9. Peter Costello, *Clongowes Wood: The History of Clongowes Wood College, 1814–1989* (Dublin 1989).
10. Charles Lever, *The Knight of Gwynne* (London 1847).
11. Molony, *A Soul Came into Ireland*.
12. *Irish People,* 17 Feb. 1900, 1.
13. Patrick Maume, 'Griffith and Young Ireland: the question of continuity', *Éire-Ireland,* autumn 1999.
14. *United Irishman,* 28 July 1900, 1.
15. 'M.A.' and J. F. Reid, *Life of William Field* (Dublin 1918), 23–5; Lane, 'The Land and Labour Association'.
16. Brian Donnelly, 'Michael Joyce: squarerigger, Shannon pilot and MP', *Old Limerick Journal,* 27 (autumn 1990), 42–4; NA, Joyce Papers, LIM23.
17. Daniel Corkery, *The Embers,* act III, in Robert Hogan and R. Burnham (eds.), *Lost Plays of the Irish Renaissance, vol. 3: Cork Dramatic Society* (New Jersey 1984);

J. M. Synge, 'National Drama: A Farce' in Anne Saddlemeyer (ed.), *J. M. Synge: Collected Works, vol. 3: Plays, book I* (Oxford 1968); R. F Foster, *Paddy and Mr Punch* (London 1993), 273–4.

18. Moran, *Tom O'Kelly; The Philosophy of Irish Ireland.*
19. *United Irishman,* 11 Mar. 1899, 3; 8 Apr. 1899, 2.
20. Maye, *Arthur Griffith,* 12–14, 313–4.
21. *United Irishman,* 11 Jan. 1902, 1.
22. *Sinn Féin,* 19 Sep. 1908, 1.
23. Maye, *Arthur Griffith,* 13.
24. Davis, *Arthur Griffith and Non-Violent Sinn Féin;* Maye, *Arthur Griffith,* 13–15.
25. O'Brien, *The Parnell of Real Life,* 27.
26. Mary-Louise Legg, *Newspapers and Nationalism: The Irish Provincial Press, 1850–1892* (Dublin 1998).
27. Bull, *Land, Politics and Nationalism,* 129–30.
28. *United Irishman,* 26 Aug. 1905, 4–5.
29. O'Callaghan, *British High Politics and a Nationalist Ireland.*
30. Bew, *Land and the National Question in Ireland,* 238–40, 243–5.
31. Jordan, *Land and Popular Politics in Ireland.*
32. *Sinn Féin,* 23 Nov. 1907, 2.
33. Larkin, *The Roman Catholic Church and the Creation of the Modern Irish State.*
34. O'Brien, *Evening Memories,* 17–32; Callanan, *T. M. Healy,* 89–91.
35. Anon., *The Times, Parnellism and Crime,* 119–20.
36. Brian Walker, *Ulster Politics: The Formative Years, 1868–86* (Belfast 1989).
37. James Loughlin, 'Constructing the political spectacle: Parnell, the press, and national leadership, 1879–86' in Boyce and O'Day (eds.), *Parnell in Perspective,* 221–41.
38. Warwick-Haller, *William O'Brien and the Irish Land War,* 100–1.
39. Tynan, *The Irish National Invincibles and their Times,* 248–9.
40. Bew, *Land and the National Question,* 50–3.
41. O'Brien to Sophie Raffalovich, 23 Mar. 1889, in Raffalovich O'Brien, *Golden Memories,* vol. 1, 32; O'Brien, *The Parnell of Real Life,* 107.
42. Bew, *Parnell.*
43. *Irish Independent,* 19 Mar. 1918.
44. O'Brien, *The Parliamentary History of the Irish Land Question; Irish Wrongs and English Remedies; Thomas Drummond.*
45. Geary, *The Plan of Campaign.*
46. Mullin, *The Story of a Toiler's Life;* Maume, 'James Mullin, the poor scholar'; Valentine, *Irish Memories;* Fielding, *Class and Ethnicity;* Tom Gallagher, *Glasgow: The Uneasy Peace* (Manchester 1987).
47. Ian Wood, *John Wheatley* (Manchester 1990).
48. Brady, *T. P. O'Connor and the Liverpool Irish; Cork Free Press,* 2 Mar. 1911, 5.
49. *Notes from Ireland,* 19 Aug. 1893, 289; 26 Aug. 1893, 304.
50. Open letter to William O'Brien, 30 Mar. 1912, in Ó Buachalla (ed.), *The Letters of P. H. Pearse,* 258–9.
51. Gordon Lucy, *The Great Convention* (Lurgan 1996).
52. F. D. Howe, *Archbishop Plunkett: A Memoir* (London 1900), 199.

53. Jackson, *Colonel Edward Saunderson,* 113–16.

54. *Cork Free Press,* 17 June 1913, 8.

55. Anon., *Newry Bridge, or Ireland in 1887* (London 1886); Edward James, 'The Anglo-Irish disagreement: past Irish futures', *Linenhall Review,* winter 1986, 5–8.

56. Anon., *Parnellism and Crime,* 117–8; Tynan, *The Irish National Invincibles,* 353 n.

57. 'Ballyhooly' [Robert Martin], *Bits of Blarney* (London 1897); *United Irishman,* 30 Mar. 1901, 1; 24 Oct. 1903, 5.

58. *Sinn Féin,* 1 Feb. 1908, 2.

59. Henry Lucy, *A Diary of the Salisbury Parliament* (London 1892), 327–31, 355, 360–2.

60. Callanan, *The Parnell Split,* 93–5, 204–26.

61. Margaret O'Callaghan, 'Parnell and crime: constructing a conservative strategy of containment' in McCartney, *Parnell.*

62. [Richard John Buckley], *Ireland As She Is and As She Would Be under Home Rule* (Birmingham 1894).

CHAPTER 1 (P. 14–39)

1. C. Woods, 'The general election of 1892: the Catholic clergy and the defeat of the Parnellites' in Lyons and Hawkins, *Ireland Under the Union,* 289–320.

2. Caroline Fox, 'Westmeath Politics in the Later Nineteenth Century', paper read at conference of Irish History Students' Association, 1992.

3. O'Brien, *Irish Ideas,* 109.

4. McMinn, *Against the Tide,* x–xi, xix–xx, xxviii–xxxviii.

5. Loughlin, *Gladstone, Home Rule and the Ulster Question.*

6. *Sinn Féin,* 11 Mar. 1911, 1.

7. *Shan Van Vocht,* 4 Sep. 1896; *United Irishman,* 4 Nov. 1899, 3.

8. 'Mr. Morley's Task' in O'Brien, *Irish Ideas,* 96–111.

9. [Frank Frankfort Moore], *Larry O'Lanigan J.P.: His Rise and Fall* (Belfast 1893).

10. Griffith, *Meagher of the Sword,* ii–iv; 'Seachránaidhe' [Frank Ryan], *Irish Emancipation* (Dublin 1929).

11. McBride, *The Greening of Dublin Castle,* 48.

12. *United Irishman,* 3 Mar. 1906, 4–5.

13. H. Mathew, *The Liberal Imperialists* (Oxford 1973).

14. *United Irishman,* 19 Oct. 1901, 6–7.

15. *Sinn Féin,* 12 Jan. 1907, 2; 16 Jan. 1909, 2.

16. *United Irishman,* 11 Nov. 1899, 4.

17. Mandle, *The Gaelic Athletic Association and Irish Nationalist Politics;* León Ó Broin, *Revolutionary Underground* (Dublin 1976).

18. Ayerst, *Garvin of the Observer; United Irishman,* 4 Mar. 1899, 2; 25 Aug. 1900, 4.

19. Kelly, 'The fall of Parnell and the rise of Irish literature', 1–23.

20. Doyle, *Justin McCarthy.*

21. William O'Brien, 'If Ireland sent her MPs to Washington', *Nineteenth Century,* May 1896, 746–55; 'Was Fenianism ever formidable?', *Contemporary Review,* May 1897, 680–93.

22. *Shan Van Vocht,* 15 Jan. 1896, 1, 8; 7 Feb. 1896, 17.

23. *Shan Van Vocht,* 12 Mar. 1897, 50. The phrase 'Ourselves alone' derives from a Young Ireland ballad by John O'Hagan attacking O'Connell's alliance with the Whigs; it was first rendered as 'Sinn Féin' by another Young Ireland poet, John Keegan.

24. Warwick-Haller, *William O'Brien and the Irish Land War,* 147–8.
25. Lyons, *The Irish Parliamentary Party,* 45 n. 1, 47 n. 1.
26. Lyons, *The Irish Parliamentary Party,* 41–5.
27. Oliver Rafferty, *Catholicism in Ulster: An Interpretative History* (London 1994).
28. Callanan, *T. M. Healy,* 21–2.
29. Callanan, *The Parnell Split,* 94–5.
30. Lyons, *The Irish Parliamentary Party,* 51; Callanan, *T. M. Healy,* 424.
31. Miller, *Church, State and Nation in Ireland,* 31–4.
32. Murphy, *Catholic Fiction and Social Reality in Ireland.*
33. *New Ireland Review,* Apr. 1906, 81–6; *Leader,* 24 Feb. 1906, 8–9.
34. The Chief Secretary was the nominal President, but control rested with the Vice-President.
35. John Muldoon to Dillon, 27 Mar. 1904, TCD, Dillon Papers, ms. 6734/98 .
36. James Pethica (ed.), *The Diaries of Lady Gregory, 1892–1902* (Gerrards Cross 1996), 135–7.
37. *Sinn Féin,* 9 Feb. 1907, 2.
38. Morrissey, *William Martin Murphy,* 25–6.
39. Dónal McCartney, 'William Martin Murphy: an Irish press baron and the rise of the popular press' in Brian Farrell (ed.), *Communications and Community in Ireland* (Dublin 1984), 30–8.
40. Callanan, *T. M. Healy,* 427, 431–2.
41. Lyons, *The Irish Parliamentary Party,* 38–67.
42. *Irish People,* 18 Aug. 1900, 4.
43. Jackson, *The Ulster Party,* 152–3.
44. Philip Marcus, *Standish O'Grady* (Cranbury, NJ, 1970); Luke Netterville [Standish O'Grady], *The Queen of the World* (London 1906).
45. MacNeill, *Shall Ireland Be Divided?*
46. Robert Hogan and James Kilroy, *The Irish Literary Theatre, 1899–1901* (Dublin 1975), 75.
47. Heuser, *Canon Sheehan of Doneraile,* 342–3.
48. Bence Jones, *Twilight of the Ascendancy.*
49. [Lord Ashtown], *The Hidden Power Behind the Irish Nationalist Party* (London 1907).
50. *Grievances from Ireland,* Sep. 1905, 441–7, 465–9.
51. *Grievances from Ireland,* June 1905, 282–3; Sep. 1909, 430.
52. *Grievances from Ireland,* Sep. 1907, 450–60; Apr. 1908, 199–211.
53. *Outlook,* 8 Feb. 1913, 16 Jan., 13 Feb., 20 Mar. and 12 June 1915; Cunningham, *Labour in the West of Ireland,* 46.
54. *Grievances from Ireland,* May 1907, 233–41.
55. *Outlook,* 11 Jan., 21 June and 1 Nov. 1913, 4 Sep. and 25 Mar. 1915.
56. 'An Irishman', *Intolerance in Ireland,* 56–9. (An inscription in the copy in QUB Library attributes this book to Rev. — Hackett, St Michael's (Church of Ireland) Parish, Limerick; see also *Leader,* 17 Dec. 1910, 446–7.)
57. Warren Nelson, *T. C. Hammond: Irish Christian* (Edinburgh 1994); 'An Irishman', *Intolerance in Ireland.*
58. Eric Gallagher, *At Points of Need: The Story of the Belfast Central Mission, 1889–1989* (Belfast 1989), 29–30.

59. *Leader,* 20 Apr. 1907.
60. *United Irishman,* 3 Jan. 1903, 3; 7 Feb. 1903, 4; 18 Feb. 1905, 1.
61. J. Boyle, 'The Belfast Protestant Association and the Independent Orange Order', *Irish Historical Studies,* 1962–3, 117–52; Gailey, *Ireland and the Death of Kindness,* 227–8.
62. Clery, 'Going to Trinity' in *The Idea of a Nation,* 29–33.
63. Loughlin, *Ulster Unionism and British National Identity,* 42–5.
64. Eric Taplin, *The Dockers' Union: A Study of the National Union of Dock Labourers* (Leicester 1986).
65. John Boyle, *The Irish Labour Movement in the Nineteenth Century* (Washington 1988).
66. Emmet O'Connor, *A Labour History of Ireland, 1824–1960* (Dublin 1992).
67. 'M.A.' and J. Reid, *Life of William Field* (Dublin 1918); Field, *Irish Industry and Treasury Tactics.*
68. Lane, 'The Land and Labour Association', 90–106.
69. *Irish Opinion/Voice of Labour,* 8 Mar. 1919.
70. Gareth and Janet Donlevy, *Douglas Hyde: A Maker of Modern Ireland* (London and Berkeley 1991).
71. Tierney, *Eoin MacNeill.*
72. O'Leary, *The Prose Literature of the Gaelic Revival.*
73. *United Irishman,* 10 Aug. 1901, 6–7.
74. O'Brien, 'The influence of the Irish language' in *Irish Ideas,* 47–77.
75. Douglas Hyde, 'The necessity of de-Anglicising Ireland' (1893), reprinted in *Language, Lore and Lyrics* (Dublin 1986).
76. X [D. P. Moran], 'Confessions of a converted West Briton', *Leader,* 8 Sep. 1900.
77. *Claidheamh Soluis,* 16 Sep. 1899, 426–9. For a protest at this denunciation of parliamentarianism and a defence of the Anglo-Irish literary tradition by the ex-MP and Quaker Gaelic Leaguer Alfred Webb see p. 429; see also the parliamentarian critique of Yorke in *Irish People,* 16 Sep. 1899, 4–5.
78. *United Irishman,* 14 Sep. 1901, 4; 14 Dec. 1901, 1. This view tends to ignore the extent to which a Welsh sense of identity found political expression in Nonconformist Liberalism and hostility to Welsh landlords as Anglicised exploiters, while Welsh Tories, like such Irish counterparts as Charles Lever and Robert Martin, portrayed landlords, with diminishing success, as defenders of hedonistic traditional culture against Nonconformist-Liberal puritanism.
79. William Rooney, 'A recent Irish literature' in *Selected Prose.*
80. Ryan, *The Pope's Green Island,* 102–15.
81. Garvin, *Irish Nationalist Revolutionaries.*
82. *United Irishman,* 23 June 1900, 1; 22 Aug. 1903, 4; 14 Jan. 1905, 1; 21 Jan. 1905, 4–5.
83. *United Irishman,* 15 July 1899, 3; 22 July 1899, 4.
84. *United Irishman,* 19 Nov. 1904, 1; *Sinn Féin,* 15 Dec. 1906, 3.
85. *United Irishman,* 25 Mar. 1899, 2; Deirdre Toomey, 'Moran's collar: Yeats and Irish Ireland' in *Yeats Annual* no. 12 (1996).
86. Steven Koss (ed.), *The Pro-Boers* (Chicago 1973).
87. *United Irishman,* 16 Dec. 1899, 4.
88. *Irish People,* 18 Nov. 1900, 7.

89. *Saturday Review,* 20 June 1908, 781–2.
90. *Irish People,* 20 Jan. 1900, 4.
91. *United Irishman,* 2 Dec. 1899, 4.
92. *Irish People,* 13 Jan. 1900, 1; 20 Jan. 1900, 2, 5.
93. *Hibernian,* 21 Aug. 1915, 1.
94. *United Irishman,* 23 Dec. 1899, 4.
95. *United Irishman,* 30 Dec. 1899, 2.
96. Seán MacBride, *A Message to the Irish People* (Cork 1985), 38; Terence MacSwiney, diary, 20 Jan. 1907, NUID, 48c/103.
97. *Irish People,* 6 Jan. 1900, 1.
98. Alvin Jackson, 'Irish unionists and the empire, 1880–1920: classes and masses' in Keith Jeffrey (ed.), *An Irish Empire?: Aspects of Ireland and the British Empire* (Manchester 1996), 123–48.
99. Killen, *John Bull's Famous Circus,* 135; McCracken, *The Irish Pro-Boers,* 48–50, 58–67, 98–11; *Cork Free Press,* 18 Apr. 1914, 7.
100. *United Irishman,* 17 Mar. 1900, 6; 24 Mar. 1900, 6.
101. McCracken, *The Irish Pro-Boers.*
102. Lynch to D. F. Cohalan, 9 Mar. 1909, in O'Brien and Ryan, *Devoy's Post Bag,* vol. 2, 378–80.
103. McCracken, *The Irish Pro-Boers,* 109–10.
104. Gailey, *Ireland and the Death of Kindness,* 40–50.
105. Bew, *Conflict and Conciliation in Ireland.*
106. *Mayo News,* 24 Dec. 1898, 7; 15 Apr. 1899, 6.
107. *Irish People,* 30 Sep. 1899, 3, 4.
108. *Mayo News,* 18 and 25 Nov. 1899.
109. Gailey, *Ireland and the Death of Kindness,* 49.
110. *Sinn Féin,* 28 Jan. 1911, 4.
111. *Cork Free Press,* 7 Aug. 1913, 6.
112. Lyons, *The Irish Parliamentary Party,* 88–91.
113. Lyons, *The Irish Parliamentary Party,* 91 n. 1.
114. Lyons, *The Irish Parliamentary Party,* 96–8.
115. *Irish People,* 27 Jan. 1900, 4–5.
116. *Irish People,* 13 Jan. 1900, 1; 3 Feb. 1900, 4–5; 30 June 1900, 5–6; 7 July 1900, 5.
117. Morrissey, *William Martin Murphy,* 29–30.
118. *Irish People,* 6 Oct. 1900, 5; *United Irishman,* 13 Oct. 1900, 4; 10 Oct. 1903, 4.
119. *United Irishman,* 29 June 1901, 4; *Irish People,* 14 Oct. 1899, 5; 20 Jan. 1900, 5; 12 May 1900, 3.
120. Miller, *Church, State and Nation in Ireland,* 52.
121. Colm Fox, *The Making of a Minority: Political Developments in Derry and the North, 1921–25* (Derry 1997).
122. Murphy, *Derry, Donegal and Modern Ulster.*
123. *Irish People,* 22 Sep. 1900, 3. Doyle's political activism went back to the Tenant League of the eighteen-fifties.
124. *Irish People,* 29 Sep. 1900, 3.
125. Alvin Jackson, 'The failure of unionism in Dublin, 1900', *Irish Historical Studies,* Nov. 1989.

126. *United Irishman,* 14 July 1900, 4; 21 July 1900, 4.

127. *Irish People,* 6 Oct. 1900, 5.

128. *United Irishman,* 5 Aug. 1899, 5.

129. *United Irishman,* 3 Nov. 1900, 7.

130. Healy, *Why Ireland Is Not Free,* 86.

131. *Cork Free Press,* 3 Mar. 1913, 3.

132. Jackson, *Colonel Edward Saunderson.*

133. O'Higgins, *My Songs and Myself,* 50–1; de Búrca, *The Soldier's Song,* 57; Terence MacSwiney, diary, 7 Mar. 1903, NUID, P48c/98, 50.

134. Philip Bull, 'A fatal disjunction, 1898–1905: Sinn Féin and the United Irish League' in Rebecca Pelan (ed.), *Irish-Australian Studies: Papers of the Seventh Irish-Australian Conference* (Sydney 1994).

135. Maye, *Arthur Griffith,* 85.

136. *United Irishman,* 30 Sep. 1899, 2; 24 Feb. 1900, 5; 3 Mar. 1900, 5.

137. *United Irishman,* 19 Oct. 1901, 4; 26 Oct. 1901, 4; 23 Nov. 1901, 4; 30 Nov. 1901, 4; 9 Aug. 1902, 4.

138. Bew, *Conflict and Conciliation in Ireland; United Irishman,* 24 Feb. 1900, 4; 10 Mar. 1900, 5.

139. *United Irishman,* 24 Feb. 1900, 4; *Irish People,* 24 Feb. 1900, 4.

140. *United Irishman,* 10 Mar. 1900, 4; 17 Mar. 1900, 4.

141. *United Irishman,* 2 Aug. 1902, 6; 6 June 1903, 4.

142. *United Irishman,* 16 May 1903, 4; 19 Nov. 1904, 5, *Sinn Féin,* 19 June 1909, 4.

143. *United Irishman,* 30 Nov. 1901, 4.

144. *Irish People,* 28 July 1900, 1; Vincent, *The Crawford Papers,* 46.

145. Denis Donoghue, *We Irish* (Brighton 1986), 155.

146. Gwynn, *Life of John Redmond.*

147. *United Irishman,* 6 Oct. 1900, 8; 13 Oct. 1900, 5.

148. Arthur Lynch, *O'Rourke the Great,* London 1924.

149. Moran, *Tom O'Kelly.*

150. Garvin, *Irish Nationalist Revolutionaries.*

151. Margaret Leamy, *Parnell's Faithful Few* (New York 1936), 136.

152. May Laffan Hartley, *Hogan, M.P.* (London 1876); *Christy Carew* (London 1880).

153. Mullin, *The Story of a Toiler's Life;* Maume, 'James Mullin, the poor scholar'.

154. *Irish People,* 19 May 1900, 5; *United Irishman,* 6 Oct. 1900, 4.

155. *United Irishman,* 29 Sep. 1900, 4; 6 Oct. 1900, 4.

156. *United Irishman,* 9 June 1900, 4; 16 June 1900, 3.

157. *Leader,* 1 Sep. 1900, 1.

158. O'Brien, 'Lost opportunities of the Irish gentry' in *Irish Ideas;* see also Maume, 'In the Fenians' wake'.

159. Fergal McGrath, *Father John Sullivan, S.J.* (London 1941), 1–17.

160. O'Brien, *When We Were Boys.*

161. O'Brien, *Recollections,* 170–1.

162. Raffalovich O'Brien, *Golden Memories,* vol. 1, 35 n.

163. O'Brien, *Recollections,* chap. 7; T. H. Ronayne to John Devoy, 24 Sep. 1881, in O'Brien and Ryan, *Devoy's Post-bag,* vol. 2, 101–2.

164. Jeremiah O'Donovan Rossa, *Rossa's Recollections* (New York 1898), 129.

165. John O'Leary, *Recollections of Fenians and Fenianism* (London 1896).

166. O'Donnell, *History of the Irish Parliamentary Party.*

167. Lyons, *John Dillon,* 200.

168. Moran, *Tom O'Kelly,* chap. 16.

169. *Irish People,* 24 Nov. 1900, 1–3; 1 Dec. 1900, 3, 5; 8 Dec. 1900, 3–5.

170. Lucy, *The Balfourian Parliament,* 13–14.

171. *Irish People,* 15 Dec. 1900, 2–3, 6.

172. United Irish League, *The Liffey at Ebb Tide.*

173. *Irish People,* 15 Dec. 1900, 2–3, 6.

174. O'Brien, *An Olive Branch in Ireland,* 131.

CHAPTER 2 (P. 40–77)

1. H. Mathew, *The Liberal Imperialists* (Oxford 1973).

2. Lucy, *The Balfourian Parliament.*

3. Gailey, *Ireland and the Death of Kindness,* 212; Lynch, *My Life Story,* 110–18.

4. *United Irishman,* 23 Nov. 1901, 4.

5. Alvin Jackson, 'The Irish Unionist Party and the Russellite threat', *Irish Historical Studies,* Nov. 1987, 376–404.

6. MacCarthy, *Five Years in Ireland; Priests and People in Ireland; Rome in Ireland.*

7. *United Irishman,* 31 Jan. 1903, 4.

8. *Irish People,* 26 July 1902, 1–2, 3; 2 Aug. 1902, 1–2; 9 Aug. 1902, 4–5; 16 Aug. 1902, 4–5; 23 Aug. 1902, 4–5.

9. *United Irishman,* 20 Apr. 1901, 6–7.

10. *Leader,* 6 Sep. 1902, 26–7.

11. Roger Blaney, *Presbyterians and the Irish Language* (Belfast 1996); 'Benmore' [John Clarke], 'Reverend Richard Lyttle' in *Thoughts from the Heart* (Belfast 1908); Robert Lyttle, *Origin of the Fight with the Boers* (London 1899); St John Ervine, *Craigavon: Ulsterman* (London 1949), 102; *United Irishman,* 29 Sep. 1900, 5; 16 Jan. 1904, 4.

12. *Irish People,* 12 July 1902, 3; 30 Aug. 1902, 2, 4–5; 6 Sep. 1902, 3, 5–6.

13. Cunningham, *Labour in the West of Ireland,* 157.

14. *Irish People,* 12 July 1902, 4–5; 26 July 1902, 4–5; 23 Aug. 1902, 4–5.

15. Murphy, *Catholic Fiction and Social Reality in Ireland.*

16. Joseph Guinan, *The Soggarth Aroon* (Dublin and New York, 1905).

17. Guinan, *The Island Parish,* 220–33.

18. Guinan, *Annaghmore.*

19. D. Akenson, *The Irish Education Experiment* (London 1969); E. Brian Titley, *Church, State and the Control of Schooling in Ireland, 1900–1944* (Dublin 1983).

20. Maume, *D. P. Moran,* 9.

21. Michael O'Riordan, *A Reply to Dr. Starkie's Attack on the Managers of National Schools* (Dublin 1903).

22. Michael O'Riordan, *Catholicity and Progress in Ireland* (London 1906).

23. Sheehan, *My New Curate.*

24. Guinan, *The Island Parish,* 77–83.

25. *Catholic,* Aug. 1906, 94.

26. *Sinn Féin,* 22 July 1911, 2.
27. *Catholic,* Dec. 1906, 141–2.
28. Birmingham, *Hyacinth.*
29. A. Hepburn, *A Past Apart: Studies in the History of Catholic Belfast, 1850–1950* (Belfast 1996), 132, 150–5, 209–10; Miller, *Church, State and Nation in Ireland;* Ian Budge and Cornelius O'Leary, *Belfast: Approach to Crisis: A Study of Belfast Politics, 1613–1970* (London 1973), 120–3.
30. Valentine, *Irish Memories,* 102–3; William Brown, *Through Windows of Memory* (London 1946), 154–6.
31. Bew, *Conflict and Conciliation in Ireland,* 54–6, 75–83.
32. *United Irishman,* 29 June 1901, 2, 5; 6 July 1901, 6; 13 July 1901, 6–7; 20 July 1901, 6–7.
33. *Irish People,* 22 Dec. 1900, 5–6.
34. *Irish People,* 29 Dec. 1900, 5–6.
35. *Irish People,* 2 Aug. 1902, 2, 4–5.
36. *United Irishman,* 7 Mar. 1903, 5; 14 Mar. 1903, 4.
37. Redmond, interviews with Barry O'Brien (3 Mar. 1905) and John O'Connor (10 Apr. 1905), NLI, ms. 15214 (3).
38. *Cork Free Press,* 27 June 1911, 7.
39. Brady, *T. P. O'Connor and the Liverpool Irish,* 157–8.
40. Ryan, *The Plough and the Cross; Cork Free Press,* 24 Mar. 1913, 5.
41. *Irish People,* 5 July 1902, 4, 6; 26 July, 6–7; 2 Aug. 1902, 1, 6; 9 Aug. 1902, 2–3; 16 Aug. 1902, 1–2; 23 Aug. 1902, 1; *United Irishman,* 11 Oct. 1902, 1.
42. Bew, *Conflict and Conciliation in Ireland,* 98; *Irish People,* 12 July 1902, 1.
43. *United Irishman,* 23 June 1900, 7.
44. Bew, *Conflict and Conciliation in Ireland,* 104.
45. Miller, *Church, State and Nation in Ireland,* 78–80, 83–5.
46. Healy, *Letters and Leaders of My Day,* vol. 1, 181; F. Bussy, *Irish Conspirators: Recollections of John Mallon* (London 1910).
47. Sheehan, *Luke Delmege,* 123–4; Guinan, *The Moores of Glynn,* 243–9.
48. Guinan, *The Curate of Kilcloon.*
49. Guinan, *The Moores of Glynn.*
50. Sheila Turner Johnston, *Alice: A Life of Alice Milligan* (Omagh 1994); Glandon, *Arthur Griffith and the Advanced Nationalist Press,* 10–12.
51. Hobson, *Ireland Yesterday and Tomorrow,* 1–3.
52. *Shan Van Vocht,* 5 Apr. 1897.
53. William Bulfin, *Rambles in Eirinn* (Dublin 1907).
54. *United Irishman,* 22 July 1905, 4–5.
55. *United Irishman,* 16 June 1900, 1; 24 May 1902, 4; 6 Aug. 1904, 1.
56. *United Irishman,* 15 July 1899, 2.
57. *United Irishman,* 11 May 1901, 1, 4; 18 May 1901, 6–8; 1 June 1901, 7; 13 Jan. 1906, 1.
58. William Rooney, *Prose Writings* (Dublin 1909), introduction.
59. 'Síoladóir' [Terence MacSwiney], *The Music of Freedom* (Cork 1907), 53–7.
60. O'Higgins, *My Songs and Myself.*

61. *Irish Freedom,* Nov. 1910, 2–3.
62. *United Irishman,* 20 July 1901, 5.
63. *United Irishman,* 17 Mar. 1900, 2–3; 9 June 1900, 2–3; *Sinn Féin,* 24 Dec. 1900, 1.
64. *United Irishman,* 9 Dec. 1899, 3; 16 June 1900, 6.
65. *United Irishman,* 24 Mar. 1900, 5.
66. *United Irishman,* 11 Nov. 1899, 5; 14 Apr. 1900, 3, 5; 26 May 1900, 2–3; 15 Sep. 1900, 6.
67. Bernard Porter, *Plots and Paranoia: A History of Political Espionage in Britain, 1790–1988* (London 1989), 81–6, 87–96 (contrast Irish situation, 96–100); Richard Thurlow, *The Secret State* (Oxford 1994).
68. *Sinn Féin,* 31 July 1909, 3.
69. *United Irishman,* 9 Jan. 1904, 4–5; 23 Apr. 1904, 3.
70. *United Irishman,* 24 Feb. 1906, 4–5; Republic, 31 Jan. 1907, 28 Feb. 1907; *Sinn Féin,* 15 Apr. 1911, 1.
71. *United Irishman,* 27 Aug. 1904, 4–5; 7 Jan. 1905, 3; 14 Jan. 1905, 2–3; 28 Jan. 1905, 3; 11 Feb. 1905, 3.
72. Griffith, *Pitt's Policy.*
73. *Sinn Féin,* 6 May 1911, 1.
74. *United Irishman,* 28 Nov. 1903, 2–3; *Nationality,* 5 Jan. 1918, 1.
75. *United Irishman,* 12 Mar. 1904, 1; Maye, *Arthur Griffith,* 313–5.
76. Arthur Griffith (ed.), *Thomas Davis: Thinker and Teacher* (Dublin 1914), x.
77. Maye, *Arthur Griffith,* 27, 29–30, 69–73.
78. *United Irishman,* 9 June 1900, 5.
79. *United Irishman,* 28 Nov. 1903, 4–5.
80. *United Irishman,* 24 Aug. 1901, 2; 7 Sep. 1901, 2–3; 8 Oct. 1904, 1; 14 Apr. 1906, 1; *Sinn Féin,* 15 June 1907, 3; 22 June 1907, 3; 21 Nov. 1908, 1; 5 Dec. 1908, 1.
81. *Sinn Féin,* 6 June 1908, 2; 24 Sep. 1910, 1.
82. *Nationality,* 27 Oct. 1917, 1.
83. Maye, *Arthur Griffith,* vi, 315–6.
84. *United Irishman,* 16 Jan. 1904, 4.
85. *Sinn Féin,* 1 June 1907, 2.
86. *Sinn Féin,* 7 May 1910, 1; 30 July 1910, 1; 25 Feb. 1911, 1.
87. *United Irishman,* 21 Sep. 1901, 2–3; 18 Nov. 1905, 4–5; *Sinn Féin,* 23 Apr. 1910, 2; 8 Apr. 1911, 1; 20 May 1911, 3.
88. *United Irishman,* 23 June 1900, 6.
89. Joseph White, *Tom Mann* (Manchester 1991), 120; *United Irishman,* 3 Feb. 1900, 7; 21 Apr. 1900, 6–7; 7 July 1900, 3; 8 Sep. 1900, 4, 5; 12 Jan. 1901, 5; 9 Mar. 1901, 7–8; 8 Apr. 1905.
90. *United Irishman,* 28 July 1900, 6–7.
91. *United Irishman,* 23 June 1900, 4; 7 July 1900, 4; 27 Oct. 1900, 4, 5; 1 June 1901, 2, 4; *Sinn Féin,* 9 June 1906, 2; 2 Feb. 1907, 2.
92. *United Irishman,* 21 Feb. 1903, 1; *Sinn Féin,* 27 Jan. 1912, 5.
93. *United Irishman,* 5 Sep. 1903, 2; 12 Sep. 1903, 5; 24 Oct. 1903, 6; 31 Oct. 1903, 6; 21 Nov. 1903, 3; *Sinn Féin,* 11 Apr. 1908, 2.
94. *United Irishman,* 4 Nov. 1899, 4; *Sinn Féin,* 24 Sep. 1910, 1.

95. *United Irishman*, 16 June 1900, 1; 24 Nov. 1900, 1; 8 June 1901, 1; 7 Oct. 1905, 4–5; *Sinn Féin*, 15 Aug. 1908, 2; 15 July 1911, 3.

96. *United Irishman*, 4 Mar. 1899, 2; 11 Mar. 1899, 2; 10 June 1899, 2 (pro–Dreyfus); 5 Aug. 1899, 4; 16 Sep. 1899, 3 (anti-Dreyfus).

97. Frank Hugh O'Donnell, *The Message of the Masters* (London 1901), 36–7.

98. *United Irishman*, 19 Mar. 1904, 4; *Sinn Féin*, 25 Aug. 1906, 2; 1 Dec. 1906, 4; 11 July 1914, 3; 1 Aug. 1914, 1–3.

99. *United Irishman*, 9 Mar. 1901, 2; 31 Oct. 1903, 6.

100. *United Irishman*, 31 Mar. 1900, 5; 23 Jan. 1904, 4–5; 23 Apr. 1904, 1; 28 May 1904, 1; *Sinn Féin*, 3 Nov. 1906, 1; 30 Jan. 1909, 2; 13 Feb. 1909, 2.

101. MacCarthy, *Rome in Ireland*, 321–3; see Loughlin, *Ulster Unionism and British Nationality*, 31–2, for Ulster Unionists joining the Tory campaign against Jewish immigration.

102. Dermot Keogh, *Jews in Twentieth-Century Ireland: Refugees, Anti-Semitism and the Holocaust* (Cork 1998), 26–53; Louis Hyman, *The Jews of Ireland* (Shannon 1972), 201, 216; Boyle, *The Irish Labour Movement in the Nineteenth Century*, 341.

103. Maye, *Arthur Griffith*, 362–72.

104. *Sinn Féin*, 24 Oct. 1908, 3.

105. *United Irishman*, 11 Nov. 1899, 5; 2 Dec. 1899, 5; 4 Aug. 1900, 1; 18 Aug. 1900, 6.

106. *United Irishman*, 31 Aug. 1901, 4; *Sinn Féin*, 22 Jan. 1910, 2; 25 Mar. 1911, 1.

107. *United Irishman*, 9 Apr. 1904, 1; 25 Mar. 1905, 1.

108. *United Irishman*, 11 Apr. 1903, 4; 25 Apr. 1903, 4; 9 Jan. 1904, 4–5; 13 Feb. 1904, 4–5; 26 Mar. 1904, 4–5.

109. *United Irishman*, 2 Apr. 1904, 4; Tierney, *Eoin MacNeill*, 72.

110. Morrissey, *William Martin Murphy*, 36–7.

111. MacSwiney diary, NUID; Terence MacSwiney, *The Revolutionist* (Dublin 1914).

112. *United Irishman*, 7 Sep. 1901, 4; 14 Sep. 1901, 2.

113. Robert Hogan (ed.), *Towards a National Theatre: The Dramatic Criticism of Frank Fay* (Dublin 1970).

114. *United Irishman*, 29 Apr. 1899, 1; *Sinn Féin*, 26 May 1907, 4.

115. *United Irishman*, 20 Dec. 1902, 3.

116. *United Irishman*, 22 Nov. 1902, 6; 29 Nov. 1902, 1–2.

117. *United Irishman*, 11 Feb. 1905, 4–5. This disproves the central thesis of Patrick Maume, 'The Ancient Constitution', 123–37.

118. *United Irishman*, 30 Dec. 1905, 1; 6 Jan. 1906, 2–3; 13 Jan. 1906, 2; Joop Leerssen, *Remembrance and Imagination* (Cork 1996), 108–46.

119. *United Irishman*, 10 May 1902, 6.

120. *United Irishman*, 28 Nov. 1903, 2; 5 Mar. 1904, 2.

121. *United Irishman*, 25 Oct. 1902, 5.

122. *Sinn Féin*, 17 Nov. 1906, 2; 24 Nov. 1906, 1–2.

123. *United Irishman*, 4 Feb. 1905, 1; 11 Feb. 1905, 4–5; *Sinn Féin*, 17 Apr. 1909, 2; 1 May 1909, 2.

124. *United Irishman*, 9 June 1900, 3, 7; 30 Apr. 1904, 1; 14 May 1904, 4–5.

125. *United Irishman*, 6 July 1901, 4; 12 July 1902, 4; 30 Aug. 1902, 4; *Sinn Féin*, 24 Oct. 1908, 2.

126. *United Irishman,* 17 Mar. 1906, 4–5; 24 Mar. 1906, 4–5; 14 Apr. 1906, 6.
127. *United Irishman,* 8 June 1900, 6; 17 Aug. 1901, 2; 24 May 1902, 5; 11 July 1903, 5.
128. Mary Butler, *The Ring of Day* (London 1906).
129. *United Irishman,* 12 Jan. 1901, 4; 26 Jan. 1901, 7–8; 2 Feb. 1901, 7; 16 Feb. 1901, 7–8.
130. *United Irishman,* 3 May 1902, 4.
131. *United Irishman,* 17 Nov. 1900, 7–8; 23 Feb. 1901, 2–3; 6 July 1901, 7; 28 Feb. 1903, 6–7; 21 Mar. 1903, 1.
132. *United Irishman,* 30 Dec. 1905, 2.
133. *United Irishman,* 6 Feb. 1904, 4–5.
134. *United Irishman,* 10 June 1905, 3.
135. *United Irishman,* 4, 11 and 25 Jan. 1902.
136. *Catholic,* Apr. 1906, 44.
137. *United Irishman,* 28 June 1902, 1, 4; 4 July 1903, 5; 11 July 1903, 5; 1 Aug. 1903, 5–7.
138. *United Irishman,* 9 Sep. 1905, 3.
139. T. M. Kettle, 'Would the Hungarian policy work?', *New Ireland Review,* Feb. 1905, 321–8.
140. *United Irishman,* 11 Aug. 1900, 6–7; *Sinn Féin,* 20 June 1914, 4–5.
141. Arthur Griffith, 'The resurrection of Hungary', serialised in the *United Irishman* from 2 January 1904; first published in book form 1904; new edition, 1918.
142. *United Irishman,* 26 Nov. 1904, 1; 3 Dec. 1904, 4–5; 10 Dec. 1904, 4–5.
143. *Irish Nation and Peasant,* 2 Apr. 1910.
144. T. M. Kettle, 'Would the Hungarian policy work?', *New Ireland Review,* Feb. 1905, 321–8.
145. *United Irishman,* 4 Feb. 1905, 4–5.
146. Irish Unionist Alliance, *The New Home Rule* (Dublin 1906–7); *United Irishman,* 20 Jan. 1905, 4.
147. Hobson, *Ireland Yesterday and Tomorrow,* 9; *Leader,* 7 Jan. 1905, 326–7; Davis, *Arthur Griffith and Non-Violent Sinn Féin,* 115.
148. *United Irishman,* 11 Feb. 1905, 4–5.
149. Manus O'Riordan (ed.), *Frederick Ryan: Sinn Féin and Reaction* (Dublin 1984).
150. *United Irishman,* 30 Jan. 1904, 4; 6 Feb. 1904, 1.
151. Ó Lúing, 'Arthur Griffith'. *Irish Opinion* (12 Jan. 1918, 76) notes that in practice Sinn Féin councillors favoured slum clearance rather than completely new developments.
152. *United Irishman,* 17 June 1905, 1; 21 Mar. 1908, 1.
153. *Sinn Féin,* 11 Jan. 1908, 2; 25 Jan. 1908, 2.
154. *United Irishman,* 10 June 1905, 4–5.
155. Cunningham, *Labour in the West of Ireland,* 140–3.
156. *United Irishman,* 27 May 1905, 5.
157. *Sinn Féin,* 23 Nov. 1907, 1; 27 June 1908, 1; 7 Nov. 1908, 1.
158. *Sinn Féin,* 19 Sep. 1908, 1.
159. Oliver St John Gogarty, *It Isn't This Time of Year at All* (London 1954), 218.
160. Birmingham, *Hyacinth,* 198–9.
161. James Murphy (ed.), *Nos Autem: Castleknock College and Its Contribution* (Dublin n.d. [1996]).

162. *Leader,* 8 Sep. 1900.
163. *United Irishman,* 17 Nov. 1900, 6–7; 15 Dec. 1900, 7; 19 July 1902, 5; 28 Nov. 1903, 5.
164. Hutchinson, *The Dynamics of Cultural Nationalism.*
165. Stanislaus Joyce, *My Brother's Keeper* (New York 1958), 169.
166. P. Curran, *Under the Receding Wave* (Dublin 1970).
167. *St. Stephen's,* Feb. 1904, 48–9; Dec. 1903, 3–5; Feb. 1904, 48–9; *Leader,* 3 Aug. 1907, 377.
168. Maume, *D. P. Moran,* 19–20.
169. *United Irishman,* 30 Aug. 1902, 5; 4 Oct. 1902, 4; 4 July 1903, 1; *Sinn Féin,* 3 Aug. 1912, 2–3.
170. Callanan, *T. M. Healy,* vol. 3, xxiii, 44–5.
171. *Irish People,* 30 Aug. 1902, 1.
172. *United Irishman,* 19 Dec. 1903, 4–5; 25 June 1904, 3; 18 Mar. 1905, 1; *Sinn Féin,* 6 Oct. 1906, 2.
173. Catholic Association, *Handbook of the Catholic Association.* Thomas Connellan, *The Catholic Association* (Dublin 1906), attributes it to Father Peter Finlay.
174. *United Irishman,* 23 Jan. 1904, 4–5; 5 Mar. 1904, 6.
175. Evelyn Bolster, *The Knights of Columbanus* (Dublin 1979).
176. *Leader,* 18 Jan. 1902.
177. *United Irishman,* 13 Apr. 1901, 4; 30 Nov. 1901, 1.
178. *Leader,* 11 Apr. 1903.
179. *United Irishman,* 6 June 1903, 4; 10 Oct. 1903, 2–3; *Sinn Féin,* 1 Apr. 1911, 2.
180. Griffith, 'The resurrection of Hungary', 10.
181. *United Irishman,* 3 Mar. 1902, 4; 21 June 1902, 4.
182. *United Irishman,* 21 Sep. 1901, 3.
183. O'Leary, *The Prose Literature of the Gaelic Revival.*
184. *United Irishman,* 15 June 1901, 7. This section is omitted by Piaras Béaslaí (ed.), *Songs, Ballads and Recitations by Famous Irishmen: Arthur Griffith* (Dublin n.d.), 6–13.
185. *United Irishman,* 23 Feb. 1901, 6–7.
186. *United Irishman,* 26 Jan. 1901, 8; 2 Feb. 1901, 7–8; 9 Feb. 1901, 7; 16 Feb. 1901, 7.
187. For a fuller discussion see Maume, *D. P. Moran.*
188. Lyons, *The Enigma of Tom Kettle,* 61–6.
189. Lyons, *The Enigma of Tom Kettle,* 67–70, 77–9.
190. Boland, *Irishman's Day;* Boland, *At My Mother's Knee;* Gaughan, *Thomas O'Donnell.*
191. William O'Brien, T. M. Healy, et al., *The All-for-Ireland League and its Calumniators* (Cork 1912).
192. James Joyce, *Stephen Hero* (London 1944), 237.
193. Clery, 'Thomas Kettle' in *Dublin Essays,* 1–14.
194. *Sinn Féin,* 25 Aug. 1906, 2; 22 Dec. 1906, 2; 13 Apr. 1907, 1; Lyons, *The Enigma of Tom Kettle,* 213.
195. O'Hegarty, *Terence MacSwiney,* 34–5.
196. W. J. Brennan-Whitmore (edited by Pauric Travers), *Dublin Burning: The Easter Rising from Behind the Barricades* (Dublin 1996), 140–1; and see review by Patrick Maume in *Studia Hibernica,* no. 29 (1995–7), 245–7.

197. Tierney, *Eoin MacNeill*, 103–6.

198. Ward, *Hanna Sheehy-Skeffington*; Maria Luddy, *Hanna Sheehy-Skeffington* (Dundalk 1995); Murphy, *The Women's Suffrage Movement*.

199. Bull, 'The significance of the nationalist response to the Irish Land Act of 1903'; Bew, *Conflict and Conciliation in Ireland*, 92–5; Lyons, *John Dillon*, 222–7.

200. *Irish People*, 26 July 1902, 2, 4–5; 2 Aug. 1902, 4; 9 Aug. 1902, 1; 6 Sep. 1902, 3.

201. *Irish People*, 6 Sep. 1902, 2.

202. Bew, *Conflict and Conciliation in Ireland*, 96–102; Lyons, *The Irish Parliamentary Party*, 99–102; Gailey, *Ireland and the Death of Kindness*, 190–2. O'Brien, *An Olive Branch in Ireland*, is euphoric and lacks detail.

203. Blunt, *My Diaries*, 102; O'Brien, *The Irish Revolution*, 74–5 n.; Loughlin, *Ulster Unionism and British National Identity*, 43–5; *Cork Free Press*, 8 July 1910, 7; *United Irishman*, 25 Feb. 1905, 4–5.

204. *United Irishman*, 2 May 1903, 1.

205. O'Higgins, *My Songs and Myself*.

206. *United Irishman*, 12 Sep. 1903.

207. *United Irishman*, 23 May 1903, 4–5.

208. Gailey, *Ireland and the Death of Kindness*, 197; Mackail and Wyndham, *George Wyndham*, vol. 1, 85–7.

209. W. Mandle, 'Sir Antony MacDonnell and Crime Branch Special' in Oliver MacDonagh and W. Mandle (eds.), *Ireland and Irish Australia* (London 1986).

210. Henry Patterson, 'Independent orangeism and class conflict in Edwardian Belfast', *Proceedings of the Royal Irish Academy*, vol. 80, section 4 (1980).

211. Gailey, *Ireland and the Death of Kindness*, 235–51; Jackson, *The Ulster Party*, 253–60.

212. Gailey, *Ireland and the Death of Kindness*, 212–5; West, *Horace Plunkett*, 12–13, 111–13; Lawrence Woods, *British Gentlemen in the Wild West* (London 1990).

213. Leslie, *Studies in Sublime Failure*; Leslie, *Mr Frewen of England*; A. Andrews, *The Splendid Pauper* (London 1968); Villiers-Tuthill, *Beyond the Twelve Bens*, 131–8; G. Searle, *Corruption in British Politics* (Oxford 1987), 205 n.

214. Gailey, *Ireland and the Death of Kindness*, 216; Dunraven, *Past Times and Pastimes*.

215. O'Brien, *An Olive Branch in Ireland*, 169–70; Heuser, *Canon Sheehan of Doneraile*; *Castletown Ego* (London 1923); *Irish Year Book, 1908* (Dublin 1908), chapters on 'Forestry' and 'Tobacco'; Dudley Edwards, *Patrick Pearse*, 31–3; Meehan, *The Members of Parliament for Laois and Offaly*, 108–10.

216. Coogan, *War and Politics in Meath*, 7; Gailey, *Ireland and the Death of Kindness*, 216–8.

217. Bew, *Conflict and Conciliation in Ireland*, 61–3, 107; O'Brien, *William O'Brien and the Course of Irish Politics*, 145; Gailey, *Ireland and the Death of Kindness*, 216–8.

218. Pierce O'Mahony to O'Brien, 7 Mar. 1909, NUIC, O'Brien Papers, AR39.

219. Gailey, *Ireland and the Death of Kindness*, 216–23.

220. Sheehy-Skeffington, *Michael Davitt*, 179–92.

221. Bew, *Conflict and Conciliation in Ireland*, 102–11.

222. Bull, 'Irish Party response to 1903 Land Act' in *Land, Politics and Nationalism*, 165–6; O'Brien, *An Olive Branch in Ireland*, 188–210, 227–9.

223. Muldoon to Dillon, n.d. [1903], TCD, Dillon Papers, ms. 6734; 21 May 1904, ms. 6734/106.

224. Niall Harrington, *Kerry Landing* (Dublin 1992), 48; *Irish Freedom*, July 1911, 1.
225. William O'Brien, *The Irish National Question and the Land Act: Speeches Delivered at Cork, 21st and 22nd September 1903* (Dublin 1903), 3.
226. O'Brien, *An Olive Branch in Ireland*, 403.
227. Bew, *Conflict and Conciliation in Ireland*, 112.
228. Devlin to Dillon, 14 Sep. 1903, TCD, ms. 6729/95; 17 Sep. 1903, ms. 6729/96; Bull, 'The significance of the nationalist response to the Irish Land Act of 1903'.
229. Matthew Keating to Dillon, TCD, ms. 6755/731; Devlin to Dillon, 27 Sep. 1903, ms. 6729/97; O'Brien, *An Olive Branch in Ireland*, 223–6, 294.
230. Sheehy-Skeffington, *Michael Davitt*, 176–84; Gaughan, *Thomas O'Donnell*, 53–4.
231. McCarthy to O'Brien, 5 Nov. 1903, NUIC, AN82.
232. John O'Donnell to O'Brien, 5 Nov. 1903, NUIC, AN86–8.
233. O'Brien to Dunraven, 18 Nov. 1903, in Schilling, 'William O'Brien and the All-for-Ireland Movement'; O'Brien to Patrick Ford, in Warwick-Haller, *William O'Brien and the Irish Land War*, 250.
234. Bew, *Conflict and Conciliation in Ireland*, 113–7.
235. Compare William Lundon to O'Brien, 11 Apr. 1903, NUIC, AN26; 7 Nov. 1903, AN93; to Dillon, n.d., TCD, Dillon Papers, ms. 6756/923–4; Sheehy to O'Brien, 12 and 19 Oct. 1903, NUIC, AN69, 72; John O'Donnell to O'Brien, 4 Mar. 1905, AO47; J. D. Condon to O'Brien, 8 Apr. 1903, AN24–5; Condon to Dillon, n.d., TCD, ms. 6752/90.
236. Haviland-Burke to O'Brien, 3 Aug. 1904, NUIC, AN198.
237. Muldoon to Dillon, n.d. [1904], TCD, ms. 6734.
238. Dr Robert Ambrose MP to Dillon, 13 and 18 Jan. 1905, TCD, ms. 6752/21; Muldoon to Dillon, 29 May 1904, ms. 6734/107.
239. For example William O'Brien, *The Land Conference and its Critics*; *Mayo News*, July 1904.
240. Muldoon to Dillon, 20 Jan. 1904, TCD, ms. 6734/89; Dillon to Redmond, 14 July 1904, NLI, ms. 15182 (6).
241. Schilling, 'William O'Brien and the All-for-Ireland Movement'.
242. John O'Donnell to O'Brien, 8 Oct. 1906, NUIC, AO314; Sir Thomas Esmonde to O'Brien, 12 Jan. 1907, AP1.
243. Margaret Banks, *Edward Blake: Canadian Statesman in Irish Politics* (Toronto 1957), 292–302.
244. Sheehan, *Ireland Since Parnell*, 140–50, 169–80; Bradley, *Farm Labourers*.
245. John Herlihy to O'Brien, 7 June 1907, NUIC, AP41; 21 July 1907, AP 64; Ó Broin, *Dublin Castle and the 1916 Rising*, 76.
246. Sophie O'Brien, obituary for Sheehan, NLI, ms. 15048.
247. Jackson, *The Ulster Party*, chap. 6.
248. Gordon Lucy, 'The Battle of Drum', *New Ulster*, July 1995, 4–6; 'The Twelfth in County Monaghan, 1923', *New Ulster*, autumn 1997, 27–9.
249. Blunt, *My Diaries*, vol. 2, 48.
250. Mackail and Wyndham, *George Wyndham*, vol. 1, 90–1; Gailey, *Ireland and the Death of Kindness*, 191–3, 205–7.
251. *United Irishman*, 9 Apr. 1904, 4–5.

252. *United Irishman,* 11 Nov. 1905, 4–5.
253. Muldoon to Dillon, 22 Feb. 1904, TCD, ms. 6734/96.
254. Muldoon to Dillon, 12 Apr. 1904, TCD, ms. 6734/111.
255. McCarthy, *Rome in Ireland,* 26–9, 59, 231–3.
256. O'Brien to Wyndham, 20 Dec. 1904, NUIC, AN238; O'Brien to J. R. Doran, n.d., AN241.
257. Harrington to O'Brien, 21 Jan. 1905, NUIC, AO3; see also Haviland-Burke to O'Brien, 23 Jan. 1905, AO4.
258. *Mayo News,* 5 Mar. 1904, 8.
259. Harrington to O'Brien, 24 Jan. 1905, NUIC, AO5.
260. O'Brien to Wyndham, n.d., NUIC, AN239–40.
261. O'Brien to Crean, 4 Feb. 1905, NUIC, AO20–6.
262. Gailey, *Ireland and the Death of Kindness,* 261–80.
263. Dillon to Redmond, 5 Mar. 1905, NLI, ms. 15182 (7).
264. Devlin to Dillon, TCD, ms. 6729/107.
265. O'Halpin, *The Decline of the Union*; Kendle, *Walter Long, Ireland and the Union.*
266. *United Irishman,* 9 Sep. 1905, 1; 23 Sep. 1905, 1; Walsh, *Old Friends,* 113–5.
267. Swift MacNeill to Redmond, NLI, ms. 15205 (1); Ullswater, *A Speaker's Commentaries,* vol. 2, 11–12.
268. *Mayo News,* 25 Mar. and 15 Apr. 1906.
269. *New Ireland Review,* Oct. 1905.
270. Clery, *The Idea of a Nation,* 62–74; Maume, 'Nationalism and partition'.
271. Bradley, *Farm Labourers,* 27–8.
272. *Mayo News,* 17 June 1905, 4, 7; 16 Dec. 1905, 5.
273. *Irish People,* 7 Nov. 1905, quoted by Schilling in 'William O'Brien and the All-for-Ireland Movement'.
274. Monica Taylor, *Sir Bertram Windle* (London 1932); John A. Murphy, *The College: A History of Queen's/University College, Cork* (Cork 1995).
275. O'Brien, *An Olive Branch in Ireland,* 375–80; Sheehan, *Ireland Since Parnell,* 187–9.
276. O'Brien, quoted by Schilling in 'William O'Brien and the All-for-Ireland Movement'; John O'Donnell to O'Brien, 9 Mar. 1905, NUIC, AO58–9.
277. Healy, *Letters and Leaders of My Day,* vol. 2, 474; *Mayo News,* 6 Jan. 1906, 3.
278. Callanan, *The Parnell Split,* 84; Healy to Maurice Healy, 19 Nov. 1900, in Callanan, *T. M. Healy,* 441.
279. Healy to Frewen, 27 Aug. 1905, NLI, ms. 8557 (5).
280. O'Brien to Frewen, 31 Aug. 1905, NLI, ms. 8557 (5).
281. Herlihy to O'Brien, 27 June 1907, NUIC, AP54; W. M. Murphy to O'Brien, 21 Jan. 1908, AQ18.
282. O'Brien to Healy, 23 Sep. 1908, NUIC, AQ99–100.
283. Dillon to Redmond, 8 Dec. 1905, NLI, ms. 15182 (8).
284. Miller, *Church, State and Nation in Ireland,* 143–4.
285. *Catholic,* Feb. 1906, 21–2.
286. Archbishop Healy to O'Brien, 1 Nov. 1904, NUIC, AN227; O'Brien to Archbishop Healy, 3 Jan. 1906, AD187; Archbishop Healy to O'Brien, 4 Jan. 1906, AD188; *United Irishman,* 5 Dec. 1903, 4; 19 Dec. 1903, 4–5; 12 Aug. 1905, 4–5.

287. Muldoon to Dillon, 13 Aug. 1904, TCD, ms. 6734/111.

288. Mooney to Redmond, 29 Mar. 1901, 28 June 1901, 7 Dec. 1904; J. A. Kavanagh to Mooney, 24 June 1901, 26 June 1901 and n.d., NLI, ms. 15206 (6).

289. Valentine, *Irish Memories*.

290. Herlihy to O'Brien, 14 June 1907, NUIC, AP44.

291. Valentine, *Irish Memories*.

292. *Leader*, 8 Jan. 1910.

293. *Irish Peasant*, 13 Jan. 1906, 5; 20 Jan. 1906, 5; *United Irishman*, 3 Feb. 1906, 1.

294. Devlin to Redmond, 20 May 1905; Redmond to Devlin, 22 May 1905, NLI, ms. 15181 (1); Fr Denis O'Halloran to Devlin, 5 Jan. 1906, ms. 15181 (2); Muldoon to Dillon, 26 Mar. 1906, ms. 15182 (10).

CHAPTER 3 (P. 78–102)

1. O'Halpin, *The Decline of the Union*, 215.

2. Dillon to Redmond, 9 Apr. 1906, NLI, ms. 15182 (10).

3. There are several in NUIC, box AO (1905–6).

4. Russell, *Liberal Landslide*, 74, 122; *United Irishman*, 13 Jan. 1906, 4–5.

5. *Sinn Féin*, 23 June 1906, 1.

6. *United Irishman*, 3 Sep. 1904, 4; 16 Dec. 1905, 4–5; 6 Jan. 1906, 4–5.

7. *United Irishman*, 27 Jan. 1906, 3–4; 3 Feb. 1906, 4–5; 17 Feb. 1906, 3–4.

8. *Outlook*, 13 July 1907, 39–40.

9. Skinnider, *Doing My Bit for Ireland*, 25–7.

10. *Leader*, 15 May 1909, 301–2; 29 May 1909, 351; 12 June 1909, 396–7.

11. *Cork Free Press*, 9 June 1913, 4.

12. Bew, *Conflict and Conciliation in Ireland*, 130, 221–2.

13. Schilling, 'William O'Brien and the All-for-Ireland Movement'; Harrington to O'Brien, 10 Oct. 1906, NUIC, AO316.

14. *Sinn Féin*, 10 Nov. 1906, 2.

15. O'Brien, *An Olive Branch in Ireland*, 404–6; Gwynn to O'Brien, 27 June 1925, NUIC, AT252; O'Brien to Gwynn, 30 June 1925, AT254–7; Gwynn, *Recollections of a Literary Man*, 285–304.

16. O'Brien, *An Olive Branch in Ireland*, 356–73; Dillon to Redmond, 31 July 1907, NLI, ms. 15182 (15).

17. *Saturday Review*, 14 Mar. 1909, 335.

18. *Catholic*, May 1906, 57–8; June 1906, 70; MacCarthy, *Church and State in England and Wales*.

19. Miller, *Church, State and Nation in Ireland*, 153–9.

20. 'The Irish National Assembly (Session of 1910)', *Independent Review*, Apr. 1905, summarised by Sheehy-Skeffington in *Michael Davitt*.

21. *Mayo News*, 27 Jan. 1906, 4, 7. Not all Davitt's support reflected non-sectarianism: the *Mayo News* simultaneously attacked bishops subordinating Ireland to English Catholic requirements and denounced the Church of Ireland rector James Hannay for criticising Catholic priests (17 Feb. 1906, 4; 24 Feb. 1906, 4; 3 Mar. 1906, 5).

22. Sheehy-Skeffington, *Michael Davitt*; Levenson, *With Wooden Sword*, 54–61, 64–73.

23. *Sinn Féin*, 10 Aug. 1907, 2.

24. James McCann, *Some Facts, Figures and Factors in the Economic and Financial Position of Ireland To-Day* (Dublin n.d. [1902?]); *Sinn Féin,* 12 May 1906, 3.
25. 'Pat' [P. D. Kenny], *The Sorrows of Ireland;* Patrick Maume, 'Between Fleet Street and Mayo: P. D. Kenny, journalism and politics in Edwardian Ireland', *Twentieth-Century British History* (forthcoming).
26. *Irish People,* 5 July 1902, 1; Ryan, *The Plough and the Cross.*
27. Kenny, *Economics for Irishmen; Leader,* 12 Jan. 1907.
28. Hutchinson, *The Dynamics of Cultural Nationalism.*
29. *Irish Peasant,* 20 Jan. 1906; 17 Feb. 1906, 7; 14 Apr. 1906.
30. Ryan, *The Pope's Green Island,* 8–10.
31. *National Democrat,* Feb. 1907, 4–5.
32. *National Democrat,* June 1907, 75.
33. Waters, 'W. P. Ryan and the Irish Ireland Movement', 368–76.
34. *Sinn Féin,* 5 Jan. 1907, 2.
35. Walsh, *Old Friends,* 53–9; Augusteijn, *From Public Defiance to Guerrilla Warfare; Sinn Féin,* 4 Aug. 1906, 1.
36. MacSwiney diary, 22 Apr. 1905, 31–2, NUID, P48c/99; 3 Dec. 1906, 20 Jan. 1907, P48c/103.
37. *Republic,* 3 Jan. 1907.
38. Davis, *Arthur Griffith and Non-Violent Sinn Féin,* 24–34.
39. Dillon to Redmond, 29 Sep. 1906, NLI, ms. 15182 (12).
40. Hazleton to Field, 17 Dec. 1906, NLI, ms. 15195.
41. *Sinn Féin,* 18 Jan. 1908, 2; 25 Jan. 1908, 2.
42. *Sinn Féin,* 5 Dec. 1908, 2; 19 Dec. 1908, 2; 26 Dec. 1908, 1; 9 Jan. 1909, 2; 9 Sep. 1911, 2.
43. *Sinn Féin,* 30 May 1908, 2; 6 June 1908, 1; 13 May 1911, 2; 2 Sep. 1911, 2; 23 Mar. 1912, 5.
44. *United Irishman,* 5 Aug. 1905, 4–5.
45. *Sinn Féin,* 20 June 1908, 3.
46. *Sinn Féin,* 2 Feb. 1907, 3; 9 Mar. 1907, 2; 6 Apr. 1907, 1.
47. *Sinn Féin,* 13 Jan. 1912, 2.
48. *Sinn Féin,* 25 Jan. 1913, 4–5.
49. *Sinn Féin,* 18 Nov. 1911, 1; 9 Dec. 1911, 1; 22 Feb. 1913, 1; 14 June 1913, 5.
50. Waters, 'W. P. Ryan and the Irish Ireland Movement', 406.
51. Waters, 'W. P. Ryan and the Irish Ireland Movement'.
52. *Sinn Féin,* 2 Jan. 1909, 2.
53. *Sinn Féin,* 1 Jan. 1910, 2.
54. Terry Eagleton, 'The Ryan Line', *Crazy John and the Bishop and Other Essays on Irish Culture* (Cork 1998), 249–72.
55. *Sinn Féin,* 12 Apr. 1913, 4.
56. *Sinn Féin,* 26 Apr. 1913, 5.
57. *Sinn Féin,* 26 Apr. 1913, 5.
58. *New Ireland Review,* Feb. 1906, 321–31; *Leader,* 20 Jan. 1906; 24 Feb. 1906; 29 Sep. 1906; 20 Oct. 1906; 1 Dec. 1906, 229–30; 12 Jan. 1907, 340; 2 Mar. 1907, 29–30; 18 May 1907, 203–4.
59. *Sinn Féin,* 8 Sep. 1906, 2; 15 Sep. 1906, 2; 18 May 1907, 2; 25 May 1907, 2.

60. Bew, *Conflict and Conciliation in Ireland*, 131 n. 35.
61. Miller, *Church, State and Nation in Ireland*, 181–8; *Leader,* 18 and 25 May 1907; Dudley Edwards, *Patrick Pearse*, 73–4.
62. A. Hepburn, 'The Irish Council Bill and the fall of Sir Antony MacDermott', *Irish Historical Studies*, vol. 17 (1971), no. 68.
63. Joyce to Redmond on Limerick City opinion, NLI, ms. 15199 (2).
64. Miller, *Church, State and Nation in Ireland*, 187–8; Bew, *Conflict and Conciliation in Ireland*, 131–3.
65. *Sinn Féin*, 15 June 1907, 1; 6 July 1907, 1; 7 Sep. 1907, 2.
66. *Sinn Féin*, 29 June 1907, 2; 27 July 1907, 1; 23 Aug. 1907, 1; 19 Oct. 1907, 1; 23 Nov. 1907, 1; 1 Feb. 1908, 1.
67. *Sinn Féin*, 18 Aug. 1906, 1; 23 Feb. 1907, 2; *Republic*, 11 Apr. 1907, 18 Apr. 1907.
68. *Sinn Féin*, 17 Aug. 1907, 2; 7 Sep. 1907, 2; 21 Sep. 1907, 2; 18 Jan. 1908, 2; 27 Feb. 1909, 2.
69. Bew, *John Redmond*, 20.
70. *Sinn Féin*, 14 Sep. 1907, 2; 12 Oct. 1907, 2; 9 Nov. 1907, 1.
71. *Sinn Féin*, 2 Nov. 1907, 2; 9 Nov. 1907, 2.
72. United Irish League, *The Irish Party and Its Assailants: Vindication of Policy, Record of Achievements* (Dublin 1907).
73. Séamas Ó Maoileoin, *B'Fhiú an Braon Fola* (1958), translated by Patrick Twohig as *Blood on the Flag: Autobiography of a Freedom Fighter* (Cork 1996), 1.
74. Ó Duibhir, *Sinn Féin*.
75. *Sinn Féin*, 3 Aug. 1907, 1–2.
76. *Sinn Féin*, 19 Oct. 1907, 2; 26 Oct. 1907, 2.
77. *Sinn Féin*, 23 Mar. 1907, 3; 20 Apr. 1907, 2; 4 May 1907, 2–3; 11 May 1907 , 1.
78. McBride, *The Greening of Dublin Castle*.
79. Davis, *The Young Ireland Movement*.
80. *Irish People,* 27 Jan.–10 Mar. 1900.
81. *Sinn Féin*, 23 Nov. 1907, 2.
82. Dillon to Redmond, 29 Mar. 1906, 31 Mar. 1906, 1 Apr. 1906, 3 Apr. 1906, NLI, ms. 15182 (10).
83. William Boyle, *The Eloquent Dempsey* (Dublin 1911).
84. *Nationality,* 16 Mar. 1918, 1.
85. Henry Robinson, *More Memories of My Official Life* (London 1924).
86. *Leader,* 11 Mar. 1911, 79–80.
87. Harriet O'Brien to Redmond, 28 Feb. 1908, TCD, ms. 6747/269; 5 Mar. 1908, ms. 6747/276; Joyce to Redmond, 29 Jan. 1906 (with Redmond's draft reply), 31 Jan. 1906, NLI, ms. 15199.
88. *Leader,* 16 Sep. 1911, 109; Jeremiah MacVeagh, *Rome Rule* (London 1911).
89. The Armour-Dougherty-Dodd connection is described by McMinn in *Against the Tide*.
90. McMinn, *Against the Tide*.
91. Clifford and Marsland (eds.), *Lovat Fraser's Tour of Ireland*, 11–12; Dudley Edwards, *Patrick Pearse* (Wilson lent money to St Enda's). There is an account of Carlisle by Jefferson in *Viscount Pirrie of Belfast*, 98–104.
92. Pirrie's politics are discussed by Jefferson in *Viscount Pirrie of Belfast*, 133–42. Michael Moss and John R. Hume, *Shipbuilders to the World* (Belfast 1986), 127–9, 151, 157.

93. *Hibernian,* 10 July 1915; McBride, *The Greening of Dublin Castle,* 141–7 (note cartoon, 144); *Sinn Féin,* 16 Nov. 1907, 2; 23 Nov. 1907, 2.
94. *Sinn Féin,* 11 Jan. 1907, 3.
95. Lyons, *The Enigma of Tom Kettle,* 113.
96. *Sinn Féin,* 2 Mar. 1907, 2; 9 Mar. 1907, 2; 16 Mar. 1907, 2; *Leader,* 16 Mar. 1907.
97. For example the Arkins case: *Sinn Féin,* 4 Jan. 1913, 4–5; 11 Jan. 1913, 5; 18 Apr. 1913, 4; 25 Jan. 1913, 7; 1 Feb. 1913, 2.
98. *Leader,* 26 Dec. 1914, 488.
99. *Sinn Féin,* 26 June 1909, 2.
100. *Sinn Féin,* 27 June 1912, 2–3.
101. *Sinn Féin,* 26 Oct. 1907, 2.
102. *United Irishman,* 28 Oct. 1905, 4–5; *Sinn Féin,* 30 Mar. 1907, 2; 27 Apr. 1907, 2; 27 July 1907, 3; 19 Dec. 1908, 3–4.
103. *Cork Free Press,* 12 Feb. 1913, 4.
104. *Sinn Féin,* 19 Jan. 1907, 1, 2; 9 Feb. 1907, 1.
105. O'Higgins, 'The Ringsend Babies' Club', *1916, Before and After,* 40–1 (jeers at microbes), 'Herself and the microbes', 41–2, and commentary, 42–3, expounds the conspiracy theory.
106. Muenger, *The British Military Dilemma in Ireland,* 68–9.
107. O'Brien, *An Olive Branch in Ireland,* chap. 19.
108. Foy, 'The Ancient Order of Hibernians'; Miller, *Church, State and Nation in Ireland,* 208–17.
109. *Spark,* 9 May 1915, 1–3.
110. *Sinn Féin,* 16 Mar. 1907, 2; 6 Apr. 1907, 2; 13 Apr. 1907, 2; 20 Apr. 1907, 1.
111. *Leader,* 6 Apr. 1907.
112. *Sinn Féin,* 30 Mar. 1907, 2.
113. *Sinn Féin,* 2 Nov. 1907, 2.
114. O'Brien, *An Olive Branch in Ireland,* 380, 418–21.
115. *Cork Free Press,* 2 May 1913, 4; 22 Aug. 1913, 8.
116. *Cork Free Press,* 16 Feb. 1911, 8.
117. *Cork Free Press,* 3 Jan. 1911, 5; 4 Jan. 1911, 7; 11 Feb. 1911, 4, 7.
118. *Cork Free Press,* 11 June 1914, 5; 12 June 1914, 4; 19 June 1914, 5.
119. *Leader,* 19 Feb. 1910, 16–17.
120. Miller, *Church, State and Nation in Ireland,* 212–4.
121. Esmonde to O'Brien, 12 Jan. 1907, NUIC, AP1.
122. John Herlihy to O'Brien, 26 Aug. 1907, NUIC, AP110; 10 Sep. 1907, AP120; 22 Oct. 1907, AP179 29 Oct. 1907 AP193; George Murnaghan MP to O'Brien, 14 Oct. 1907, AP157.
123. Harrington to O'Brien, 12 Oct. 1907, NUIC, AP152–3; O'Brien to Harrington, 17 Sep. 1906, AO295–7; Herlihy to O'Brien, 5 Sep. 1907, AP119.
124. Bew, *Conflict and Conciliation in Ireland,* 141–3.
125. Guinan, *The Curate of Kilcloon.*
126. Bew, *Conflict and Conciliation in Ireland,* 165–8.
127. Bew, *Conflict and Conciliation in Ireland,* 165–6, 168.
128. Dillon to Redmond, 2 Jan. 1907, NLI, ms. 15182 (17); Devlin to Dillon, quoted by Foy in 'The Ancient Order of Hibernians', 102–3.

129. Bew, *Conflict and Conciliation in Ireland*, 186.
130. Farrell to O'Brien, 15 Oct. 1903, NUIC, AN70.
131. O'Callaghan to Redmond, 15 Jan. 1907, quoted by O'Brien in *William O'Brien and the Course of Irish Politics*, 172; O'Callaghan to Redmond, 31 Jan. 1908, TCD, ms. 6747/258.
132. O'Brien to C. J. Dolan, 19 Jan. 1908, NUIC, AQ7–8.
133. Ó Duibhir, *Sinn Féin*, 60–4, 113; *Sinn Féin*, 22 Feb. 1908, 2.
134. *Sinn Féin*, 29 Feb. 1908, 2–3.
135. *Sinn Féin*, 23 Jan. 1909, 2.
136. *Sinn Féin*, 1 Oct. 1910, 1.
137. *Nationality*, 4 Jan. 1919, 1.
138. Cunningham, *Labour in West of Ireland*, 140–3.
139. Davis, *Arthur Griffith and Non-Violent Sinn Féin*, 60–1; *Sinn Féin*, 10 Aug. 1907, 1; 27 June 1908, 3.
140. Bew, *Conflict and Conciliation in Ireland*, 171–2.
141. O'Brien, *An Olive Branch in Ireland*, 435–40.
142. *Sinn Féin*, 8 Aug. 1908, 1.
143. Ginnell, *Land and Liberty*.
144. *Cork Free Press*, 2 Jan. 1913, 6; 10 Jan. 1913, 4; Bamford and Banks, *Vicious Circle*; Hobson, *Ireland Yesterday and Tomorrow*, 85–90.
145. *Sinn Féin*, 4 Apr. 1908, 2; 15 Aug. 1908, 2.
146. *Leader*, 2 July 1910.
147. *Sinn Féin*, 24 Dec. 1909, 2.
148. *Sinn Féin*, 20 Aug. 1910, 1; 6 May 1911, 3–4.
149. Miller, *Church, State and Nation in Ireland*, 234–42; Ryan, *The Pope's Green Island*, 137–84.
150. *Sinn Féin*, 19 Dec. 1908, 2.
151. *Sinn Féin*, 30 May 1908, 2; 9 Jan. 1909, 1.
152. Boland, *Irishman's Day*, chap. 9; *Sinn Féin*, 30 Jan. 1909, 1; *Leader*, 25 Sep. 1909.
153. Lyons, *The Enigma of Tom Kettle*, 141–2; *Sinn Féin*, 12 Sep. 1908, 2.
154. Bew, *Conflict and Conciliation in Ireland*, 181–5.
155. Joseph Devlin to C. Buckley, 13 Jan. 1909, NUIC, AR2 .
156. *Sinn Féin*, 20 Feb. 1909, 4.
157. O'Brien, *An Olive Branch in Ireland*, 441–53; letter from eyewitness to the assault on Crean to 'Ned' [Edward Sheehan], 21 Feb. 1909, NUIC, AR19; Foy, 'The Ancient Order of Hibernians', 105–13; *Cork Examiner*, 16 Apr. 1909, quoted by Schilling in 'William O'Brien and the All-for-Ireland Movement'.
158. Levenson, *With Wooden Sword*, 86–9.
159. Boland, *Irishman's Day*, 133–4.
160. Muldoon to Redmond, n.d. [1909], NLI, ms. 15208.
161. Schilling, 'William O'Brien and the All-for-Ireland Movement'.
162. Fr T. Dawson to O'Brien, 31 Mar. 1909, NLI, ms. 8557 (3).
163. Schilling, 'William O'Brien and the All-for-Ireland Movement'; Healy, *Letters and Leaders of My Day*, vol. 2, 485.
164. *Sinn Féin*, 3 Apr. 1909, 2.

165. Sheehan, *Ireland Since Parnell*, 228.
166. Schilling, 'William O'Brien and the All-for-Ireland Movement'.
167. Lundon to Dillon, 22 Oct. 1909, TCD, ms. 6756/927.
168. *Cork Free Press*, 18 July 1910, 4.
169. *Sinn Féin*, 28 Aug. 1909, 3; 8 Jan. 1911, 3.
170. *Sinn Féin*, 1 Feb. 1908, 2; 8 Feb. 1908, 2.
171. *Sinn Féin*, 1 Jan. 1910, 2.
172. *Sinn Féin*, 8 May 1909, 2.
173. *Sinn Féin*, 29 May 1909, 2; 2 Oct. 1909, 2; 12 Feb. 1910, 4.
174. *Sinn Féin*, 22 May 1909, 2; 13 Nov. 1909, 1.
175. Sheehan, *Ireland Since Parnell*, 224.
176. Schilling, 'William O'Brien and the All-for-Ireland Movement'.
177. Davis, *Arthur Griffith and Non-Violent Sinn Féin*, 64; O'Brien, *William O'Brien and the Course of Irish Politics*; Edward Sheehan to O'Brien, 2 Feb. 1908, NUIC, AR18, *Sinn Féin*, 13 Mar. 1909, 4; 11 Mar. 1911, 1.
178. *Sinn Féin*, 14 Dec. 1907, 2.
179. Crawford to O'Brien, 17 Feb. 1908, NUIC, AQ32–3; 5 Mar. 1909, AR34–7; 9 Mar. 1909, AR39–40.
180. O'Brien to Alderman Forde, 28 Nov. 1909, NUIC, AR54–5.
181. *Leader*, 15 Jan. 1910, 510; O'Brien, *An Olive Branch in Ireland*, 464–6.

CHAPTER 4 (P. 103–119)

1. *Leader*, 12 Feb. 1910, 617–8; 7 Jan. 1911, 515–6.
2. *Cork Free Press*, 2 Mar. 1911, 7; 31 Jan. 1914, 4.
3. Lennox Robinson, Tom Robinson, and Nora Dorman, *Three Homes* (London 1938), 178–80.
4. *Cork Free Press*, 18 Mar. 1911, 7.
5. *Sinn Féin*, 5 Feb. 1910, 5.
6. Schilling, 'William O'Brien and the All-for-Ireland Movement'.
7. Lane, 'The Land and Labour Association', 94.
8. *Cork Free Press*, 8 May 1911, 8; 13 Oct. 1913, 4–5; 14 Oct. 1913, 5–6.
9. 'An Irishman', *Intolerance in Ireland*, 95–8.
10. *Leader*, 8 Jan. 1910.
11. *Leader*, 12 Feb. 1910, 617–8.
12. *Leader*, 19 Feb. 1910, 16–17; 26 Mar. 1910.
13. Healy, *Letters and Leaders of My Day*, vol. 2, 491–2.
14. *Leader*, 29 Jan. 1910, 568–70.
15. Miller, *Church, State and Nation in Ireland*, 259–60; *Pall Mall Gazette*, 7 Feb. 1910, 5.
16. O'Sullivan to Sheehan, 3 Apr. 1906, NUIC, AO251; Sheehan to William O'Brien, 11 Oct. 1907, AP50; O'Sullivan to Sheehan, n.d. [Oct. 1907], AP151.
17. *Cork Free Press*, 27 Sep. 1913, 7.
18. *Leader*, 29 July 1911, 575–6; Joyce statement of costs, NA, LIM 23/2/5.
19. *Leader*, 22 Jan. 1910; Morgan, *Labour and Partition*, 31.
20. Lane, 'The Land and Labour Association', 94.
21. Bew, *Conflict and Conciliation in Ireland*, 198–9; *Cork Free Press*, 18 July 1910, 4.

22. *Cork Free Press,* 16 June 1910, 2.

23. *Leader,* 8 Jan. and 29 Jan. 1910.

24. *Sinn Féin,* 22 Mar. 1913, 1; 29 Mar. 1913, 1.

25. In 1910 O'Brien thought Egan was the party candidate (*An Olive Branch in Ireland,* 468–70). For Egan's later support see *National Conference of the All-for-Ireland League* (Cork 1912).

26. Sheehan, *Worthies of Westmeath;* Bew, *Conflict and Conciliation in Ireland,* 197–8.

27. O'Brien, 'The new power in Ireland'.

28. *Leader,* 29 Jan. and 18 June 1910.

29. *Sinn Féin,* 19 Sep. 1914, 1; 26 Sep. 1914, 1; *Leader,* 22 Mar. 1913, 133.

30. *Cork Free Press,* 3 Feb. 1911, 5.

31. *United Irishman,* 23 Jan. 1904, 4–5; *Sinn Féin,* 15 Jan. 1910, 2; 29 Jan. 1910, 1.

32. Sir John Ross, *Pilgrim Scrip* (London 1927), 128–9; *Cork Free Press,* 22 Apr. 1914, 8.

33. Crawford to O'Brien, 25 May 1910, NUIC, AR99–102.

34. *Leader,* 18 June 1910.

35. *Leader,* 29 Jan. 1910.

36. O'Brien, 'The new power in Ireland'; *Mayo News,* 1 Jan. 1910, 5; *Sinn Féin,* 23 Feb. 1907, 2.

37. Schilling, 'William O'Brien and the All-for-Ireland Movement'.

38. Lane, 'The Land and Labour Association', 98.

39. Herlihy to O'Brien, 7 June 1907, NUIC, AP41; Sheehan to Herlihy, 30 June 1907, AP55; Herlihy to O'Brien, 21 July 1907, AP64.

40. Bradley, *Farm Labourers,* 28–9.

41. Healy to O'Brien, 29 Oct. 1907, 30 Oct. 1907, 20 Dec. 1907, NLI, ms. 8556 (2), for this interpretation of the pledge. Bew, *Conflict and Conciliation in Ireland,* overestimates such professions of loyalty.

42. Redmond to Dillon, TCD, ms. 6748/433; O'Brien, 'The new power in Ireland', 441.

43. McKean to O'Brien, 15 Feb. 1910, NUIC, AR78; Healy to O'Brien, 22 Oct. 1910, NLI, ms. 8556 (3).

44. E. P. O'Kelly to O'Brien, 13 Mar. 1910, NUIC, AR84–5.

45. Healy to O'Brien, 5 May 1910, NLI, ms. 8556 (3).

46. Clifford, *Reprints from the 'Cork Free Press',* 21; *Cork Free Press,* 17 June 1910, 4.

47. *Leader,* 2 July 1910; *Cork Free Press,* 16 June 1910, 4; *Sinn Féin,* 28 May 1910, 1.

48. *Sinn Féin,* 11 June 1910, 1; 18 June 1910, 1.

49. *Leader,* 22 Jan. 1910, 534.

50. Hardcastle and O'Malley, *Election Petition Reports,* vol. 6, 58–95; *Cork Free Press,* 30 June 1910, 4–5.

51. Dillon to Redmond, 17 Feb. 1907, NLI, ms. 15182 (14).

52. Miller, *Church, State and Nation in Ireland,* 265; Healy to O'Brien, 18 Mar. 1910, O'Brien to Healy 19 Mar. 1910, NLI, ms. 8556 (3).

53. Muldoon to Dillon, 27 Mar. 1904, TCD, ms. 6734/98.

54. Fr Richard Barrett to O'Brien, 23 Nov. 1904, NUIC, AN232; Appeal of AFIL MPs to Cardinal Merry del Val, 1914, NLI, ms. 8506 (1).

55. Muldoon to Dillon, 3 Nov. 1911, TCD, ms. 6734/111.

56. Heuser, *Canon Sheehan of Doneraile;* Clifford, *Reprints from the 'Cork Free Press',* 9–18; *Cork Free Press,* 15 May 1911, 7–9; Sophie O'Brien, *In Mallow; Around Broom Lane.*

57. Miller, *Church, State and Nation in Ireland*, 264–6.
58. Healy to O'Brien, 14 May and 17 Dec. 1910, NLI, ms. 8556 (3).
59. *Leader*, 7 Sep. 1912.
60. Schilling, 'William O'Brien and the All-for-Ireland Movement'; O'Brien, *William O'Brien and the Course of Irish Politics*, 199–200.
61. *Cork Free Press*, 4 Aug. 1910, 4; 15 May 1911, 4.
62. *Cork Free Press*, 11 June 1910, 7–8.
63. *Cork Free Press*, 12 Aug. 1910, 5.
64. *Cork Free Press*, 27 July 1910, 5–6.
65. Bradley, *Farm Labourers*. For Keane and censorship see Adams, *Censorship*, 53, 59, 69–70, 84–6, 208 n. 32–3.
66. *Cork Free Press*, 9 July 1910, 7–8.
67. Schilling, 'William O'Brien and the All-for-Ireland Movement'.
68. O'Brien to Sir Horace Plunkett, 25 Feb. 1904, NUIC, AN178–81.
69. *Leader*, 10 Sep. 1910, 80; 17 Sep. 1910.
70. *Cork Free Press*, 15 July 1910, 4–5.
71. Horgan, *Parnell to Pearse*, 188–9; *Leader*, 28 May 1910.
72. *Sinn Féin*, 11 June 1910, 1; *Leader*, 4 June 1910, 364; 11 June 1910, 389; *Cork Free Press*, 11 June 1910, 11.
73. *Leader*, 20 Aug. 1910, 8; 1 Apr. 1911, 149; *Cork Free Press*, 25 Mar. 1911, 7–8.
74. United Irish League, *The Liffey at Ebb Tide*.
75. A. C. Murray, *Master and Brother* (London 1945), 40–1.
76. Gilbert, *Lloyd George: Architect of Change*, 403–10.
77. Healy to O'Brien, 5 May 1910, 4 Aug. 1910, NLI, ms. 8556 (3); *Irish Freedom*, Apr. 1911, 1.
78. *Sinn Féin*, 5 Feb. 1910, 4; 2 Apr. 1910, 4.
79. *Sinn Féin*, 22 Jan. 1910, 2; 29 Jan. 1910, 1.
80. *Sinn Féin*, 15 Jan. 1910; 5 Feb. 1910, 1.
81. *Sinn Féin*, 8 Oct. 1910, 2.
82. *Sinn Féin*, 22 Oct. 1910, 2.
83. *Sinn Féin*, 21 May 1910, 1; 4 June, 1; 11 June, 1.
84. O'Brien, *William O'Brien and the Course of Irish Politics*, 195–6.
85. Austen to Joseph Chamberlain, 12 Apr. 1910, Chamberlain, *Politics from Inside*, 248.
86. *Cork Free Press*, 19 and 20 July and 1 Aug. 1910.
87. Ward, 'Moreton Frewen's Anglo-American campaign for federalism'.
88. *Sinn Féin*, 15 Oct. 1910, 1–2; 22 Oct. 1910, 1.
89. Alan Ward, *Ireland and Anglo-American Relations* (London 1969), 18.
90. Shannon, *Arthur J. Balfour and Ireland*, 148–53; Gollin, *The 'Observer' and J. L. Garvin*.
91. John Marlowe, *Milner: Apostle of Empire* (London 1976), 218–9.
92. Vincent, *The Crawford Papers*, 166.
93. Alfred Lyttelton to Balfour, 16 Oct. 1910, BL, add. ms. 49775, fol. 66.
94. Shannon, *Arthur J. Balfour and Ireland*, 150, 154–6.
95. Austen Chamberlain to Garvin, 21 Oct. 1910, in Chamberlain, *Politics from Inside*, 282.
96. Sophie O'Brien memoirs, quoted by Schilling in 'William O'Brien and the All-for-Ireland Movement'.

97. Shannon, *Arthur J. Balfour and Ireland*; Kendle, *Walter Long, Ireland and the Union*; Gwynn, *Life of John Redmond*, 182.

98. O'Brien, *An Olive Branch in Ireland*, 439 n.; O'Brien to Long, 3 Oct. 1908, NUIC, AQ108; Long to O'Brien, 5 Oct. 1908, AQ109.

99. O'Brien, *The Irish Revolution*, 74.

100. Gollin, *The 'Observer' and J. L. Garvin*, 248–50.

101. *Cork Free Press*, 31 Jan. 1911, 5.

102. *Sinn Féin*, 1 Jan. 1910, 2.

103. *Leader*, 28 Jan. 1911, 582.

104. *Leader*, 21 Jan. 1911, 558.

105. Gaughan, *Thomas O'Donnell*, 63.

106. *Leader*, 7 Jan. 1911.

107. *Cork Free Press*, 20 June 1910, 5–7.

108. Ó Broin, *No Man's Man*, 6; Stenton and Lees, *Who's Who of British Members of Parliament*, vol. 2, 362.

109. *Leader*, 17 Sep. 1910, 101; Hardcastle and O'Malley, *Election Petition Reports*, vol. 6, 103–78.

110. *Leader*, 31 Dec. 1910, 496–7.

111. Madden to O'Brien, 3 Jan. 1911, NUIC, AR124.

112. Ned Buckley, 'The All-for-Ireland League', in Clifford and Lane (eds.), *Ned Buckley's Poems*; *Cork Free Press*, 2 May 1911, 4–5.

113. O'Brien, *The Irish Revolution*, 378.

114. Healy to O'Brien, 25 Nov. 1916, NLI, ms. 8556 (11).

115. *Grievances from Ireland*, Feb. 1909, 86; *United Irishman*, 20 May 1905, 6.

116. *Leader*, 24 Dec. 1910, 463; *Sinn Féin*, 24 Nov. 1906, 3.

117. *Leader*, 4 Feb. 1911, 605.

118. Gaughan, *Thomas O'Donnell*, 82–6; *Cork Free Press*, 2 Jan. 1911, 7; 4 Jan. 1911, 8.

119. *Clongownian*, June 1918, 199–200.

120. D. D. Sheehan to John Herlihy, 30 June 1907, NUIC, O'Brien Papers, AP55; O'Brien, *An Olive Branch in Ireland*, 443 n.

121. *Cork Free Press*, 4 July 1910, 5, 8; 31 Jan. 1911, 5, 8.

122. Healy to Herlihy, 27 Oct. 1909, NUIC, AR49; Gollin, *The 'Observer' and J. L. Garvin*, 249.

123. *Cork Free Press*, 19 Jan. 1911, 7.

124. Healy to O'Brien, 22 June 1911, NLI, ms. 8556 (4).

125. *Cork Free Press*, 6 Feb. 1911, 7; 20 Mar. 1911, 7.

126. *Leader*, 24 Dec. 1910, 462.

127. *Sinn Féin*, 3 Dec. 1910, 1; 10 Dec. 1910, 1, 4.

128. *Leader*, 24 Dec. 1910.

129. *Morning Post*, 28 Sep. 1910.

130. Sophie O'Brien memoirs, NLI, ms. 4210–3, 1910 section.

131. *Cork Free Press*, 24 Jan. 1911, 7; 31 Jan. 1911, 4; 1 Feb. 1911, 5; 12 Apr. 1911, 2; 1 June 1911, 6.

132. Irish Times, *Sinn Fein Rebellion Handbook*, 141.

133. *Cork Free Press*, 27 Apr. 1911, 5–6.

134. *Leader,* 4 Mar. 1911, 57; 27 May 1911, 345; 5 Aug. 1911, 587.
135. Callanan, *T. M. Healy,* 474–5.
136. Redmond to Dillon, 5 July 1911, TCD, ms. 6748/476.
137. Healy, *Letters and Leaders of My Day,* vol. 2, 503.
138. *Cork Free Press,* 2 June 1911, 4.
139. *Cork Free Press,* 18 Jan. 1911.
140. *Cork Free Press,* 14 Mar. 1911, 7; 5 June 1911, 4; 13 June 1911, 4, 7; 20 June 1911, 5.
141. *Cork Free Press,* 7 Jan. 1911, 7–9; 6 Feb. 1911, 5; 17 Feb. 1911.
142. Healy to O'Brien, 21 July 1911, NLI, ms. 8556 (4); O'Brien, *William O'Brien and the Course of Irish Politics,* 202–5.
143. *Leader,* 19 Aug. 1911, 7–8.
144. *Lady Gregory's Journals,* books 30–44 (Gerrards Cross 1987). I owe this reference to Dr Brian Murphy.
145. Healy, *Letters and Leaders of My Day,* vol. 2, 503.
146. Maume, 'In the Fenians' wake'.
147. *Sinn Féin,* 7 Oct. 1911, 3.

CHAPTER 5 (P. 120–146)

1. *Irish Freedom,* Nov. 1911, 1; *Sinn Féin,* 23 Mar. 1912, 1.
2. *Sinn Féin,* 28 Jan. 1911, 2.
3. *Cork Free Press,* 13 Jan. 1913, 6; 3 Mar. 1914, 5–6.
4. *Sinn Féin,* 15 Feb. 1913, 7; 22 Feb. 1913, 2–3.
5. *Cork Free Press,* 13 Jan. 1913, 6.
6. *Cork Free Press,* 10 Feb. 1913, 4–5; 4 Mar. 1914, 8.
7. *Irish Freedom,* July 1911; *Cork Free Press,* 9 June 1911, 4–6.
8. *Leader,* 17 June 1911, 422; *Sinn Féin,* 17 June 1911, 1.
9. Glandon, *Arthur Griffith and the Advanced Nationalist Press,* 83–4.
10. *Irish Freedom,* Feb. 1911, 4–5; Jan. 1913, 1.
11. *Sinn Féin,* 5 Aug. 1911, 3.
12. *Irish Freedom,* Jan. 1912, 1; Aug. 1912, 1.
13. Mitchel, *Jail Journal*; Michael Doheny, *The Felon's Track* (Dublin 1913); Griffith, *Meagher of the Sword*; Griffith, *Thomas Davis: Thinker and Teacher* (Dublin 1914).
14. *Sinn Féin,* 29 Oct. 1910, 2; 12 Nov. 1910, 1; Arthur Griffith, *Pitt's Policy* (1911). Griffith's suggestion that Pitt sincerely wished to benefit Ireland by his trade proposals of 1785 (defeated by Grattan and English Whigs) gestures towards tariff reformers and denigrates the IPP-Liberal alliance, *Sinn Féin,* 14 Mar. 1911, 4–5.
15. Davis, *Arthur Griffith and Non-Violent Sinn Féin,* 106–7, 119–20; Maume, 'The Ancient Constitution', 123–37.
16. *Sinn Féin,* 11 May 1907, 2; 9 Oct. 1909, 2.
17. O'Brien, *The Irish Revolution,* 147.
18. Michael Farrell, *Arming the Protestants* (London 1980); S. Rosenbaum (ed.), *The Case Against Home Rule* (London 1911).
19. *Freeman's Journal,* 3 Jan. 1913, quoted by Chauvin in 'The Parliamentary Party and the Revolutionary Movement in Ireland', 202.
20. *Leader,* 27 Apr. 1912, 250–1; *Sinn Féin,* 20 Apr. 1912, 3.

21. *Leader,* 13 Apr. 1912, 211.
22. *Leader,* 27 Apr. 1912, 260; Schilling, 'William O'Brien and the All-for-Ireland Movement'.
23. *Sinn Féin,* 8 Dec. 1906, 2.
24. Davis, *Arthur Griffith and Non-Violent Sinn Féin,* 24; Dudley Edwards, *Patrick Pearse,* 157–9.
25. Levenson, *With Wooden Sword,* 121–3.
26. *Cork Free Press,* 24 Feb. 1911, 5, 8.
27. *Irish Freedom,* Aug. 1912, 1; *Leader,* 27 July 1912.
28. Scott, *Diaries,* 64–6.
29. *Sinn Féin,* 20 Mar. 1909, 4.
30. *Sinn Féin,* 15 Apr. 1911, 1 (for Hanna Sheehy-Skeffington's reply see *Sinn Féin,* 22 Apr. 1911, 1), 6 Apr. 1912, 4–5; 13 Apr. 1912, 1 (with Jenny Wyse Power's dissent).
31. *Irish Citizen,* 17 May 1913, 410, 416; 24 May 1913, 3; Chauvin, 'The Parliamentary Party and the Revolutionary Movement in Ireland', 231 (Glasnevin AOH resolution, from *Freeman's Journal,* 10 May 1913).
32. *Cork Free Press,* 7 May 1913, 4; 8 May 1913, 7.
33. Murphy, *The Women's Suffrage Movement,* 178–89.
34. Dudley Edwards, *Patrick Pearse,* 219–20; *Cork Free Press,* 30 Apr. 1913, 4.
35. Maume, *D. P. Moran,* 31–2.
36. *Leader,* 22 June 1912, 437; 3 Aug. 1912, 584–5; 16 Nov. 1912, 329.
37. *Leader,* 1 Feb. 1913, 614; 8 Feb. 1913, 637, 641.
38. Gailey, *Ireland and the Death of Kindness,* 100–20.
39. Thomas Kennedy, *Ireland's Revolt Against Overtaxation* (Dublin 1897).
40. Lyons, *The Enigma of Tom Kettle,* 122–3; O'Brien, *Dear Old Dirty Dublin,* 172–3.
41. Garvin to Balfour, 20 Oct. 1910, in Chamberlain, *Politics from Inside,* 279–81.
42. Kettle, *Home Rule Finance.*
43. *Sinn Féin,* 22 Jan. 1911, 2; 28 Jan. 1911, 1; *Cork Free Press,* 17 Jan. 1911, 4–5; 2 Feb. 1911, 5; 1 Apr. 1911, 2.
44. *Leader,* 25 Feb. 1911, 29–30; *Irish Freedom,* Apr. 1911, 1.
45. *Irish Freedom,* Apr. 1911, 1.
46. J. J. Horgan, *Home Rule: A Critical Consideration* (Dublin 1911).
47. Horgan, *Parnell to Pearse,* 250–1.
48. *Cork Free Press,* 8 Jan. 1913, 4.
49. Patricia Jalland, 'Home rule finance: a neglected dimension of the Irish question, 1910–14' in Alan O'Day (ed.), *Reactions to Irish Nationalism* (Dublin 1987), 297–318.
50. *Cork Free Press,* 3 Apr. 1913, 4–5.
51. Horgan, *Parnell to Pearse,* 250–1; Kettle, *The Open Secret of Ireland.*
52. Begbie, *The Lady Next Door,* 25–33.
53. *Cork Free Press,* 4 July 1913, 4–5.
54. *Cork Free Press,* 3, 10, 17, 24 and 31 May 1913, 7, 14, 21 and 28 June 1913, 5 July 1913.
55. *Cork Free Press,* 3 June 1911, 9; 21 May 1913, 6.
56. Miller, *Church, State and Nation in Ireland,* 274–6; Gwynn, *John Redmond's Last Years,* 55; *Cork Free Press,* 27 May 1911, 7; 6 June 1911, 2, 5.

57. *Hibernian,* 10 July 1915.
58. *Irish Freedom,* Feb. 1912, 1.
59. *Sinn Féin,* 8 July 1911, 1.
60. *Sinn Féin,* 20 May 1911, 2; 27 May 1911, 1; 3 June 1911, 1, 2; 10 June 1911, 1.
61. *Sinn Féin,* 3 June 1911, 2; 17 June 1911, 1.
62. Devlin to Horgan, 27 Oct. 1911, in Horgan, *Parnell to Pearse,* 208.
63. O'Brien, *The Irish Revolution,* 105–7.
64. *Cork Free Press,* 1 June 1911, 5.
65. Bradley, *Farm Labourers,* 29.
66. *Irish Freedom,* May 1912, 1.
67. Healy, *The Old Munster Circuit,* 185.
68. *Hibernian,* 11 Dec. 1915, 1.
69. Muldoon to Dillon, TCD, ms. 6734/128–34, 138, 140–5; 18 Sep. 1911, 6734/143; 19 Sep. 1911, ms. 6734/145.
70. *Leader,* 26 Aug. 1911, 36.
71. McMinn, *Against the Tide,* 94–6.
72. Healy to O'Brien, 20 Aug. 1911, 14 Sep. 1911, NLI, ms. 8556 (5).
73. *Leader,* 21 Oct. 1911, 240.
74. Muldoon to Dillon, 18 Sep. 1911, TCD, ms. 6734/143; 19 Sep. 1911, 6734/145.
75. *Sinn Féin,* 23 Sep. 1911, 1; 30 Sep. 1911, 2.
76. Muldoon to Dillon, 20 Sep. 1911, TCD, ms. 6734/146; 31 Aug. 1911, ms. 6734/136; 13 Sep. 1911, ms. 6734/139; 16 Sep. 1911, ms. 6734/141.
77. *Leader,* 14 Oct. 1911, 212–3; 21 Oct. 1911, 240.
78. *Outlook,* 14 Oct. 1911, 488; Harris, *The Catholic Church and the Foundation of the Northern Ireland State,* 12.
79. *Leader,* 21 Oct. 1911, 240.
80. *Leader,* 2 Nov. 1912, 288–9.
81. Day, *The Amazing Philanthropists,* 146.
82. Gwynn, *The Case For Home Rule,* 73–6.
83. For example *Leader,* 23 Sep. 1911, 129.
84. *Leader,* 5 Feb. 1910, 582–3; Lysaght [MacLysaght], *Sir Horace Plunkett,* 128, 155–6; Seumas O'Kelly, *The Bribe* (Dublin 1914).
85. Carroll, *They Have Fooled You Again,* 201.
86. MacVeagh to Redmond, 28 Oct. 1913, NLI, ms. 15205 (4).
87. McBride, *The Greening of Dublin Castle,* 200–1.
88. Day, *The Amazing Philanthropists.*
89. Murray Fraser, *John Bull's Other Homes: State Housing and British Policy in Ireland, 1883–1922* (Liverpool 1996), 93–4. Field was prominent in the Town Tenant organisation; its secretary, J. C. M. Briscoe, regularly sought nomination as a parliamentary candidate. For vampirisation of the Town Tenant Association by the Irish Party see *Cork Free Press,* 12 Apr. 1913, 7; 22 May 1913, 4.
90. Schilling, 'William O'Brien and the All-for-Ireland Movement'. The *Cork Free Press* published articles on the housing situation throughout 1913.
91. O'Brien, *Dear Old Dirty Dublin,* 98; *Hibernian,* 20 Nov. 1915, 1.
92. O'Brien, *Dear Old Dirty Dublin,* 14–15, 76, 82–3.

93. *Catholic,* Jan. 1906, 3–4; *United Irishman,* 16 Dec. 1905, 1.

94. *Leader,* 11 Nov. 1911, 299–300; 2 Dec. 1911, 373–4; 9 Dec. 1911, 406; 20 Jan. 1912, 567; 27 Jan. 1912, 590.

95. *Leader,* 9 Nov. 1912, 305.

96. *Cork Free Press,* 7 Jan. 1913, 4; 11 Feb. 1913, 4; Don Lynch and Ken Marshall, *Titanic: An Illustrated History* (Toronto 1992), 187.

97. Meehan, *The Members of Parliament for Laois and Offaly,* 71.

98. J. P. Hayden Memoirs, chap. 33, MDA.

99. Healy to O'Brien, 11 Sep. 1911, NLI, ms. 8556 (5).

100. *Leader,* 30 Mar. 1912, 152.

101. J. P. Hayden Memoirs, MDA.

102. Murphy, *Patrick Pearse and the Lost Republican Ideal,* 53; Flann Campbell, *The Dissenting Voice: Protestant Nationalists in Ireland* (Belfast 1991).

103. Eileen Reilly, 'Rev. J. O. Hannay, the home rule controversy, and the Church of Ireland Synod, April 1912', *Retrospect,* 1993, 9–17; *Sinn Féin,* 10 Feb. 1912, 5.

104. Joseph McMinn, 'Liberalism in North Antrim, 1900–14', *Irish Historical Studies,* May 1982.

105. Jefferson, *Viscount Pirrie of Belfast.*

106. *Leader,* 3 Jan. 1914, 513; McMinn, *Against the Tide.*

107. Muldoon to Dillon, 15 Aug. 1912, TCD, ms. 6734/158.

108. Healy, *The Old Munster Circuit,* 54.

109. *Leader,* 28 Jan. 1911, 581.

110. *Leader,* 20 Apr. 1912, 228–9.

111. For example *Leader,* 4 Jan. 1913, 535.

112. *Nationality,* 3 July 1915, 4; 22 Jan. 1916, 2.

113. *Sinn Féin,* 2 Nov. 1912, 3.

114. Tierney, *Eoin MacNeill,* 117.

115. 'One of the Tolerant Majority' [Father — Coleman], *Grievances in Ireland.* Coleman's authorship is revealed by L. M. Cullen in *Eason and Son,* 256. As editor of the *Irish Rosary,* Coleman joined Moran in supporting the Catholic Association and the pro-censorship Irish Vigilance Association, the latter heavily influenced by Dominican confraternities.

116. *United Irishman,* 5 Aug. 1905, 3.

117. 'An Irishman', *Intolerance in Ireland,* 180, 188.

118. Cullen, *Eason and Son,* 248–57.

119. Maume, *D. P. Moran,* 31; Father Thomas Murphy, *The Literature Crusade in Ireland* (Limerick 1912); O'Leary, *The Prose Literature of the Gaelic Revival,* 36–45.

120. *Cork Free Press,* 18 Mar. 1911, 7; 24 Mar. 1914, 7.

121. O'Leary, *The Prose Literature of the Gaelic Revival,* 40–2; *Sinn Féin,* 13 Jan. 1912, 1.

122. *Leader,* 9 Dec. 1911, 402–3; 16 Dec. 1911, 445–6.

123. *Hibernian,* 18 Sep. 1915, 4; *Leader,* 14 Aug. 1915, 9.

124. *Catholic Bulletin,* Jan. 1911, 1–5.

125. *Cork Free Press,* 10 June 1913.

126. *Sinn Féin,* 13 Jan. 1912, 5; 27 Jan. 1911, 4–5.

127. *Sinn Féin,* 24 Aug. 1912, 4–5.

128. Carson to Curzon, 21 Aug. 1911, BL, India Section, Curzon ms. EUR.F112/18.
129. Lyons, *The Enigma of Tom Kettle*, 221.
130. *Sinn Féin*, 19 July 1913, 4–5.
131. Birrell, *Things Past Redress*.
132. Jalland, *The Liberals and Ireland*, 214.
133. Asquith memorandum on visit to Ireland, 21 May 1916, quoting Lord Mayor of Belfast.
134. Law to O'Brien, 30 Oct. 1925, NUIC, AT271.
135. Alvin Jackson, 'Unionist myths, 1912–85', *Past and Present*, Aug. 1992, 164–95.
136. 'An Irishman', *Is Ulster Right?*, 246.
137. Gilbert, *Lloyd George: Organiser of Victory*, 101.
138. *Cork Free Press*, 15 July 1913, 5; 3 Jan. 1914, 10.
139. *Cork Free Press*, 30 Dec. 1913, 4–5; 9 Jan. 1914, 4, 6; 10 Jan. 1914, 5.
140. MacCarthy, *The Nonconformist Treason*.
141. Joseph Hocking, *Is Home Rule Rome Rule?* (London 1912).
142. Begbie, *The Lady Next Door*, 79–81.
143. 'An Irishman', *Intolerance in Ireland*, 178–90, 197.
144. Matthew Fforde, *Conservatism and Collectivism, 1886–1914* (Edinburgh 1990).
145. *Sinn Féin*, 1 Feb. 1913, 4–5.
146. *Cork Free Press*, 5 Feb. 1913, 7; 22 Feb. 1913, 7; 19 Mar. 1913, 5; 3 June 1913, 5; 15 Oct. 1913, 4; 4 Feb. 1914, 8; 7 Feb. 1914, 7.
147. *Cork Free Press*, 26 Mar. 1913, 5.
148. *Leader*, 5 June 1915.
149. James Connolly, 'Mr. John E. Redmond, M.P.: His Strengths and Weaknesses', *Collected Works*, vol. 1, 360.
150. Miller, *Queen's Rebels*, 78–9.
151. Loughlin, *Gladstone, Home Rule and the Ulster Question*, 148–50.
152. *Leader*, 5 Oct. 1912, 189–90; 2 Nov. 1912, 286–7; 9 Nov. 1912, 303–4; 16 Nov. 1912, 325–6; 23 Nov. 1912, 350–1; 30 Nov. 1912, 380–1; 7 Dec. 1912, 398–400; 14 Dec. 1912, 441–2; 21 Dec. 1912, 479–80; 28 Dec. 1912, 507–8.
153. *Leader*, 19 July 1913, 539–41.
154. *Leader*, 1913–14 (starts 22 Feb. 1913).
155. *Leader*, 5 July 1913, 495–7.
156. *Leader*, 19 May 1917, 354; [Coleman], *Grievances in Ireland*.
157. *Leader*, 28 Sep. 1912, 158–60; 6 Jan. 1917, 549.
158. McMinn, *Against the Tide*, 111–12.
159. Bew, *Ideology and the Irish Question*, 56–8.
160. *Leader*, 13 July 1912, 511–2.
161. *Leader*, 10 Aug. 1912, 605; Bew, *Ideology and the Irish Question*, 59–62.
162. Boyd, *Holy War in Belfast*, 149–51.
163. *Leader*, 7 Mar. 1914, 88–90.
164. Alec Wilson to Asquith, Bodleian Library, Oxford, Asquith Papers, 39, fol. 13–19 (Nov. 1913), fol. 237.
165. *Leader*, 10 Aug. 1912, 615; 23 Aug. 1913, 33.
166. *Leader*, 21 Sep. 1913, 133, 140; John Kennedy, *Belfast Celtic* (Belfast 1989), 21.

167. *Leader,* 9 Aug. 1913, 611–12.
168. *Leader,* 10 Aug. 1912, 609; 24 Aug. 1912, 34–5; 31 Aug. 1912, 58; 28 Dec. 1912, 508–11; *Cork Free Press,* 20 Apr. 1914, 5.
169. Clifford and Marsland (eds.), *Lovat Fraser's Tour of Ireland,* 9, 10.
170. For example *Leader,* 16 June 1917, 441.
171. *Leader,* 28 Feb. 1914, 53–4, 57.
172. *Leader,* 23 Aug. 1913, 35–6; 30 Aug. 1913, 58, 61.
173. Carroll, *They Have Fooled You Again,* 72–4.
174. Claire O'Halloran, *Partition and the Limits of Irish Nationalism* (Dublin 1987), 59.
175. *Leader,* 28 Nov. 1914, 374–5.
176. Clery, *The Idea of a Nation,* 71.
177. Compare Clifford and Marsland (eds.), *Lovat Fraser's Tour of Ireland,* 15, 17.
178. *Cork Free Press,* 11 Apr. 1914, 7; O'Brien, *The Irish Revolution,* chap. 6.
179. Hansard, 4 Nov. 1912.
180. O'Brien, *The Irish Revolution,* 165–6; *Cork Free Press,* 1 Jan. 1913, 4.
181. *Cork Free Press,* 25 Feb. 1914, 4.
182. Jeremy Smith, 'Bluff, bluster and brinkmanship: Andrew Bonar Law and the third Home Rule Bill', *Historical Journal,* vol. 36 (1993), 161–78.
183. Ward, 'Moreton Frewen's Anglo-American campaign for federalism'.
184. *Cork Free Press,* 16 Aug. 1913, 7–11; 11 Sep. 1913, 4; 20 Jan. 1914, 5–6; 10 Feb. 1914, 5.
185. Healy to O'Brien, 15 Nov. 1911, NLI, ms. 8556 (5); Beaverbrook, *Men and Power,* 296; Healy, *Letters and Leaders of My Day,* vol. 2.
186. Loreburn to Healy, quoted by Healy to O'Brien, 21 Mar. 1913, NLI, ms. 8556 (6).
187. Schilling, 'William O'Brien and the All-for-Ireland Movement'; Jalland, *The Liberals and Ireland,* 126–9.
188. Redmond interview with Lloyd George, 27 Nov. 1913, TCD, ms. 6748/508.
189. Begbie, *The Lady Next Door,* 53.
190. Healy, *Letters and Leaders of My Day,* vol. 2, 532.
191. Healy, *Letters and Leaders of My Day,* vol. 2, 532, 537, 604–5.
192. Jalland, *The Liberals and Ireland,* 156–7.
193. Mark Bonham-Carter and Mark Pottle (eds.), *Lantern Slides: The Diaries and Letters of Lady Violet Bonham-Carter, 1904–1914* (London 1996), 391–2.
194. Colvin and Marjoribanks, *Life of Lord Carson,* vol. 2, 213–4; Gilbert, *Lloyd George: Organiser of Victory,* 65, 106; memorandum of conversation between Bonar Law and Asquith, 14 Oct. 1913, HLRO, Bonar Law Papers, 33/6/80.
195. *Cork Free Press,* 10 June 1913, 5–6.
196. MacNeill to Horgan, 17 Dec. 1913, in Tierney, *Eoin MacNeill,* 127.
197. Lyons, *The Enigma of Tom Kettle,* 111, 114–5, 219–21.
198. *Cork Free Press,* 16 June 1910, 5; 29 June 1910, 5; 12 July 1910, 5.
199. Jalland, *The Liberals and Ireland,* 63–72.
200. Gilbert, *Lloyd George: Organiser of Victory,* 95.
201. *Sinn Féin,* 21 Sep. 1912, 4–5; 21 Feb. 1914, 4–5; 14 Mar. 1914, 4–5.
202. *Cork Free Press,* 1 Jan. 1913, 4; 3 Jan. 1913, 4; 4 Jan. 1913, 7; 12 Feb. 1913, 5.
203. *Leader,* 1 Mar. 1913, 709–10.

204. Gwynn, *Life of John Redmond*, 232; Clifford and Marsland (eds.), *Lovat Fraser's Tour of Ireland*, 18.
205. O'Hegarty, *John Mitchel*.
206. *Irish Freedom*, July 1913, 1.
207. Terence MacSwiney, *Principles of Freedom* (Dublin 1921).
208. For example Pearse, 'From a hermitage', *Irish Freedom*, Nov. 1913, in Dudley Edwards, *Patrick Pearse*, 214.
209. *Irish Freedom*, Dec. 1910, 7.
210. *Irish Freedom*, Nov. 1910, 5; *Sinn Féin*, 25 Jan. 1913, 4–5; 31 Jan. 1914, 2–3.
211. Kickham, *Knocknagow*, chap. 42.
212. Muenger, *The British Military Dilemma in Ireland*, 142–63.
213. Sullivan, *Old Ireland*, 149–51, 163.
214. De Búrca, *The Soldier's Song*, 95; Skinnider, *Doing My Bit for Ireland*, 6.
215. Foy, 'The Ancient Order of Hibernians'; Ned Buckley, 'The Mollies', in Clifford and Lane (eds.), *Ned Buckley's Poems*, 51.
216. *Leader*, 6 Apr. 1912, 174; 13 Apr. 1912, 198.
217. F. X. Martin, 'MacNeill and the Irish Volunteers' in Martin and Byrne (eds.), *Eoin MacNeill*, 123–8.
218. F. X. Martin, 'MacNeill and the Irish Volunteers' in Martin and Byrne (eds.), *Eoin MacNeill*, 121–3.
219. Bourke, *The O'Rahilly*, 70–2; F. X. Martin, 'MacNeill and the Irish Volunteers' in Martin and Byrne (eds.), *Eoin MacNeill*, 129–43.
220. John Ryan (ed.), 'A Patrician Problem: Bury versus Slemish by Eoin MacNeill' in Martin and Byrne (eds.), *Eoin MacNeill*, 323.
221. Louis Walsh, *On My Keeping—and in Theirs* (Dublin 1921), 96; compare Mary Harris, *Prejudice and Tolerance in Ulster* (Manchester 1972).
222. MacNeill, *Shall Ireland Be Divided?*
223. Eoin MacNeill, 'The north began' in *An Claidheamh Soluis*, 1 Nov. 1913, 4, reproduced by Martin and Byrne in *Eoin MacNeill*, 381–4.
224. F. X. Martin, 'MacNeill and the Irish Volunteers' in Martin and Byrne (eds.), *Eoin MacNeill*.
225. MacNeill to Redmond, 2 June 1914, in Tierney, *Eoin MacNeill*, 136–7; see also p. 115.
226. Callanan, *The Parnell Split*, 214; MacCarthy, *The Irish Revolution*.
227. Martyn to Horgan, in Horgan, *Parnell to Pearse*, 232.
228. Muldoon to Horgan, 16 Dec. 1913, in Horgan, *Parnell to Pearse*, 229.
229. Horgan, *Parnell to Pearse*, 229–30.
230. Dudley Edwards, *Patrick Pearse*, 208.
231. Fitzpatrick, *Politics and Irish Life*, 104.
232. Flor O'Donoghue, *Tomás MacCurtain* (Tralee 1958); Horgan, *Parnell to Pearse*, 227–8.
233. F. X. Martin, 'MacNeill and the Irish Volunteers' in Martin and Byrne (eds.), *Eoin MacNeill*, 167–8.
234. F. X. Martin, 'The McCartan documents, 1916', *Clogher Historical Record*, 1966.
235. Fitzpatrick, *Politics and Irish Life*, 104.
236. Maurice Moore in Anon., *Major Willie Redmond* (London 1917).
237. Martin (ed.), *The Irish Volunteers*.

238. *Cork Free Press,* 18 Aug. 1913, 2; 21 Aug. 1913, 4; 9 Sep. 1913, 5–6; 11 Dec. 1913, 4–5.
239. Claire Murphy, 'The ranch war in Ireland', paper read to seminar, Department of Politics, Queen's University, Belfast, Nov. 1991.
240. *Sinn Féin,* 4 Oct. 1913, 5; 11 Oct. 1913, 1; 18 Oct. 1913, 5; 25 Oct. 1913, 2–3.
241. *Cork Free Press,* 18 Jan. 1913, 8.
242. *Cork Free Press,* 28 Oct. 1913, 8; 6 Nov. 1913, 4–5.
243. Gwynn to Archbishop Walsh, 29 Oct. 1913; Keogh, *The Rise of the Irish Working Class,* 263–4. J. J. Mooney's brother sat on the board of the *Independent.*
244. *Cork Free Press,* 8 Sep. 1913, 5; 29 Sep. 1913, 5; 7 Oct. 1913, 4; 8 Oct. 1913, 4, 8; 3 Nov. 1913, 5; 8 Nov. 1913, 4; 21 Nov. 1913, 4.
245. *Cork Free Press,* 21 Oct. 1913, 5; 27 Oct. 1913, 5; 6 Nov. 1913, 5.
246. *Cork Free Press,* 4 Jan. 1911, 5; 30 Jan. 1911, 7.
247. Peter Murray, 'Electoral politics and the Dublin working class before the First World War', *Saothar,* 6 (1982), 8–24.
248. *Leader,* 24 Jan. 1914, 593–4.
249. *Cork Free Press,* 17 Jan. 1914, 4; 21 Feb. 1914, 7.
250. Schilling, 'William O'Brien and the All-for-Ireland Movement'.
251. Horgan, *Parnell to Pearse,* 253.
252. *Cork Free Press,* 19 Feb. 1914, 5–8.
253. Gwynn, *Life of John Redmond,* 264–7.
254. *Leader,* 13 June 1914, 415; 20 June 1914, 438–9.
255. Dudley Edwards, *Patrick Pearse,* 212.
256. Hobson, *Ireland Yesterday and Tomorrow,* 50–3.
257. *Cork Free Press,* 2 June 1914, 4; 3 June 1914, 4; 10 June 1914, 4; 13 June 1914, 5; 16 June 1914, 4; 17 June 1914, 4–6.
258. *Cork Free Press,* 7 July 1914, 2, 7; 27 Aug. 1914, 2.
259. *Cork Free Press,* 1 June 1914, 4.
260. *Cork Free Press,* 13 Feb. 1914, 4.
261. Jalland, *The Liberals and Ireland,* 200.
262. Lynch to O'Brien, 2 Dec. 1925, NUIC, AT284; *Cork Free Press,* 9 Mar. 1914, 4–5; 18 July 1914, 7.
263. *Leader,* 3 Apr. 1915, 183–5.
264. Maud Gonne to W. B. Yeats, 19 Mar. 1914, in Anna MacBride White and A. Norman Jeffares (eds.), *The Gonne-Yeats Letters, 1893–1938* (London 1992), 339; Lynch, *My Life Story,* 261–4.
265. *Cork Free Press,* 10 Mar. 1914, 5–7.
266. *Cork Free Press,* 22 Apr. 1914, 3.
267. *Leader,* 4 Apr. 1914, 177.
268. Blunt, *My Diaries,* vol. 2, 444–5.
269. J. J. Scollan (secretary of Irish-American Alliance) to O'Brien, 25 Mar. 1914, NUIC, AS79–8; 31 Mar. 1914, AS81; O'Brien to Scollan, 3 Apr. 1914, AS82.
270. Healy to O'Brien, 1 Oct. 1910, NLI, ms. 8556 (1).
271. *Cork Free Press,* 16 Mar. 1914, 5–9.
272. R. M. Henry, *The Evolution of Sinn Féin* (London 1920), 150–1; *Sinn Féin,* 25 Apr. 1914, 2.

273. *Sinn Féin*, 9 May 1914, 4–5. Griffith adapted a proposal by a Dublin Tory in the eighteen-forties that the British Parliament should move between London, Dublin, and Edinburgh (*Sinn Féin*, 4 Feb. 1911, 2).
274. *Sinn Féin*, 11 Apr. 1914, 4–5.
275. *Cork Free Press*, 26 May 1914, 4–8; 29 May 1914, 5; 23 June 1914, 4; 26 June 1914, 4; 3 July 1913, 4–5; 7 July 1914, 5; 9 July 1914, 4.
276. Gilbert, *Lloyd George: Organiser of Victory*, 81–6.
277. *Cork Free Press*, 19 Feb. 1914, 4–5.
278. *Cork Free Press*, 5 June 1914, 4–8.
279. *Cork Free Press*, 10 June 1914, 4–7.
280. *Sinn Féin*, 18 July 1914, 1–3; Desmond Ryan, 'Sinn Féin Policy and Practice, 1916–26' in T. Desmond Williams (ed.), *The Irish Struggle, 1916–26* (London 1966), 38.
281. *Leader*, 2 May 1914, 274; for Dillon's advice see Scott, *Diaries*, 84–5; Horgan, *Parnell to Pearse*, 224.
282. Memorandum of informal conversations between Bonar Law, Carson, Asquith, and Lord Murray, 17 July 1914, HLRO, Bonar Law Papers, BL 39/4/44.
283. Memorandum of conference proceedings, 21 July 1914, HLRO, Bonar Law Papers, BL 39/4/44.
284. Asquith to Venetia Stanley, 22 July 1914, in Michael and Eleanor Brock (eds.), *H. H. Asquith: Letters to Venetia Stanley* (revised edition, Oxford 1985), 109.
285. *Cork Free Press*, 22 July 1914, 5–6; 23 July 1914, 4–5; 27 July 1914, 4.
286. Gilbert, *Lloyd George: Organiser of Victory*, 105–6; Laffan, *The Partition of Ireland*, 45–6.
287. Martin, *The Howth Gun-Running*.
288. *New Ireland*, 24 July 1915, 163–4.
289. Scott, *Diaries*, 90–1.
290. *Cork Free Press*, 28 July 1914, 4–5; 30 July 1914, 4–5; *Sinn Féin*, 1 Aug. 1.
291. Lyons, *The Enigma of Tom Kettle*, 249–52; Horgan, *Parnell to Pearse*, 259.
292. Pádraig Ó Snodaigh, *Comhghuaillithe na Réabhlóide, 1913–1916* (Dublin 1966), 64.
293. Pearse to J. McGarrity, 17 July 1914, in Ó Buachalla (ed.), *The Letters of P. H. Pearse*, 319.

CHAPTER 6 (P. 147–178)

1. J. P. Hayden Memoirs, 71, MDA; Gwynn, *Life of John Redmond*, 354–5; Horgan, *Parnell to Pearse*, 259–61.
2. For example O'Higgins, *1916, Before and After*, 54–5, 57.
3. Gwynn, *Life of John Redmond*, 353.
4. MacDonagh, *The Irish at the Front*, 1–15.
5. Herbert O. Mackey (ed.), *The Crime Against Europe* (Dublin 1958), reprints Casement's pro-German essays of 1912–14.
6. H. Koch (ed.), *The Origins of the First World War* (second edition, London 1984); Ferguson, *The Pity of War*; Aodhagán O'Rahilly, *Winding the Clock: O'Rahilly and the 1916 Rising* (Dublin 1991), 141; Clifford and O'Donnell, *Ireland and the Great War*.
7. Corcoran to Horgan, 12 Oct. 1914, in Horgan, *Parnell to Pearse*, 264–5.
8. O'Brien, *The Irish Nuns at Ypres*, 137.
9. Kettle, *The Ways of War*; Lyons, *The Enigma of Tom Kettle*, 251–67. Clifford and O'Donnell, *Ireland and the Great War*, 30, note the perverse element in Kettle's response.

10. Hobhouse, *Inside Asquith's Cabinet*, 183.
11. Clifford and O'Donnell, *Ireland and the Great War*, 42–3.
12. Scott, *Diaries*, 99.
13. Levenson, *With Wooden Sword*, 161, 163, 182–3; *Sinn Féin*, 8 Aug. 1914, 5; 15 Aug. 1914, 1–3.
14. For Connolly's pro-German utterances see Clifford, *James Connolly*, but also Desmond Ryan, *The Rising* (Dublin 1949), 14, 16.
15. Lynch, *My Life Story*, 268; *Sinn Féin*, 22 Aug. 1914, 3.
16. *Sinn Féin*, 17 Oct. 1914, 1; *New Ireland*, 4 Dec. 1915, 51–2.
17. MacNeill to Casement, 15 Aug. 1914, in Martin, *The Howth Gun-Running*, 183.
18. Gwynn, *Life of John Redmond*, chap. 10.
19. *Cork Free Press*, 25 Aug. 1914, 3.
20. *Leader*, 5 Sep. 1914, 80; Lynch, *My Life Story*, 70–85, 119–25, 265–74.
21. *Cork Free Press*, 1 Apr. 1913, 5.
22. *Cork Free Press*, 3 Sep. 1914, 5–6.
23. Hogan [Gallagher], *The Four Glorious Years*.
24. O'Brien, *The Irish Revolution*, 229–32, 237–8.
25. Gwynn, *Life of John Redmond*, 380–1; *Leader*, 26 Sep. 1914, 151–2.
26. Gwynn, *John Redmond's Last Years*, 154–5.
27. Gwynn, *Life of John Redmond*, 393–4.
28. Mac Giolla Choille, *Intelligence Notes*, 107–8.
29. *Cork Free Press*, 1 Jan. 1916, 4.
30. Fitzgerald, *Memoirs of Desmond Fitzgerald*, 46–8.
31. *Leader*, 26 May 1915, 471; 3 July 1915, 497–8.
32. *Leader*, 9 Aug. 1915, 205–6; 21 Aug. 1915, 36–7.
33. *New Ireland*, 6 Nov. 1915, 404–5; 4 Dec. 1915, 51–2.
34. Dillon to O'Connor, 26 Sep. 1916, TCD, ms. 674/344; 19 Aug. 1916, ms. 6741/339.
35. Gaughan, *Austin Stack*, 35.
36. *Leader*, 24 Apr. 1915, 259.
37. O'Hegarty, *The Victory of Sinn Féin*.
38. *Leader*, 29 Aug. 1914, 57.
39. *Leader*, 29 Sep. 1914, 154–7.
40. *Leader*, 29 Aug. 1914, 60; 12 Sep. 1914, 109–10; 19 Sep. 1914, 130–1.
41. *Leader*, 17 Oct. 1914, 222–3.
42. *Leader*, 22 Aug. 1914, 39–40.
43. *Leader*, 22 Aug. 1914, 33.
44. *Leader*, 6 Feb. 1915, 630.
45. For example *Leader*, 14 Nov. 1914, 329–31; 12 Dec. 1914, 6 Feb. 1915, 631; 20 Feb. 1915, 36; 27 Feb. 1915, 67; 6 Mar. 1915, 89–90; 27 Mar. 1915, 165.
46. *Leader*, 14 Oct. 1916, 235; 28 Oct. 1916, 281–2; 28 Nov. 1914, 377–9.
47. *Leader*, 16 Oct. 1915, 222–3; 23 Oct. 1915, 246, 251; 30 Oct. 1915, 269–70; *New Ireland*, 2 Oct. 1915, 322–3; 16 Oct. 1915, 353–4.
48. *New Ireland*, 18 Dec. 1915, 91. For southern unionists see Buckland, *Irish Unionism*, vol. 1, chap. 2.
49. Brian Barton, *Brookeborough: The Making of a Prime Minister* (Belfast 1988), 24.

50. Scott, *Diaries*, 14.
51. *Leader*, 10 Oct. 1914, 204–6; 17 Oct. 1914, 221–2.
52. Pearse to McGarrity, 12 Aug. 1914, in Ó Buachalla, *The Letters of Patrick Pearse*, 327.
53. Gwynn, *John Redmond's Last Years*, 159–63.
54. Redmond, foreword to MacDonagh, *The Irish at the Front*, 1–15.
55. Denman, *Ireland's Unknown Soldiers*, 47.
56. O'Malley, *Glancing Back*, 162–7.
57. Bew, *Ideology and the Irish Question*, 139; MacDonagh, *The Irish at the Front*, 96; *Clongownian*, June 1916, 324–5; June 1918, 177; June 1919, 303–4.
58. *Clongownian*, June 1917, 21.
59. 'A Norman' [Esmonde], *Gentlemen! The Queen!*, 89–97.
60. Albert White, *The Irish Free State* (London n.d. [1923?]), 114, 118.
61. Newspaper cutting, NA, LIM23.
62. Eugene Sheehy, *May It Please the Court* (Dublin 1951); Lyons, *The Enigma of Tom Kettle*, 267.
63. Callanan, *T. M. Healy*, 511, 515.
64. *Clongownian*, June 1921, 193–4.
65. Gwynn, *John Redmond's Last Years*, 183.
66. Gaughan, *Thomas O'Donnell*, 92–107, 108, 135.
67. Carroll, *They Have Fooled You Again*, 95.
68. *Leader*, 7 Nov. 1914, 295–6.
69. *Spark*, 20 June 1915, 3.
70. *Spark*, 20 June 1915, 3.
71. Fitzpatrick, *Politics and Irish Life*, 101.
72. *Honesty*, 13 Nov. 1915.
73. *Leader*, 16 Jan. 1915, 557; Horgan, *Parnell to Pearse*, 267–70.
74. *New Ireland*, 21 Aug. 1915, 237.
75. Denman, *Ireland's Unknown Soldiers*, 47–8.
76. Fitzpatrick, *Ireland and the First World War*, 57.
77. Gwynn, *John Redmond's Last Years*, 195–6.
78. Johnstone, *Orange, Green and Khaki*, 62, 148–52.
79. *New Ireland*, 26 June 1915 to 31 July 1915 ff, 20 Nov. 1915 ff. (Second series incorporated in *The Irish at the Front*.)
80. *New Ireland*, 4 Sep. 1915, 257.
81. Terence Denman, 'The Catholic Irish soldier in the First World War: the "racial environment"', *Irish Historical Studies*, Nov. 1991, 352–65.
82. *New Ireland*, 5 June 1915, 53–4; 19 June, 80–90; 26 June 1915, 103.
83. *Nationality*, 1 Jan. 1916.
84. For example *Leader*, 19 Sep. 1914, 129; 10 Apr. 1915, 203; 24 Apr. 1915, 252. Redmond, quoted by Hobhouse, *Inside Asquith's Cabinet*, 220.
85. *Spark*, 25 July 1915, 3; *Irish Volunteer*, 3 July 1915.
86. Ó Broin, *Dublin Castle and the 1916 Rising*, 25.
87. Johnstone, *Orange, Green and Khaki*, 14–15.
88. O'Connor to Dillon, 7 July 1915, TCD, ms. 6741/265a.
89. Gwynn, *Life of John Redmond*, 368.

90. Hobhouse, *Inside Asquith's Cabinet,* 72.
91. McBride, *The Greening of Dublin Castle,* 182.
92. *Leader,* 17 Oct. 1914.
93. *Hibernian,* 11 Mar. 1916.
94. *Leader,* 14 Nov. 1914, 322–3; 28 Nov. 1914, 370–1.
95. *Leader,* 10 Oct. 1914, 211–2; 17 Oct. 1914, 230–1; 7 Nov. 1904, 306–7.
96. *Leader,* 20 Mar. 1915, 131; 24 Apr. 1915, 252; 11 Sep. 1915.
97. *Sinn Féin,* 12, 19 and 26 Sep. 1914; 3 Oct. 1914, 1; 7, 14 and 21 Nov. 1914.
98. Glandon, *Arthur Griffith and the Advanced Nationalist Press,* 79–80.
99. Anthony P. Haydon, *Sir Matthew Nathan: British Colonial Governor and Civil Servant* (St Lucia: University of Queensland Press 1976).
100. Riordan, *Modern Irish Trade and Industry;* George Kelleher, *Gunpowder to Guided Missiles: Ireland's War Industries* (Cork 1993).
101. *Leader,* 8 May 1915, 297–8; Gilbert, *Lloyd George: Organiser of Victory,* 167–8.
102. O'Connor to Dillon, 13 June 1916, TCD, ms. 6741/318; *Leader,* 8 May 1915, 297–8, 301.
103. Gilbert, *Lloyd George: Organiser of Victory,* 455 n. 100.
104. Scott, *Diaries,* 188.
105. *Leader,* 8 May 1915, 298.
106. Gilbert, *Lloyd George: Organiser of Victory,* 168–9.
107. Stevenson, *Lloyd George: A Diary,* 49.
108. *Leader,* 22 May 1915, 348.
109. *New Ireland,* 15 May 1915, 2–3.
110. *Leader,* 31 July 1915, 588; O'Connor to Redmond, TCD, ms. 6741/262.
111. Lynch, *My Life Story,* 284–6.
112. Ferguson, *The Pity of War,* chap. 13.
113. Ginnell, *D.O.R.A. at Westminster,* 30–3.
114. *Leader,* 17 Feb. 1917, 31.
115. *Irish Opinion,* 9 Sep. 1916, 1–2.
116. *Leader,* 29 May 1915, 369–70.
117. O'Connor to Dillon, 25 May 1915, TCD, ms. 674/252; Scott, *Diaries,* 188.
118. *Spark,* 18 July 1915, 3.
119. Gwynn, *Life of John Redmond,* 423–5; O'Connor to Dillon, 25 May 1915, TCD, ms. 6741/252.
120. Gwynn, *Life of John Redmond,* 498.
121. Asquith memorandum, 21 May 1916 (quoting Lord Mayor of Belfast), BL, India Section, Curzon Papers, EUR F112/176.
122. Gwynn, *John Redmond's Last Years,* 192–3.
123. O'Brien to Healy, 22 May 1915, NLI, ms. 8556 (9).
124. Healy to O'Brien, 25 Apr. 1915, NLI, ms. 8556 (9).
125. Healy to O'Brien, 28 May 1915, NLI, ms. 8556 (9).
126. *Leader,* 19 June 1915, 441, 445.
127. Walter Long memorandum, 19 May 1916, BL, India Section, Curzon Papers, EUR F112/176.
128. *Hibernian,* 21 Aug. 1915, 4.
129. *New Ireland,* 12 June 1915, 75–6.

130. *New Ireland*, 13 Nov. 1915, 1.
131. *Cork Examiner*, 11 Nov. 1915; Chauvin, 'The Parliamentary Party and the Revolutionary Movement in Ireland'.
132. *Hibernian*, 27 Nov. 1915, 1.
133. *Leader*, 18 Sep. 1915, 130.
134. Coogan, *War and Politics in Meath*, 24, 27–8, 31–2; editorial, *Catholic Bulletin*, June 1915 (for earlier covert opposition see *Catholic Bulletin*, Oct. 1914, 658, 681).
135. *New Ireland*, 15 May 1915, 1–2, 3–4.
136. *New Ireland*, 12 June 1915, 65–7; 19 June 1915, 82–3; 26 June 1915, 97–9; 3 July 1915, 113–5; 17 July 1915, 145–6; 24 July 1915, 161–2.
137. *New Ireland*, 31 July 1915, 177–8; *Hibernian*, 24 July, 1.
138. Mac Giolla Choille, *Intelligence Notes*, 163–4.
139. *Mayo News*, 3 Apr. 1915, 2.
140. Condon to Dillon, 30 Aug. 1915, TCD, ms. 6752/93.
141. Lynch, *Ireland*; Fitzpatrick, *Politics and Irish Life*, 113.
142. Lyons, *John Dillon*, 362–3.
143. *Kilkenny People*, 21 Dec. 1927; *Grievances from Ireland*, Feb. 1906, 104.
144. *Hibernian*, 10 July 1915, 2; *Cork Free Press*, 25 Sep. 1915, 3 (National Insurance Act).
145. *Cork Free Press*, 30 May 1911.
146. *Leader*, 4 Dec. 1915, 390; *New Ireland*, 21 Aug. 1915, 226; *Hibernian*, 13 Nov. 1915, 2; 27 Nov. 1915, 1.
147. *Hibernian*, 13 Nov. 1915, 2.
148. Gwynn, *Life of John Redmond*, 422–50.
149. *Cork Free Press*, 25 May 1915, 3.
150. Mac Giolla Choille, *Intelligence Notes*, 147–8.
151. Bew, *Conflict and Conciliation in Ireland*, 213.
152. Lyons, *The Enigma of Tom Kettle*, 278; *New Ireland*, 7 Aug. 1915, 194.
153. *Spark*, 27 Feb. 1916, 2; 5 Mar. 1916, 2–3, *Honesty*, 22 Jan. 1916.
154. Farry, *Sligo*, 42.
155. *Spark*, 20 Feb. 1915, 2–3; 13 Feb. 1916, 3–4.
156. *Spark*, 9 Apr. 1916, 3.
157. *Spark*, 6 June 1915, 4; 4 July 1915, 1.
158. Patrick Twohig, *Green Tears for Hecuba* (Cork 1994), 262–3.
159. Farry, *Sligo*, 57–9.
160. *Leader*, 17 July 1915, 539–40; 24 July 1915, 561.
161. Ó Broin, *Dublin Castle and the 1916 Rising*.
162. Glandon, *Arthur Griffith and the Advanced Nationalist Press*, 151–2.
163. *Irish Volunteer*, 26 June 1915; 30 Oct. 1915; 8 Apr. 1916.
164. *Irish Volunteer*, 27 Mar. 1915; 7 Aug. 1915, 9; 16 Oct. 1915; León Ó Broin, *The Prime Informer: A Suppressed Scandal* (London 1971).
165. *Irish Volunteer*, 30 Jan. 1915; 19 June 1915; 27 Nov. 1915; 8 Jan. 1916; 19 Feb. 1916; 11 Mar. 1916.
166. *Irish Volunteer*, 17 July 1915; 30 Oct. 1915; 15 and 22 Jan. 1916; 15 Apr. 1916.
167. *Irish Volunteer*, 2 Jan., 3 May, 18 Sep. 1915.
168. Eoin MacNeill, *Daniel O'Connell and Sinn Féin, part 1: O'Connell's Alternative* (Dublin

1915); *part 2: How Ireland is Plundered* (Dublin 1915).
169. Arthur Griffith, *When the Government Publishes Sedition* (Dublin 1915).
170. Herbert Moore Pim, *What It Feels Like* (Dublin 1915); 'Adventures in the land of Sinn Féin', *Plain English,* 10 July–25 Sep. 1920.
171. A. Newman [Herbert Moore Pim], *What Emmet Means in 1915* (Dublin 1915); review, *Spark,* 2 May 1915.
172. Glandon, *Arthur Griffith and the Advanced Nationalist Press,* 130–1, 271.
173. *Spark,* 19 Dec. 1915, 102.
174. *Spark,* 9 Apr. 1916, 3–4.
175. Brennan, *Allegiance,* 76–8.
176. *Spark,* 26 Dec. 1915, 1–2.
177. *Spark,* 13 Feb. 1916. For O'Flanagan and Sinn Féin see Davis, *Arthur Griffith and Non-Violent Sinn Féin,* 67, 175–6. Carroll, *They Have Fooled You Again,* ignores it.
178. *Spark,* 27 Feb. 1916, 1–2; 12 Mar. 1916.
179. *Cork Free Press,* 14 June 1915, 4.
180. *Spark,* 11 Apr. 1915, 3.
181. *Spark,* Mar. 28 1915.
182. J. de L. Smyth (ed.), *Ireland and France* (Dublin 1916); *Ireland, France, and Prussia: A Selection from the Speeches and Writings of John Mitchel* (Dublin 1918).
183. *Honesty,* 6, 13 and 27 Nov. 1915; 18 Dec. 1915.
184. *Honesty,* 25 Mar. 1916.
185. *Honesty,* 10 Oct. 1915; *Spark,* 2 May 1915, 3–4.
186. *Spark,* 13 June 1915, 3.
187. *Hibernian,* 18 Dec. 1915, 4.
188. *Hibernian,* 7 Aug. 1915, 1.
189. *Hibernian,* 4 Mar. 1916, 1, 8.
190. *Hibernian,* 13 Nov. 1915, 4.
191. *Spark,* 10 Oct. 1915, 1–2.
192. *Nationality,* 10 Oct. 1915, 1–2.
193. O'Higgins, 'Who is Ireland's enemy?' in *1916, Before and After,* 55–6; Derry Records, *Irish Revolutionary Songs, vol. 1* (tape, 1973).
194. Pearse, *Ghosts* (Dublin 1915).
195. *Nationality,* 7 Aug. 1915, 2–3.
196. *Spark,* 8 Aug. 1915, 1–2; Chauvin, 'The Parliamentary Party and the Revolutionary Movement in Ireland', 439–43.
197. *Spark,* 8 Aug. 1915, 3; *Freeman's Journal,* 2 Aug. 1915, 8.
198. *Outlook,* 14 Aug. 1915; 11 and 18 Sep. 1915.
199. *Outlook,* 28 Aug. 1915; 11, 18 and 25 Sep. 1915.
200. *Sinn Féin,* 3 Oct. 1914, 1.
201. John Pius Boland, *The European Crisis and Ireland's Commercial Interests* (Dublin 1915).
202. O'Higgins, *1916, Before and After,* 65.
203. *Sinn Féin,* 26 Sep. 1914, 2–3; *Nationality,* 22 June 1918, 1.
204. O'Higgins, 'A nail in the Kaiser's coffin', *1916, Before and After,* 64–5.
205. *Nationality,* 9 Mar. 1918, 4; 24 Nov. 1917, 1; *Honesty,* 15 Jan. 1916; *Spark,* 13 Feb. 1916, 1–3.

206. *Gael,* 12 Feb. 1916, 7–8; *Nationality,* 7 Sep. 1918, 1.
207. *Gael,* 26 Feb. 1916, 5–6; *Studia Hibernica,* 1995–7, 245–7.
208. *Gael,* 11 Mar. 1916, 1–2.
209. *Spark,* 9 May 1915, 1–2; *Sinn Féin,* 10 Oct. 1914, 1.
210. *Hibernian,* 20 Nov. 1915, 6.
211. *Leader,* 24 Oct. 1914, 245–6; *Nationality,* 10 Nov. 1917, 1.
212. For example *Leader,* 31 Oct. 1914, 274–5.
213. Dillon to O'Connor, 11 Jan. 1915, TCD, ms. 6741/235; 30 Mar. 1915, ms. 6741/242; O'Connor to Dillon, 1 Apr. 1915, ms. 3741/243; 5 Apr. 1915, ms. 6741/244; 6 Apr. 1915, ms. 6741/245; Dillon to O'Connor, 6 Apr. 1915, ms. 6741/246; O'Connor to Dillon, 25 Apr. 1915, ms. 6741/249.
214. *Spark,* 2 May 191, 4.
215. *Nationality,* 18 Aug. 1917, 1.
216. *Spark,* 18 July 1915, 4.
217. *Leader,* 3 Oct. 1914, 183–4.
218. Ginnell, *D.O.R.A. at Westminster,* 37–40; *Catholic Bulletin,* Nov. 1914, 751–7.
219. *Hibernian,* 25 Mar. 1916, 6.
220. *Catholic Bulletin,* Apr. 1915, 261–5; May 1915, 372–7.
221. *Hibernian,* 24 Aug. 1915, 5; *Honesty,* 30 Oct. 1915.
222. O'Connor to Dillon, 3 July 1915, TCD, ms. 6741/261; Dillon to O'Connor, 4 July 1915, ms. 6741/263; 7 July 1915, ms. 6741/205.
223. *Leader,* 21 Aug. 1915, 1–2.
224. *Nationality,* 21 Aug. 1915.
225. Miller, *Church, State and Nation in Ireland,* 345.
226. For example *Spark,* 21 Feb. 1915; *Nationality,* 15 Apr. 1916, 2; 18 Aug. 1917, 1; *Sinn Féin,* 26 Sep. 1914, 2–3.
227. *Nationality,* 18 Dec. 1915, 4–5.
228. *Spark,* 5 Sep. 1915, 3.
229. For example *Hibernian,* 24 July 1915.
230. *Spark,* 19 Dec. 1915, 8.
231. *Hibernian,* 30 Oct. 1915, 1.
232. *Honesty,* 15 Apr. 1916.
233. *Honesty,* 27 Nov. 1915.
234. Patrick O'Farrell, *Ireland's English Question.*
235. Charles Moss (ed.), *Frank Duff: A Living Biography* (Dublin 1983), 21–2.
236. Law, *Why Is Ireland at War?,* 14.
237. *Gael,* 26 Feb. 1916, 2.
238. 'Old Martin's blessing on the *Freeman',* *Gael,* 26 Feb. 1916, 7–8.
239. Mac Giolla Choille, *Intelligence Notes,* 163.
240. *Spark,* 26 Dec. 1915, 1–2.
241. Carroll, *They Have Fooled You Again,* summarises these.
242. Carroll, *They Have Fooled You Again,* overlooks the *Spark* articles.
243. Carroll, *They Have Fooled You Again,* 27–8, 37–8.
244. Bew, *Ideology and the Irish Question,* 144–50.
245. Bew, *Ideology and the Irish Question,* 144–5.

246. Healy to O'Brien, 14 Dec. 1914, NLI, ms. 8556 (8).

247. *Leader,* 18 Nov. 1916, 353; 25 Nov. 1916, 374–5.

248. *Leader,* 19 Dec. 1914, 461.

249. *Sinn Féin,* 31 Oct. 1914, 1, 4.

250. Healy to O'Brien, 24 Dec. 1914, NLI, ms. 8556 (8).

251. *Mayo News,* 20 Feb. 1915, 3.

252. *Spark,* 13 June 1915, 3; Keogh, *The Rise of the Irish Working Class,* 263–4 n. 86.

253. *Cork Free Press,* 2 June 1915, 6; 5 June 1915, 7.

254. Healy to O'Brien, 2 June and 4 June 1915, NLI, ms. 8556 (10).

255. *Leader,* 19 June 1915, 44; *Cork Free Press,* 14 June 1915, 4; Cody, *The Parliament of Labour,* 111–3.

256. *New Ireland,* 26 June 1915, 98–9; 28 Aug. 1915, 241–2.

257. D. R. O'Connor Lysaght, 'County Tipperary: class struggle and national struggle, 1916–24' in William Nolan and T. G. McGrath (eds.), *Tipperary: History and Society* (Dublin 1985), 469 n. 6.

258. *Leader,* 12 June 1915, 417–8; *Cork Free Press,* 22 May 1915, 3.

259. *Clongownian,* June 1919, 303–4.

260. *Leader,* 7 Dec. 1918, 428.

261. *Cork Free Press,* 9 Oct. 1915, 4.

262. Cody, *The Parliament of Labour,* 113.

263. *Leader,* 18 Sep. 1915, 130; 21 Aug. 1915, 32; *Freeman's Journal,* 30 Aug. 1915, 8. Byrne's opposition to Larkin: *Leader,* 9 Oct. 1915, 198–9; Emmet Larkin, *James Larkin: Irish Labour Leader, 1876–1947* (London 1965), 105.

264. *Leader,* 16 Oct. 1915, 226.

265. O'Mahony to O'Brien, 7 Mar. 1909, NUIC, AR39.

266. Bamford and Banks, *Vicious Circle.*

267. *Cork Free Press,* 10 Nov. 1913, 4; 30 Dec. 1913, 6.

268. *Leader,* 4 Sep. 1915, 79; *Cork Free Press,* 2 Oct. 1915, 3; 9 Oct. 1915, 4.

269. *Cork Free Press,* 2 Oct. 1915, 3.

270. *Leader,* 9 Oct. 1915, 198–9.

271. *Spark,* 17 Oct. 1915, 2–3; *Nationality,* 9 Oct. 1915, 2.

272. *Cork Free Press,* 9 Oct. 1915, 4.

273. *Honesty,* 16 Oct. 1915, 4; *New Ireland,* 9 Oct. 1915, 337.

274. *Irish Homestead,* 23 Oct. 1915, in Henry Summerfield (ed.), *Collected Works of Æ: Selections from the Contributions to the Irish Homestead* (Gerrards Cross 1978), vol. 2, 496.

275. *Leader,* 22 Jan. 1916, 586.

276. *Nationality,* 3 Nov. 1917, 1.

277. Hazleton to Redmond, 9 Jan. 1915; J. J. Scallan [solicitor] to Hazleton, 20 Nov. 1915; Hazleton to Redmond, 30 Nov. 1915, 13 Dec. 1915, 17 Dec. 1915, NLI, ms. 15195; Healy to O'Brien, 10 Feb. 1916, ms. 8556 (11).

278. *Hibernian,* 1 Jan. 1916, 1; *Cork Free Press,* 8 Jan. 1916, 5; 12 Feb. 1916, 5; *Leader,* 12 Feb. 1916, 8.

279. *Leader,* 12 Feb. 1916, 7; 19 Feb. 1916, 34, 45; 26 Feb. 1916, 54, 56, 58.

280. Healy to O'Brien, 10 Feb. 1916, NLI, ms. 8556 (11).

281. Murphy to Harrington, 23 Feb. 1916, NA, Harrington Papers, 4/4.

282. *Leader,* 6 Jan. 1917, 541; 26 Feb. 1916.
283. Bew, *Conflict and Conciliation in Ireland,* 202; *Ideology and the Irish Question,* 146.
284. *Cork Free Press,* 4 Mar. 1916; *Leader,* 4 Mar. 1916.
285. Bew, *Ideology and the Irish Question,* 146; Healy to O'Brien, 13 May 1910, NLI, ms. 8556 (3).
286. *Cork Free Press,* 4 Mar. 1916.
287. *Mayo News,* 26 Feb. 1916, 7; 11 Mar. 1916, 3; *Nationality,* 4 Mar. 1916, 2–3.
288. *Leader,* 4 Mar. 1916.
289. Hazleton to Redmond, 3 Oct. 1916, NLI, ms. 15195 (3). Settlement: TCD, ms. 6755/687d, h, 688–95.
290. Healy to O'Brien, 24 Dec. 1914, saying Aird is 'now a strong Redmondite,' NLI, ms. 8556 (8). Meehan, *The TDs and Senators for Laois and Offaly,* gives a brief description of Aird.
291. Gaughan, *Thomas O'Donnell,* 100–3; *Honesty,* 1 Apr. 1916, 3–4; *Hibernian,* 4 Mar. 1916, 5; *Mayo News,* 26 Feb. 1916, 4.
292. *Mayo News,* 9 Jan. 1915, 7; 23 Jan. 1915, 7; 20 Feb. 1915, 3; 15 Jan. 1916, 8; 29 Jan. 1916, 6; 26 Feb. 1916, 7.
293. Lysaght [MacLysaght], *Sir Horace Plunkett,* 124–42.
294. *Plain English,* 27 Aug. 1920.
295. *Irish Volunteer,* 13 Feb. 1915, 29 Aug. 1915, 9 Oct. 1915 (MacNeill's analysis of by-elections).
296. *Leader,* 7 Nov. 1914, 301–2.
297. Hart, *The IRA and Its Enemies,* 187–9, 205.
298. *Spark,* 2 Jan. 1916, 4.
299. *Spark,* 26 Sep. 1915, 1–2.
300. Dunraven, *Past Times and Pastimes,* vol. 2, 52–3.
301. Healy to O'Brien, 21 May 1915; O'Brien to Healy, 22 May 1915, NLI, ms. 8556 (9).
302. O'Brien to Sophie O'Brien, 3 June 1915, in Schilling, 'William O'Brien and the All-for-Ireland Movement'.
303. Hogan [Gallagher], *The Four Glorious Years,* 225.
304. *Hibernian,* 26 June 1915, 4, 3 July 1915.
305. *Hibernian,* 4 Mar. 1916, 4; O'Hegarty, *Terence MacSwiney.*
306. *Hibernian,* 26 June 1915, 1.
307. Batt O'Connor, *With Michael Collins in the Fight for Irish Independence* (London 1929), 28–9; but see Callanan, *T. M. Healy,* 512.
308. Gwynn, *Life of John Redmond,* 466–8.
309. O'Connor to Dillon, 3 Nov. 1915, TCD, ms. 6741/781.
310. *Hibernian,* 4 Dec. 1915, 1; *Honesty,* 4 Dec. 1915, 2.
311. O'Connor to Dillon, 7 July 1915, TCD, ms. 6741/265a (Kitchener); 14 July 1915, ms. 6741/267; *New Ireland,* 30 Oct. 1915, 385–6.
312. *Honesty,* 29 Jan. 1914.
313. Turner, *British Politics and the Great War,* 74–5; O'Connor to Dillon, 22 Nov. 1915, TCD, ms. 6741/288.
314. F. X. Martin, 'Eoin MacNeill on the 1916 Rising', *Irish Historical Studies,* Mar. 1961, 240–1 n. 3, 246, 253 n. 8, 258 n. 29.

315. *New Ireland,* 11 Dec. 1915, 65–7; 18 Dec. 1915, 90.
316. *New Ireland,* 4 Dec. 1915, 49–51; 11 Dec. 1915, 65–7; 18 Dec. 1915, 90.
317. *Leader,* 11 Dec. 1915, 423, 425–6.
318. *Leader,* 25 Dec. 1915, 486–7; *Cork Free Press,* 22 Jan. 1916, 8.
319. O'Sullivan, *The Irish Free State and its Senate,* 94, 268; *Leader,* 25 Apr. 1914, 24–6.
320. T. P. Dooley, *Irishmen or English Soldiers?: The Times and World of a Southern Catholic Irishman (1876–1916) Enlisting in the British Army During the First World War* (Liverpool 1995), 28, 33, 120, 123, 149–53.
321. *Leader,* 1 Apr. 1916, 173–4.
322. *Leader,* 1 Apr. 1916, 179.
323. *Leader,* 11 Mar. 1916, 101.
324. *Leader,* 26 Feb. 1916, 59; 11 Mar. 1916, 101, 105–6.
325. *Irish Opinion,* 9 Sep. 1916, 2.
326. McBride, *The Greening of Dublin Castle,* 207–8.
327. Scott, *Diaries,* 188.
328. *Cork Free Press,* 15 Jan. 1916, 1, 5.
329. Scott, *Diaries,* 169.
330. Dillon to O'Connor, 5 July 1915, TCD, ms. 6741/264; 7 July 1915, ms. 6741/265; 27 Sep. 1915, ms. 6741/275; O'Connor to Dillon, 20 Nov. 1916, ms. 6741/287.
331. *Honesty,* 22 Jan. 1916, 4.
332. *New Ireland,* 22 Jan. 1916, 176.
333. *Hibernian,* 5 Feb. 1916, 4.
334. *Hibernian,* 5 Feb. 1916, 4; 12 Feb. 1916, 1; 26 Feb. 1916, 1.
335. *New Ireland,* 15 Jan. 1916, 153–4; 22 Jan. 1916, 176.
336. *Honesty,* 8 Jan. 1915.
337. Gwynn, *Life of Redmond,* 464.
338. *Mayo News,* 1 Jan. 1916, 5.
339. *Mayo News,* 8 Jan. 1916, 3; 15 Jan. 1916, 8.
340. *New Ireland,* 19 Feb. 1916, 233–5.
341. *New Ireland,* 12 Feb. 1916, 217–9.
342. *Honesty,* 1 Apr. 1916; *Hibernian,* 8 Jan. 1916, 2.
343. *Hibernian,* 8 Apr. 1916, 1; *Spark,* 28 Nov. 1915, 3–4.
344. Martin, 'Eoin MacNeill on the 1916 Rising', *Irish Historical Studies,* Mar. 1961, 234–40.
345. *Spark,* 2 Apr. 1916, 1, 4; *Honesty,* 8 Apr. 1916.
346. *Spark,* 19 Mar. 1916, 3–5. The *Cork Free Press,* 22 Jan. 1916, reports similar hopes by O'Flanagan.
347. For example Lee, *Ireland,* 24–8.
348. *Sunday Press,* 31 Mar. 1991, 1, 8–9.
349. Inglis, *Roger Casement,* charts his disillusionment.
350. Townshend, *Political Violence in Ireland,* 282–98.
351. William Irwin Thompson, *The Imagination of an Insurrection* (London 1967).
352. O'Hegarty, *The Victory of Sinn Féin,* 10.
353. Morgan, *James Connolly,* 163–70. Connolly overestimated the ability of urban insurrectionists to defeat regular troops.
354. O'Hegarty, *The Victory of Sinn Féin*; Clarke, *Revolutionary Woman.*

CHAPTER 7 (P. 179–214)

1. *Leader,* 1 July 1916.
2. Stephens, *The Insurrection in Dublin,* 36; C. Desmond Greaves, *1916: The Myth of the Blood Sacrifice* (Dublin 1966); Bew, *Ideology and the Irish Question,* 143.
3. Phillips, *The Revolution in Ireland,* 108.
4. Hart, *The IRA and Its Enemies,* 204–5.
5. Ginnell, *D.O.R.A. at Westminster,* 179–201.
6. Murphy, *Patrick Pearse and the Lost Republican Ideal,* 6–7.
7. *Nationality,* 13 Oct. 1917, 1.
8. O'Connor to Dillon, 13 June 1916, TCD, ms. 6741/318; Dillon to O'Connor, 19 June 1916, ms. 6741/322; memorandum by Sir Neville Chamberlain (Inspector-General, RIC), 15 May 1916, BL, India Section, Curzon Papers, EUR F112/176.
9. Figgis, *Recollections of the Irish War,* 46, 51.
10. Lee, *Ireland,* 36.
11. J. Anthony Gaughan (ed.), *Memoirs of Senator J. G. Douglas: A Concerned Citizen* (Dublin 1998), 53.
12. Memorandum by Sir Neville Chamberlain, 15 May 1916.
13. Hogan [Gallagher], *The Four Glorious Years,* 5–6; O'Brien to Gallagher, 26 Apr. 1916, NUIC, AS112; O'Brien to Frewen, 5 May 1916, quoted by Schilling in 'William O'Brien and the All-for-Ireland Movement'.
14. Ginnell, *D.O.R.A. at Westminster,* 25–7; O'Brien, *The Irish Revolution,* 6–9.
15. Scott, *Diaries,* 261.
16. *Irish Opinion,* 25 Nov. 1916, 2.
17. O'Mahony, *Frongoch,* 158–9.
18. Clarke, *Revolutionary Woman,* 126–7, 130–9; Murphy, *Patrick Pearse and the Lost Republican Ideal,* 71.
19. Memorandum by Arnold White, 5 June 1916, BL, India Section, Curzon Papers, EUR F112/178.
20. *Plain English,* 7 Aug. 1920.
21. Buckland, *Irish Unionism,* vol. 1, 52–82.
22. Gilbert, *Lloyd George: Organiser of Victory,* 328–9.
23. *Outlook,* 1 July 1916.
24. *Leader,* 24 June 1916, 1 July 1916; O'Brien to Healy, 14 July 1917, NLI, ms. 8556 (13).
25. Hogan [Gallagher], *The Four Glorious Years,* 227; O'Brien to Father Clancy, 29 June 1916, NLI, ms. 8506; O'Brien, *The Irish Revolution,* 45 n.
26. Lynch to O'Brien, 2 Dec. 1925, NUIC, AT284.
27. Miller, *Church, State and Nation in Ireland,* 344.
28. Gwynn, *Life of John Redmond,* 511–12; Anon., *Ireland's Path to Freedom.*
29. Harris, *The Catholic Church and the Foundation of the Northern Ireland State,* 54–6.
30. Memorandum by J. H. Campbell, 19 June 1916, BL, India Section, Curzon Papers, EUR F112/176; Cabinet minutes, 27 June 1916, Public Record Office (London), CAB 41/37/24.
31. Gilbert, *Lloyd George: Organiser of Victory,* 333; memorandum by Lansdowne, 17 July 1916, BL, India Section, Curzon Papers, EUR F112/176.
32. Gwynn, *Life of John Redmond,* 519–23.

33. Stevenson, *Lloyd George: A Diary*, 110–11; Gilbert, *Lloyd George: Organiser of Victory*, 333.
34. Scott, *Diaries*, 354; John Grigg, *Lloyd George: From Peace to War* (London 1985).
35. *Irish Opinion*, 12 Aug. 1916, 1, 2.
36. O'Connor to Dillon, 23 Dec. 1916, TCD, ms. 67741/360. White's recruiting speech: *Honesty*, 11 Mar. 1916, 2.
37. Ginnell, *D.O.R.A. at Westminster*, 521.
38. Ginnell, *D.O.R.A. at Westminster*, 208.
39. Ginnell, *D.O.R.A. at Westminster*, 338.
40. Ginnell, *D.O.R.A. at Westminster*, 519–21.
41. Boland, *At My Mother's Knee*, 66–7.
42. *Irishman*, 16 Sep. 1916; *Irish Opinion*, 17 Feb. 1917, 5; *Nationality*, 12 May 1917, 6; 7 July 1917, 1.
43. *Mayo News*, 26 Aug. 1916, 3; O'Mahony, *Frongoch*, 147; *Nationality*, 2 June 1917, 1.
44. Middlebrook, *The First Day on the Somme*.
45. Lyons, *The Enigma of Tom Kettle*.
46. Lyons, *The Enigma of Tom Kettle*, 298, 303–4.
47. *Clongownian*, June 1916, 431.
48. *Clongownian*, 332 n. 37, 333 n. 5, 287.
49. *Clongownian*, 303.
50. *Nationality*, 11 Aug. 1917, 1–2.
51. Dillon to O'Connor, 6 June 1916, TCD, ms. 6741/313; O'Connor to Dillon, 7 July 1916, ms. 6741/314; Dillon to O'Connor, 8 June 1916, ms. 6741/315.
52. Dillon to O'Connor, 1 Nov. 1916, TCD, ms. 6741/357; *Irish Opinion*, 14 Oct. 1916, 4; *Mayo News*, 14 Oct. 1916, 4–5.
53. Dillon to O'Connor, 11 Aug. 1916, TCD, ms. 6741/335; 12 Aug. 1916, ms. 6741/336; 26 Sep. 1916, ms. 6741/344.
54. *Nationality*, 2 Feb. 1918, 1.
55. William O'Brien, 'The Irish sibyl's books', *Nineteenth Century and After*, Apr. 1917, 945–60.
56. Scott, *Diaries*, 283.
57. Chauvin, 'The Parliamentary Party and the Revolutionary Movement in Ireland', quoting *Freeman's Journal*, 19 Dec. 1914 and 4 Jan. 1915; Bulmer Hobson, quoted by Martin in *The Irish Volunteers*, 39.
58. Murphy, *Patrick Pearse and the Lost Republican Ideal*, 73.
59. *Plain English*, 4, 11,18 and 25 Sep. 1920.
60. *Irish Opinion*, 25 Nov. 1916, 3.
61. Murphy, *Patrick Pearse and the Lost Republican Ideal*, 74–5; Carroll, *They Have Fooled You Again*, 52.
62. Hogan [Gallagher], *The Four Glorious Years*, 40–3.
63. Miller, *Queen's Rebels*, 112; Herbert Moore Pim, 'Adventures in the land of Sinn Féin', *Plain English*, 10 July–25 Sep. 1920; Morgan, *Labour and Partition*, 207–8; *Nationality*, 20 Oct. 1917, 1; 22 Sep. 1917, 1; *New Ireland*, 30 Mar. 1918.
64. Herbert Moore Pim, *Unconquerable Ulster* (Belfast 1919).
65. J. Anthony Gaughan (ed.), *Memoirs of Senator Joseph Connolly* (Dublin 1996), 134–8.

66. Murphy, *Derry, Donegal and Modern Ulster,* 244–5; Harris, *The Catholic Church and the Foundation of the Northern Ireland State,* 56–9.

67. *Mayo News,* 22 July 1916, 4; 12 Aug. 1916, 4.

68. Murphy, *Patrick Pearse and the Lost Republican Ideal,* 72–3.

69. *Leader,* 22 July 1916, 546–7; 12 and 26 Aug., 9 Sep., 16, 23 and 30 Sep. 1916, etc.

70. *Irish Opinion,* 25 Nov. 1916.

71. Carroll, *They Have Fooled You Again;* Bew, *Conflict and Conciliation in Ireland,* 218–9; Maume, 'Arthur Clery'.

72. Chauvin, 'The Parliamentary Party and the Revolutionary Movement in Ireland'.

73. *Irish Opinion,* 14 Oct. 1916, 3; 21 Oct. 1916, 3.

74. *Leader,* 25 Dec. 1916, 488.

75. Rumpf and Hepburn, *Nationalism and Socialism in Twentieth-Century Ireland,* 236.

76. *United Irishman,* 17 Mar. 1900, 5.

77. *Leader,* 25 Nov. 1917, 366–7.

78. *Irish Opinion,* 7 Oct. 1916, 1.

79. William O'Brien to M. O'Brien, 15 June 1916, NUIC, AS135–6.

80. *Cork Free Press,* 20 Nov. 1913, 2.

81. Letters from Casey to O'Brien, NUIC, box AS; George Murnaghan (junior) to O'Brien, 7 Oct. 1916, NUIC, AS111–2.

82. 'Red Hand', *Through Corruption to Dismemberment;* J. D. Nugent et al., *A Challenge and What Came of It* (Dublin 1937), 4.

83. Ward, 'Moreton Frewen's Anglo-American campaign for federalism', 273; O'Brien to Frewen, 7 Oct. 1916, NLI, ms. 8557.

84. O'Connor to Dillon, 10 Aug. 1916, TCD, ms. 6741/334; Dillon to O'Connor, 1 Oct. 1916, ms. 6741/345; *Leader,* 7 and 14 Oct. 1916.

85. O'Brien to Casey, 26 Sep. 1916, AS160–1; Casey to O'Brien, 28 Oct. 1916, NUIC, AS183.

86. O'Brien to Frewen, 21 Oct. 1916, NLI, ms. 8557 (5).

87. Liam Ó Coileáin, 'Nuala Healy: a lifetime of struggle', *An Phoblacht/Republican News,* 16 July 1992, 8–9; McCarthy and Christensen, *Cóbh's Contribution to the Fight for Irish Freedom,* 16–17.

88. J. J. Walsh, *Recollections of an Irish Rebel* (Tralee 1944); Hogan [Gallagher], *The Four Glorious Years,* 222.

89. Liam Ó Coileáin, 'Nuala Healy: a lifetime of struggle', *An Phoblacht/Republican News,* 16 July 1992, 8–9; McCarthy and Christensen, *Cóbh's Contribution to the Fight for Irish Freedom,* 37–9, 44.

90. Healy to O'Brien, 22 Nov. 1916, NLI, ms. 8556 (II); Sullivan to O'Brien, 18 Oct. 1916, NUIC, AS175; O'Brien to Sullivan, 20 Oct. 1916, AS176–9; Sullivan to O'Brien, AS180, 22 Oct. 1916.

91. *Cork Examiner,* 3 Nov. 1916, in Schilling, 'William O'Brien and the All-for-Ireland Movement'; F. J. O'Connor to O'Brien, 11 Nov. 1916, NUIC, AS189.

92. D. D. Sheehan to O'Brien, 17 Nov. 1916, NUIC, AS191; *Leader,* 25 Nov. 1916, 365.

93. Frank Healy to Canon Cohalan, 11 Nov. 1916, NUIC, AS188; Cohalan to O'Brien, 12 Nov. 1916, AS190.

94. Muldoon to Dillon, 13 Nov. 1916, TCD, Dillon Papers, ms. 6734/170; *Leader,* 9 Sep. 1916, 101–2.

95. *Cork Free Press*; Canon Cohalan to O'Brien, 12 Nov. 1916, NUIC, AS190.
96. Pim to O'Brien, 25 Oct. 1916, NUIC, AS181–2; 30 Oct. 1916, AS184–5; n.d., AS186; Murphy, *Patrick Pearse and the Lost Republican Ideal,* 74; Schilling, 'William O'Brien and the All-for-Ireland Movement'; *Plain English,* 25 Sep. 1920.
97. O'Brien, *The Irish Revolution,* 282–3.
98. O'Brien to F. J. Healy, 22 Oct. 1916, NLI, ms. 8556 (II).
99. O'Brien, *The Irish Revolution,* 383.
100. O'Brien to William MacDonald, 12 Dec. 1916, NUIC, AS198–9.
101. Financial statement, 21 Dec. 1916, NUIC, AS200–1.
102. Healy to O'Brien, 25 Nov. 1916, NLI, ms. 8556 (12).
103. *Irish Opinion,* 25 Nov. 1916, 3.
104. *Irish Opinion,* 2 Dec. 1916, 5.
105. Bew, *Conflict and Conciliation in Ireland,* 212; *Irish Opinion,* 18 Nov. 1916; *Sinn Féin,* 29 Nov. 1913, 3.
106. Dillon to Redmond, 8 May 1917, NLI, ms. 15182 (1).
107. Healy to O'Brien, 28 Nov. 1918, NLI, ms. 8556 (22).
108. Dillon to O'Connor, 29 Oct. 1916, TCD, ms. 6741/354; 1 Nov. 1916, ms. 6741/357; O'Connor to Dillon, 4 Nov. 1916, ms. 6741/359; *Irish Opinion,* 4 Nov. 1916; *Mayo News,* 11 Nov. 1916.
109. Dillon to O'Connor, 5 Oct. 1916, TCD, ms. 6741/349.
110. Dillon to O'Connor, 23 Jan. 1917, TCD, ms. 6741/370.
111. Scott, *Diaries,* 239.
112. Gilbert, *Lloyd George: Organiser of Victory*; Colvin and Marjoribanks, *Life of Lord Carson,* vol. 3, 215.
113. O'Mahony, *Frongoch,* 163–8.
114. Murphy, *Patrick Pearse and the Lost Republican Ideal,* 125–6.
115. Geraldine Plunkett-Dillon, 'Joseph Plunkett: origin and background', *University Review,* 1958.
116. Muldoon to Dillon, 22 Feb. 1904, TCD, ms. 6734/96.
117. *Leader,* 6 May 1911, 270–1; 13 May 1911, 310; *Sinn Féin,* 15 July 1911, 1.
118. *Leader,* 10 Mar. 1917, 104.
119. *Irish Press,* 26 May 1933, in Close, *Jesuit Plots,* 43–6.
120. *New Ireland,* 25 Aug. 1917, 259.
121. Ó Broin, *No Man's Man,* 49.
122. Carroll, *They Have Fooled You Again,* 57, too readily assumes that these statements were false.
123. *Leader,* 27 Jan. 1917, 606; *New Ireland,* 27 Jan. 1917, 189.
124. Carroll, *They Have Fooled You Again,* 55.
125. Dillon to Redmond, 26 Apr. 1906, NLI, ms. 15182 (10); Healy, *Letters and Leaders of My Day,* vol. 2, 578; *Mayo News,* 6, 27 Jan. 1917.
126. Dillon to O'Connor, 23 Jan. 1917, TCD, ms. 647/370.
127. Healy, *Letters and Leaders of My Day,* vol. 2, 578; *Nationality,* 28 Apr. 1917, 1.
128. *Nationality,* 12 May 1917, 1–2.
129. Michael O'Flanagan, 'The Roscommon election', *Catholic Bulletin,* Mar. 1917, 146–51; James Meenan (ed.), *History of the Literary and Historical Society, UCD,* 89.

130. Augusteijn, *From Public Defiance to Guerrilla Warfare*, 55–86; Hart, *The IRA and Its Enemies*, 134–83.
131. Lee, *Ireland*, 33–5.
132. *Leader*, 10 Feb. 1917, 8.
133. *Nationality*, 3 Mar. 1917, 1; Maye, *Arthur Griffith*, 67.
134. Lyons, *John Dillon*, 410–11.
135. *Irish Opinion*, 21 Apr. 1917, 1.
136. *New Ireland*, 21 Apr. 1917, 380.
137. *Nationality*, 7 Sep. 1918, 8 (Sinn Féin advised those affected to complain to the government-run National Health Insurance Commission).
138. 'Father O'Flanagan's suppressed speech', *Heart of Bréifne*, vol. 2 (1983), 55–61. During the 1918 election O'Flanagan promised that Sinn Féin would raise the old age pension from 7s 6d to 10s (Lee, *The Modernisation of Irish Society*, 162).
139. *Leader*, 6 Apr. 1918, 208–9. *Catholic Bulletin*, May 1918, 239, predicts that free and wealthy Ireland will abolish 'that dishonouring dole', the old age pension.
140. Tom Garvin, *1922: The Birth of Irish Democracy* (Dublin 1996); Mary Daly, *The Buffer State: The Historical Roots of the Department of the Environment* (Dublin 1997).
141. Bew, *Ideology and the Irish Question*.
142. Turner, *British Politics and the Great War*, 171–4.
143. Fitzpatrick, *Politics and Irish Life*, 68–71.
144. D. R. O'Connor Lysaght, *The Republic of Ireland* (Cork 1970), 61.
145. *Leader*, 10 Feb. 1917, 11; 24 Feb. 1917, 53–4; 3 Mar. 1917, 82.
146. *Nationality*, 3 Mar. 1917, 1.
147. Jose Harris, *William Beveridge* (Oxford 1977), 235–7.
148. *Nationality*, 5 May 1917, 1.
149. *Leader*, 10 Mar. 1917, 104.
150. Farrell, *The Founding of Dáil Éireann*, 13.
151. *Nationality*, 12 May 1917, 1–2.
152. *Nationality*, 29 Sep. 1917, 1.
153. Farry, *Sligo*, 90, 102.
154. List of delegates and organisations, *New Ireland*, 21 Apr. 1917.
155. Murphy, *Patrick Pearse and the Lost Republican Ideal*, 82–4; Farrell, *The Founding of Dáil Éireann*, 16–17.
156. Murphy, *Patrick Pearse and the Lost Republican Ideal*, 84–7; Farrell, *The Founding of Dáil Éireann*, 16–17.
157. Scott, *Diaries*, 264–5.
158. Gwynn, *Life of John Redmond*, 541–2.
159. Ginnell, *D.O.R.A. at Westminster*, 482–8.
160. Miller, *Church, State and Nation in Ireland*, 352–3, 540 n. 89.
161. Kenneth Griffith and Timothy O'Grady, *Curious Journey* (London 1982), 16, 59–60, 108–9.
162. Ó Lúing, *I Die in a Good Cause*, 121–3.
163. Miller, *Church, State and Nation in Ireland*, 353.
164. Farrell to Redmond, 21 May 1917; Redmond to Farrell, 22 May 1917, NLI, ms. 15188.

165. Scott, *Diaries*, 290.

166. Scott, *Diaries*, 282 and n.

167. *Leader*, 12 May 1917, 318.

168. *Leader*, 23 and 30 Sep. 1916; 7 Oct. 1916.

169. *Leader*, 5 May 1917, 293; 12 May 1917, 318; 16 Dec. 1916, 443–4.

170. Scott, *Diaries*, 289–90.

171. *New Ireland*, 31 Mar. 1917, 339.

172. Scott, *Diaries*, 289.

173. Lyons, *John Dillon*, 415.

174. O'Connor to Dillon, n.d. [Jan. 1917], TCD, ms. 6741/367; Dillon to O'Connor, 23 Jan. 1917, ms. 6741/370.

175. Scott, *Diaries*, 290.

176. P. J. Walsh, *Life of Archbishop Walsh* (London 1928), 572–3, 593.

177. Scott, *Diaries*, 291.

178. Scott, *Diaries*, 290–1.

179. Gwynn, *Life of John Redmond*, 547–51.

180. TCD, ms. 6741/375–97.

181. Lynch to Redmond, 11 May 1917, 31 July 1917, NLI, ms. 15202 (2).

182. *Nationality*, 18 Aug. 1917, 6.

183. O'Brien, *The Irish Revolution*, 325; O'Brien, *William O'Brien and the Course of Irish Politics*, 231; West, *Horace Plunkett*, 163.

184. Healy to O'Brien, 11 and 13 June 1917, NLI, ms. 8556 (12).

185. O'Brien to Healy, 5 July 1917, NLI, ms. 8556 (13).

186. O'Brien to Healy, 10 and 18 Jan. 1918, NLI, ms. 8556 (17).

187. Gwynn, *Life of John Redmond*, 556.

188. William Redmond, *Trench Pictures from France* (London 1917).

189. Gwynn, *John Redmond's Last Years*, 265–6.

190. Gwynn, *John Redmond's Last Years*, 265.

191. Johnstone, *Orange, Green and Khaki*, 278.

192. Gwynn, *Life of John Redmond*, 562.

193. Scott, *Diaries*, 293.

194. Gwynn, *John Redmond's Last Years*, 268–9.

195. Fitzpatrick, *Politics and Irish Life*, 116.

196. Midleton to Curzon, 20 June 1917, BL, India Section, Curzon papers, EUR F112/178, 28–34.

197. C. S. Andrews, *Dublin Made Me* (Dublin 1979), 102.

198. *Nationality*, 9 June 1917, 1.

199. Chauvin, 'The Parliamentary Party and the Revolutionary Movement in Ireland', quoting *Freeman's Journal*, 8 and 23 June 1917, 2 July 1917, and *Irish Weekly Independent*, 7 July 1917.

200. Browne, *Éamon de Valera and the Banner County*, 42.

201. Devlin to Redmond, 1 Aug. 1917, NLI, ms. 15181.

202. Denman, 'A voice from the cold grave', 286–96.

203. R. F. Foster (ed.), *Illustrated History of Ireland* (Oxford 1989), 242.

204. Browne, *Éamon de Valera and the Banner County*, 39–40, 52.

205. *Leader,* 3 Feb. 1917, 629–30.
206. *Leader,* 17 Aug. 1918, 40–1.
207. *Leader,* 19 May 1917, 341, 347.
208. *Leader,* 2 June 1917.
209. *Leader,* 30 June 1917, 487–8.
210. *Leader,* 29 Sep. 1917, 175–6.
211. *Leader,* 7 July 1917, 513, 525; 14 July, 534–5.
212. Browne, *Éamon de Valera and the Banner County,* 59–60, 63.
213. Fitzpatrick, *Politics and Irish Life,* 120–1.
214. *Catholic Bulletin,* Aug. 1923, 497–500; *Nationality,* 23 Mar. 1918, 1.
215. Dillon to O'Connor, 4 Sep. 1917, TCD, ms. 6741/416.
216. Murphy, *Patrick Pearse and the Lost Republican Ideal,* 80–1.
217. *Leader,* 20 Apr. 1918, 245.
218. Ginnell, *D.O.R.A. at Westminster.*
219. Scott, *Diaries,* 308–9.
220. *Nationality,* 9 Mar. 1918, 2.
221. *Nationality,* 28 July 1917, 2–4; 4 Aug. 1917, 4–5; 18 Aug. 1917, 2–3.
222. Pauric Travers, *Settlements and Divisions: Ireland, 1870–1922* (Dublin 1988), 87–8.
223. *Nationality,* 11 Aug. 1917, 2–3.
224. Lyons, *John Dillon,* 389–90, 418, 451–8.
225. Hamilton Fyfe, *Life of T. P. O'Connor,* 272–4.
226. O'Connor to Dillon, 29 Dec. 1917, NLI, ms. 15182 (24).
227. O'Connor to Lloyd George, 13 July 1917, TCD, ms. 6741/412.
228. Hazleton to Thomas Lundon, 17 Oct. 1917, TCD, ms. 6756/935.
229. O'Connor to Dillon, 3 Oct. 1917, TCD, ms. 6741/419.
230. O'Connor to Dillon, 29 Oct. 1917, NLI, ms. 15182 (24).
231. *Nationality,* 29 Dec. 1917, 1; O'Brien to *Times,* 26 Dec. 1917, NUIC, AS220–2.
232. Ó Lúing, *I Die in a Good Cause,* 184.
233. Midleton to Curzon, 11 Oct. 1917, BL, India Section, Curzon Papers, EUR F112/118, fol. 42–4.
234. *Leader,* 27 Oct. 1917, 280, 2.
235. Arthur Mitchell and Pádraig Ó Snodaigh (eds.), *Irish Political Documents, 1916–49* (Dublin 1985), 31.
236. *Leader,* 6 Oct. 1917, 197–8; Ó Lúing, *I Die in a Good Cause,* 194–6.
237. *Leader,* 20 Oct. 1917, 245; Lord Midleton, *Ireland: Dupe or Heroine?* (London 1932), 116.
238. Joseph Sheehan, 'Killing Landlords by Kindness', paper read to conference of Irish Historical Students' Association, 1993.
239. Gwynn, *Life of John Redmond,* 582; Lord Midleton, *Records and Reactions* (London 1939), 243–4.
240. Ullswater, *A Speaker's Commentaries,* vol. 2, 227–8.
241. *Leader,* 31 Mar. 1917, 183–4; 2 June 1917, 400–1; 27 Apr. 1918, 281–2; 18 July 1918, 547–8.
242. Murphy, *Patrick Pearse and the Lost Republican Ideal,* 91–6; Farrell, *The Founding of Dáil Éireann,* 20–1.

243. *Leader,* 6 July 1918, 511–12; *New Ireland,* 14 Apr. 1917.
244. J. H. Bernard to Randall Davidson, 28 Nov. 1917, BL, India Section, Curzon Papers, EUR F112/178, fol. 61–4.
245. Miller, *Church, State and Nation in Ireland,* 376; Scott, *Diaries,* 277.
246. *Leader,* 5 Jan. 1918, 544–6.
247. *Leader,* 2 Feb. 1918, 632.
248. *Nationality,* 22 Dec. 1917, 1; *Leader,* 19 Jan. 1918, 583, 585.
249. Diarmuid Lynch (edited by Flor O'Donoghue), *The IRB and the 1916 Rising* (Cork 1957).
250. *Leader,* 23 Feb. 1918, 65–8.
251. *Mayo News,* 9 Feb. 1918, 4.
252. Coogan, *War and Politics in Meath,* 23–4.
253. *Leader,* 19 Jan. 1918, 581–2.
254. Villiers-Tuthill, *Beyond the Twelve Bens,* 167–71.
255. *Leader,* 19 Jan. 1918, 581–2.
256. Healy to O'Brien, 18 Sep. 1917, NLI, ms. 8556 (15); 6 Jan. 1918, ms. 8556 (17).
257. Healy to O'Brien, 4 Jan. 1918, NLI, ms. 8556 (17).
258. Healy to O'Brien, 19 Sep. 1917, NLI, ms. 8556 (15).
259. *Nationality,* 9 Feb. 1918, 4.
260. Gwynn, *John Redmond's Last Years,* 332.
261. Redmond to Dillon, 26 Feb. 1918, NLI, ms. 15182 (24).
262. Gwynn, *Life of John Redmond,* 593–4.
263. Gwynn, *John Redmond's Last Years,* 312–23.
264. R. B. MacDowell, *The Irish Convention*; Miller, *Church, State and Nation in Ireland,* chap. 17.
265. Horgan, *Parnell to Pearse,* 324.
266. *Nationality,* 16 Mar. 1918, 1; Chauvin, 'The Parliamentary Party and the Revolutionary Movement in Ireland'.
267. *Irishman,* 16 Mar. 1918, 1, 5, 8.
268. Phoenix, *Northern Nationalism.*
269. *Catholic Bulletin,* Mar. 1918, 114–5; *Nationality,* 25 Aug. 1917, 1.
270. *Leader,* 2 June 1917, 400–1.
271. *Leader,* 9 Feb. 1918, 11–12.
272. *Leader,* 9 Mar. 1918, 117; 23 Feb. 1918, 69; 2 Mar. 1918, 84–6.
273. *Leader,* 16 Feb. 1918, 37–9.
274. For example *Nationality,* 10 Mar. 1917, 3; 12 May 1917, 4–5; *New Ireland,* 16 Feb. 1918; *Mayo News,* 2 and 9 Feb. 1918, 2 Mar. 1918.
275. O'Connor, *Tomorrow Was Another Day,* 44.
276. *Catholic Bulletin,* Mar. 1918, 112–5; *Nationality,* 9 Mar. 1918, 1; 9 Feb. 1918, 1.
277. Figgis, *Recollections of the Irish War,* 187–8.
278. *Nationality,* 23 Mar. 1918, 1.
279. *Nationality,* 30 Mar. 1918, 2; *Leader,* 13 Apr. 1918, 221.
280. *Nationality,* 23 Mar. 1918, 1; *Leader,* 23 Mar. 1918, 150–1; O'Connor, *Tomorrow Was Another Day,* 43–5.
281. Margaret O'Callaghan (ed.), *Memoirs of Senator Edward Maguire* (privately printed). Maguire's employer, Alderman Richard Hearne, was a leading Redmond supporter (*Leader,* 23 Mar. 1918, 150–1).

282. *Leader,* 30 Mar. 1918, 176.
283. *Leader,* 23 Mar. 1918, 150–1.
284. *Leader,* 23 Mar. 1918, 150–1; *Nationality,* 23 Mar. 1918, 1.
285. *Catholic Bulletin,* Mar. 1918, 106–7.
286. *Nationality,* 30 June 1917, 1.
287. Healy to O'Brien, 20 Jan. 1918, NLI, ms. 8556 (17).
288. *Nationality,* 2 Feb. 1918, 1.
289. O'Brien to Healy, 27 Jan. 1918, NLI 8556 (17).
290. Ullswater, *A Speaker's Commentaries,* vol. 2, 222; Healy to O'Brien, 20 Jan. 1918, NLI, ms. 8556 (17).
291. O'Brien to Healy, 3 Aug. 1917, NLI, ms. 8556 (14).
292. William O'Brien, *The Party: Who They Are and What They Have Done* (Dublin 1917); *Sinn Féin and Its Enemies; The Downfall of Parliamentarianism: A Retrospect for the Accounting Day.*
293. Beaverbrook, *Men and Power,* 295–9.
294. Healy to O'Brien, 18 Oct. 1918, with draft reply, NLI, ms. 8556 (21).
295. *Leader,* 13 Apr. 1918, 236; *Nationality,* 13 Apr. 1918, 4.
296. Healy to O'Brien, 20 Jan. 1918, NLI, ms. 8556 (17).
297. Lyons, *John Dillon,* 433.
298. Hazleton to Lundon, 12 Apr. 1918, TCD, ms. 6756/936; 7 May 1918, ms. 6756/937.
299. *Leader,* 27 Apr. 1918, 269–70, 272, 273; McNeill, *Ulster's Stand for Union,* 287–95; J. Anthony Gaughan, *Thomas Johnson: Irish Labour Leader* (Dublin 1980).
300. McNeill, *Ulster's Stand for Union,* 296–9 (Redmond quotation, 298).
301. Scott, *Diaries,* 349.
302. Close, *Jesuit Plots.*
303. *Nationality,* 27 Apr. 1918, 1.
304. *Leader,* 15 June 1918, 440, 451; 18 May 1918, 342.
305. *Catholic Bulletin,* Sep. 1918, 411.
306. *New Ireland,* 4 May, 20 July 1918.
307. *Nationality,* 22 June 1918, 1.
308. Miller, *Church, State and Nation in Ireland,* 413–4.
309. *Leader,* 3 Aug. 1918, 607; 15 June 1918, 439.
310. *Nationality,* 3 Aug. 1918, 1.
311. Horgan, *Parnell to Pearse,* 329–32; Sullivan, *Old Ireland,* 217–24.
312. Lynch, *My Life Story,* 296–306.
313. *Nationality,* 27 June 1918, 1.
314. Ward, 'Moreton Frewen's Anglo-American campaign for federalism'.
315. Horgan to Stephen Gwynn, in Horgan, *Parnell to Pearse,* 329–32; *Nationality,* 27 July 1918, 1.
316. *Leader,* 18 May 1918, 343; *Nationality,* 11 May 1918, 3.
317. Hogan [Gallagher], *The Four Glorious Years,* 33.
318. Dillon to O'Connor, 4 Sep. 1917, TCD, ms. 6741/416; Figgis, *Recollections of the Irish War,* 200–2.
319. Lyons, *John Dillon,* 438.
320. *Leader,* 11 May 1918, 343.

321. *Nationality,* 4 May 1918, 1.
322. Figgis, *Recollections of the Irish War,* 207–8; O'Brien, *The Irish Revolution,* 367–8. Hansard shows that Crean moved the writ.
323. Lyons, *John Dillon,* 438.
324. *Leader,* 25 May 1918, 378–9; *Nationality,* 25 May 1918, 2–3.
325. Figgis, *Recollections of the Irish War,* 207–8.
326. *Nationality,* 29 June 1918, 1.
327. Lyons, *John Dillon,* 440.
328. Coogan, *War and Politics in Meath,* 75.
329. Carroll, *They Have Fooled You Again,* 83–6.
330. *Nationality,* 29 June 1918, 1; *New Ireland,* Sep. 14 1918, 397–8.
331. *Leader,* 13 Apr. 1918, 221.
332. *Leader,* 18 May, 341, 351–3.
333. *Irish Opinion,* 28 Dec. 1917.
334. Phillips, *The Revolution in Ireland,* 146.
335. Robert O'Loughran, *Cain's Rival* (London 1916), 116–28.
336. *New Ireland,* 29 June 1918, 126.
337. Frank Gallagher to William O'Brien, 31 Dec. 1917, NUIC, AS223–4.
338. Sir James O'Connor, *History of Ireland, 1798–1924* (London 1925), vol. 2, 248–51; de Blácam, *Towards the Republic*; Aodh de Blácam, *What Sinn Féin Stands For* (Dublin 1921); Darrell Figgis, *The Gaelic State: The Crown of a Nation* (Dublin 1920); William Ferris, *The Gaelic Commonwealth* (Tralee 1922).
339. De Blácam, *Towards the Republic.*
340. Emmet O'Connor, *Syndicalism in Ireland.*
341. Coogan, *War and Politics in Meath,* 79, 85; Meehan, *The TDs and Senators for Laois and Offaly,* 25.
342. *Irish Opinion/Voice of Labour,* 16 Nov. 1918, 488; 14 Dec. 1918, 523.
343. Hart, *The IRA and Its Enemies,* 143–6; Maume, *D. P. Moran,* 40.
344. Bishop Fogarty, *Cork Examiner,* 25 Apr. 1918; Bishop Morrisroe of Achonry (Irish Party supporter), *Irish Weekly Independent,* 11 May 1918, in Chauvin, 'The Parliamentary Party and the Revolutionary Movement in Ireland', chap. 8.
345. *Leader,* 22 June 1918, 461–2, 465; *Catholic Bulletin,* July 1918, 315.
346. *Leader,* 20 July 1918, 564–5.
347. *Nationality,* 7 Dec. 1918, 1.
348. *Catholic Bulletin,* May 1918, 223; *Nationality,* 9 Mar. 1918, 1.
349. *New Ireland,* 6 Apr. 1918.
350. Stephens, *The Insurrection in Dublin,* 76.
351. *Nationality,* 7 Dec. 1918.
352. Lyons, *The Enigma of Tom Kettle,* 336 n. 20.
353. Morgan, *Labour and Partition,* 209–10.
354. For example *Nationality,* 20 Oct. 1917, 1; 26 Oct. 1918, 1.
355. *Nationality,* 10 Nov. 1917, 1; 30 Mar. 1918, 1.
356. *Nationality,* 30 June 1917, 2; 17 Aug. 1917, 2; 1 Sep. 1917, 2–3; 27 Oct. 1917, 1; 17 Nov. 1917, 1; 8 Dec. 1917, 1.
357. *Nationality,* 20 Oct. 1917, 1; 3 Nov. 1917, 1.

358. *Nationality,* 14 Dec. 1918, 4; 6 July 1918, 5; *Leader,* 20 July 1918, 564–5.
359. Horgan, *Parnell to Pearse,* 349.
360. *Mayo News,* 2 Nov. 1918, 2; *Irish Opinion,* 7 Dec. 1918.
361. Maurice Cowling, *The Impact of Labour, 1920–1924* (London 1971).
362. *Catholic Bulletin,* Aug. 1918, 383; *New Ireland,* 27 July 1918.
363. *Nationality,* 27 July 1918, 2.
364. Kenneth Morgan (ed.), *Lloyd George: Family Letters* (London and Cardiff 1973), 30 July 1918.
365. *Nationality,* 21 Sep. 1918, 1; 3 Aug. 1918, 4.
366. *Nationality,* 23 Nov. 1918, 4.
367. Healy to O'Brien, 13 Oct. 1918, O'Brien to Healy, 14 Oct. 1918, Healy to O'Brien, 18 Oct. 1918, 28 Oct. 1918, 30 Oct. 1918, NLI, ms. 8556 (21); 3 Nov. 1918, ms. 8556 (22).
368. Healy to O'Brien, 11 Nov. 1918, 12 Nov. 1918, O'Brien to Healy, 13 Nov. 1918, NLI, ms. 8556 (22).
369. O'Brien to Healy, 13 Nov. 1918, 18 Nov. 1918, NLI, ms. 8556 (22).
370. Chauvin, 'The Parliamentary Party and the Revolutionary Movement in Ireland', quoting *Irish Weekly Independent,* 19 Oct. 1918.
371. *Leader,* 14 Dec. 1918, 439–40.
372. *Nationality,* 5 Oct. 1918, 4; *Catholic Bulletin,* Jan. 1918, 25–31, Healy to O'Brien, 19 Sep. 1918, NLI, ms. 8556 (20).
373. Coogan, *War and Politics in Meath,* 82–7; Farry, *Sligo,* 146–8.
374. Boyle to Dillon, 20 Nov. 1918, TCD, ms. 6752/66.
375. *Mayo News,* 7 Dec. 1918, 3.
376., TCD, ms. 6752/112–6; the catalogue wrongly identifies Conway as a former Leitrim MP; see Desmond Ryan, *Remembering Sion* (London 1934).
377. Dillon to Scott, Dec. 1918, in Scott, *Diaries,* 350.
378. Horgan, *Parnell to Pearse,* 345–8, 350–3.
379. *Nationality,* 19 Oct. 1918.
380. Lyons, *John Dillon,* 442–3.
381. *Nationality,* 3 Aug. 1918, 1.
382. *Leader,* 7 Dec. 1918, 414, 428.
383. *Nationality,* 7 Dec. 1918, 1.
384. Carroll, *They Have Fooled You Again,* 93.
385. Chauvin, 'The Parliamentary Party and the Revolutionary Movement in Ireland': Cohalan from *Cork Examiner,* 11 Feb. 1918, and *Irish Weekly Independent,* 26 Oct. 1918.
386. *Nationality,* 30 Nov. 1918, 1.
387. *Leader,* 19 Oct. 1918, 249.
388. O'Brien, *The Irish Revolution,* 390.
389. *Leader,* 14 Dec. 1918, 437.
390. *Nationality,* 14 Sep. 1918, 1.
391. Brady, *T. P. O'Connor and the Liverpool Irish,* 246.
392. Scott, *Diaries,* 352.
393. Morgan, *Labour and Partition,* 208–12.

394. Tierney, *Eoin MacNeill*, 274.
395. Anita Gallagher, 'Nationalism in east Down' in Fitzpatrick, *Ireland and the First World War.*
396. Devlin to Dillon, 22 May 1919, TCD, ms. 6729/226.
397. *Nationality*, 16 Nov. 1918, 1.
398. *Leader*, 7 Dec. 1918, 419.
399. Farry, *Sligo*, 152–3.
400. Murphy, *Derry, Donegal and Modern Ulster*, 248–51; Liam Brady, *Glenties and Inniskeel* (Ballyshannon 1986).
401. Farry, *Sligo*, 152.
402. Coogan, *War and Politics in Meath*, 86–7. For a general discussion see Lee, *The Modernisation of Irish Society*, 158–61.
403. *Nationality*, 23 Nov. 1918, 1.
404. *Nationality*, 7 Dec. 1918, 1; *Leader*, 7 Dec. 1918.
405. *Leader*, 14 Dec. 1918, 1; *Leader*, 7 Dec. 1918.
406. Rumpf and Hepburn, *Nationalism and Socialism in Twentieth-Century Ireland*, 56 (map).
407. Letter to Joyce from his agent, NA, LIM23.
408. Villiers-Tuthill, *Beyond the Twelve Bens*, 192–4.
409. Lily MacManus, *White Light and Flame*, 136.
410. Lyons, *John Dillon*, 452.

EPILOGUE (P. 215–222)

1. Gwynn, *John Redmond's Last Years*.
2. Warre B. Wells, *John Redmond* (London 1919); *Irish Indiscretions*.
3. *Catholic Bulletin*, Mar. 1919, 109.
4. *Leader*, 14 Jan. 1922.
5. Lyons, *John Dillon*, 468.
6. Arthur Lynch to William O'Brien, 11 Feb. 1924, NUIC, AT205.
7. O'Sullivan, *The Irish Free State and its Senate*.
8. John Regan, 'The politics of reaction: the dynamics of Treatyite government and policy, 1922–33', *Irish Historical Studies*, Nov. 1997, 542–63.
9. *Irish Times*, 14 Nov. 1998, 8.

Bibliography

Manuscript sources

Meath [Catholic] Diocesan Archive
    J. P. Hayden Memoirs
National Archives, Dublin
    Lundon Papers
    Michael Joyce Papers
    T. R. Harrington Papers
National Library of Ireland
    Redmond Papers
    William O'Brien Papers
    Sophie O'Brien Papers
National University of Ireland, Cork
    William O'Brien Papers
National University of Ireland, Dublin
    Terence MacSwiney Papers
Trinity College, Dublin
    Dillon Papers

Contemporary periodicals

Catholic Bulletin
Cork Free Press
An Gael
Hibernian
Honesty
Irish Freedom
Irishman
Irish Opinion
Irish Peasant
Irish People
Leader
Mayo News
Nationality
New Ireland
Outlook
Plain English
Republic

Saturday Review
Shan Van Vocht
Sinn Féin
Spark
United Irishman

CONTEMPORARY BOOKS, PAMPHLETS, AND ARTICLES

ANON., *Ireland's Path to Freedom: Why Lloyd George's Proposals Should Be Accepted*, [Dublin?] 1916.

BEAVERBROOK, Lord [Max Aitken], *Men and Power*, London 1956.

BEGBIE, Harold, *The Lady Next Door*, London 1914.

BIRMINGHAM, George A. [James Hannay], *Hyacinth*, London 1906.

BIRRELL, Augustine, *Things Past Redress*, London 1937.

BLUNT, Wilfred Scawen, *My Diaries, 1890–1914*, 2 vols., London 1919.

BOLAND, Bridget, *At My Mother's Knee*, London 1978.

BOLAND, John Pius, *The Great War and Irish Commercial Opportunities*, Dublin 1915.

BOLAND, John Pius, *Some Memories*, Dublin 1928.

BOLAND, John Pius, *Irishman's Day: A Day in the Life of an Irish M.P.*, London 1944.

BRENNAN, Robert, *Allegiance*, Dublin 1950.

BUSSY, F. M., *Irish Conspirators: Recollections of John Mallon*, London 1910.

CASTLETOWN, Viscount [Barnaby Fitzpatrick], *Ego*, London 1923.

CATHOLIC ASSOCIATION, *Handbook of the Catholic Association*, Dublin n.d. [c. 1902/3].

CHAMBERLAIN, Austen, *Politics from Inside*, London 1936.

CLARKE, Kathleen (edited by Helen Litton), *Revolutionary Woman: Kathleen Clarke, 1878–1972: An Autobiography*, Dublin 1991.

CLERY, Arthur, *The Idea of a Nation*, Dublin 1907.

CLERY, Arthur, *Dublin Essays*, Dublin 1920.

CLIFFORD, Brendan (ed.), *Reprints from the 'Cork Free Press'*, Belfast 1984.

CLIFFORD, Brendan, and Lane, Jack (eds.), *Ned Buckley's Poems*, Millstreet 1987.

CLOSE, Albert, *Jesuit Plots from Elizabeth to George V*, London n.d. [1935?].

CONNOLLY, James, *Collected Works*, 2 vols., Dublin 1987.

CURRAN, Constantine, *Under the Receding Wave*, Dublin 1970.

DAY, Suzanne, *The Amazing Philanthropists*, London 1916.

DE BLÁCAM, Aodh, *Towards the Republic*, Dublin 1919.

DE BÚRCA, Séamus, *The Soldier's Song: The Story of Peadar Kearney*, Dublin 1957.

DUNRAVEN, Earl of [Windham Thomas Wyndham-Quin], *Past Times and Pastimes*, 2 vols., London 1923.

FIELD, William, *Governments in Ireland*, Dublin n.d.

FIELD, William, *Treasury Tactics and Irish Industry*, Dublin n.d.

FIGGIS, Darrell, *Memories of the Irish War*, London 1927.

FITZGERALD, Fergus (ed.), *Memoirs of Desmond Fitzgerald*, London 1968.

GAUGHAN, J. Anthony (ed.), *Memoirs of Senator Joseph Connolly: A Founder of Modern Ireland*, Dublin 1996.

GINNELL, Laurence, *Land and Liberty*, Dublin 1908.

GINNELL, Laurence, *D.O.R.A. at Westminster*, Dublin 1917.

GRIFFITH, Arthur, *Pitt's Policy*, Dublin 1911; 1918.

GRIFFITH, Arthur (ed.), *Thomas Davis: Thinker and Teacher*, Dublin 1914.

GRIFFITH, Arthur, *The Resurrection of Hungary*, Dublin 1905; 1918.

GUINAN, Joseph, *Priests and People in Doon*, Dublin 1903.

GUINAN, Joseph, *The Soggarth Aroon*, Dublin 1905.

GUINAN, Joseph, *The Moores of Glynn*, Dublin 1907.

GUINAN, Joseph, *The Island Parish*, Dublin 1908.

GUINAN, Joseph, *The Curate of Kilcloon*, Dublin 1912.

GUINAN, Joseph, *Annaghmore, or The Tenants at Will*, Dublin 1922.

GWYNN, Stephen, *The Case for Home Rule*, Dublin 1911.

GWYNN, Stephen, *John Redmond's Last Years*, London 1919.

GWYNN, Stephen, *Recollections of a Literary Man*, London 1925.

HARDCASTLE, Henry, and O'Malley, Edward Loughlin (eds.), *Election Petition Reports*, vol. 6, London 1911.

HEALY, Maurice, *The Old Munster Circuit*, Dublin 1939.

HEALY, T. M., *Why Ireland is Not Free*, Dublin 1898.

HEALY, T. M., *Letters and Leaders of My Day*, 2 vols., London 1928.

HEUSER, H., *Canon Sheehan of Doneraile*, London 1918.

HOBHOUSE, Charles (edited by Edward David), *Inside Asquith's Cabinet: From the Diaries of Charles Hobhouse*, London 1977.

HOBSON, Bulmer, *Ireland Yesterday and Tomorrow*, Tralee 1968.

HORGAN, J. J., *Parnell to Pearse*, Dublin 1948.

'An Irishman' [Rev. — Hackett?], *Intolerance in Ireland*, London 1913.

'An Irishman', *Is Ulster Right?*, London 1913.

IRISH TIMES, *Sinn Fein Rebellion Handbook* (second edition), Dublin 1916.

Irish Yearbook, 1908, Dublin.

KENNY, P. D., *Economics for Irishmen*, Dublin 1906.

KENNY, P. D., *My Little Farm*, Dublin 1915.

KETTLE, T. M., *Home Rule Finance: An Experiment in Justice*, Dublin 1911.

KETTLE, T. M., *The Day's Burden*, Dublin 1912.

KETTLE, T. M., *The Open Secret of Ireland*, Dublin 1912.

KETTLE, T. M., *The Ways of War*, London 1917.

KICKHAM, Charles, *Knocknagow, or The Homes of Tipperary*, Dublin and New York 1873.

KILLEN, John, *John Bull's Famous Circus: Ulster History through the Postcard*, Dublin 1985.

LAW, Hugh, *Why is Ireland at War?*, Dublin 1915.

LESLIE, Shane, *Studies in Sublime Failure*, London 1932.

LESLIE, Shane, *The Film of Memory*, London 1938.

LEVER, Charles, *The Knight of Gwynne*, London 1847.

LUCY, Henry, *The Balfourian Parliament, 1900–1905*, London 1906.

LYNCH, Arthur, *Ireland: Vital Hour*, London 1915.

LYNCH, Arthur, *My Life Story*, London 1924.

LYSAGHT [MacLysaght], Edward, *Sir Horace Plunkett*, Dublin 1916.

MACCARTHY, Michael, *Five Years in Ireland*, London 1901.

MACCARTHY, Michael, *Priests and People in Ireland*, Dublin 1902.

MACCARTHY, Michael, *Rome in Ireland*, London 1904.

MacCarthy, Michael, *Church and State in England and Wales, 1829–1906*, Dublin and London 1906.

MacCarthy, Michael, *The Irish Revolution*, Edinburgh 1912.

MacCarthy, Michael, *The Nonconformist Treason*, London and Edinburgh 1912.

MacDonagh, Michael, *The Irish at the Front*, London 1916.

Mac Giolla Choille, Breandán (ed.), *Intelligence Notes, 1913–16, Preserved in the State Paper Office*, Dublin 1966.

Mackail, J., and Wyndham, Guy, *George Wyndham*, 2 vols., London 1925.

MacManus, Lily, *White Light and Flame*, Dublin 1929.

McMinn, Joseph (ed.), *Against the Tide: J. B. Armour, Irish Presbyterian Minister and Home Rule*, Belfast 1985.

MacNeill, Eoin, *Shall Ireland Be Divided?*, Dublin 1915.

MacNeill, Eoin (ed.), *An Ulsterman for Ireland*, Dublin 1917.

McNeill, Ronald, *Ulster's Stand for Union*, London 1922.

Meagher, Thomas Francis (edited by Arthur Griffith), *Meagher of the Sword: Speeches of Thomas Francis Meagher in Ireland, 1846–1848* ... Dublin 1916.

Messinger, Betty, *Picking Up the Linen Threads*, Belfast 1978.

Mitchel, John (edited by Arthur Griffith), *Jail Journal* [1854], Dublin 1913.

Moran, D. P., *The Philosophy of Irish Ireland*, Dublin 1905.

Moran, D. P., *Tom O'Kelly*, Dublin 1905.

Mullin, James, *The Story of a Toiler's Life*, Dublin 1921.

'A Norman' [Sir Thomas Esmonde], *Gentlemen! The Queen!: An Irish Reverie*, Dublin 1926.

O'Brien, George, *An Economic History of Ireland in the Eighteenth Century*, Dublin 1918.

O'Brien, R. Barry, *The Parliamentary History of the Irish Land Question from 1829 to 1869*, London 1880.

O'Brien, R. Barry, *Irish Wrongs and English Remedies*, London 1887.

O'Brien, R. Barry, *Thomas Drummond, Under-Secretary in Ireland, 1835–40: Life and Letters*, London 1889.

O'Brien, R. Barry, *Dublin Castle and the Irish People*, Dublin 1910.

O'Brien, R. Barry (ed.), *Speeches by John Redmond*, London 1911.

O'Brien, R. Barry (ed.) (compiled by Dame M. Columba, with introduction by John Redmond), *The Irish Nuns at Ypres: An Episode of the War*, London 1915.

O'Brien, Sophie Raffalovich, *Unseen Friends*, London 1912.

O'Brien, Sophie Raffalovich, *In Mallow*, London 1920.

O'Brien, Sophie Raffalovich, *Around Broom Lane*, London 1931.

O'Brien, Sophie Raffalovich, *My Irish Friends*, London 1937.

O'Brien, William, *When We Were Boys: A Novel*, London 1890.

O'Brien, William, *Irish Ideas*, London 1893.

O'Brien, William, *The Land Question and the National Question*, Dublin 1903.

O'Brien, William, *The Land Conference and Its Critics*, Dublin 1904.

O'Brien, William, *Recollections*, London 1905.

O'Brien, William, *An Olive Branch in Ireland and its History*, London 1910.

O'Brien, William, 'The new power in Ireland', *Nineteenth Century*, March 1910.

O'Brien, William, 'The Party': *Who They Are and What They Have Done*, Dublin 1911.

O'Brien, William, et al., *The All-for-Ireland League and Its Calumniators*, Cork 1912.

O'BRIEN, William, *Sinn Féin and Its Enemies*, Dublin 1918.

O'BRIEN, William, *The Downfall of Parliamentarianism*, Dublin 1918.

O'BRIEN, William, *Evening Memories*, Dublin 1920.

O'BRIEN, William, *The Irish Revolution and How It Came About*, London 1923.

O'BRIEN, William, *Edmund Burke as an Irishman*, Dublin 1924.

O'BRIEN, William, *The Parnell of Real Life*, London 1926.

O'BRIEN, William, *Irish Fireside Hours*, Dublin 1927.

O'BRIEN, William (edited by Sophie Raffalovich O'Brien), *Golden Memories: The Love Letters and the Prison Letters of William O'Brien*, 2 vols., Dublin 1929–30.

Ó BUACHALLA, Séamas (ed.), *Letters of P. H. Pearse*, Dublin 1980.

O'CONNOR, Séamus, *Tomorrow Was Another Day*, Tralee 1970.

O'CONNOR, T. P., *The Parnell Movement* (revised edition), London 1890.

O'CONNOR, T. P., *Memories of an Old Parliamentarian*, 2 vols., London 1929.

O'DONNELL, Frank Hugh, *History of the Irish Parliamentary Party*, 2 vols., London 1910.

O'HEGARTY, P. S., *John Mitchel*, Dublin 1913.

O'HEGARTY, P. S., *Terence MacSwiney*, Dublin 1922.

O'HEGARTY, P. S., *The Victory of Sinn Féin*, Dublin 1924.

O'HIGGINS, Brian (ed.), *My Songs and Myself: Wolfe Tone Annual, 1949*, Dublin 1949.

O'HIGGINS, Brian (ed.), *1916, Before and After: Wolfe Tone Annual, 1950*, Dublin 1950.

O'LEARY, John, *Recollections of Fenians and Fenianism*, 2 vols., London 1891.

O'MALLEY, William, *Glancing Back*, London 1933.

'One of the Tolerant Majority' [Father — Coleman], *Grievances in Ireland*, Dublin 1913.

O'RIORDAN, Michael, *Catholicity and Progress in Ireland*, Dublin 1905.

PARNELL, Anna (edited by Dana Hearne), *The Tale of a Great Sham* [1907], Dublin 1986.

'Pat' [P. D. KENNY], *The Sorrows of Ireland*, Dublin 1907.

PEARSE, Patrick, *Collected Works*, Dublin 1917–24.

PHILLIPS, W. Allison, *The Revolution in Ireland*, London 1925.

PLUNKETT, Horace, *Ireland in the New Century* (revised edition), London 1905.

PLUNKETT-DILLON, Geraldine, 'Joseph Plunkett: life and origins', *University Review*, 1958.

'Red Hand', [?John Herlihy], *Through Corruption to Dismemberment: A Story of Apostasy and Betrayal*, Athlone n.d. [1916].

REDMOND-HOWARD, L. G., *John Redmond: The Man and the Demand*, London 1910.

REID, J. F. (with addenda by M.A.), *Life of William Field*, Dublin 1918.

RIORDAN, E. J. (ed.), *Modern Irish Trade and Industry*, Dublin 1920.

ROLLESTON, T. W. (ed.), *Writings of Thomas Davis*, London 1889.

RYAN, Desmond, and O'Brien, William (eds.), *Devoy's Postbag*, 2 vols., Dublin 1958.

RYAN, W. P., *The Plough and the Cross*, Dublin 1910.

RYAN, W. P., *The Pope's Green Island*, London 1912.

SCOTT, C. P. (edited by Trevor Wilson), *The Diaries of C. P. Scott*, London 1970.

'Seachránaidhe' [Frank Ryan], *Irish Emancipation*, Dublin 1929.

SHEEHAN, D. D., *Ireland Since Parnell*, London 1921.

SHEEHAN, P. A., *Geoffrey Austin, Student*, London 1895.

SHEEHAN, P. A., *The Triumph of Failure*, London 1899.

SHEEHAN, P. A., *My New Curate*, London 1899.

SHEEHAN, P. A., *Luke Delmege*, London 1901.

SHEEHAN, P. A., *The Graves of Kilmorna*, London 1915.
SHEEHY-SKEFFINGTON, Francis, *Michael Davitt*, London 1908.
SKINNIDER, Margaret, *Doing My Bit for Ireland*, New York 1917.
STEPHENS, James, *The Insurrection in Dublin*, Dublin 1916.
STEVENSON, Frances (edited by A. J. P. Taylor), *Lloyd George: A Diary*, London 1971.
SULLIVAN, A. M., Sullivan, T. D., and Sullivan, D. B. (eds.), *Speeches from the Dock*, Dublin 1868.
SULLIVAN, A. M., *Old Ireland*, New York 1928.
The 'Times', *Parnellism and Crime* [reprinted from the *Times*, 7 June 1887], London 1887.
TYNAN, P. J. P., *The Irish National Invincibles and Their Times*, London 1894.
ULLSWATER, Viscount, *A Speaker's Commentaries*, 2 vols., London 1925.
UNITED IRISH LEAGUE, *The Liffey at Ebb Tide*, Dublin 1910.
VALENTINE, John, *Irish Memories*, Bristol n.d. [1927?].
WALSH, Louis, *Old Friends*, Dundalk, 1934.
WELLES, Warre B., *Irish Indiscretions*, Dublin 1923.

LATER WORKS

UNPUBLISHED THESES

CHAUVIN, Guy, 'The Parliamentary Party and the Revolutionary Movement in Ireland, 1912–18', PhD dissertation, Trinity College, Dublin, 1976.
FOY, M., 'The Ancient Order of Hibernians: An Irish Political-Religious Pressure Group, 1884–1975', MA thesis, Department of Politics, Queen's University, Belfast, 1976.
KELLY, Charles, 'Laurence Ginnell', PhD thesis, St Patrick's College, Maynooth, 1970.
SCHILLING, F., 'William O'Brien and the All-for-Ireland Movement', PhD dissertation, Trinity College, Dublin, 1956.
WATERS, M., 'W. P. Ryan and the Irish Ireland Movement', PhD dissertation, University of Connecticut, 1970.

BOOKS

ADAMS, Michael, *Censorship: The Irish Experience*, Dublin 1968.
AUGUSTEIJN, Joost, *From Public Defiance to Guerrilla Warfare*, Dublin 1996.
AYERST, David, *Garvin of the Observer*, London 1985.
BAILYN, Bernard, *The Ideological Origins of the American Revolution*, Cambridge (Mass.) 1967.
BAMFORD, Francis, and Banks, Viola, *Vicious Circle: The Case of the Missing Irish Crown Jewels*, London 1965.
BARDON, Jonathan, *History of Ulster*, Belfast 1992.
BENCE JONES, Mark, *Twilight of the Ascendancy*, London 1987.
BEW, Paul, *Land and the National Question in Ireland, 1858–1882*, Dublin 1978.
BEW, Paul, *C. S. Parnell*, Dublin 1980.
BEW, Paul, *Conflict and Conciliation in Ireland, 1890–1910*, Oxford 1987.
BEW, Paul, *Ideology and the Irish Question: Ulster Unionism and Irish Nationalism, 1912–1916*, Oxford 1994.
BEW, Paul, *John Redmond*, Dundalk 1996.
BOURKE, Marcus, *The O'Rahilly*, Tralee 1967.

BOYCE, D., and O'Day, Alan (eds.), *Parnell in Perspective*, London 1991.

BOYD, Andrew, *Holy War in Belfast* (third edition), Belfast 1987.

BRADLEY, Dan, *Farm Labourers: Irish Struggle*, Belfast 1988.

BRADY, Liam, *T. P. O'Connor and the Liverpool Irish*, London 1983.

BROWNE, Kevin, *Éamon de Valera and the Banner County*, Dublin 1982.

BUCKLAND, Patrick, *Irish Unionism, vol. 1: The Anglo-Irish and the New Ireland*, Dublin 1972.

BULL, Philip, 'The significance of the nationalist response to the Irish Land Act of 1903', *Irish Historical Studies*, May 1993.

BULL, Philip, *Land, Politics and Nationalism: A Study of the Irish Land Question*, Dublin 1996.

CALLANAN, Frank, *The Parnell Split*, Cork 1992.

CALLANAN, Frank, *T. M. Healy*, Cork 1996.

CANDY, Catherine, *Priestly Fictions*, Dublin 1995.

CARROLL, Denis, *'They have fooled you again': Michael O'Flanagan, 1876–1942: Priest, Republican, Social Critic*, Blackrock (Co. Dublin) 1993.

CHAVASSE, Moirin, *Terence MacSwiney*, Cork 1962.

CLARKSON, J. D., *Labour and Nationalism in Ireland*, New York 1925.

CLIFFORD, Brendan, *James Connolly: The Polish Aspect*, Belfast 1984.

CLIFFORD, Brendan, and Marsland, Jane (eds.), *Lovat Fraser's Tour of Ireland in 1913*, Belfast 1992.

CLIFFORD, Brendan, and O'Donnell, C., *Ireland and the Great War*, Belfast 1992.

CODY, Séamus (with John O'Dowd and Peter Rigney), *The Parliament of Labour: 100 Years of the Dublin Council of Trade Unions*, Dublin 1986.

COLUM, Pádraic, *Sinn Féin: The Story of Arthur Griffith and the Origin of the Irish Free State*, New York 1959.

COLVIN, Ian, and Marjoribanks, Edward, *Life of Lord Carson*, 3 vols., London 1932–6.

COMERFORD, R., *The Fenians in Context*, Dublin 1985.

COOGAN, Oliver, *War and Politics in Meath, 1912–23*, Dublin 1983.

CRUISE O'BRIEN, Conor, *States of Ireland*, London 1972.

CULLEN, L. M. (ed.), *The Development of the Irish Economy*, Dublin 1978.

CULLEN, L. M., *Eason and Son: A History*, Dublin 1989.

CUNNINGHAM, John, *Labour in the West of Ireland: Working Life and Struggle, 1890–1914*, Belfast 1995.

DALY, Mary, *Dublin: The Deposed Capital*, Cork 1985.

DAVIS, Richard, *Arthur Griffith and Non-Violent Sinn Féin*, Dublin 1974.

DAVIS, Richard, *The Young Ireland Movement*, Dublin 1987.

DENMAN, Terence, *Ireland's Unknown Soldiers: The 16th (Irish) Division in the Great War*, Dublin 1992.

DENMAN, Terence, 'A voice from the cold grave: the death in action of Major William Redmond MP', *Irish Sword*, summer 1992.

DOYLE, Eugene, *Justin McCarthy*, Dundalk 1996.

DUDLEY EDWARDS, Ruth, *Patrick Pearse: The Triumph of Failure*, London 1977.

FARRELL, Brian, *The Founding of Dáil Éireann*, Dublin 1971.

FARRELL, Brian, *The Irish Parliamentary Tradition*, Dublin 1973.

FARRY, Michael, *Sligo, 1914–1921: A Chronicle of Conflict*, Trim 1992.

FERGUSON, Niall, *The Pity of War*, London 1998.

FIELDING, Steven, *Class and Ethnicity: Irish Catholics in England, 1880–1939*, Buckingham 1993.

FITZPATRICK, David, *Politics and Irish Life, 1913–21*, Dublin 1977.

FITZPATRICK, David (ed.), *Ireland and the First World War*, Dublin 1986.

FOSTER, R. F., 'Anglo-Irish literature, Gaelic nationalism and Irish politics in the 1890s' in *Ireland under the Union*, Oxford 1989.

FYFE, Hamilton, *Life of T. P. O'Connor*, London 1934.

GAILEY, Andrew, *Ireland and the Death of Kindness: The Experience of Constructive Unionism*, Cork 1987.

GARVIN, Tom, *Irish Nationalist Revolutionaries, 1858–1928*, Oxford 1987.

GAUGHAN, J. Anthony, *Austin Stack: Portrait of a Separatist*, Dublin 1977.

GAUGHAN, J. Anthony, *Thomas O'Donnell: A Political Odyssey*, Dublin 1983.

GEARY, Laurence, *The Plan of Campaign, 1886–1891*, Cork 1986.

GILBERT, Bentley Brinkerhoff, *Lloyd George: Architect of Change*, London 1986.

GILBERT, Bentley Brinkerhoff, *Lloyd George: Organiser of Victory, 1912–16*, London 1992.

GLANDON, Virginia, *Arthur Griffith and the Advanced Nationalist Press*, New York 1985.

GOLLIN, Alfred, *The 'Observer' and J. L. Garvin, 1908–1914: A Study in a Great Editorship*, London 1960.

GREAVES, C. Desmond, *The Life and Times of James Connolly*, London 1961.

GWYNN, Denis, *Life of Edward Martyn*, London 1932.

GWYNN, Denis, *Life of John Redmond*, London 1932.

HARRIS, Jose, *William Beveridge*, Oxford 1977.

HARRIS, Mary, *The Catholic Church and the Foundation of the Northern Ireland State*, Cork 1993.

HART, Peter, *The IRA and Its Enemies: Violence and Community in Cork, 1916–1923*, Oxford 1998.

HEALY, T. M., *Why Ireland Is Not Free*, Dublin 1898.

HOGAN, David [Frank Gallagher], *The Four Glorious Years*, Dublin 1953.

HUTCHINSON, John, *The Dynamics of Cultural Nationalism*, London 1987.

HYDE, H. Montgomery, *Carson*, London 1953.

INGLIS, Brian, *Roger Casement*, London 1973.

JACKSON, Alvin, *The Ulster Party: Irish Unionists in the House of Commons, 1884–1911*, Oxford 1989.

JACKSON, Alvin, *Edward Carson*, Dundalk 1993.

JACKSON, Alvin, *Colonel Edward Saunderson: Land and Loyalty in Victorian Ireland*, Oxford 1995.

JALLAND, Patricia, *The Liberals and Ireland*, Brighton 1980.

JEFFERSON, Herbert, *Viscount Pirrie of Belfast*, Belfast n.d.

JOHNSTONE, Tom, *Orange, Green and Khaki: The Irish Regiments in the Great War*, Dublin 1992.

JORDAN, Donald, *Land and Popular Politics in Ireland: County Mayo from the Plantation to the Land War*, Cambridge 1994.

KELLY, John, 'The fall of Parnell and the rise of Anglo-Irish literature', *Anglo-Irish Studies*, 2, 1976.

KENDLE, J., *Ireland and the Federal Solution*, Montréal 1989.

KENDLE, J., *Walter Long, Ireland and the Union, 1905–20*, Dublin 1992.

KEOGH, Dermot, *The Rise of the Irish Working Class: The Dublin Trade Union Movement and Labour Leadership, 1890–1914*, Belfast 1982.

KERR, Dónal, *A Nation of Beggars?*, Oxford 1994.

LAFFAN, Michael, *The Partition of Ireland*, Dundalk 1983.

LANE, Pádraig, 'The Land and Labour Association, 1894–1914', *Journal of the Cork Historical and Archaeological Society*, 1993.

LARKIN, Emmet, *The Roman Catholic Church and the Creation of the Modern Irish State*, Philadelphia and Dublin 1975.

LEE, J. J., *The Modernisation of Irish Society, 1848–1918*, Dublin 1973.

LEE, J. J., *Ireland, 1912–85*, Cambridge 1989.

LESLIE, Anita, *Mr Frewen of England*, London 1978.

LEVENSON, Leah, *With Wooden Sword: A Life of Francis Sheehy-Skeffington*, Boston 1983.

LOUGHLIN, James, *Gladstone, Home Rule and the Ulster Question, 1882–93*, Dublin 1986.

LOUGHLIN, James, 'Constructing the political spectacle' in Boyce and O'Day (eds.), *Parnell in Perspective*, 1991.

LOUGHLIN, James, *Ulster Unionism and British National Identity since 1885*, London 1996.

LYONS, F. S. L., *The Irish Parliamentary Party, 1890–1910*, London 1951.

LYONS, F. S. L., *John Dillon: A Biography*, London 1968.

LYONS, F. S. L., *Charles Stewart Parnell*, London 1977.

LYONS, F. S. L., and Hawkins, R. (eds.), *Ireland Under the Union: Varieties of Tension*, Oxford 1980.

LYONS, J. B., *The Enigma of Tom Kettle*, Dublin 1983.

McBRIDE, Laurence, *The Greening of Dublin Castle*, Washington 1991.

McCARTHY, Kieran, and Christensen, Maj-Britt, *Cóbh's Contribution to the Fight for Irish Freedom, 1913–1992*, Cóbh 1992.

McCARTNEY, Dónal (ed.), *Parnell: The Politics of Power*, Dublin 1991.

McCRACKEN, Dónal, *The Irish Pro-Boers, 1877–1902*, Cape Town 1989.

MACDONAGH, Michael, *The Home Rule Movement*, London 1920.

MACDONAGH, Michael, *The Life of William O'Brien*, London 1928.

McDOWELL, R. B., *The Irish Administration, 1800–1914*, London 1964.

McDOWELL, R. B., *The Irish Convention*, London 1970.

MACINTYRE, Angus, *The Liberator: Daniel O'Connell and the Irish Party, 1830–47*, London 1965.

McTERNAN, John, *Worthies of Sligo*, Sligo 1994.

MANDLE, W., *The Gaelic Athletic Association and Irish Nationalist Politics, 1884–1924*, Dublin 1987.

MARTIN, F. X. (ed.), *The Irish Volunteers, 1913–1915: Recollections and Documents*, Dublin 1963.

MARTIN, F. X. (ed.), *The Howth Gun-Running, 1914*, Dublin 1964.

MARTIN, F. X., and Byrne, F. J. (eds.), *Eoin MacNeill: The Scholar Revolutionary*, Shannon 1973.

MAUME, Patrick, *Life that Is Exile: Daniel Corkery and the Search for Irish Ireland*, Belfast 1993.

MAUME, Patrick, *D. P. Moran*, Dundalk 1995.

MAUME, Patrick, 'The ancient constitution: Arthur Griffith and his ideological legacy to Sinn Féin', *Irish Political Studies*, 1995.

MAUME, Patrick, 'James Mullin, the poor scholar: a self-made man from Carleton's country', *Irish Studies Review*, April 1999.

MAUME, Patrick, 'Nationalism and partition: the political thought of Arthur Clery', *Irish Historical Studies*, November 1998.

MAUME, Patrick, 'Anti-Machiaveli: three Ulster nationalists of the age of Devlin and Craig', *Irish Political Studies*, 1999.

MAUME, Patrick, 'In the Fenians' wake: the crises of fin de siècle Ireland in the rhetoric of Canon Sheehan and William O'Brien MP', *Bullan*, autumn 1998.

MAUME, Patrick, 'Young Ireland, Arthur Griffith and republican ideology: the question of continuity', in *Éire-Ireland* (special issue), autumn 1999.

MAUME, Patrick, 'P. D. Kenny: agrarianism, anti-clericalism and economic development in Edwardian Ireland', *Twentieth-Century British History* (forthcoming).

MAYE, Brian, *Arthur Griffith*, Dublin 1997.

MEEHAN, P., *The Members of Parliament for Laois and Offaly, 1800–1921*, Port Laoise 1983.

MEEHAN, P., *The TDs and Senators for Laois and Offaly, 1921–86*, Port Laoise 1987.

MEENAN, James (ed.), *History of the Literary and Historical Society, UCD*, Tralee 1955.

MEENAN, James, *George O'Brien*, Dublin 1980.

MIDDLESBROOK, Martin, *The First Day on the Somme*, London 1971.

MILLER, D., *Church, State and Nation in Ireland, 1898–1921*, Dublin 1973.

MILLER, D., *Queen's Rebels*, Dublin 1978.

MOLONY, John, *A Soul Came into Ireland: Thomas Davis: A Biography*, Dublin 1995.

MORGAN, Austen, *James Connolly: A Political Biography*, Manchester 1988.

MORGAN, Austen, *Labour and Partition: the Belfast working class, 1905–1923*, London 1990.

MORRISSEY, Thomas, *William Martin Murphy*, Dundalk 1997.

MUENGER, Elizabeth, *The British Military Dilemma in Ireland: Occupation Politics, 1886–1914*, Lawrence (Kansas) 1991.

MURPHY, Brian P., *Patrick Pearse and the Lost Republican Ideal*, Dublin 1991.

MURPHY, Clíona, *The Women's Suffrage Movement and Irish Society in the Early Twentieth Century*, New York and London 1989.

MURPHY, Desmond, *Derry, Donegal and Modern Ulster, 1721–1921*, Derry 1981.

MURPHY, James, *Catholic Fiction and Social Reality in Ireland, 1873–1922*, London 1997.

Ní DHONNCHADHA, Máirín, and Dorgan, Theo (eds.), *Revising the Rising*, Derry 1991.

NORSTEDT, Johann, *Thomas MacDonagh*, Charlottesville (Va) 1980.

O'BRIEN, J., *William O'Brien and the Course of Irish Politics, 1881–1918*, Berkeley (Calif.) 1976.

O'BRIEN, J., *Dear Old Dirty Dublin*, Berkeley (Calif.) 1982.

Ó BROIN, León, *Dublin Castle and the 1916 Rising*, Dublin 1966.

Ó BROIN, León, *Revolutionary Underground*, Dublin 1976.

Ó BROIN, León, *No Man's Man: A Biographical Memoir of Joseph Brennan*, Dublin 1982.

Ó BUACHALLA, Séamas (ed.), *The Letters of P. H. Pearse*, Gerrards Cross (Bucks) 1980.

O'CALLAGHAN, Margaret, *British High Politics and a Nationalist Ireland: Criminality, Land and the Law under Forster and Balfour*, Cork 1994.

O'CONNOR, Emmet, 'The influence of Redmondism on the trade union movement in Waterford', *Decies*, 10, January 1979.

O'CONNOR, Emmet, *Syndicalism in Ireland*, Cork 1988.

O'CONNOR, Emmet, *A Labour History of Waterford*, Waterford 1989.

O'CONNOR, Emmet, *A Labour History of Ireland*, Dublin 1992.

Ó DUIBHIR, Ciarán, *Sinn Féin: The First Election, 1908*, Manorhamilton 1993.

Ó FAOLÁIN, Seán, *King of the Beggars*, Dublin 1938.

O'FARRELL, Patrick, *Ireland's English Question*, London 1971.

O'HALPIN, Eunan, *The Decline of the Union: British Government in Ireland, 1892–1920*, Dublin 1987.

O'HEGARTY, P. S., *The Victory of Sinn Féin*, Dublin 1924.

O'HEGARTY, P. S., *History of Ireland Under the Union*, London 1952.

O'LEARY, Philip, *The Prose Literature of the Gaelic Revival, 1881–1921: Ideology and Innovation*, University Park (Pennsylvania) 1994.

Ó LÚING, Seán, *I Die in a Good Cause: A Life of Thomas Ashe*, Tralee 1970.

Ó LÚING, Seán, 'Arthur Griffith: thoughts on an anniversary', *Studies*, summer 1971.

O'MAHONY, Seán, *Frongoch: University of Revolution*, Dublin 1987.

ORR, Philip, *The Road to the Somme*, Belfast 1987.

O'SULLIVAN, Dónal, *The Irish Free State and Its Senate*, London 1940.

PATTERSON, Henry, *Class Conflict and Sectarianism*, Belfast 1980.

PHOENIX, Éamon, *Northern Nationalism: Nationalist Politics, Partition and the Catholic Minority in Northern Ireland, 1890–1940*, Belfast 1994.

RUMPF, Eberhard, and Hepburn, A., *Nationalism and Socialism in Twentieth-Century Ireland*, Liverpool 1977.

RUSSELL, A., *Liberal Landslide: The General Election of 1906*, Newton Abbot (Devon) 1973.

RYAN, Desmond, *The Phoenix Flame*, London 1937.

SCOTT, C. P. (edited by Trevor Wilson), *The Diaries of C. P. Scott*, London 1970.

SHANNON, Catherine, *Arthur J. Balfour and Ireland, 1874–1922*, Washington 1988.

SHEEHAN, Jeremiah, *Worthies of Westmeath: a Biographical Dictionary*, Moate 1987.

STENTON, Michael, and Lees, Stephen (eds.), *Who's Who of British Members of Parliament*, Brighton, 1978.

TIERNEY, Michael, *Eoin MacNeill: Scholar and Man of Action, 1867–1945*, Oxford 1980.

TOWNSHEND, Charles, *Political Violence in Ireland*, Oxford 1983.

TURNER, John, *British Politics and the Great War: Coalition and Conflict, 1915–1918*, New Haven (Conn.) 1992.

VILLIERS-TUTHILL, Kathleen, *Beyond the Twelve Bens*, Clifden 1986.

VINCENT, John (ed.), *The Crawford Papers: The Journals of David Lindsay, 27th Earl of Crawford and 10th Earl of Balcarres*, Manchester 1984.

WALKER, Brian M., \ *Election Results in Ireland, 1800–1921*, Dublin 1978.

WARD, Alan, 'Moreton Frewen's Anglo-American campaign for federalism, 1910–21', *Irish Historical Studies*, Mar. 1967.

WARD, Margaret, *Hanna Sheehy-Skeffington: A Life*, Cork 1997.

WARWICK-HALLER, Sally, *William O'Brien and the Irish Land War*, Dublin 1990.

WELLES, Warre B., *John Redmond*, London 1919.

WEST, Trevor, *Sir Horace Plunkett: Co-operation and Politics*, Gerrards Cross (Bucks) 1986.

INDEX

Page references in bold indicate an entry in the *Who's Who* section.